Eye-Tracking

Eye-tracking is quickly becoming a valuable tool in applied linguistics research as it provides a real-time, direct measure of cognitive processing effort. This book provides a straightforward introduction to the technology and how it might be used in language research. With a strong focus on the practicalities of designing eye-tracking studies that achieve the standard of other well-established experimental techniques, it provides valuable information about building and designing studies, touching on common challenges and problems, as well as solutions. Importantly, the book looks at the use of eye-tracking in a wide variety of applied contexts including reading, listening and multimodal input, writing, testing, corpus linguistics, translation, stylistics and computer-mediated communication. Each chapter finishes with a simple checklist to help researchers use eye-tracking in a wide variety of language studies. Discussion is grounded in concrete examples, which will allow users coming to the technology for the first time to gain the knowledge and confidence to use it to produce high-quality research.

Kathy Conklin is an associate professor in psycholinguistics at the University of Nottingham. She has expertise in the use of eye-tracking to understand processing in a first and a second language.

Ana Pellicer-Sánchez is a senior lecturer in applied linguistics and TESOL at the UCL Institute of Education. Her research centres on the teaching and learning of vocabulary in a second and foreign language and makes use of eye-tracking.

Gareth Carrol is a lecturer in psycholinguistics and a researcher in figurative and formulaic language at the University of Birmingham. His work focuses on idioms and utilises psycholinguistic methods, principally eye-tracking, to investigate questions relating to processing, learning and use in first and second language speakers.

Eye-Tracking

A Guide for Applied Linguistics Research

KATHY CONKLIN
University of Nottingham

ANA PELLICER-SÁNCHEZ
UCL Institute of Education

GARETH CARROL
University of Birmingham

CAMBRIDGE
UNIVERSITY PRESS

CAMBRIDGE
UNIVERSITY PRESS

University Printing House, Cambridge CB2 8BS, United Kingdom

One Liberty Plaza, 20th Floor, New York, NY 10006, USA

477 Williamstown Road, Port Melbourne, VIC 3207, Australia

314–321, 3rd Floor, Plot 3, Splendor Forum, Jasola District Centre, New Delhi – 110025, India

79 Anson Road, #06–04/06, Singapore 079906

Cambridge University Press is part of the University of Cambridge.

It furthers the University's mission by disseminating knowledge in the pursuit of education, learning, and research at the highest international levels of excellence.

www.cambridge.org
Information on this title: www.cambridge.org/9781108415354
DOI: 10.1017/9781108233279

© Cambridge University Press 2018

First published 2018

Printed in the United Kingdom by Clays, St Ives plc

A catalogue record for this publication is available from the British Library.

Library of Congress cataloging-in-publication Data
Names: Conklin, Kathryn author. | Pellicer-Sánchez, Ana author. | Carrol, Gareth author.
Title: Eye-tracking : a guide for applied linguistics research / Kathryn Conklin, University of Nottingham ; Ana Pellicer-Sánchez, UCL Institute of Education; Gareth Carrol, University of Birmingham.
Description: Cambridge ; New York, NY: Cambridge University Press, 2018. | Includes bibliographical references.
Identifiers: LCCN 2017043873 | ISBN 9781108415354
Subjects: LCSH: Applied linguistics – Research.
Classification: LCC P129.C625 2018 | DDC 418.0072–dc23
LC record available at https://lccn.loc.gov/2017043873

ISBN 978-1-108-41535-4 Hardback
ISBN 978-1-108-40120-3 Paperback

Contents

Figures

Tables

Preface

The eyes provide a window into the mind.

Eye-tracking can in part make this statement a reality. More specifically, by tracking people's eye-movements, we can determine what they are attending to and for how long. By extension, we can make inferences about what they might be thinking about and how much cognitive effort they expend in doing so. We don't need to set an additional task (although we often do); we can simply ask participants to read a text, look at an image or watch a video as they normally would on a computer screen. Importantly, eye-tracking provides a rich moment-to-moment data source. Because of its advantages, it is an essential and well-established research tool in psychology and psycholinguistics, as well as in more applied fields like translation studies. Increasingly, it is being used more widely in a range of applied linguistics domains. While it might seem that eye-tracking is a magic potion that can make our studies more natural, authentic, less contrived, etc., it is simply a tool. Like all tools, it is only as good as the uses we put it to. Even with the best equipment and high-quality materials, with no training we are far more likely to build a rickety shack than a good, sturdy house. Without a clear understanding of the limitations of eye-tracking technology and a good foundation in experimental design and data analysis, eye-tracking technology will likely tell us very little. The goal of this book is to provide readers with a good foundation so that eye-tracking can become a useful and valuable research tool in applied linguistics research.

One aim of this book is to provide researchers with a good understanding of what eye-tracking is and what it can do given the current technical constraints of the equipment. Our focus is on the main eye-tracking systems that are used in language research: SR Research EyeLink, Tobii and SensoMotoric Instruments (SMI)[1] systems. We do not advocate the use of any one system over and above the others. We simply provide information about technical specifications and the dedicated software that the systems use to design experiments and analyse data. This should help readers gain an awareness of the kinds of studies that are appropriate and/or easier to carry out with particular systems.

The book is intended to be broad and inclusive, to make eye-tracking understandable, accessible and achievable for any language researcher coming to the technology for the first time. We expect the primary audience of the book to be applied linguists, and it covers a range of topics that will be of particular interest to them. However, the book can also be a resource for people in fields where eye-tracking is well established, but the researchers themselves are making a start with the technology. The sheer volume of language research making use of the technology will prove daunting for anyone starting out with it, no matter the field. Thus, in this book, we explain the basic assumptions of eye-tracking, which are

---

[1] Eye-tracking manufacturers and software developers are constantly updating to ensure that their methods are advanced and up-to-date, which means that the landscape is constantly shifting. After the book was written, Apple acquired SensoMotoric Instruments. This will likely pose challenges for SMI users, as the level of support and the pace of developments may change or even cease entirely.

often not fully spelled out. Understanding these is the first step in producing good research with the technology.

A predominant theme throughout the book is the methodological considerations we should take into account when designing studies. We try to relate all of our discussions to concrete examples. In Chapters 1, 4 and 5 we spell out methodological concerns largely in regard to existing research. This serves two purposes. First, it provides some sense of the existing eye-tracking literature. Second, it lays out some well-established means for dealing with a range of methodological concerns. In Chapter 6, we turn to more uncharted territory and provide a discussion of methodological considerations when using eye-tracking in very applied fields, which have generally been less explored. We have tried to describe a range of 'test cases' where we think eye-tracking could be fruitfully employed, as well as a few examples where it has already been used. Importantly, the focus in this chapter is on how we can meaningfully use eye-tracking with 'authentic' materials. A recurring topic is the trade-off between maintaining authenticity and modifying the experimental input in various ways so that we can acquire particular kinds of data.

In this book we walk people through eye-tracking from start to finish, and it can be read from cover to cover to gain a comprehensive overview of eye-tracking technology and its use in (applied) language research. However, the book is also written in such a way that it can be used as a resource for studying particular topics. Thus, if a reader already has some knowledge about eye-tracking in reading, he/she may not need to read Chapter 4 on reading research before diving into the discussion of eye-tracking reading tests in Chapter 6. Because we intend sections of the book to be somewhat self-contained, this means that there is some repetition in places. Similarly, in Chapters 2 and 7, where we talk about the different eye-tracking systems, readers may want to read them from start to finish if they want to learn more about the available systems – maybe because they are considering buying one. However, in many cases researchers may only have access to a particular eye-tracker. Thus, they may only want to read the sections that are specifically relevant to their system. Again, allowing the discussion to be, at the same time, inclusive and compartmentalised leads to a certain level of repetition.

This book would have been difficult to write without the help and support of manufacturers and colleagues. Thanks to people who have either read and commented on sections of the book, or helped with guidance on and demonstration of certain aspects of the system: Kurt Debono, William Schmidt, Sam Hutton, Marcus Johnson and Jiye Shen of SR Research; Ricardo Matos and Cecilia Lago Albright of Tobii; Meike Mischo and Stefanie Gehrke of SMI; and Richard Lilley of Tracksys Ltd. We would also like to thank our colleagues Steven Frisson and Bodo Winter (University of Birmingham) and Walter van Heuven (University of Nottingham) for their comments on different parts of the book and guidance on the use of some systems, as well as Dave Evans for his attentive proofreading.

Finally, we believe that we have produced a comprehensive overview of (1) the current state of eye-tracking technology for language research; (2) what measuring eye-movement behaviour can tell us in various domains; and (3) how we might extend it to more applied contexts. Our discussion is grounded in concrete examples to allow new users of the technology to gain the knowledge and confidence to use the 'tool' to produce high-quality research. We hope that you find it a good and helpful resource.

Chapter 1

Introduction to Eye-Tracking

1.1   What Is Eye-Tracking?

Have you ever watched someone's eyes as they read or look at a scene? What do you notice about the eyes' behaviour from simple observation? There are descriptions of eye-movements, as well as what they might tell us, that go back as far as Aristotle (Wade, 2010). However, this kind of observation only provides a limited understanding of eye-movements, and historically led to the erroneous conclusion that eyes 'glide over scenes and to alight on objects of interest, which they would fix with unmoved accuracy' (Wade and Tatler, 2011, p. 37). It was not until the late nineteenth and early twentieth centuries, when early eye-trackers were developed, that we gained insight into the rapid discontinuous nature of eye-movements.

We fancy that we can move our eyes uniformly, that by a continuous motion like that of a telescope we can move our eyes along the sky-line in the landscape or the cornice of a room, but we are wrong in this. However determinedly we try to do so, what actually happens is, that our eyes move like the seconds hand of a watch, a jerk and a little pause, another jerk and so on; only our eyes are not so regular, the jerks are sometimes of greater, sometimes of less, angular amount, and the pauses vary in duration, although, unless we make an effort, they are always short. During the jerks we practically do not see at all, so that we have before us not a moving panorama, but a series of fixed pictures of the same fixed things, which succeed one another rapidly. (Brown, 1895, pp. 4–5)

The 'twitches' and 'jerks' of the eye – in other words their movements – are what we commonly refer to as *saccades*. The interval between the eyes' movements, when the eyes 'stop', are called *fixations*. Both are a type of automatic, physiological response, which means that they are not under our conscious control (Rayner et al., 2012). In reading, saccades do not always move the eye forward in a text. About 10–15 per cent of the time, readers move their eyes back (regress) to previously encountered sections of text. These backward movements are referred to as *regressions*. Regressions can be short or long. Short regressions are usually due to overshooting a target. If we look at the first example in Figure 1.1, the intended eye-movement was to the word 'normally'. However, the eye 'overshot' and landed on 'safe'. The short regression moves the eye back to the intended target. Longer regressions are usually attributed to the difficulty of the text, which can be due to a range of factors. Looking at the second example in Figure 1.1, a reader might not associate 'infect' with 'violence' and go back and check that the word was indeed 'violence' and not perhaps 'virus' instead.

In very basic terms, when we read or look at a scene or images, our eyes stop to process the information at that location and then move to another point where other information is available. During fixations, the cognitive system perceives and processes the visual input, as well as planning when and how far to move the eyes next. Under most normal circumstances, during a saccade the eyes move so quickly that we do not obtain new visual information (Rayner, 2009). While new visual information is not encoded during saccades,

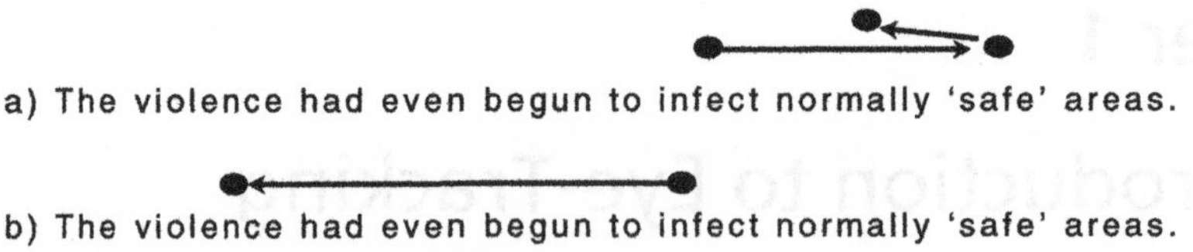

a) The violence had even begun to infect normally 'safe' areas.

b) The violence had even begun to infect normally 'safe' areas.

Figure 1.1 Examples of regressions due to different factors: (a) overshooting the target; and (b) difficulty. The oval depicts a fixation, while the arrows illustrate saccades, with the right-pointing arrow indicating a forward saccade (generally simply referred to as a saccade) and the left-pointing arrows indicating a backward saccade (referred to as a regression).

the processing of already perceived information can continue (Irwin, 1998; Irwin and Carlson-Radvansky, 1996). Fixations, saccades and regressions generally occur 'automatically', without our conscious awareness. Thus, tracking eye-movements provides a window into a largely unconscious behaviour. Crucially, *eye-tracking* technology tells us where people's eyes land, how many times they land in that position or region (*fixation count*), and how long each fixation lasts (*fixation duration*), as well as measuring saccade duration and length. To sum this up simply, eye-tracking is a technology that measures fixations, saccades and regressions in response to visual input, while an eye-tracker is the device that does this. The data that is produced by an eye-tracker will depend on what we are using it for, and we go into much more detail about the different eye-tracking measures throughout the book, and qualitative analyses (heat maps, cluster maps, scan paths) that can be undertaken in Chapter 7.

Why would being able to track and measure people's eye-movements be of any interest to applied linguists? It appears that in complex processing tasks, like reading and scene perception, eye location provides an index of attention (Rayner, 2009). This means that our eyes indicate what we are paying attention to and how much cognitive effort is being expended to process the input at the fixation point. Thus, the difficulty and complexity of what the eyes are looking at influences fixations and saccades (Castelhano and Rayner, 2008). When the input is more difficult, fixation durations and regressions increase, while saccade size decreases. This means that in reading, more difficult texts elicit more and longer fixations and regressions, while saccades get shorter. When looking at scenes or images that are more crowded, cluttered or dense, fixations also get longer and saccades get shorter. It is important to note that the difficulty we are talking about here is in 'global' terms – so it is a property of a text, image or scene as a whole. We can also talk about 'local' properties, and in reading we can look at effects of individual words or short sections of text. For example, we can look at eye-movements to a specific word, like 'infect' in Figure 1.1. There are a set of standard measures that are used in eye-tracking to look at local effects; these measures will be presented in detail in Section 3.2 and will be the main focus of the discussion in the remainder of the book when talking about reading tasks. It is important to keep in mind that factors other than difficulty can influence both global and local eye-tracking measures – for example, the reader's/viewer's goals (Rayner and Pollatsek, 1989). Reading a text for understanding produces a different pattern of eye-movement behaviour from skimming a text, as does looking at images on a page to understand what is being depicted compared to memorising images and their location.

Global eye-tracking measures give us an indication of typical looking behaviour. An overview of fixation time and saccade length and duration for silent reading, oral reading and scene perception is presented in Table 1.1. It is important to keep in mind that

Table 1.1 'Global' characteristics of fixations and saccades in reading and scene perception for skilled English readers (based on Castelhano and Rayner, 2008; Rayner, 1978, 1998), with line indicating unspecified information.

Task	Mean fixation duration (ms)	Mean saccade size	Mean saccade duration (ms)
Silent reading	225–250	2° / 7–9 letter spaces	30
Oral reading	275–325	1.5° / 6–7 letter spaces	—
Scene perception	260–330	4°–5°	40–50

this table simply depicts average behaviour. For example, saccades can span anywhere from two to more than eighteen characters and fixation duration can vary from 50 to 600+ ms for a single reader in one passage (Rayner, 1998, 2009). The table highlights that there is a considerable range in terms of fixations and saccades depending on the visual input and the task. For skilled, adult readers, a scientific paper will elicit longer fixations and shorter saccades than a Harry Potter novel. Crucially, these global measures will underscore group differences. If we consider a standard newspaper article intended for a general audience, the text should not prove challenging for educated native-speaker adult readers with no history of vision or language processing difficulties. This same text will be more challenging for ten-year-olds, less proficient non-native speakers, participants with dyslexia, etc. For these groups, we would expect more and longer fixations, more regressions, and shorter saccades. Although it has not been rigorously investigated (yet), it is likely that global eye-tracking measures can provide a metric for identifying the skill of readers. In other words, because global measures provide a metric of 'difficulty', we would expect a highly proficient group of non-native speakers to have fewer and shorter fixations, fewer regressions and longer saccades than less proficient non-native speakers on a particular text.

As Table 1.1 indicates, eye-movement behaviour varies depending on whether participants are reading silently or orally or viewing a scene. As Rayner (2009) points out, 'It is actually somewhat hazardous to generalise across these tasks in terms of eye-movement behaviour' (p. 1459). He goes on to hypothesise that the differences in eye-movements are due to the cognitive mechanisms involved in the different tasks, as well as because of the interaction between the cognitive and oculomotor systems differing as a function of the task. Again, we can ask ourselves why this might be important for applied linguists. In general, applied linguistics work with 'real-world' and 'authentic' materials. This might involve presenting children or second language learners with a reading test, a range of readers with a story or novel, storybooks accompanied by images, films with subtitles, etc. Chapters 4–6 will discuss some of these types of authentic materials and the methodological considerations when using them. Crucially, if we use materials that have image and language components, we would expect different patterns of fixations and saccades for the image and text portions of the stimuli simply because the eyes behave differently when they encounter these sources of information. This makes any direct comparison of images and text somewhat complicated.

Further, Table 1.1 points to some specific differences between tasks. First, fixations tend to be longer in oral reading than silent reading. Skilled readers can read words more quickly than they can say them aloud, which means that our eyes outpace our word production. In oral reading, our eyes fixate longer and make shorter saccades, likely so that they do not get too far ahead of what we are saying. Second, fixations and saccades in scene perception

```
   210    172    386  172          133   187        180
The most recent statistics showed that crime rates were

   253           400  335    197    260       285  225
increasing. The epidemic was out of control. The violence had

   179         333  172   179         375         267
even begun to infect normally `safe´ areas. The police were

   180         130         192         375
desperately looking for a cure to the problem.
```

Figure 1.2 Hypothetical fixations for a skilled reader during silent reading. Fixations (in ms) are indicated above the word where they occurred.

tend to be longer than in either type of reading because the eyes take in information from a wider area in an image than in reading. Again these differences highlight potential issues with comparing eye-movement behaviour across task types and different visual sources.

It is important to note that the averages presented in Table 1.1 and the discussion thus far have been focused on skilled readers in English. Crucially, eye-movement behaviour is comparable in skilled readers of other similar alphabetic languages. However, in a language like Hebrew, where information is more densely packed than English, largely because vowels are not generally spelled out, there tend to be shorter saccades (about 5.5 letter spaces), while fixation durations are similar (Pollatsek et al., 1981). In Chinese, which has a very different writing system, again average fixation durations are quite similar to those presented in Table 1.1 and regression rates do not differ markedly (Rayner, 2009). However, average saccade length is much shorter and is typically only two to three characters.

The global effects that have been discussed thus far with regard to reading are informative because they tell us something about overall performance and they can be used to differentiate difficulty in terms of texts and for various groups of readers. However, they are somewhat limited because they do not tell us where a difficulty may arise. As mentioned above, they do not reveal any local effects. More precisely, in a text, some words will be read more than once, while others will not have a fixation associated with them at all – in other words they are skipped. There is good reason to believe that skipped words are processed on the fixation prior to the skip (Rayner, 2009). English readers can acquire useful information from an asymmetrical region around the fixation point that extends about three to four letter spaces to the left of the fixation and fourteen to fifteen character spaces to the right. Information that can be used for word identification is obtained from a smaller region extending to about seven to eight character spaces to the right of a fixation. If we look at the text in Figure 1.2,[1] this means that when the eyes land on the word 'even', they will also see and identify the word 'begun'. This will make a fixation on the word 'begun' unnecessary. Unfortunately, global measures (e.g. number and length of fixations on a text as a whole) do not provide this level of information. It is the local measures that provide more precise information about reading and viewing behaviour.

---

[1] This passage is loosely based on the materials from Allbritton, McKoon and Gerrig (1995). They investigated metaphorical language processing, but did not make use of eye-tracking. We will use this example passage, or parts of it, throughout the book.

Figure 1.2 can demonstrate some important differences between a global and local examination of eye-movement data. We can see that there are twenty-four individual fixations to the text and can calculate the mean fixation duration, which is 241 ms. Based on the information in Table 1.1, this is within the expected range of fixation duration for a skilled reader during silent reading. The global data would be useful for comparing skilled and unskilled readers. Thus, the expectation would be that unskilled readers would have more fixations and that their mean fixation duration would be longer. However, what a global assessment will not tell us is that for our (hypothetical) reader, the words 'statistics', 'epidemic' and 'infect' all have two fixations, and that the fixations at the end of sentences, where sentence integration occurs, are all above the expected average. Local measures – the fixation pattern to individual words or small regions – would be used to explore processing effort within the text itself.

Finally, before turning to the next section, we will briefly discuss scene perception. As we will see in Chapter 5, we do not talk about eye-movement measures in terms of being global and local when examining looking patterns for images. However, as with reading, the average values depicted in Table 1.1 vary depending on the task and the exact nature of the scene. Viewers do not fixate every part of a scene (Rayner, 2009). It appears that viewers can very quickly obtain the gist of a scene in a single glance in as short as 40 ms (Castelhano and Henderson, 2008; De Graef, 2005). This initial fixation is used to point to the appropriate or interesting regions for subsequent fixations (Rayner, 2009). Overall, viewers primarily fixate on informative areas of a scene (Antes, 1974; Mackworth and Morandi, 1967), as well as on salient aspects, which are generally defined in terms of features like contrast, colour, intensity, brightness, spatial frequency, etc. (Mannan, Ruddock and Wooding, 1995, 1996; Parkhurst and Niebur, 2003). Viewing is also influenced by the task and by real-world knowledge. For example, in a visual search task of a scene containing the sky and a road, when participants are asked to look for a 'jeep', fixations are largely constrained to the road, which is where a jeep is likely to be found (Neider and Zelinksy, 2006). Finally, viewers tend to fixate near the centre of an object (Henderson, 1993), and when looking at scenes they look at people (or characters like Mickey Mouse) and concentrate their fixations on the face (Henderson and Hollingworth, 1999).

1.2   Why Use Eye-Tracking?

It is quite apparent that research utilizing eye-movements to examine cognitive processing tasks is burgeoning as more and more researchers have started to use eye tracking techniques in the last few years. (Rayner, 2009, p. 1458)

The quote by Rayner describes the rapid increase in the use of eye-tracking in cognitive psychology at the turn of the twenty-first century. This sentiment is echoed by Liversedge, Gilchrist and Everling (2011) who point out that in the early 1980s the number of eye-tracking laboratories in psychology departments in UK universities could be counted on the fingers of one or two hands, while three decades later almost all such departments had an eye-tracking device. What led to the rise of eye-tracking research in psychology, and why might this be relevant to applied linguists? Part of the explanation for the spread of eye-tracking is a practical one. Eye-tracking systems have become more readily available, cheaper (although they can still be quite expensive), and more user-friendly (even though they might not seem so upon a first encounter). While affordability and usability are not reasons to use eye-tracking technology, they mean that eye-tracking systems are increasingly accessible to applied linguists.

The main driver behind the rise in eye-tracking research in psychology and psycholinguistics is the belief that there is a tight relationship between eye-movements and cognitive processing. Put another way, there is a belief that the eyes provide a 'window' into the mind, which is sometimes referred to as the *eye–mind hypothesis* or *eye–mind assumption* (Just and Carpenter, 1980). This means that eye-movements tell us about cognitive processing. Importantly, as was discussed in the previous section, eye-movements reflect cognitive processes that operate automatically, giving eye-tracking some important advantages over other behavioural measures (discussed in more detail in Scherr, Agaus and Ashby, 2016).

Advantages of eye-tracking:

1 Eye-tracking provides a 'direct' measure of processing effort during a task, rather than at the output of a decision, recall or production task, which are often subject to strategic effects.

2 Eye-movements have little variance due to individual differences in memory, deliberate decision-making processes and recognition strategies, which are generally implicated in explicit judgement tasks.

3 The temporal precision of eye-tracking provides a record of behaviour from the first moment a visual stimulus (text, image, scene, etc.) is perceived until the stimulus is removed or a participant stops looking at it. For example, eye-tracking allows us to measure the cognitive effort that is expended the first time readers encounter a word, as well as when and if they go back to re-read the word at some point.

4 Although it generally occurs in a laboratory setting, eye-tracking allows readers and viewers to engage with visual stimuli as they normally would (when they are presented on a computer screen). This means that participants can read and re-read at their own pace and look where they want, *without* the need to impose an additional task.

Because of its advantages, eye-tracking research has become the 'gold standard' for studying reading in psycholinguistics and cognitive psychology (Rayner, 2009, p. 1474), and an ever-increasing number of researchers in applied linguistics are beginning to use it. However, it is important to note that the eye–mind assumption relies on two underlying beliefs (Pickering et al., 2004). First, there is the supposition that what is being fixated is what is being considered. This means that when the eyes fixate the word 'infect' in Figure 1.3, the processing system is working to decode and understand this word and not the word 'even' that occurred three words before. In other words, readers try to interpret words as they are encountered. However, this assumption is somewhat of an

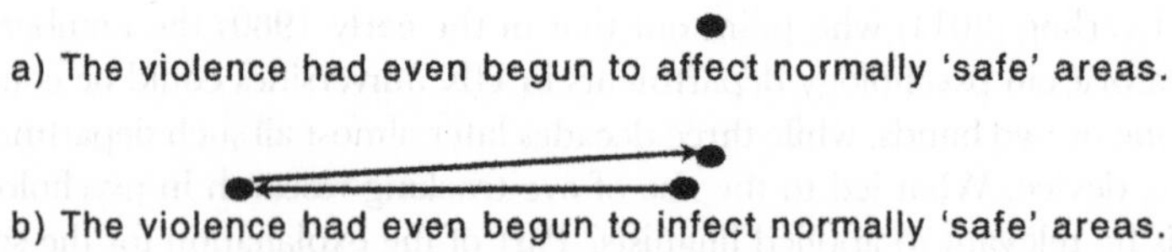

a) The violence had even begun to affect normally 'safe' areas.

b) The violence had even begun to infect normally 'safe' areas.

Figure 1.3 Fixations (depicted by circles) used to assess cognitive effort to two matched words: 'affect' and 'infect'. The word 'affect' has one fixation, while 'infect' has two, indicating that greater cognitive effort was expended in processing it.

oversimplification (Ehrlich and Rayner, 1983). For example, in a sentence like 'Jill sold her horse to Jack because she decided to quit riding,' when the eyes land on the word 'she', in order to interpret it, the processing system will need to consider previously encountered entities that could be potential referents of the pronoun. Thus, when the eyes land on 'she', the processing system is indeed working on this word; however, it is also considering previous elements of the sentence that could be potential referents (e.g. 'Jill').

The second part of the eye–mind assumption is that the amount of time spent fixating an item or region reflects the cognitive effort required to process it. This means that longer and more fixations indicate greater processing effort, and shorter fixations and/or more skipping indicate less processing effort. Importantly, these terms are relative: longer/ shorter duration and more/less processing effort need to be in comparison to something. In general, cognitive effort is linked to a particular region of interest (ROI, sometimes referred to as area of interest (AOI)) using local measures. Thus, if we want to explore how using metaphorical language influences processing, readers could be presented with sentences like those in Figure 1.3. In this example the ROIs are the words 'affect' and 'infect'. The number (fixation count) and length (fixation duration) of fixations to the ROIs would be measured to determine processing effort. In the example, we see that 'infect' has two fixations, while 'affect' only has one; this could be taken as an indication that 'infect' requires more processing effort.

So far much of the discussion and the examples have been focused on reading. While investigations of reading can tell us a lot about language representation and processing, they have clear limitations. For example, we cannot use reading studies to tell us about the linguistic skills of pre-literate children. Further, reading is only one element of language competence; thus limiting ourselves to reading studies will never give us a complete picture of linguistic ability. Importantly, in addition to presenting written text, eye-tracking technology can present static images and visual scenes (often referred to as the *visual-world paradigm*), as well as visual media like films and television programmes. Such stimuli are often used to explore auditory processing – or listening. In this type of research, eye-movements and fixations to visual input are time-locked to a particular linguistic variable (a word, pronoun, syntactic structure, etc.) that is presented auditorily. The different areas/images on the screen are defined as ROIs. Data are usually reported in terms of total fixation duration, as well as the proportion of saccades directed to or the proportion of time spent looking at a target ROI compared to competitor ROIs (see Section 5.1 for a discussion). As with reading, the eye–mind assumption holds. Thus, what is being looked at is what is being processed and the number of fixations and fixation time indicate processing effort.

Figure 1.4 provides some examples of how the visual-world paradigm works (from Altmann and Kamide, 1999 and Chambers and Cooke, 2009). In Example A, static images are presented on a visible grid, while in B the scene is more 'natural'. In both cases eye-movements and fixations to the depicted objects are measured and assessed relative to each other. As can be seen in A, Chambers and Cooke (2009) presented English–French bilinguals with a screen containing static images of a swimming pool, a chicken ('la poule' is a near homophone of pool) and two distractor objects (a strawberry and a boot). Participants listened to sentences like 'Marie va décrire la poule' ('Marie will describe the chicken') and their eye-movements were monitored time-locked to the noun 'poule'. So what happens when English–French bilinguals hear the word 'poule'? Do they only think about the French word 'poule', or do they also consider the homophone 'pool' from their other language? To assess this, Chambers and Cooke (2009) calculated both the

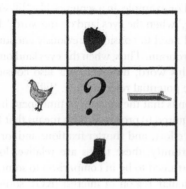 

Example A

◀ 'Marie va décrire la poule'
'Marie will describe the chicken'

Example B

◀ 'The boy will eat the cake'

Figure 1.4 Examples of the visual-world paradigm presenting images and auditory stimulus (◀). In Example A, the images are presented in a visible grid, while in B they are presented as a more 'natural' scene. The ROIs would be the individual objects and entities.

mean number of saccades and the probability of fixating the target (pool) and near homophone (chicken). In Example B, Altmann and Kamide (1999) wanted to know what people think about when they hear the word 'eat'. If they primarily consider edible things, there should be more looks to the cake relative to the other objects on the screen. Both of these studies utilise eye-tracking in the visual-world paradigm as a way to investigate the behaviour of listeners in real time. Finally, it is important to note that ROIs can be defined for other types of visual material. Thus, for films the ROIs could be some aspect of the image that appears at a given point in the video and the subtitle regions during the same time period.

In general, what the eyes are looking at *is* what is being processed. However, we have highlighted some caveats to this assertion; and it is important to note that this belief has been challenged by some. Central to the eye–mind hypothesis is the view that the amount of time and number of times that the eyes look at something provide an indication of processing effort. Because of this, a significant effort has been made to try to relate local fixation measures to specific cognitive processes. To do this we would need very specific evidence linking particular eye-movement measures with underlying cognitive events. Importantly, at this point we do *not* have such evidence and we do *not* know how to uniquely map cognitive events to the different eye-movement measures (Pickering et al., 2004). In other words, we cannot use the eye-movement record to pinpoint, for example, exactly when a word's meaning is accessed, or when it was integrated into our unfolding understanding of a sentence or discourse. What exactly we can conclude from various eye-tracking data and measures will be touched upon in the next section and will be the focus of Chapters 4, 5 and 6.

1.3 Basic Considerations When Doing Eye-Tracking

It is probably already clear that eye-tracking is potentially a useful technology. Importantly, it is increasingly being used by researchers in applied linguistics. The growth of eye-tracking means that researchers who have not previously encountered the technology are coming into contact with it in presentations and papers, as well as possibly wanting to try it out for themselves. In order to establish it on a sound footing in the field, it is important to come to an understanding about (1) what eye-tracking is; (2) what it can and cannot tell us; and (3) how it might be meaningfully used in applied linguistics research. Over the course of this book we will address all of these.

By this point, we should have a basic idea of eye-tracking. Eye-tracking systems, as well as their associated software, differ in certain ways. An important consideration when we start out doing eye-tracking research is choosing the 'right' system or understanding the capabilities of one that we may have access to. Chapter 2 will discuss some of the basic properties of eye-tracking systems and software, as well as things to consider when choosing or using one. The remainder of the book, as well as this chapter, will provide insight into what eye-tracking technology can tell us, how to use it and how we might integrate it into our research in a meaningful way. As we have seen, while the technology can provide a window into the mind, we need to be cautious about overstating what it tells us. Importantly, eye-tracking's capacity to tell us anything about cognitive processing is largely dependent on designing good studies. Thus, experimental design, as well as the methodological considerations associated with different paradigms, will be a predominant focus of the book.

As was touched on in Section 1.2, eye-tracking can be used for the examination of participants' processing of different types of verbal and non-verbal stimuli, and a combination of different types of stimuli. Importantly, as we have seen, one of the attractions of eye-tracking is its ability to tell us what the mind is thinking about – which is whatever we are looking at – and how much cognitive effort is being expended on this. In general, more and longer fixations indicate that more processing effort is needed, while fewer and shorter fixations and/or skipping indicate that less processing effort is required. As mentioned previously, short and long are relative terms. If we think about this in relation to a 'real-world' comparison, this becomes clearer. If we want to know whether a three-year-old boy is of tall/short/average height for his age, which of the following statements would help us assess this: 'the three-year-old boy is short compared to giraffes' or 'the three-year-old boy is short compared to other three-year-old boys'? Clearly to say anything meaningful about the child's height we want to assess this with a reasonable comparison set – other three-year-old boys and not giraffes (which are apparently already six feet tall at birth).

Thus, if we want to know whether more/less/equal processing effort is required for words that we encounter frequently versus words that we rarely encounter, we need to first make sure that our comparison set is right. In Example 1.1 sentences (a), (b) and (c) provide potential stimuli to address our question; they will allow us to compare the reading pattern for the high-frequency word 'house' versus low-frequency words 'protractor' or 'louse'. While in (a) the word 'house' is more frequent than 'protractor', 'protractor' is also a longer word. Thus, greater processing time for 'protractor' could be due to its frequency, length or both. In other words, 'protractor' does not provide convincing evidence that we spend longer reading low-frequency words than high-frequency ones. In the second example, the words 'house' and 'louse' are well matched for length, as well as for phonological properties, and simply differ in frequency. However, in (b) the words are in very different sentence frames. Any longer reading times for 'louse' in (b) could be due to its frequency, the general parsing difficulty for the sentence or both. Finally, in (c) we see a 'fair' comparison, where the only thing that differs is the frequency of the words 'house' and 'louse'; thus shorter fixations for 'house' can convincingly be attributed to less processing effort being required for higher-frequency words.

Example 1.1 Hypothetical stimuli exploring the effect of word frequency on reading times when words *are not* well matched on other properties like word length (a) or sentence structure (b) and when they *are* well matched on these properties (c).

(a) She found a <u>house</u> yesterday. vs She found a <u>protractor</u> yesterday.
(b) She found a <u>house</u> yesterday. vs I was told that what was found yesterday by the barber was a <u>louse</u> and not dandruff.
(c) She found a <u>house</u> yesterday. vs She found a <u>louse</u> yesterday.

Potentially more challengingly, we may want to determine whether test-takers spend longer, in other words expend more processing effort, reading gist questions or questions asking about details. If we conduct a study and find that on average test-takers spend 500 ms longer reading detail questions, we might conclude that detail questions require greater cognitive processing. However, if the detail questions in the study are systematically four words longer than the gist questions, the difference in fixations could be entirely due to the length of the questions, as sentences or questions that have more words take longer to read. Thus, in this case the comparison is not reasonable because differences in question length and type are confounded. In order to ensure that the conclusions that are drawn from the study are warranted, we would either need to match our question types on factors like length and syntactic complexity, which are known to influence reading time, or use an analysis technique that could take into account these differences (e.g. mixed-effects modelling or multiple regression analyses), which will be discussed in Section 7.2.

Typically, in eye-tracking studies involving reading we are interested in particular phenomena, for example the influence of word frequency on processing, as in the 'house'/'louse' example. We show readers complete sentences or texts and not simply the individual words 'house' and 'louse'. This means that we are interested in eye-movements made to a very specific ROI in a sentence or longer discourse. For instance, if we wanted to look at how using metaphorical language influences reading and comprehension we could show readers passages like those in Example 1.2. (Usually the two versions would be presented in different experimental lists, so that a single participant would only see one version, but each version would be seen by an equal number of participants – see Section 3.1.2 for more on counterbalancing in eye-tracking studies.) In each version keywords would be set as ROIs, which are indicated by the underlining in the example.[2] The ROIs correspond to words that make the metaphor of 'crime as a disease' apparent, which are matched to ensure that comparisons are fair/appropriate. We would count and measure the number of fixations to our ROIs. This would show us whether there is a difference in reading time, in other words processing effort, for the metaphorical and non-metaphorical language. We could also explore whether readers performed better on a comprehension task following the different versions and examine whether this correlated with reading times. We could also look at whether metaphorical versus non-metaphorical language impacted reading time in the rest of the passage. Because processing effort is relative, an analysis will determine whether more or less processing effort is required for the metaphorical compared to the non-metaphorical

---

[2] In all of the examples in this chapter, the ROIs are underlined to make them easier to identify, but they would not be indicated in any way to participants in a study.

words and passages, and how this relates to the ability to answer questions about the passage. More specifically, an average fixation duration of 300 ms for the word 'infect' does not tell us anything by itself. It is in comparison to the reading time of 'affect' that we can tell if an average fixation duration of 300 ms is long, short or neither.

Example 1.2 Passage to compare reading when metaphorical (Version A) versus non-metaphorical (Version B) language is used. ROIs are indicated with underlining, which would not be visible to participants.

Version A
```
The most recent statistics showed that crime rates were
increasing. The epidemic was out of control. The violence had
even begun to infect normally 'safe' areas. The police were
desperately looking for a cure for the problem.
```

Version B
```
The most recent statistics showed that crime rates were
increasing. The situation was out of control. The violence had
even begun to affect normally 'safe' areas. The police were
desperately looking for a solution to the problem.
```

As we see, in order to draw meaningful conclusions, we need to make sure that we are making reasonable comparisons – a three-year-old boy to other three-year-old boys and not giraffes. So what kinds of things should we consider to ensure that our eye-movement data can actually tell us something meaningful? Various linguistic and non-linguistic variables, which often are *not* of interest to researchers, can impact saccades and fixations (Leow et al., 2014). Thus, stimuli should be matched on as many factors as possible that have been shown to influence reading time. Looking at Example 1.2, critical words ('epidemic'/'situation', 'infect'/'affect', 'cure'/'solution') should be matched on properties like word class, length, frequency, familiarity, age of acquisition, number of meanings/ polysemy, plausibility, contextual constraint, etc. (for more on this see Section 4.1, and for a detailed discussion of factors demonstrated to influence eye-movement patterns see Clifton, Staub and Rayner, 2007). If the words are well matched, any differences in the eye-movement record can be attributed to the use of metaphorical language and not to other properties of the words. Similarly, when investigating longer stretches of text, or things like question types, it is important that these are well matched on factors like length and syntactic complexity, etc.

Further, ROIs should be placed in similar positions in a text and should not end a sentence. A word that ends a sentence is typically read more slowly, as are sentences at the end of a passage, because this is where meaning integration occurs. More specifically, if the word 'cure' ended the sentence, as in (a) in Example 1.3, this would likely lead to long reading times and could elicit regressions. If we simply showed readers (a) this might lead to the conclusion that metaphorical language requires a lot of processing effort, when in fact it is the sentence integration that occurs here that leads to the considerable processing effort. To conclude that metaphorical language underpins any processing effort, we would need to compare this to non-metaphorical language that also ends a sentence, as in (b). If 'cure' at the end of the sentence elicits significantly greater fixations and increased regressions relative to 'solution' at the end of the sentence, we could feel confident that this was due to the metaphorical language and not simply the position in the sentence.

However, the best scenario is the one illustrated in (c) and (d), where sentence integration effects would not contaminate reading measures to our ROI. It is good to avoid placing an ROI at the end of a sentence, clause or line break (for a discussion see Section 3.1.2). Finally, critical stimuli should appear in contexts that are the same or as similar as possible. Looking back at Example 1.2, the critical words (ROIs) are in identical passages in the two versions. This is the ideal situation for making comparisons. However, if the contexts are different they should be matched on variables like syntactic complexity, length, predictability of the context, etc.

Example 1.3 Hypothetical ROIs (indicated by underlining) which could be subject to end-of-sentence integration effects, (a) and (b), and ROIs for which this is not an issue, (c) and (d).

(a) The police were desperately looking for a <u>cure</u>.
(b) The police were desperately looking for a <u>solution</u>.
(c) The police were desperately looking for a <u>cure</u> for the problem.
(d) The police were desperately looking for a <u>solution</u> to the problem.

Just as in reading, longer/shorter fixations to images are relative, and therefore comparisons need to be made between well-matched items. Looking back at Example B from Figure 1.4, if the image of the cake had been ten times larger than those of the ball, car or train set, then more and longer fixations to it upon hearing the word 'eat' could be attributed to its size and not the fact that it is the only edible object in the image. This means that the target images in our ROIs should be matched for size. Similarly, salience influences eye-movements and looking patterns. If the cake in Figure 1.4 had been presented in colour while everything else was black and white, this would draw attention to it and increase the number and/or the duration of looks to it. Thus, image salience for our ROIs should be matched as far as possible. Considerations for matching visual stimuli will be taken up in Section 5.1.

Further, we tend to scan a screen with images from left to right (for speakers of languages where reading is from left to right), so it is important to counterbalance the location of objects. If the target object is disproportionately on one side of the screen or the other, participants' looking patterns could reflect this. For example, if condition x always appears on the right side of the screen and condition y on the left side, condition y would likely always be fixated first, not because of the experimental manipulation, but because of its position on the screen. Returning to Example A in Figure 1.4, this means that the homophones like 'poule' should appear equally in the different positions on the grid. If the homophones always appeared on the left-hand side participants may 'notice' this (potentially unconsciously), which could influence looking patterns. We discuss these kinds of experimental considerations further in Chapter 3.

In studies that make use of images, eye-movements show a systematic relationship between what is being listened to and where the eyes tend to go (and how quickly they go there) in the visual array (Rayner, 2009). However, the visual-world paradigm is somewhat less natural than eye-tracking studies involving reading. More precisely, when faced with a text, participants can read as they normally would on a computer screen. We do not need to impose any additional task on them. However, as Rayner (2009) points out, when faced with a visual array of images like those in Figure 1.4, participants may be uncertain about what they are supposed to do. They probably assume that they are supposed to look at the pictures and may search for connections (even subconsciously) between the visual and auditory stimuli. This type of paradigm does not present a situation we are typically faced with in the real world and has much more of an experimental flavour to it. However, in studies making use of authentic audio and visual material, like films, this is natural in the same way that eye-tracking while reading is.

While eye-tracking allows for natural reading and viewing, and has many advantages over traditional behavioural techniques, this does not mean that we can simply present participants with authentic materials (e.g. newspaper article, Test of English as a Foreign Language (TOEFL)/International English Language Testing System (IELTS) reading passage, episode from a television show) and draw conclusions directly from eye-movement data. We need to carefully define our ROIs and make sure that we are making comparisons that will justify any conclusions that we draw from our data. In instances where we cannot carefully control and design our materials because we are using authentic ones, the eye-movement data will be influenced by various factors like word frequency or the visual salience of images, thereby calling into question any conclusions that are drawn from the data. If researchers would like to use authentic materials, more sophisticated analyses that allow us to account for a variety of factors may be required. For example, mixed-effects modelling or multiple regression analyses allow researchers to account for the factors detailed above when they have not been explicitly controlled or manipulated (e.g. Carrol and Conklin, 2017; Conklin and Pellicer-Sánchez, 2016; McDonald and Shillcock, 2003a; Siyanova-Chanturia, Conklin and van Heuven, 2011).

In sum, eye-tracking is a valuable tool in applied linguistics research because it provides a real-time, direct measure of cognitive processing and processing effort. Crucially, the eye-movement record is generally not subject to strategic effects, individual differences in memory, deliberate decision processes or recognition strategies that are problematic for many other types of tasks. Finally, in many cases, eye-tracking allows for natural behaviour. Readers can read as they normally would and viewers can watch as they normally would, all without the need to impose an additional, often artificial task.

Chapter 2
Choosing the Equipment

2.1 Introduction

A number of different eye-tracking systems are currently available to researchers. Despite the apparent similarity of the physical components of some of the current systems, important differences in their technical specifications mean that some systems are more suited to certain types of research questions than others. Some eye-tracking systems are presented as easy and effortless to use, and do indeed allow users to run an experiment with almost no knowledge of the system and limited understanding of experimental design. However, eye-trackers make advanced physiological measurements, and therefore knowing a system, its technical aspects and their impact on the quality of the data collected is crucial for determining whether a study will be feasible with a particular system (Holmqvist et al., 2011). Thus, choosing the right equipment and understanding its features and capabilities are of paramount importance for conducting high-quality eye-tracking research. The aim of this chapter is to provide an overview of the different types of eye-tracking systems available and of the main technical specifications that need to be considered when planning eye-tracking research. For practical reasons, it is not possible to review all eye-tracking systems currently available, so we will review the features of some of the most commonly used ones:[1] EyeLink II, 1000/1000 Plus, Portable Duo (SR Research, www.sr-research.com); Tobii T/X series, Tobii Pro TX300 (Tobii, www.tobii.com); and iView X RED, RED and X Hi-Speed series (SensoMotoric Instruments (SMI),[2] www.smivision.com).[3]

2.2 Types of Eye-Trackers

Performing an eye-tracking experiment involves acquiring a continuous record of the eye's position relative to a visual stimulus, such that the recorded eye gaze is matched with the time course of the stimulus (Sedivy, 2010). For example, if we present participants with two images – x and y – we may want to know at specific time points where a participant was looking: at image x, image y or somewhere else. Most of the commercially available eye-trackers currently on the market are video-based systems, with eye-movements monitored by an infra-red camera directed at a participant's eyes.[4] Recordings of the locations of the

---

[1] Although some of these systems have been discontinued by manufacturers, we have included them as they are still used by research groups.

[2] Apple recently acquired SensoMotoric Instruments, which will likely pose challenges for SMI users; the level of support and pace of developments may change or cease entirely.

[3] A draft of this chapter has been checked by the three main manufacturers referred to here: SR Research, Tobii and SensoMotoric Instruments (SMI).

[4] Alternative methods for recording eye-movements include electro-oculography, photo/video-oculography and scleral contact lenses/search coil. However, these methods are mainly used in clinical settings and have therefore not been included in this chapter. See Duchowski (2007) for a review of them.

eyes are based on pupil-only detection or pupil and corneal reflection detections, with the latter being the predominant method. Pupil with corneal reflection tracking has the advantage of compensating for small head movements, which has made it the dominant tracking method (Holmqvist et al., 2011). Additionally, systems differ in whether the pupil is visualised as bright or dark. Different illumination methods make the pupil appear dark or bright in the eye image. Although both are used by some systems, dark pupil tracking is the most common (see Table 2.1 at the end of Section 2.3). If the pupil is large, both light and dark tracking seem to work in a similar way. However, as Holmqvist et al. (2011) explain, with small pupil sizes, the bright pupil tracking method may fail.

Video-based eye-trackers work by analysing the video images of the tracked eye(s), which are illuminated by an infra-red light source. The eye-tracker then outputs (to a data file or in some cases to a real-time data stream) the eye's *x* and *y* coordinates on the screen where the stimulus is displayed (Duchowski, 2007). Using predefined algorithms, the system's software translates the analysed eye-image information to specific gaze position data. The recorded gaze data are then matched up with the experimental stimuli so that eye-gaze data can be mapped onto the identified regions of interest (ROIs).

As we will see in Chapter 3, eye-tracker software varies in its ability to compute and extract different kinds of measures. The eye positions sampled by eye-trackers are parsed into eye-movement events (e.g. fixations, saccades, blinks). These eye-movements are then used to compute different types of measures. Thus, it is important to be familiar with the different eye-movement measures that are the most appropriate to address a specific research question, and to make sure that the software can compute and export the data we require. For example, the software for SR Research and SMI systems can export specific metrics for regressions (movements back to an ROI), whereas Tobii systems can only output measures of fixations and saccades. Regressions can still be calculated from the information on absolute and relative saccadic direction between fixations in the data export, although this makes the extraction of regression data more laborious. The use of publicly available R scripts (R Development Core Team, 2016) might help with this task.

We can distinguish three main types of eye-trackers based on the position of the camera in relation to the eye, the zoom level of the lens (with greater magnification meaning a better quality signal than wide-angle lenses with lower magnification) and the algorithms used to parse eye-movement events): (1) high-precision, head-stabilised eye-trackers; (2) remote, head-free-to-move eye-trackers; and (3) head-mounted eye-trackers. We will talk about each in turn.

High-precision, head-stabilised eye-trackers have zoomed-in views of the eyes and use algorithms that assume a constant distance and steady illumination. The camera and infra-red light can be positioned remotely near the monitor (desktop mounting) with a head support (see Figure 2.1) or in close contact with the participant, usually integrated in a head-rest (tower mounting option, see Figure 2.2).

In *remote, head-free-to-move* eye-trackers the camera and infra-red light are placed remotely on or near the monitor (Figure 2.3). The camera and illumination can be integrated in the monitor (e.g. Tobii T60/120), or can be a separate device that is located typically below the monitor (e.g. SR Research EyeLink 1000/1000 Plus, Portable Duo, Tobii Pro X2-60/X3-120, SMI RED5, REDn Scientific, RED250mobile). When it is a separate device, it can be placed on the desk (desktop mounting option) or on an LCD arm mounting in some eye-trackers (see Table 2.1). It can also be used with other screens. Many eye-trackers offer these two set-up options, i.e. they can be attached to

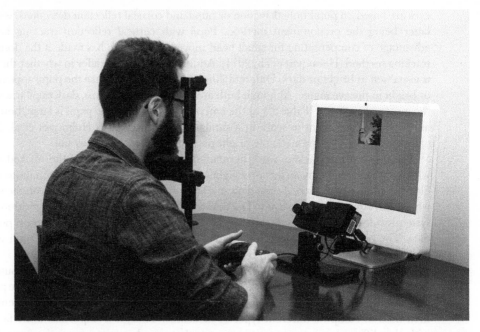

Figure 2.1 SR Research EyeLink 1000 Plus with desktop mount being used with head support in its high-precision mode (SR Research, www.sr-research.com).

a monitor and function as an integrated screen set-up or they can be removed to function as a stand-alone eye-tracker, increasing flexibility in the studies that can be run (e.g. SR Research EyeLink 1000/1000 Plus and Portable Duo, Tobii Pro TX300, SMI RED series).

Remote, head-free-to-move systems need a zoomed-out, low-magnification view of the eye to allow for a large visual field. The image of the eye will consequently be poorer than when a high-power zoom lens is used. Because of the free head movement, the illumination and distance are constantly changing. Therefore, dynamic algorithms must be used to compensate for the changing conditions, which produces noisier sample-level data. A common misconception is that researchers can get a remote tracker and add a head support to achieve high-precision tracking. However, certain technical specifications (e.g. the system's lens/zoom/algorithm combination) would also need to be adapted to the head-stabilised option and not all remote systems can do this. It is also important to note that not all remote systems are head-free-to-move systems, nor do they have to have lower-quality data. The camera can be placed remotely but we can have a good zoom lens to compensate.

Some remote eye-trackers can collect data in both head-stabilised, high-precision tracking and remote, head-free-to-move tracking modes. The SR Research EyeLink 1000/1000 Plus with desktop mounts, for example, is a remote tracker that allows high accuracy and low noise in both head-stabilised and head-free-to-move options.

An important source of missing data in remote, head-free-to-move eye-trackers is tracking recovery time, i.e. the time that it takes an eye-tracker to recover when the eye is lost. Remote, head-free-to-move eye-trackers with a long recovery time should be avoided as it will lead to a lot of missing data.

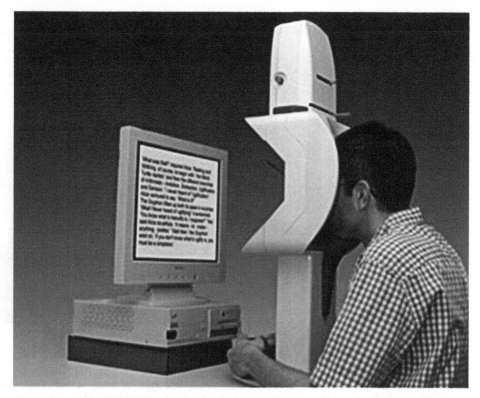

Figure 2.2 SMI iView X Hi-Speed tower-mounted eye-tracker (SMI, www.smivision.com).

The majority of remote eye-trackers have portable functionality (e.g. SR Research EyeLink 1000/1000 Plus and Portable Duo, Tobii systems, SMI RED5, RED250mobile, REDn Scientific). This is particularly advantageous when conducting research with children and participants from specific locations, since it avoids having to ask participants to come to a laboratory. However, this doesn't mean that experiments can be conducted anywhere. Often the location of the experiment still needs to be carefully controlled, avoiding set-up in a noisy room with distractors or with direct sunlight, unless the examination of the effect of these factors on eye-movement behaviour is one of the research aims (see discussion in Section 3.5.1).

While remote eye-trackers allow for head movement, they can only account for a certain degree of head movement without having a negative impact on data quality. Technical specifications usually include information about the specific amount of head movement that the system can account for. Since exceeding these measures might have an impact on data quality, we should use a system that allows for the right degree of head movement for our experiment.

The selection of remote eye-trackers is often based on the argument that they allow for a more natural experience, adding ecological validity to the experiment (Holmqvist et al., 2011). However, as Holmqvist et al. state, this superiority is still to be empirically proven. Some systems also offer the possibility of a remote camera upgrade that tracks the position of the head even during eye blinks (e.g. SR Research EyeLink 1000/1000 Plus Remote with camera upgrade, EyeLink Portable Duo). This allows for precision in the recording

Figure 2.3 Tobii Pro TX300 remote, desktop-mounted eye-tracker (Tobii AB).

without the need to use a chin-rest or any other type of head stabilisation. The SR Research EyeLink Portable Duo and the EyeLink 1000/1000 Plus systems in remote mode measure head distance independent of the eye by placing a small target sticker on the participant's forehead. The position of the head is tracked even during very quick head movements. This is particularly useful for those experiments in which high levels of precision and accuracy are necessary, but the use of a head/chin-rest is not desirable. If we plan to use a remote eye-tracker it is advisable to ask manufacturers if they offer any options for tracking head position.

The third type of eye-trackers, *head-mounted eye-trackers*, are those that place the camera and infra-red light on the head of the participant, in a helmet or cap (Figure 2.4). Some head-mounted eye-trackers also include a head camera to record the position of the head in relation to the display, which facilitates data analysis (Holmqvist et al., 2011). Head-mounted eye-trackers provide greater accuracy and are more tolerant of head movements than remote eye-trackers, but they can be quite heavy and may not be appropriate for research with children or for very long experiments. Eye-tracking glasses are another type of head-mounted eye-tracker (see specifications of Tobii Pro Glasses 2 and SMI Eye-Tracking Glasses 2 Wireless in Table 2.1). Here, the camera and infra-red light are placed on a pair of glasses or goggles that participants wear, allowing them to move freely and to interact more easily with the environment (Figure 2.5). However, they tend to have low accuracy and lower sampling rates which has an impact on the quality of the data recorded (see Section 2.3). Importantly, when using glasses or goggles, there is no control over what the subject is looking at, which becomes a major undertaking for data analysis. Eye-tracking glasses are currently used in a wide range of research fields (e.g. sports psychology, media consumption, commercial market research). In the future, they might be used by applied linguists to investigate, for example, participants'

Figure 2.4 SR Research EyeLink II head-mounted eye-tracker (SR Research, www.sr-research.com).

Figure 2.5 SMI Eye-Tracking Glasses (SMI, www.smivision.com).

attention to the interlocutor's gestures and other non-verbal codes in spoken interaction, but accuracy and difficulty of data analysis will still be important constraints. Very recently a new trend has emerged that has been termed 'immersive research', which presents participants with 360° still images or video as stimuli in order to make the

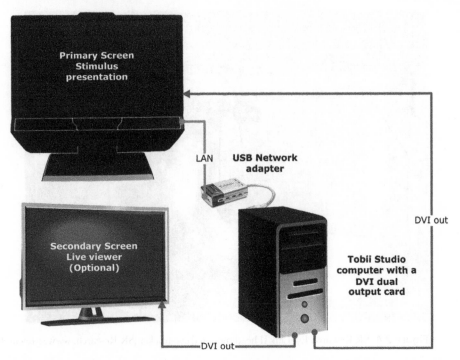

Figure 2.6 Tobii Pro TX300 system set-up with two screens. The primary screen is used for stimulus presentation and the second screen is used to monitor eye-movements in real time (Tobii AB).

participant feel physically present inside the stimulus (SMI HTC Vive Head Mounted Display at 250 Hz).

Most eye-tracking systems have a computer screen that participants sit in front of and which displays the stimuli to them. Towers and the remote tracking devices are positioned on or near this monitor. Often, there will be an additional monitor, sometimes referred to as the 'host' PC. The host PC processes and records eye-movement data, and this second computer screen allows the operator to observe the experiment and the participant's eye-movements in real time. This will help the experimenter monitor the calibration accuracy, which is important for maintaining data quality (see Section 2.3). Most systems allow both laptops and desktops as the host PC (e.g. SR Research EyeLink 1000 Plus, SMI RED series). Some eye-tracking systems do not need a host PC and can be set up with only one screen, i.e. the screen where the eye-tracker is integrated (e.g. Tobii Pro TX300). However, this means that the experimenter cannot monitor the data as they are acquired (see Section 3.4 for more on setting up an eye-tracker). In Tobii systems, a second screen can be connected to the computer on which we run the recording software, and can be used to view the eye-movements in real time. The Tobii Pro Studio software can also be connected remotely (using the Remote Viewer software) to another computer in the same or in a different room. Figure 2.6 illustrates a typical set-up of a Tobii Pro TX300 eye-tracking remote system with two screens.

2.3 Technical Specifications (Hardware Properties)

The technical specifications of eye-tracking systems can be daunting. When starting out using the technology, it can be difficult to know what is important for a particular kind of study. In this section, we go through the key technical specifications that should be considered when selecting an eye-tracking system and the implications that those specifications have for the design of experiments and the analysis of eye-movement data.

2.3.1 Monocular or Binocular Recording

The list of technical features of a system specifies whether an eye-tracker records from one eye only (*monocular eye-tracking*) or from both eyes (*binocular eye-tracking*). Some systems allow us to select monocular or binocular tracking, whereas other systems only offer binocular tracking (see Table 2.1). If choosing the monocular tracking option, it is important to decide which eye to use. This needs to be specified in the settings before outputting the data, as the default setting for data export in most of these systems is binocular and the output is an average of the data recorded from both eyes. The common procedure is to track the same eye for all participants, but some researchers prefer to record participants' dominant eye, in which case a quick test to determine visual dominance would be needed (e.g. the Miles Test; Miles, 1930).

Some systems that perform the recording binocularly can output separate data streams for each eye (e.g. Tobii and SMI systems). This has the advantage of allowing the researcher to choose data from the eye with the best accuracy for the analysis (Raney, Campbell and Bovee, 2014), which may be particularly useful when collecting data from children. This involves checking the accuracy of all the data (the data recorded with the right and left eyes for each participant) to decide which eye to select for the analysis. However, not all binocular eye-trackers can output separate data streams for each eye. Other binocular systems calculate the average location of the right and left eyes and output an averaged data stream. This could in principle lead to better precision if both eyes are correctly tracked, but could also be problematic if one of the eyes is not correctly recorded. The main disadvantage of binocular tracking is that the eye-tracker may operate at a lower sampling rate, which may lead to lower-quality data (Conklin and Pellicer-Sánchez, 2016). In fact, some configurations that allow for both types of recording (e.g. SR Research EyeLink systems operating in high-precision, head-stabilised modes and the SMI iView Hi-Speed) capture fewer data samples when binocular tracking is chosen (see Section 2.3.2). Further, calibration with binocular recording might take longer. Importantly, the eyes are believed to move more or less in synchrony – moving at the same time to approximately the same location. Fixations by the left and right eyes are generally to the same position, but may vary by one or two letter spaces (Liversedge et al., 2006). However, this slight disparity would generally not be of concern in the kinds of studies we would do, and therefore there is normally no advantage in recording binocularly for the kinds of language research that we will discuss in the book. In general, monocular recording is common practice in eye-movement research (Raney et al., 2014).

2.3.2 Data Quality

One of the main criteria in the selection of an eye-tracking system is the quality of the data. As Holmqvist, Nyström and Mulvey (2012) state, 'The validity of research results based on eye movement analysis are clearly dependent on the quality of eye movement data' (p. 45). We therefore need to ensure that the data recorded are of sufficient quality. Data quality is determined by several properties of the eye-tracker, so we will now discuss some of the most important properties: *sampling rate, accuracy, precision* and *latency*.

Sampling Rate

One of the key features that determines data quality is the *sampling rate* or *sampling frequency* of the equipment. Sampling rate is the speed with which eye-movements are recorded, i.e. the number of samples captured per second, and is measured in hertz (Hz). If an eye-tracker has a sampling rate of 300 Hz, this means that eye-movements are recorded 300 times per second. Any sampling errors will have a larger impact on data recorded with a system with a low sampling rate than with a system with a high sampling rate (provided that all the other features of the systems are the same), which may therefore result in lower-quality data. Usually, the higher the speed, the more expensive the system, which can make deciding on a sampling rate a less than straightforward decision. We can currently find eye-trackers with sampling rates ranging from 30 Hz to 2000 Hz. The required sampling rate depends on what is being measured in the experiment and the specific research questions we want to answer. Sampling rate will be less of an issue if our ROIs are large areas of the screen, and thus systems with a high or low sampling rate would be suitable. However, when recording eye-movements to smaller areas of the screen, like individual words, phrases or sentences, a higher sampling rate will be one of the factors that contributes to the required level of data quality. For reading, systems with sampling rates of 500 Hz or 1000 Hz are best, but imprecision does not seem to be a problem with systems recording at 250 Hz, which is often considered the threshold between low speed and high speed (Holmqvist et al., 2011). A sample rate of less than 250 Hz does not mean that eye-movements to smaller ROIs cannot be examined and that the experiment cannot be run, but a larger amount of data is needed to overcome the imprecision introduced by the low sampling rate.

The negative impact of a low sampling rate can be compensated for to *some extent* with more data (Holmqvist et al., 2011), which translates into having to record data from more participants and adding more stimuli. Andersson, Nyström and Holmqvist (2010) calculated the relationship between sampling frequency and data requirements and explained how to determine the amount of data points needed to account for the sampling error introduced by systems with lower sampling rates. They also provide a graph with estimates of the required data points per sampling frequency, which makes this calculation even easier (see Andersson et al., 2010, for a detailed explanation of this method). As an example, if we are looking at fixation durations recorded by a system with a 60 Hz sampling rate, a total of 675 data points would be needed. The Andersson et al. equation can also be used to check if we have the appropriate amount of data for our experiment and to determine whether more data need to be collected to find an effect. If we are using a system with a low sampling rate, knowing how much data will be needed to accurately answer the intended research questions before designing the experiment is crucial, as the amount of data points needed might be impractical, resulting in experiments which are too long and which require too large a participant sample given the number of potential research participants available.

It is important to note that low sampling rate is only one contributor to poor data quality. Collecting more data allows us to overcome the temporal uncertainty over saccade latencies and fixation durations, but it doesn't address other issues associated with low-speed systems such as low-quality lenses.

Some eye-trackers can operate with two or more different sampling rates. For example, the SR Research EyeLink 1000 with the 2000 Hz option can operate at 2000 Hz, 1000 Hz or 500 Hz; the Tobii T120 can run with a sampling rate of 120 Hz or 60 Hz. When we have a choice, we always need to make sure that we are running an experiment with the appropriate sampling rate. In the majority of cases, a higher sampling rate is preferred so we would need to make sure that this is the one selected in the recording settings of the equipment. It is also important to note that the systems that allow for monocular and binocular tracking might operate at a different sampling rate for each tracking option, with sampling rates reduced in some systems when both eyes are tracked (see Table 2.1).

In sum, because of its effect on data quality, the sampling rate of the system (together with the features described in the next section) determines the type of research questions that can be investigated, as well as having implications for the size of our ROIs (individual-word-level precision vs large sections of text), making it one of the key technical features when choosing an eye-tracking system, and one of the main selling points used by manufacturers.

Accuracy, Precision and Latency

Data quality is also determined by the *accuracy* of the system. Accuracy is defined as the average difference between the true and the measured gaze position (see Figure 2.7). This distance between the measured fixation locations and the true fixation locations is measured in degrees of visual angle. The gaze position recorded by eye-trackers does not always correspond to the exact position of the eye, and a certain level of mismatch is expected. High accuracy is particularly needed for studies in which we have smaller ROIs, for instance when we want to make claims about participants' reading of specific words. Accuracy can depend on the distance between the participant and the eye-tracker, with the optimum operating distance depending on the eye-tracking system. We therefore need to make sure that participants are placed at the recommended distance from the eye-tracker (usually provided in the technical specifications and user manuals; see Section 3.4 for more information about the eye-tracker set-up).

There are different ways of checking and reporting the accuracy of the equipment. In the technical specifications of the eye-tracking systems, manufacturers report the accuracy of the system in degrees of visual angles (see Table 2.1). Referring to the information provided by the manufacturer is therefore the most common way to report accuracy values. This might make us think that all experiments conducted with a specific eye-tracker have the same accuracy. However, the accuracy values reported by most manufacturers have been calculated at ideal conditions and, when calculated under some non-ideal conditions (including head movement and ambient-light-induced pupil size changes, as can happen in Tobii systems), we cannot assume that the accuracy of our experiment will be the same as what appears in the manufacturer's report. Accuracy is determined on a per-subject basis based on calibration and it needs to be assessed per individual participant. As Holmqvist et al. (2012) state, 'This assumption of optimal accuracy across all recording conditions and participants is unlikely to be correct and may lead to invalid results even when data loss is accounted for and the data look reasonable' (p. 51).

The lack of standardisation in reporting accuracy on a participant and/or item basis has led researchers to report the accuracy values provided by manufacturers, without measuring the data quality of a particular dataset. Although it is important to report the accuracy of the equipment as reported by the manufacturer, it is also crucial to ensure that the experimental data have been recorded within those accuracy levels. In some systems the accuracy of gaze positions can be checked in the initial calibration of the equipment (see Section 3.4.2). The degree of error is reported after the calibration and validation procedure and most systems state whether the calibration is good/acceptable or if it needs to be recalibrated. Average gaze error should be within 0.5° and 1.0°. However, a good calibration and validation do not ensure that accuracy is going to be maintained at that level throughout the experiment. Thus, it is important to monitor the experiment to identify when accuracy has dropped and decide whether and when to recalibrate. As explained in Section 2.2, the use of a second screen makes this kind of monitoring possible. When we have this second screen, the eye-tracking system allows us to watch in real time what the participant is doing. Some tools let researchers not only observe the experiment but also annotate behaviour in real time (e.g. the annotation feature in SMI Experiment Center).

An important difference among systems that affects the accuracy of the data is the possibility to perform drift corrections. Obtaining a successful initial calibration and validation does not guarantee that a participant's eye gaze will remain at the same level of accuracy throughout the experiment. Many different factors, such as changes in head position or pupil size across a recording session, can lead to cases of drift, i.e. deviations from the calibrated gaze positions, which can be corrected during the experiment. SR Research EyeLink systems, for example, allow the researcher to include drift corrections as often as needed during the experiment. Tobii systems, however, do not have this functionality and data accuracy therefore relies on the initial calibration and subsequent pre-set calibrations throughout the experiment.

Despite these attempts to calculate and maintain accuracy, there will always be a certain amount of data that needs to be excluded because of tracking difficulties with specific participants which lead to poor accuracy and precision or to data that are not available at all. The percentage of data losses reported by studies varies significantly, with reports ranging from 2 to 60 per cent (Holmqvist et al., 2012). Since data accuracy depends on many different factors pertaining to a particular experiment and participant, no specific threshold for what constitutes an expected percentage of data loss is generally provided. However, in our experience, it is usual to see a data loss of between 3 and 10 per cent with adult participants. Seeing a data loss of more than 10 per cent may raise 'red flags' about the equipment set-up and therefore about the quality of the data that have been acquired. Importantly, the amount of data loss could increase with groups like children, who may have difficulty sitting fairly still for the duration of a study.

Accuracy is very often discussed together with *precision*. Precision is defined as the ability to reproduce a measurement in a reliable way, and refers to the spatial variation between the different data samples that are recorded when a participant if fixating a point (see Figure 2.7). As Holmqvist et al. (2012) explain, 'Precision refers to how consistent calculated gaze points are' (p. 46). Although the terms 'accuracy' and 'precision' are sometimes used interchangeably, they are in fact two different technical specifications of eye-tracking systems. Precision can be calculated as the average root mean square (RMS) of inter-sample distances in the data. RMS values of current eye-trackers range from 1° to 0.01°. For very accurate measurement of fixation durations and saccades, we should aim at

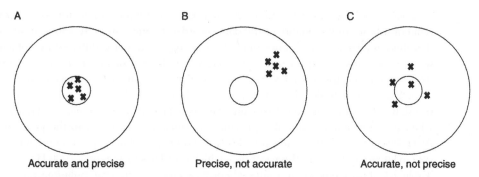

Figure 2.7 Depiction of the difference between accuracy and precision with crosses representing fixation points. In A the recorded fixations are precise and accurate; in B they are precise but not accurate; and in C they are accurate but not precise.

a RMS lower than 0.05° (Holmqvist et al., 2011). Precision is a consequence of many factors, one of which is camera focus. In systems where we can adjust the focus of the camera, we may be able to improve precision in some situations. Of course, this is only possible in eye-tracking systems in which the researcher is in charge of setting up the camera (e.g. SR Research EyeLink systems, SMI iView series), but cannot be adjusted in systems in which the camera set-up is done automatically (e.g. Tobii systems, SMI RED series). Not all manufacturers report precision, but this is certainly another important feature to check when choosing a system.

It is important not only to check the accuracy and precision values reported by the manufacturers, but also to understand how they were calculated. As Holmqvist et al. (2011) point out, different manufacturers use different terms for measuring quality and have different ways of calculating and reporting the performance of their systems, which makes comparison and standardisation between systems very difficult. Some manufacturers calculate the values using an artificial eye, which eliminates noise other than that generated by the eye-tracker. However, as explained by Holmqvist et al. (2011), values calculated with artificial eyes might be misleading as they don't have the properties of human eyes. For this reason, some manufacturers also calculate accuracy and precision values based on a large sample of real participants. The distribution of values calculated with real participants is more representative of the values we will get in an actual experiment. Some manufacturers report both values (calculated with artificial eyes and with real participants), and this is the preferred option as it provides a clearer estimation of the values of our experiment.

Ideally, we should not only report the accuracy and precision values reported by manufacturers and ensure that accuracy and precision are maintained throughout the experiment, but also calculate accuracy and precision values for our own experiment. This can be done by having participants fixate a set of targets and comparing the exact position of the targets with the recorded fixation positions in the exported raw data. It is beyond the scope of this chapter to explain the different methods for calculating accuracy and precision values, so for a more detailed description see Holmqvist et al. (2011).[5]

---

[5] Reporting the actual accuracy and precision values for a study is the ideal, as it makes research more transparent. However, it is not currently standard practice to do so in language research.

Total system latency (or *end-to-end sample delay*) is another important feature of eye-trackers that contributes to the quality of the data recorded by the system. It is important to note that there is a lack of consistency in the terminology used by the different manufacturers, which makes this a complex issue. The total system latency of an eye-tracker is defined as 'the average end-to-end delay from an actual movement of the tracked eye until the recording computer signals that a movement has taken place' (Holmqvist et al., 2011, p. 43). In other words, it refers to the time between the real eye-movement and the moment when the experimental stimulus presentation software has access to the position data. As Holmqvist et al. (2011) indicate, ideally a good eye-tracking system should have a total system latency of less than three samples, which translates to 3 ms on a 1000 Hz system (see Table 2.1). Low latency determines whether gaze-contingent manipulations are possible. Thus, it is particularly important if the experimental manipulations depend on the stimulus changing based on the ongoing gaze position, such as in the boundary paradigm (see Section 4.5 for a detailed discussion of this paradigm), but it does not have a direct impact on recorded data quality.

It is important to note that data quality is not only affected by the specifications of the system used. Other situational factors also impact the quality of the data recorded, including: the participants (whether they are wearing glasses, contact lenses, mascara, etc.); how skilled the operators are; the lab environment (e.g. the presence of sunlight and noise); and the requirements of the task. The experimental design also affects the required level of data quality. For example, experiments with smaller ROIs require better data quality. More precisely, when doing research on reading, where we want to pinpoint fixations to words or small sections of the text, we would need a system with sampling rates greater than 250 Hz, accuracy values within 0.5° and precision better than 0.05° to be able to record high-quality data. When examining the processing of larger areas, such as pictures and quadrants on a screen, a system of a lower sampling rate (below 250 Hz), lower accuracy and lower precision would be enough to record data of sufficient quality. It is crucial that we choose a system that is accurate and precise enough and with a good enough latency for our research questions.

2.4 Software Properties

Each eye-tracker is supported by different software packages that are used to build the experiment, and record and analyse the data. Checking the properties of the software can be as important as checking the technical specifications of the hardware, since ultimately the software will make the design of the experiment and the data analysis more or less difficult (or possible in some cases). Some eye-tracking systems have separate software for creating the experiment and for analysing the data (e.g. SR Research and SMI systems), whereas other systems have one single software program supporting the entire research process (e.g. Tobii systems), including the design, recording of the data and presentation of results (see Table 2.2).

The stimulus presentation software offered by the eye-tracking manufacturers works in different ways. As with any software and computer program, in order to fully understand how it works, we need to start using it. The different software packages allow us to add more or less the same types of stimuli, but the specific approach varies and sometimes we will need to use workarounds to build the study exactly as we want. In what follows, we summarise some features that are different across the software that may be important to applied linguistics researchers. A more detailed discussion of how the

Table 2.1 Main technical specifications of some of the eye-tracking systems by SR Research, Tobii and SensoMotoric Instruments.

	Manufacturer	Eye-tracking method	Mounting options	Type of recording	Sampling rate	Accuracy	Precision (RMS)	End-to-end sample delay/Total system latency
EyeLink II	SR Research	Dark pupil-CR[b] or Dark pupil only	Head-mounted	Binocular or monocular	250 Hz (pupil-CR mode) 500 Hz (dark pupil only mode)	0.25°–0.5°	0.01° RMS (pupil-only mode) 0.022° (pupil-CR mode)	< 3 ms
EyeLink 1000 Plus	SR Research	Dark pupil-CR (pupil only available with head fixed conditions)	Desktop Tower LCD arm	Binocular or monocular	Head supported: 1000 Hz (monocular); 500 Hz (binocular) With 2000 Hz upgrade: 2000 Hz (monocular); 1000 Hz (binocular) Remote/head free: 500 Hz binocular	Head supported: 0.25°–0.5° With 2000 Hz upgrade: 0.25°–0.5° Remote/head free: 0.25°–0.5°	Head supported: < 0.01° With 2000 Hz upgrade: < 0.01° Remote/head free: 0.01°	Head supported: 1.95 ms @ 1000 Hz With 2000 Hz upgrade: 1.68 ms @ 2000 Hz Remote/head free: 2.98 ms @ 500 Hz
EyeLink Portable Duo	SR Research	Dark pupil-CR (pupil only available with head fixed conditions)	Desktop Laptop	Binocular or monocular	Head supported: 500 Hz (binocular) Remote/head free: 500 Hz binocular	Head supported: 0.25°–0.5° Remote/head free: 0.25°–0.5°	Head supported: < 0.01° Remote/head free: < 0.01°	< 3 ms @ 500 Hz
EyeLink 1000[a]	SR Research	Dark pupil-CR	Desktop Tower LCD arm	Binocular or monocular	Head supported: 2000 Hz (monocular); 1000 Hz (binocular) Remote/head Free: 500 Hz monocular	Head supported: 0.25°–0.5° Remote/head free: 0.25°–0.5°	Head supported: < 0.01° Remote/head free: < 0.05°	Head supported: 1.4 ms @ 2000 Hz Remote/head free: 3 ms @ 500 Hz
Tobii T Series (T60/T120[a], T60 XL)	Tobii	Dark and bright pupil tracking	Desktop (integrated in the monitor)	Binocular	60 Hz (T60 system and T60 XL) 120 Hz (T120 system)	0.5°	0.2°	< 33 ms
			Desktop	Binocular	60 Hz (X2 60 system)	0.4° (both systems)	0.34° (X2 60 system)	< 33 ms

Table 2.1 (cont.)

	Manufacturer	Eye-tracking method	Mounting options	Type of recording	Sampling rate	Accuracy	Precision (RMS)	End-to-end sample delay/Total system latency
Tobii Pro X series (X2 60/X3 120)		Dark and bright pupil tracking			120 Hz (X3 120 system)		0.24° (X3 120 system)	
Tobii Pro TX300	Tobii	Dark pupil tracking	Desktop	Binocular	60, 120, 300 Hz	0.4°	0.14°	< 10 ms
Tobii Pro Glasses 2	Tobii	Dark pupil-CR	Head-mounted	Binocular	50, 100 Hz	N/A	N/A	N/A
iView X RED series	SMI	Dark pupil-CR	Desktop Laptop	Binocular	60, 120, 250, 500 Hz	0.4°	0.03°	< 4 ms
iView RED series (REDn Scientific / RED250mobile) (RED250mobile)	SMI	Dark pupil-CR	Desktop Laptop	Binocular or monocular	60 Hz (REDn Scientific) 60, 120, 250 Hz (RED250mobile)	0.4°	0.05° (REDn Scientific) 0.03° (RED250mobile)	< 25 ms (REDn Scientific) < 8 ms (RED250mobile)
iView X Hi-Speed	SMI	Dark pupil only Or Dark pupil-CR	Tower	Binocular or monocular	1250, 500 Hz (monocular) 500 Hz (binocular)	0.25–0.5°	< 0.01	< 2 ms (typical)
SMI Eye-Tracking Glasses 2 Wireless	SMI	N/A	Head-mounted	Binocular	60, 120 Hz	0.5°	N/A	N/A

[a] These systems are discontinued now but have been included here as they might still be used by some research groups. The SR Research EyeLink 1000 has been replaced by the SR Research EyeLink 1000 Plus and EyeLink Portable Duo; Tobii T series have been replaced by Tobii Pro X series.

[b] Corneal reflections.

Table 2.2 Software and operating systems supported by the three main types of eye-trackers discussed in this chapter.

Eye-tracker	Stimulus presentation software	Analysis software	Operating systems
SR Research EyeLink systems	Experiment Builder	Data Viewer	Experiment Builder: Windows and OS X Data Viewer: Windows, OS X and Linux
Tobii systems	Tobii Pro Studio		Windows (The free software development kit Tobii Pro Analytics SDK is compatible with OS and Ubuntu)
SMI systems	Experiment Center	BeGaze	Windows

different types of stimuli can be added in each of the three main software programs is provided in Section 3.1.3. Text, static images and videos are the main stimulus types for all of the systems we have mentioned in this chapter (although they are added in different ways). Using separate audio files as a stimulus source is possible in Experiment Builder (SR Research) and Experiment Center (SMI). Dynamic webpages are one of the main stimulus elements in Tobii Pro Studio and Experiment Center, whereas in EyeLink systems we would need to use the free Screen Recorder software, which allows for a video screen capture of whatever is happening on the screen. Another difference is the possibility of including questionnaires in the experimental design. Tobii Pro Studio and Experiment Center have specific resource tools which allow us to easily create multiple-choice questionnaires, whereas in Experiment Builder we would need to use the text resource tool or have a component specifically designed for the purposes of our study.

After designing the experiment and collecting the data, the analysis software is used to process and analyse the data. The analysis software used by each of the eye-tracking systems also varies. It is important to know the basic characteristics of the analysis software to make sure that the tools for data analysis allow us to access the data we need. For example, as we touched on previously in this chapter, the Tobii system does not output regression metrics. If we need to analyse data from regressions to answer a particular research question, we would need to calculate this based on the order of fixations and the saccadic information between fixations. The different analysis software packages offer a range of visualisation options (see Section 7.1.3 for more on the options available and how to create them in each software package). However, it should be noted that visualisations do *not* constitute an analysis of the data and should not be used as a report of findings in papers and academic publications without additional supporting statistical analysis (see Section 7.3 for a more detailed discussion on different types of visualisations).

Another important software feature to consider is the tools offered for exporting the eye-movement data. Some software programs offer more advanced tools for exporting and analysing the data, whereas others have more limited options, which makes the data analysis phase more time-consuming and laborious. The three software programs referred to in this chapter offer the possibility of producing some descriptive statistics for all of the trials recorded in an experiment without the need for other statistical analysis programs. This is particularly useful to get an initial idea about our data and some preliminary insights into eye-movement patterns. However, in the majority of cases we will need a complete report of the gaze events made within our selected ROIs so that the data can be examined using more sophisticated statistical analyses, often using software like SPSS (IBM SPSS Statistics, 2016) or R (R Development Core Team, 2016; see Section 7.2 for a more detailed discussion of data analysis). Although the eye-movement measures that can be exported vary among systems, all software programs offer the option of exporting the average values of the selected eye-movement measures per ROI. This ROI report would create a columnar output (usually in Excel or a text file) of eye-movement data for each ROI in a trial, with one row/column for each ROI.

Importantly, very often we need to work with the raw data of individual fixations, as opposed to averaged values per ROI, to be able to identify and discard outliers and to normalise the data (see Section 7.1). The raw data reports generated by different software programs differ in terms of the amount of information that is included, which can affect how easy or difficult it is to work with the data file. With Data Viewer (SR Research) and Experiment Center, for example, apart from an ROI report we can also output individual fixation/saccade reports and create a columnar output of fixation events/saccades, with each row of the report representing a fixation/saccade made within the selected ROIs. This is particularly useful when we would like, for example, to identify fixations in our data that are too short or too long that we might want to remove (see Section 7.1.3). Tobii Pro Studio, on the other hand, only produces a report including all gaze events, regardless of whether they fall within the identified ROIs. Extra columns for each ROI are provided and the numbers 0 and 1 indicate whether the ROI has been fixated or not. A report that outputs all fixations, not only those to our ROIs, can take more time and effort to sort and identify relevant data. It is therefore important to have a clear idea of the type of data reports that the software can export, as well as an idea of what we will need for any analyses. Notably, some of the data analysis tools are only available with a specific version of a program or with an optional upgrade, so it is also important to find out what the software package includes.

These software programs are revised and updated frequently so it is advisable to be aware of the changes and developments in the latest versions, and download software updates when useful functionalities are added. Most manufacturers have demo versions of the software packages that can be downloaded for free for a trial period. Although these demo versions don't allow us to use all of the tools and functions, they provide a good idea of what the software offers and how it works.

Overall, the functionality offered by the different software packages will influence the design of certain experiments and/or the ease of performing different types of analyses. However, ease of use should not be the sole determining factor when selecting an eye-tracking system. If we are going to conduct research that requires high-quality data and precise data analysis, the properties of the hardware and software should override the ease of use. Even the seemingly most complex eye-tracking software can be used within a relatively short period of time. Learning how to use the software and equipment takes time and practice, but does not require any previous programming or computing background (unless additional plug-ins and additional functionality are required; see Chapter 3).

2.5 Conclusions and Final Checklist

As illustrated by the discussion in this chapter, the choice of eye-tracking system can dictate the kind of research studies that can be conducted and will impact the quality of the data collected. It is not the aim of this book to make recommendations about specific systems. Each of the eye-tracking systems has different strengths and weaknesses. As discussed above, systems of lower accuracy and precision (e.g. Tobii Pro X2-60) can be appropriate for experimental studies that measure eye-movements to bigger areas of the screen, such as pictures or real-world stimuli. They are also suitable if we only need to look at more general measures of eye-movements, without the need to measure short saccades or regressions. However, systems of higher accuracy (e.g. SR Research EyeLink II/1000/1000 Plus/Portable Duo, Tobii Pro TX300, SMI Hi-Speed/RED5/RED250mobile) are required for research examining eye-movements to smaller ROIs, such as fixations made to individual words or short phrases, where data of higher quality is needed. The discussion provided in this chapter should support researchers in evaluating the appropriateness of a system for a specific research purpose. This final checklist aims to help researchers in this evaluation.

Final checklist	
• Consider the characteristics of the task, the participants and the location of your research; which type of eye-tracker and mounting options do you need for your research?	⇨ If you are conducting experiments with children, remote, head-free-to-move equipment might be better. For other populations, high-precision, head-stabilised equipment will be best.
	⇨ If you are conducting experiments that involve typing, a head-free-to-move system might also be better.
	⇨ If you are conducting research in different locations, a portable eye-tracker is needed.
• What type of recording does the eye-tracker offer: monocular and/or binocular?	⇨ Monocular recording is common practice in the type of eye-movement research that we discuss in this book.
	⇨ Systems that offer both types of recording (and separate data streams for each eye) provide more flexibility.
• Can the eye-tracker provide the data quality you need? (Check sampling rate, accuracy, precision and latency.)	⇨ For bigger ROIs, lower sampling rate, precision and accuracy might be acceptable.
	⇨ For smaller ROIs, higher data quality is needed. Systems with a sampling rate >250 Hz, accuracy values <0.5° and precision >0.05° should be used.
	⇨ Lower precision can be compensated for with more data to some extent. However, this will only account for one type of imprecision caused by the low sampling rate.
• Does the data presentation software allow you to use the type of stimuli you need for your experiment?	⇨ Text, static images and videos can be used as stimuli in all the systems we have mentioned in this chapter.

(cont.)

Final checklist	
	⇨ Separate audio files can only be used in certain systems.
	⇨ The different types of stimuli will be added in different ways depending on the software package. You might need to use workarounds to build the study exactly as you want.
• Does the analysis software output the measures that you need?	⇨ Not all systems output the same metrics. The Tobii system, for example, does not output regression metrics. These can be calculated based on the saccadic information between fixations. This would be an important step in data preparation and analysis and should be considered before running the experiment.
• Finally, become familiar with the functioning of a system.	⇨ There are many online training courses and tutorials provided by manufacturers. These, together with the demo versions of the software available online, will give you a good idea of what using the system will be like.
	⇨ Many companies – the eye-tracking manufacturers as well as some suppliers – will offer a range of services to help you make the right choice, such as advice and support, software updates, and even equipment loans to try out the systems.

Chapter 3

Practicalities of Eye-Tracking

3.1   Designing an Experiment

Designing and building an eye-tracking study can be a daunting task. In this chapter we will walk through the practicalities of planning, creating and running a study from beginning to end. The specifics of how to actually build an experiment vary according to the type of study we want to run and the eye-tracking system we are using. Our aim is not to provide a 'how-to' guide as such, but to talk about the key components and general issues that will be important to most studies. We will also give a brief introduction to the three systems that were discussed in Chapter 2: SR Research EyeLink (www.sr-research .com), Tobii (www.tobii.com) and SMI (www.smivision.com)[1] eye-trackers. As with most things, the best way to learn how to build an eye-tracking study on any of these systems is to dive in and try for ourselves. A good approach is to first look at an existing, similar study – if possible observing an experienced user as he/she builds an experiment – to see the 'dos' and 'don'ts', then to try editing and building a study of our own.

The first question we should ask is whether eye-tracking is even the best methodology to use. It is tempting to adopt new technologies even when a different approach might produce more useful data, so we should first consider the alternatives to decide whether this is the best option for our research purposes. As with any experiment in any field, the research question should inform the methodology and design, rather than the other way around. Reading extensively around our topic will show us how other researchers have chosen to study it, and this should help us to decide whether eye-tracking is a good choice. Assuming that this decision has been made (and that the answer was yes), this chapter addresses some of the things we will need to consider to get started. We will begin by describing the process of preparing stimuli and building an experiment, then discuss factors such as selecting suitable participants, setting up and calibrating the eye-tracker, and collecting and saving data.

First of all, we need to try to conceptualise our experiment as clearly as we can. Normally we start with a set of general questions that are not specific to eye-tracking, but which are important when designing any language study. Jiang (2012, Chapter 2) provides an introduction to the kinds of things we should consider in reaction time research, as do Colantoni, Steele and Escudero (2015, Chapter 3) in the context of investigating spoken language. These include identifying a research topic and question, preparing stimuli and finding suitable participants, all of which we will deal with here.

3.1.1   Choosing the Type of Experiment

Most eye-tracking studies will follow a fairly uniform structure. Participants will be shown a series of visual stimuli and the eye-tracker will record the eye-movement patterns for each

---

[1] As noted elsewhere, SMI has been purchased by Apple. It is unclear how their systems and software will be updated and supported in the future.

person, along with any other user inputs such as key or button presses, mouse movements and any verbal responses made during the experiment. These could include the participant 'naming' something on the screen, or our study might be interested in using a 'think-aloud' approach, where the participant describes his/her thought processes during the experiment.

The first step is to decide on the type of stimuli we are interested in using and the 'task' we will be presenting to participants (that is, what exactly we will be asking them to do). Broadly, stimuli will be either 'static' or 'dynamic'. Static stimuli will be things such as text or still images, while dynamic stimuli will include moving images. In a typical text-based study, the task will be simply to read the text on screen. This might be made up of single sentences or of longer extracts, depending on our research question (see Chapter 4 for more on the questions we can address with text-based studies). Very often we will want to include comprehension questions, either after every item or at certain points in the study. These can be included to genuinely test how well the participant has understood the text, or they can just be there as a way of ensuring that people actually read the items properly – people tend to pay more attention when they know they will be tested on what they are reading. As we will see in Section 3.2.1, reading studies can generate a lot of different eye-tracking data that we can use to understand how the text is processed. This makes it important to understand what variables we are manipulating and what we will be measuring before we begin, which in turn will help us decide which of the various eye-tracking measures are appropriate.

Image-based studies can take a number of forms. In applied linguistics, it is unlikely that our experiment will just use images and nothing else; a more common scenario would be a study that uses multimodal input (see Chapter 5 for some examples). This might be in the form of a 'storybook' study, where we are interested in whether including images alongside a piece of text improves comprehension for children or second language learners. Alternatively, a reading-while-listening task would present each piece of text on the screen and play a pre-recorded spoken version at the same time. As with text-only studies, we might want to include regular comprehension questions as a way of checking either understanding or attention, and we might also want to include some kind of test after the main experiment. This can be integrated into what we present using the eye-tracking software, or in some cases it might be easier to present it as an offline paper and pencil test after the eye-tracking is completed.

Some studies will combine visual stimuli with an audio track either by using static images or video. The 'visual-world' paradigm is discussed in more detail in Chapter 5 and will involve either a set of images (as in the Chambers and Cooke (2009) example in Chapter 1) or a visual scene (as in the Altmann and Kamide (1999) example in Chapter 1). Some studies (e.g. Holsinger, 2013) use a text-based variant, presenting different words on the screen to see which one participants are more likely to look at in response to the audio stimulus. In any study combining visual and audio stimuli, the data will normally need to be 'time-locked' to a specific point in the audio. This means that we will be interested in what our participants look at when they hear a specific word and for a specific period of time immediately afterward (typically a few hundred milliseconds). We can also define different time windows (often 50 or 100 ms time windows starting at the onset of a critical word) to see how listening unfolds over time. We address this more in Chapters 5 and 7.

Dynamic stimuli will generally either involve the presentation of a video or require the participant to interact with the display in some way, for example by looking at a website,[2]

---

[2] Not all websites will be 'dynamic', since in some instances we might just ask participants to view a static webpage that does not change. In other cases, we might need participants to scroll up or down a page, click on

Table 3.1 Main stimulus types in applied linguistics eye-tracking studies.

Stimulus type	Example study	Other possible elements
Text only	Reading study	Comprehension questions, during or after main study.
Text + image	Illustrated storybook	Comprehension questions, during or after main study.
Text + audio	Reading while listening	Comprehension questions, during or after main study.
Image + audio	Visual-world paradigm	Questions about the scene and/or audio input.
Video	Learning new vocabulary from watching videos	Comprehension questions after the video; pre- and post-video vocabulary test.
Website	Surfing to find information	Think-aloud recording.
External software	Using a corpus tool	Think-aloud recording.

Note: In most studies we are also likely to want to collect some background information on our participants (demographic data such as gender and age), which can be done either as part of the study or separately. We are also likely to need to use this data to match participants on a number of variables, which is discussed in detail in Section 4.3.2.

taking an online test, or using a piece of software to achieve a specific task (such as taking part in a chat session or using a corpus tool to produce concordance lines). Video-based studies are similar to visual-world studies in that we are interested in what the participants look at during specific time windows, or when they hear certain things in the audio track. We might also be interested in how participants make use of features like subtitles (e.g. Bisson et al., 2014). Here the task is likely to simply involve participants watching a video. We might want to include some questions afterward either to test their comprehension or to test understanding of newly introduced words. Again, this could be included as part of the experiment (administered by the eye-tracking software) or conducted separately afterward. For stimuli such as websites or external software where we are interested in the interaction of the participant with the stimulus, we might need to consider what to measure and analyse based on broad questions or hypotheses.

In any task, what we ask participants to do will have a big influence on their behaviour. If the task is to take a reading test or use a corpus tool to produce concordance lines, the instructions should be clear in informing participants of this, and of any time limits or other restrictions. For potentially less directed tasks, such as looking at a website, a task should be clearly defined, for example, 'Find *x* piece of information as quickly as possible.' This will be important to avoid participants simply surfing aimlessly, and therefore producing data that is difficult to interpret. Such tasks may also involve a think-aloud protocol or retrospective recall. Participants can be asked to commentate on what they are doing during the task, or else be shown the recording of their eye-movements afterward and be asked to commentate on it. Audio recording of this commentary can be done concurrently in some of the eye-tracking systems, but in others it will be necessary to make the recording ourselves using a separate device. The broad types of experiment likely to come up in applied linguistics research are summarised in Table 3.1.

links, etc. For ease of reference here, we consider all websites as 'dynamic' stimuli, unless static screenshots are used as the stimuli – see Section 3.1.2 for more on this.

3.1.2 Selecting and Controlling Stimulus Materials

The stimuli we use are a key part of any experiment, so it is vital that we spend ample time choosing, developing and refining an appropriate pool of items. This is where reading around the research topic can be of great use. It can be very helpful to see what stimuli other researchers have used, and this can be used to help develop our own items. All published research should be replicable, so there is no problem with using stimuli from an existing study, provided we reference these appropriately to acknowledge where they were taken from.

Text Stimuli

In most text-based studies, we will identify a linguistic feature of interest and create stimuli that manipulate this. The analysis will focus on reading patterns for a word, sequence of words or longer stretch of text. A long history of research in psychology has shown us that eye-movements are affected by a range of features at the lexical or single-word level, the syntactic or sentence level, and the discourse or paragraph level. This is discussed in detail in Chapter 4. Clearly, controlling every possible variable in our study is not going to be possible, but we should certainly aim to balance the major factors that could have an unintended effect on our data.

Broadly, this means we should try to match critical words on features like length, frequency and part of speech.[3] We should also aim to compare different words in the same or similar contexts. When we manipulate a variable of interest and hold everything else constant, we can be confident that any difference in reading patterns is due to our manipulation. For example, in the study looking at the effects of metaphorical language introduced in Chapter 1, we are specifically interested in the reading patterns for the critical word in each sentence (which are underlined),[4] and everything else is the same (Example 3.1).

Example 3.1 Comparison of reading for a literal word ('affect') and a metaphorical word ('infect'), keeping all other aspects of the sentence the same.

The violence had even begun to <u>affect</u> normally 'safe' areas.
The violence had even begun to <u>infect</u> normally 'safe' areas.

If we are using longer stretches of text – paragraphs, or full-page extracts – we need to consider the position of critical words in the passage itself. Words tend to be read more slowly at the end of a sentence or paragraph due to 'wrap-up' effects (Rayner, Raney and Pollatsek, 1995). Effects of 'spillover' are also often seen, where the processing of one word or sentence carries over to the next, for example when an ambiguous word causes a reader to move forward in search of information that might be helpful. We should make sure that our stimuli are designed so that reading patterns for critical words aren't 'contaminated' by such effects. This means that where possible we should avoid having critical words at either the start or end of sentences, or in the first or last sentence of a paragraph. In

---

[3] Assuming our focus is individual words. If we are interested in phrases or longer sequences, we should consider the factors that are specific to these – see Chapter 4 for an in-depth discussion of this.

[4] Regions of interest are underlined in our examples but in a real study would not be visible to participants. See Section 3.1.4 for more about adding ROIs to experiments.

Example 3.2, 'even begun to' would be the pre-critical region, 'affect'/'infect' our critical word, and 'normally "safe" areas' the spillover region.

Example 3.2 Critical words ('affect'/'infect'), pre-critical regions ('even begun to') and spillover regions ('normally "safe"') are all areas that we might want to analyse.

The violence had <u>even begun to</u> <u>affect</u> <u>normally 'safe'</u> areas.
The violence had <u>even begun to</u> <u>infect</u> <u>normally 'safe'</u> areas.

The general layout of the text is also something we should consider. The font style and size, line spacing, line breaks and margins should all be set in such a way that will ensure clear presentation and accurate data collection. For most studies black text on a white background will help make the presentation as 'natural' as possible, but for some specific contexts the colour scheme may need to be altered (e.g. a study with dyslexic participants might use pastel colours for the background to help reduce contrast levels). A font such as Courier New is often chosen since all letters take up the same amount of horizontal space. For most studies a font size of around 14–18 pt will be appropriate. Participants will be reading from a distance of between 40 and 70 cm from the screen (this varies by system; see Section 3.4 on setting up an eye-tracker), so the text needs to be big enough to be read, but not so big that it appears unnatural on the screen. Some testing will help to find the right balance. For multi-line reading, we may also need to edit the text a little to ensure that critical words are not at the start or end of a line. Aside from the problem of sentence wrap-up effects, fixations are not always stable when readers move from one line to the next, and often there is a tendency to under- or overshoot the target (the first word of the next line). In other words, a participant's gaze may not always move perfectly to the first word of the next line, hence minor corrective saccades may be made to this word, which would influence reading times. Some careful editing of the text size and the position of line breaks should help to avoid this for our critical words.

Eye-trackers are generally less accurate towards the edges of the computer screen, so we should set appropriate margins to avoid any problems. For single-line reading, each stimulus item can be presented across the centre of the screen, with a good size indent before and after. For full-screen text we can set margins all around the screen to ensure that there is no data loss as a result of the participant exceeding the trackable range of the eye-tracker. Since eye-trackers are less accurate at measuring vertical than horizontal movement, the line spacing should also be considered. Double line spacing, or even triple line spacing, is recommended to ensure that fixations can be reliably attributed to one line or another. In Figure 3.1, the fixation in version A cannot reliably be attributed to any particular line and could be on 'violence' or 'affect', whereas in version B we can be much more confident that the fixation is on the critical word 'affect'.

Some of the issues of font size and line spacing are only really relevant when we are investigating reading at the word, phrase or sentence level. If we are interested in the general reading of a text then we may not need to control the layout so closely. For example, if we are simply interested in global measures of reading and which part of the text readers spend most time on (rather than word- or even sentence-level processing), then having smaller text with less line spacing would not be a problem. See Chapters 4 and 6 for more on the different types of text stimuli we might use in eye-tracking and some of the methodological considerations that will be important.

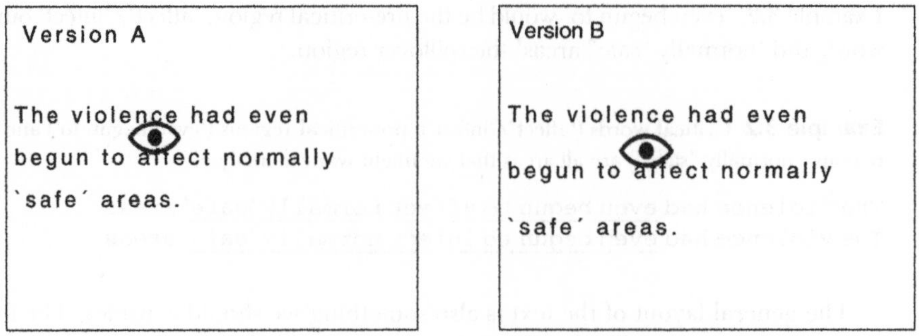

Version A	Version B
The violence had even begun to affect normally 'safe' areas.	The violence had even begun to affect normally 'safe' areas.

Figure 3.1 Example stimuli with single (left) and double (right) line spacing.

Image Stimuli

Any images we want to include in an eye-tracking study also need to be prepared carefully. This means that we should consider any potential confounding or distracting factors and do our best to minimise or balance these. Obvious considerations here are the size and quality or salience of the images we use (for a discussion of salience and other visual properties that should be considered when creating visual stimuli see Section 5.1). For example, we would not include some images that are simple black and white line drawings and some that are full colour photographs, since the photographs are more visually salient and would be likely to attract more attention. The choice of what type of image to include will probably be determined by our research question and the participants we will be using. For a storybook study looking at whether adding images to a piece of text helps with overall comprehension, we might choose different images for children than we would for adult second language learners. For children, colourful cartoon characters might be essential if they are going to take any interest in our study, but adults might find images like this distracting. There is also the practical question of where to get our images from. Clipart or royalty-free images can often be found online, but if we have specific requirements then we might need to consider whether we have the time and resources to either create these ourselves or commission someone else to do so. We should always consider the range of possible confounds (e.g. visual complexity, size, position on the screen) when using images to ensure that our materials are as balanced as possible. (See also the section 'Dynamic Stimuli' on preparing and balancing dynamic stimuli later in this chapter, and the discussion in Chapter 5.)

For images such as those used in a visual-world study, we need to consider the types of item we are interested in. Typically studies include one 'target' item (the picture we expect participants to look at), potentially a 'competitor' that is related in some way to the target, and then one or more distractors that are unrelated to the other items. In some cases, the other images may need to have specific properties, such as being semantically or phonologically related to the target item in some way (e.g. if the word 'beaker' is the target then 'beetle' would be a phonological competitor). As we have seen in Chapter 1, Chambers and Cooke (2009) investigated looking patterns to a target like 'poule' ('chicken' in English) and interlingual homophone competitors like 'pool'. However, unless this is the focus of our study, we need to ensure that our items do not contain any unintended cross-language overlap when working with language learners. Similarly, if we do not intend to study the effect of semantic or phonological overlap, we should make sure that our 'distractor' images are completely unrelated to the target images for all of the items we prepare.

For any images we want to present, the visual appearance should be balanced as far as possible. If we are combining objects in a visual-world study or visual scene, we need to make sure that the stimuli are all the same size and style, with no item appearing as more visually salient than any other. The different objects in the display should be spaced far enough apart that there is no confusion over what a participant is looking at. In the Chambers and Cooke (2009) stimuli, the images were placed at cardinal points (north, south, east and west) so fixations should be easy to identify. If we are combining text and images, we need to consider the position of the various elements and try to construct our stimuli in such a way that no one element is made more salient than any other. As with text-based stimuli, it is important to situate images in such a way that no data is lost at the edges or corners of the screen. Good tracker set-up will help to minimise this (see Section 3.4), but in general we should avoid any stimuli that will require the participant to fixate very close to the periphery of the monitor. This does not mean that we can't present images or videos full-screen, but we should try to ensure that 'critical' areas of the display are not close to the edge if we can help it.

Any images we want to include in our study can be prepared in advance using standard picture-editing software, then saved as single files for use in our experiment. Images should be of sufficient quality and resolution that participants will have no difficulty recognising what they are supposed to be, so we need to avoid using small or poor-quality pictures that will look grainy or blurred if we increase the size. Of course, while we can control many aspects of our stimuli when we are creating our own, if we want to use authentic materials such as a real illustrated storybook, we have less control. In these cases, selecting which aspects of the stimulus to analyse will be crucial, i.e. we may only want to select certain pages or extracts to compare.

Audio Stimuli

If our study also contains audio stimuli, some thought should be given to the recording of this. Will we record all items in the same voice? Are there any prosodic or phonetic cues that participants might subconsciously pick up on? For example, native speakers are able to discriminate short words ('cap') from the same syllables embedded in longer words ('captain') based on acoustic cues alone (Davis, Marslen-Wilson and Gaskell, 2002). Similarly, native speakers can reliably differentiate figurative and literal meanings of ambiguous idioms based on subtle prosodic contrasts (Van Lancker and Canter, 1981; Van Lancker Sidtis, 2003). We therefore need to consider how such cues could influence our results, and if so whether we need to modify the sound files in some way to remove these cues. Some studies record all stimuli, then cut the items up and re-edit them to minimise this possibility, although this may lead to items sounding slightly less natural. We should aim to avoid any systematic differences that might introduce additional variables into our study, such as having all of the critical stimuli recorded in a male voice and the other items in a female voice. Recordings should be clear and paced appropriately to ensure that participants will be able to hear and understand the stimuli as intended. See Section 5.2 for more on creating audio stimuli.

Importantly, when preparing a study that will combine audio prompts with eye-movement recording, the two elements will need to be accurately synchronised to allow us to analyse the data. This may involve specific sound drivers, so we need to check the system requirements for both the computer set-up and the eye-tracker software we will be using. Some of the systems can combine visual and audio stimuli within the experiment (see Section 3.1.3 for more on this), otherwise we may need to prepare each stimulus item as a video where we add the audio recording over the static image. Video-editing software such as Windows Movie Maker can be used to create these so that the files can be added to the eye-tracker software when we come to build the experiment.

Dynamic Stimuli

For most studies using dynamic stimuli such as videos, webpages or an online test, it is likely that we are primarily interested in using authentic materials. This means that controlling our stimuli to the degree that we would with text or image stimuli is less of a priority, but there may still be areas that we need to consider (see Chapters 4, 5 and 6 for methodological considerations that might be relevant here).

Video stimuli can either be items that we have selected to suit the purposes of our study, or can be items that we specifically create with a purpose in mind. The first type is likely to be films or TV shows (or extracts from these). For example, we might want to show these stimuli to language learners or children as a way of testing their uptake of new vocabulary. In this case, it is likely that we will have selected something of an appropriate level and identified keywords in the video that we are interested in studying. We might therefore measure how much attention participants pay to areas of the display that correspond to these key vocabulary items, in which case we would need to ensure that they appear on screen for roughly the same amount of time and are roughly the same size, or that we have accounted for any such differences in our analysis (see Section 7.2). If subtitles are used, the language of the subtitles might be something we want to vary; for example, we could show learners of English a video with subtitles either in their first language or in the target language.

Alternatively, we might choose to create our own stimuli, for example by recording a lecture where new vocabulary items are introduced both verbally by the presenter and in writing on the screen. Controlling the position and duration of words would be an important consideration here, and all critical words should appear in comparable positions and for the same amount of time. Ultimately, we may need to decide whether using authentic material is more important than being able to control the stimuli as much as we would in other types of studies. The same may be true if we want to use other authentic materials, such as real texts (see Chapters 4 and 6 for more on this kind of study).

For other types of dynamic stimuli, how we control visual and linguistic aspects will depend on our research question and the materials we are using. We will need to decide whether creating something ourselves that can be carefully controlled is more important than using authentic material. For example, if we want to compare how participants process information on different websites, we will likely want to use real webpages. To do this we will need to be clear about the similarities and differences of the webpages in terms of the text, images, layout etc. For example, are we comparing a webpage with ten images to one with three images? If there are more looks to images in the former, this may be driven by the fact that there are simply more images. Using real websites and allowing participants to surf them freely is possible in some of the eye-tracking systems, but an alternative is to simply take a screenshot of the webpage we want to use and present this as a static image.

In a similar vein, using corpus software to see how users interact with concordance lines might require us to give very specific instructions (e.g. for all participants to complete the same search), otherwise behaviour may be too diverse for us to draw any clear conclusions. In this case we might want to present participants with the software interface for a corpus search tool, then ask them to generate concordance lines for specific words or phrases. By doing this, we can ensure that their eye-movements and behaviour are in response to more or less the same stimuli. While there are good reasons to want to maintain the authenticity of our materials – for example if we are asking participants to take a standardised online language test – we should also be aware that how items are presented will have an important effect on eye-movements. This means that if we don't control the visual aspects of our stimuli – number and frequency of words, position and number of images, overall visual salience of critical aspects of the display, etc. – then the findings we can draw from the eye-tracking will be limited. Chapter 6 provides further discussion and examples of the kinds of studies we can undertake using authentic and dynamic stimuli.

Study Design and Counterbalancing

The type of design is an important choice in any study and will affect things like how we will present our items, and how we will analyse the data. In a lot of cases a 'factorial' design might be the best approach. This means that we will identify one or more 'factors' or 'conditions' and compare them using statistical tests (see Chapter 7 for more on working with your data). Examples of factors might be 'sentence type' (metaphorical or literal) in our earlier example of a text-based study, or word frequency (high vs low). Factors can also be related to our participants as opposed to our stimuli. Examples would be 'language status' (native speaker or language learner) in a study comparing two groups in a reading task, or 'reading ability' (high vs intermediate vs low) if we wanted to compare the reading speeds of school-age children according to the scores they had previously obtained on a standardised test. Often item factors and participant factors will be combined, so we might see a design described as two (sentence type) by two (language status), where we would show our metaphorical and literal sentences to a group of native speakers and a group of language learners to compare performance for each sentence type.

In some cases, a factorial experiment might not be as useful. This is likely for the dynamic stimuli we discussed previously, since carefully controlling the items to make two conditions might be much harder. It is still possible to create a factorial design, for example by showing videos with or without subtitles to see whether one leads to better comprehension and retention of newly introduced words. An alternative would be to take reading patterns for critical parts of the video and relate these to subsequent scores on a vocabulary test using either correlation analysis or linear regression. Baayen (2010) demonstrates how this kind of analysis is a good alternative for variables that have traditionally been analysed using a factorial approach, such as word frequency, but it would also be relevant for factors like language proficiency that can be graded.

A second important choice is whether our design will be within-subjects or between-subjects. In a within-subjects design, all participants will see all items, whereas in a between-subjects study, different participants will see different items. An example of a within-subjects design could be the video-based study mentioned in the previous paragraph. We could use two episodes of a cartoon and identify ten words (of comparable frequency) in each episode that we wanted to teach to children or language learners. We could show one episode with subtitles and the second without, then test whether the presence of subtitles was beneficial when we tested the participants on a post-video vocabulary test. In an example like this, all participants would see both videos, so the design would be within-subjects.

Conversely, we might want to only show one video to each participant, but we might want to avoid showing the same video twice (once with subtitles, once without). In this case, we would show half of the participants the video with subtitles, and half without, then test the two groups to see if there was a difference in the uptake of vocabulary. In this case, the study would be between-subjects, since the two groups saw different versions of the stimuli. The same would be true in our example study of metaphorical language. We want to compare 'infect' and 'affect' in the same sentence contexts, but we would not want any one person to see both versions of the same sentence because repetition effects would be very likely to confound the results. To avoid this, we would aim to create multiple stimuli for each condition (multiple metaphorical and multiple literal sentences) and 'counterbalance' them over two separate presentation lists, as in Example 3.3.

Example 3.3 Counterbalancing of stimuli, so that participants do not see more than one version of the same item, but do see items from both conditions.

List A
The violence had even begun to <u>affect</u> normally 'safe' areas.
(Literal condition)
After all the rain the sunlight was <u>bursting</u> through the clouds.
(Metaphorical condition)

List B
The violence had even begun to <u>infect</u> normally 'safe' areas.
(Metaphorical condition)
After all the rain the sunlight was <u>shining</u> through the clouds.
(Literal condition)

Participants would be randomly assigned to one of the lists, therefore each person would see *either* the metaphorical *or* the literal version of each sentence. Crucially, because each sentence pair is matched so that the only manipulation is the critical word, the effect of metaphorical language (whether it requires greater processing effort than literal language) should be observable when we look at reading times/reading patterns across all trials.

The principle of counterbalancing is the same no matter how many conditions we have and no matter what stimuli we are using. In our between-subjects video example, we could easily introduce a second video and counterbalance the items, as in Figure 3.2. Participants would see *either* Version 1 *or* Version 2. Each person would therefore see one subtitled and one non-subtitled video, to enable the whole group to be tested on whether subtitles improved their vocabulary retention scores.

In some experiments we may want to include more than two conditions or factors. In a three-condition study there would be three versions of each stimulus item, so three presentation lists would be required and each participant would be randomly assigned to one list. Likewise, a four-condition study would require four lists, and so on. Items would be arranged in a 'Latin square' configuration so that each item appeared once and only once per condition across the required number of lists. Table 3.2 demonstrates how items

Table 3.2 Items counterbalanced in a Latin square arrangement. Each item appears once, and only once, per condition and per list. Each participant would see one list, and equal numbers of participants would see each list, i.e. 40 participants = 10 participants per list.

	Condition 1	Condition 2	Condition 3	Condition 4
List A	Item 1	Item 2	Item 3	Item 4
List B	Item 2	Item 1	Item 4	Item 3
List C	Item 3	Item 4	Item 1	Item 2
List D	Item 4	Item 3	Item 2	Item 1

Figure 3.2 Counterbalancing in a video study with subtitles. Participants would see either Version 1 (left) or Version 2 (right). All participants would see one video with subtitles and the other without.

would be distributed according to a Latin square design in a four-condition counterbalanced study. Each item appears once per condition and once per list.

Counterbalancing of this sort is only required when we have multiple conditions in our study and it is important that people are not exposed to more than one version of the same item. Within-subjects design of the type described previously are fine in many cases, and the decision is often not clear-cut. If we show different items to different participants, we run the risk that either specific items or specific subjects might be driving differences in our data. On the other hand, in a counterbalanced design the actual number of experimental items seen by each participant is smaller, hence statistical power is reduced. For a between-subjects study we will therefore generally need to prepare more items and plan to collect data from more participants than for a within-subjects design. The more conditions we intend to include, the more items we will need to prepare and the more participants we will need.

Counterbalancing can also be applied to other aspects of how we prepare our stimuli. If we are asking participants to do several tasks, we can counterbalance the order to make sure that this is not an unwanted effect (e.g. participants might always complete the first task more slowly than subsequent tasks). In the within-subjects version of our video example, all participants would see one episode of a cartoon with subtitles and a different episode without. In this case, we would want to ensure that half of the participants saw the subtitled episode first, and the other half saw the non-subtitled episode first. The same principle is true for any of the types of stimulus item discussed so far. For example, if we are asking participants to look at two different websites, we would counterbalance the order in which they were displayed; if we were presenting two extracts from a novel, we would show extract 1 first to 50 per cent of the participants and extract 2 first to the other 50 per cent, etc.

For any image-based studies we should ensure that the position of critical images is counterbalanced across all trials. In the visual-world example from Chambers and Cooke (2009), objects appeared at the four cardinal points. In order to ensure that no effect of 'position' emerged, we should ensure that the critical target word appeared in each position an equal amount of times over the course of the study. That is, 25 per cent of the time it should be in the north position, 25 per cent in east, 25 per cent in south and 25 per cent in west.

How Many Stimuli?

The number of stimuli we need is largely determined by the nature and design of our experiment. We should aim to include an appropriate number of items to ensure that our analysis will have sufficient statistical power. Colantoni et al. (2015) suggest that a minimum of ten items per experimental condition should be the aim. What constitutes an item, however, will vary according to what we are presenting to participants.

In a text-based study presenting single sentences, or a visual-world study showing a picture plus audio stimulus, each stimulus will contain one 'item'. In other words, each critical word we are interested in will represent one data point in our analysis. For longer pieces of text – paragraphs or full-page extracts – we might include several 'items' in each page of text. If our stimulus was made up of a ten-page story, with two keywords and one image per page, this would provide us with twenty word- and ten image-based items. A video-based study might also contain multiple 'items', if the aim of our study is to test how well keywords that appear in the video are learned. For a subtitled video, the aim of the study will dictate what we are considering to be an 'item'. If we are interested in keywords, each word will represent one 'item'. If we are more concerned with general looking behaviour – how much attention readers pay to the subtitles in general – then we may want to define the occurrence of one 'set' of subtitles as one item, i.e. the period of time from when one set of subtitles appears on the screen to when it disappears is one 'item'. If the video lasts several minutes then we will have multiple individual 'items' to base our analysis on. If we are asking participants to view a series of webpages, each one might constitute one 'item', so we would want to include several different examples to ensure that we collect a usable amount of data. Example studies using a range of stimuli are discussed in more detail in Chapters 4, 5 and 6.

We therefore need to carefully consider the aims of our study, what we will be measuring and how we will analyse the data in order to decide precisely how many stimuli we will need to prepare. We also need to remember that for a between-subjects design, each factor in the experiment will double the number of items we need. For example, in our reading study comparing metaphorical and literal language, producing ten stimulus sentences would mean that each participant saw only five of each type once the items had been counterbalanced over two lists. We would therefore need to aim for a minimum of twenty sentence pairs to begin with to ensure that participants saw ten items per condition.

In many cases we will also need to include a number of filler items (non-experimental distractors) to mask the true purpose of our study. In both our reading and visual-world examples, filler trials would be included to ensure that participants were not able to spot any patterns in the stimuli (such as noticing that a lot of sentences contained metaphors). The number of fillers is normally equal to the number of experimental items in our study, so a study with twenty experimental trials will likewise require twenty fillers. Fillers will not be needed in every kind of study. For example, showing participants an authentic video will not require fillers (we would not also show them other unrelated videos). If we are presenting text-plus-image stimuli or reading-while-listening studies, our stimuli are likely to be stories or longer texts, where including fillers may not be appropriate. In such cases we should ensure that our critical words are spaced far enough away from each other and evenly throughout the texts to avoid any participant spotting a pattern. In general, fillers are most likely to be needed in any study where we will present multiple stimuli in different conditions, such as a single sentence reading study, and where we think it is likely that a participant might spot a pattern if too many critical stimuli were presented in close proximity.

It is important to strike a balance when preparing our stimuli so that our study does not end up being overly long. If we include too many items, participant fatigue could adversely affect our results, but too few items will limit the analysis that we can perform. For studies where the length of each item is fixed (such as visual-world studies where the audio for each item is the same length for each participant, or video-based studies) we know in advance how long the study will take. For text-based studies or those where participants are given more freedom (such as using a website or external piece of software), participants will vary in how quickly they perform the task so the length of our study will vary. Pilot testing will be useful for establishing what an appropriate number of items to include is.

We should also consider who our participants are when planning the length of our study. Less skilled readers (language learners, children, and people with certain language impairments) will in general read more slowly than skilled readers. Similarly, young children will not sit through as many trials as adult participants, so we should plan to collect less data, and also to make the study as appealing and interesting as possible. For people with language impairments, reading page after page of text may be very challenging. In all cases, we need to carefully consider who our participants will be when we are designing our study. (See Section 3.3 for more on choosing participants.)

As a general rule of thumb, an eye-tracking study should be no longer than one hour. Most will be much shorter, and some may be necessarily longer. For example, if we are asking participants to watch a whole movie, the session will be determined by the length of the video we are showing. If we want participants to read a whole book, we might need to plan for participants to come in for several sessions spread over a number of days. We should always consider including breaks in our study if we will be asking participants to sit and attend to a computer screen for any longer than around thirty minutes.

Order of Presentation of Stimuli

The order of presentation can be an important variable and is one we should try to control. There are some contexts where the order of stimuli must be fixed, for example in the case of a text-based study where we want to display sequential extracts from a book or show a story over several pages. Videos are necessarily fixed in the order they will present stimuli (unless we design and edit them ourselves). However, in many cases having a fixed order will not be important, and it may be desirable to present our items in random order to minimise the chance of participants spotting any patterns. We should also consider that trial order is a variable that could potentially affect performance. In general participants will speed up over the course of an experiment and respond to later trials more quickly than earlier ones, so randomising stimuli will help to mitigate against this. Trial order is often a covariate that is included in analysis to ensure that any such effects are minimised (see Section 7.2 for more on data analysis). Stimuli can be randomised in advance (using a random number generator), or pseudo-randomised, where we arrange the items into a specific order to ensure that items from the same condition do not appear next to each other. Alternatively, all three eye-tracking systems considered in Chapter 2 provide in-built methods of randomisation for stimuli. If our stimuli are divided into separate blocks, we may wish to either randomise or counterbalance the order of presentation for each block to further minimise any trial order effects. In cases where this is not possible (storybooks, movies), we could incorporate the order into our analysis. For example, if we are interested in keywords that appear during a movie, we could number them sequentially and include the order as a covariate in our analysis.

Other Aspects of the Study

Some other features of our study that will need to be considered in advance are the instructions, whether we will include any additional tasks (such as answering comprehension questions) and any additional information (demographic data, language background or proficiency information) we may require from our participants.

How we phrase the task instructions will be important. In other words, what will we actually ask the participants to do? In reading studies this may seem fairly obvious, but patterns of reading may differ according to whether the reading is silent or out loud (Rayner, 2009), and also according to whether the participant is reading for comprehension, skimming the text, reading with the intention of memorising, etc. If it is important that participants read each stimulus item only once, then we should tell them this before the experiment. For visual-world studies, participants may respond very differently according to the task and what they are told to do (Tanenhaus, 2007a). For example, the pattern of results will differ depending on whether it is an action-based task where a response is required (e.g. naming some aspect of the stimulus or finding a particular image as quickly as possible), or a passive task where the participant simply has to listen to a stimulus while viewing the image on the screen. Asking participants to perform a specific task may reduce variability in their behaviour and therefore make the results more comparable and reliable, so we should give careful thought to how we phrase our instructions.

In some studies – especially text-based studies – we may want to include regular comprehension questions as a way of ensuring that participants pay attention throughout. Typically, these are included after every few trials (e.g. one-third of items will have a question after them) and can be used simply to encourage attention throughout, or can be designed to actually probe understanding. Some studies may require participants to answer longer questions, for example reading studies combining eye-tracking with a more qualitative investigation. The three systems considered in the following section have different ways of including questions in an experiment. We may also want to record participants' verbalisations during the study as part of a think-aloud protocol (or afterward as part of a retrospective recall). Some of the systems we discuss in the next section allow us to build this in, otherwise we might have to think about a way to record participant verbalisations separately and match the recording to the eye-movement pattern once all data has been recorded.

Finally, in many cases it is useful to collect additional data about our participants, such as gender, age, etc. Depending on our participant population, we may need to think carefully about this. Information about child participants may be better collected from parents or teachers. For language-impaired subjects we may need to collect information specific to their impairment, such as type of dyslexia. Some information, such as the location of a lesion in brain-damaged or stroke patients, may need to be collected in conjunction with a medical professional, and we should be mindful of the need for confidentiality.[5] For non-native speakers we will generally want to collect details about their first language and language learning background. Some studies may also find it useful to include some method for collecting additional information, such as a vocabulary test, a test of working memory capacity or a test of non-verbal intelligence. Some of these tests can be incorporated into the experiment for ease of collection (see the following section on what can be included in each of the eye-tracking systems), but in many cases it may be just as easy to prepare paper or electronic tasks in advance.

Other data that we may require can be collected in the same way; for example, if we need to collect familiarity ratings for our stimuli then participants can be asked to rate words or phrases for how well they know them. If this is required, we should ensure that it is done after the eye-tracking data collection so that we do not give participants any information in advance that might affect how they approach the main task. Finally, if our aim is to use our study to examine the relationship between eye-movements and linguistic performance (e.g. vocabulary knowledge, grammatical learning, comprehension), we need to think carefully about those post-task measures, and in some cases administering a pre-test might also be necessary. We could use an immediate post-test, or we might want to use a delayed post-test, in which case we would need to arrange for participants to come back for an additional session. Thinking through all possible aspects of our study is essential if we are to design and run productive, successful experiments.

3.1.3 Building and Testing the Experiment

Once we have decided on the type of study (text, image, video, etc.), and the nature and number of stimuli we will need, the next step is to build the experiment using the software provided with our eye-tracking system. In this section we provide a brief introduction to building an experiment in Experiment Builder (SR Research), Tobii Pro Studio (Tobii) and Experiment Center (SMI). Each of these software packages allows us to include a variety of tasks and stimulus types. Detailed guidance for all three systems is provided in their relevant user manual. In this chapter we refer to Experiment Builder version 1.10.1630 (SR Research, 2015b), Tobii Pro Studio version 3.4.5 (Tobii AB, 2016) and Experiment Center version 3.6 (SMI, 2016b). References to specific sections may vary slightly depending on the version of the manual being used.

Building a study from scratch can seem challenging at first, so a good place to start is to look at an existing experiment to get an idea of what the structure looks like. Both Experiment Builder and Experiment Center come with example files for text, image and video display studies (as well as some others). Sample experiments within Experiment Builder are helpfully annotated to explain what each element does, so working through the structure is a good way to get to grips with the process of creating a study. These sample experiments are also described in detail in the user manual. Demo files for Tobii Pro Studio are available from the Tobii website. In all three systems, example files can be

---

[5] Confidentiality is important for all populations, but when dealing with patients or medical data, there may be additional considerations and ethical procedures.

re-saved and edited, so an easy way to start making our own studies is simply to find one that uses the same structure and add our own stimuli in. Projects should be saved with new filenames and if necessary unlocked before any changes can be made (the relevant documentation on setting up new projects in each system will provide more explanation of this). In all three systems, it is important not to add or remove files manually, e.g. in Windows Explorer, so any changes such as adding files should be made from within the software itself.

Building the Experiment and Adding Stimuli

Once our stimuli are prepared and we have created a new project (or re-saved an existing one), we can begin constructing the experiment itself. Almost all applied linguistics studies, regardless of the type of stimuli, will follow the same basic structure. There will be a set-up phase, which will include welcoming and seating the participant, providing initial instructions, then checking and calibrating the camera (see Section 3.4 for more details on setting up the eye-tracker). Next comes the experimental phase, where each stimulus item is presented. The basic workflow for the experimental phase is Stimulus → Trigger → Optional Follow-up, where the 'trigger' is any action that causes the current display to move on. Triggers are generally manual responses (such as a button or key press) or can be timed so that the display remains for a specified length of time. If we have included a follow-up task such as a comprehension question after each item, the trigger will cause this to be shown, then the participant will need to make a response before the next trial begins.

The experimental sequence will often involve a practice session where a small number of non-experimental items are shown to the participant to ensure that he/she understands the task. This is also useful as it will ensure that any teething issues occur during practice trials rather than during any trials where data are being collected. The practice session can be recorded if required, although this is generally not necessary as the data will not be included in our analysis. Following any practice trials, the main recording sequence will take place. This is the part of the experiment where we will show our stimuli to participants and record their eye-movements and any other responses they make (button presses, spoken responses, etc.).

Once all items have been displayed, we would normally include a final 'Thank you' screen to inform participants that the experiment has finished. We would then collect any other information we might require, such as demographic data, or (for language learners) information about language proficiency and use. In some of the systems this kind of data collection can be built into the experiment, but it might be more straightforward to simply collect this separately before or after the eye-tracking experiment using paper and pencil materials.

The basic structure of any eye-tracking study is summarised in Figure 3.3. The first part (welcome and set-up) and the final part (experiment end) will be the same for almost all studies. The experimental phase will vary according to the type of stimuli. Comprehension questions are often inserted between items in a reading study and may also be used in visual-world or other 'passive' viewing tasks, but are less common in 'action' tasks (where the participant needs to perform a specific action in response to a stimulus) or video studies.

We might choose to include a longer set of comprehension questions after each video as a way of measuring how well participants have understood what they have seen and heard. Depending on the type and number of stimuli we have and the amount of time it takes to

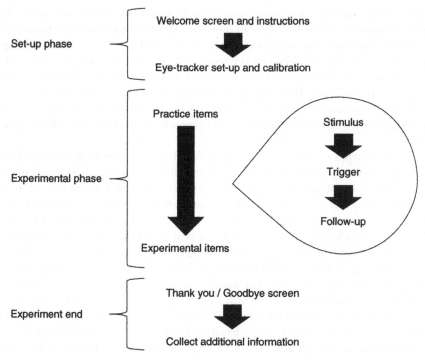

Figure 3.3 Structure of a typical eye-tracking experiment. The experiment will include an introduction and set-up phase, then the stimuli will be presented during the experimental phase. Each trial will consist of a Stimulus → Trigger → Optional follow-up, until all items have been seen. Usually we will include a set of practice items first, then show the experimental items. A final screen allows us to thank participants and inform them that the study has ended, then any additional information we may need can be collected.

present them, we might want to separate them into blocks and have a short break in between each block to prevent participants from becoming too fatigued (or bored) with a long sequence of items. This also allows us to build extra calibrations into the experiment to help ensure a high level of accuracy throughout. For example, if we have 150 sentences (experimental and filler items combined) in a text-based study, we might choose to present these in three separate blocks (and possibly counterbalance the order in which the blocks are shown to participants). If we are showing three extracts from a book, with each extract lasting ten pages, or if we are showing three five-minute videos, it would make sense for us to have a short pause and recalibration after each one. As with a lot of the considerations when building a study, a bit of trial and error is often required to figure out the best procedure.

Triggers

The triggers we use will be determined by the type of study we are running. In a text-based study we would normally want the text to stay on screen until the participant has finished reading, so we would include a manual trigger (button, key or mouse press) for participants to move on at their own pace. Since people read at different speeds, this is usually preferable to having the text on screen for a fixed period of time. In some studies we might want to include a gaze trigger, whereby fixating a particular point (or word) on the screen causes the display to change or move on. This technique has been used extensively in the 'boundary paradigm' discussed in Section 4.5.2. Often more than one trigger may be used, for example combining a key press and a timer trigger. In this case the stimulus would remain on screen until a key is pressed, or if no key is pressed within a specified time limit, the trial will end. If this happens, it is usually an indication that something went wrong (e.g. loss of concentration on the part of the participant or a minor technical issue with that trial) so the individual trial should generally be removed from the analysis of the results.

For other types of studies, the timing of the display and the trigger required will vary according to the specific task. For a 'visual search' study, where participants must find a certain object within an image as quickly as possible, a manual trigger (e.g. a mouse press on an object) will be required in order to record how long each person took. Alternatively, a gaze-contingent trigger could be used, whereby fixating in a specific area for a pre-determined length of time will cause a display change or other action. In a storybook study combining text and images, again a manual trigger (e.g. press a button when you get to the end of the page) will be required to allow participants to read at their own pace and then move on when they are ready. Any image-based study that combines an audio stimulus (such as a visual-world task) will usually display each image for the duration of the audio plus a pre-determined amount of time afterward (e.g. one second after the offset of the audio) to allow us to examine how participants' eye-movements unfold over time.

Video stimuli will almost always be displayed for the duration of the video. No additional triggers will be required, although we could add one in case we wanted the option to abort the trial for any reason. For other dynamic stimuli, the type of task will again be important. Depending on what we are asking participants to do, we might want to present stimuli for a specified amount of time or until the user presses a specific key/button. See Chapter 6 for further information on how we might set up studies that use dynamic stimuli in this way.

The common trigger types are summarised in Table 3.3. This list only covers the trigger options that are available in each system by default. Additional functionality (e.g. using a button box in Tobii or SMI systems) can be achieved using certain plug-ins or by interfacing with additional software. These include plug-ins for commonly used programs such as E-Prime and Matlab and also open-source software such as EyeTrack or PsychoPy that can be of use in building experiments or adapting the basic capabilities of each system. We do not consider this here, but information on this kind of expanded functionality is provided on the manufacturer websites.

Building the Study

The three different systems we consider in this book (SR Research EyeLink, Tobii, SMI) have very different approaches to creating a study. In the following sections we provide a basic introduction to the process in each one. Working through the process of building an experiment is the best way to learn how to do it, and the user manuals provide much greater detail on all of the aspects we address here.

Experiment Builder (SR Research EyeLink)

Experiment Builder uses a drag-and-drop interface to design the basic layout of an experiment. The Graph Editor window is the main workspace and allows us to add in

Table 3.3 Common trigger types and their availability in the three eye-tracking systems discussed in this chapter.

Trigger type	Description	EyeLink	Tobii	SMI
Keyboard	Stimulus will display until a specified key is pressed on the keyboard.	Yes	Yes	Yes
Mouse	Stimulus is displayed until the mouse button is clicked, or until the mouse cursor enters a specified area of the display.	Yes	Yes (click only)	No
Button box	Stimulus is displayed until a specified button on a button response box is pressed.	Yes	No	No
Controller	Stimulus is displayed until a specified button on a hand-held controller is pressed.	Yes	No	No
Gaze	Stimulus will display until a fixation is made for a specified minimum length of time in a specific area of the display.	Yes	No	Yes
Voice	Stimulus is displayed until a pre-configured microphone detects an audio response (e.g. naming something on the screen).	Yes	No	No
Timer	Stimulus will display for a specified amount of time.	Yes	Yes	Yes

actions or triggers as required to create a flow chart. Separate 'blocks' (also referred to as 'sequences' in the user manual) are created containing each of the elements required to run our study. Figure 3.4 reproduces the useful schematic provided in the Experiment Builder user manual.

Within each block, dedicated 'nodes' represent each of the functions that we want to include. Each 'node' represents an action we want the software to perform, and is added to the Graph Editor workspace by dragging it into place. Nodes are connected to each other to create a sequence and generally consist of Actions (such as a Display Screen) and Triggers. The stimulus presentation sequence of an EyeLink experiment is shown in Figure 3.5, and represents the third 'Trial' and fourth 'Recording' blocks in Figure 3.4.

In this example, when each trial begins the software will automatically prepare the stimulus item (pre-load any graphics, reset triggers from the previous trial), then require a drift correct (a check on the participant's gaze position) to verify accuracy (see Section 3.5.2 for more on this). The recording sequence consists of a display screen (labelled here as 'STIMULUS ITEM' but by default called 'DISPLAY SCREEN' in Experiment Builder) showing the stimulus, which will remain until the participant responds by pressing any key (keyboard trigger) or until a specified length of time has elapsed (timer trigger). If a comprehension question is required, a second display screen could be added below the existing nodes within the Recording block. A second set of triggers would then be required, with the keyboard trigger specified to allow only certain responses (e.g. the 'y' and 'n' keys to allow participants to answer a yes/no question).

Any additional actions are added into the structure in the same way. For example, adding in the procedure to set up and calibrate the eye-tracker simply requires an EL CAMERA SETUP node to be added at the appropriate point (as part of the second block – 'Block' – in Figure 3.4). This set-up node should be added in at the beginning of

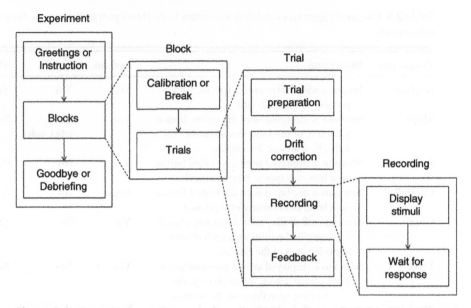

Figure 3.4 Hierarchical nested structure in an EyeLink experiment. Each 'block' is self-contained and forms part of the block above it in the structure. This allows an experimental block to be repeated as many times as required, i.e. the 'Trial' block would be repeated until all stimuli have been shown. Adapted from *SR Research Experiment Builder User Manual, Version 1.10.1630*, p. 36 (SR Research, 2015b).

any experiment we build, and by inserting it at this point rather than in the 'Experiment' block, a calibration procedure will be automatically included before each block of trials. This means that if we split our stimuli into separate blocks over the course of an experiment, each one will automatically include a set-up and calibration before the next set of stimuli are shown. All nodes and actions are detailed in the Experiment Builder manual, which provides a thorough explanation of the full functionality of the software.

Adding Stimuli   In Experiment Builder we can easily add text, image, audio and video stimuli to our study. Once we have built the basic structure for our trial (as in Figure 3.5), we double-click the DISPLAY SCREEN node to open the 'Screen Builder' resource. Here, we add the required stimuli by selecting the corresponding icon, then edit the specific properties in the left-hand 'Properties' menu. If we want to include image, audio or video files in our study, these need to be added to Experiment Builder's library in advance to allow us to select them from within the project.

Text stimuli are added using either the Text Resource tool (for single-line reading) or Mutliline Text Resource tool (for multi-line reading). The text editor allows us to type in our text and set the properties such as font type, size and position on the screen. Image-based studies are created by using the Image Resource tool, selecting the required file from the library and then setting the properties such as width, height and location on the screen. We can combine text and image resources on the same screen if this is required, for example in a storybook study comparing the effect of pictures on reading patterns. Alternatively, text (with or without images) can be prepared and saved as an image file in

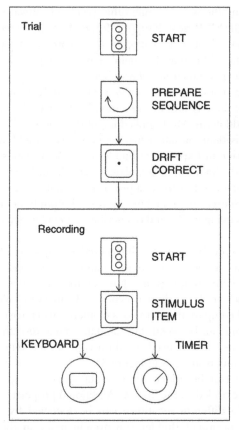

Trial START, PREPARE SEQUENCE, DRIFT CORRECT	The 'Trial' block specifies what will happen for each trial within the experiment. The basic structure of this trial involves the preparation of any required resources (via the PREPARE SEQUENCE node) and a DRIFT CORRECT action to ensure accuracy before each trial. Each item is then presented in turn until all items have been seen. Required nodes are dragged into place in the Graph Editor Window then connected by clicking and dragging an arrow between icons.
Recording START, STIMULUS ITEM, KEYBOARD, TIMER	The 'Recording' block is contained within the larger 'Trial' block. The recording sequence involves the presentation of each item (labelled as STIMULUS ITEM here) which could be text, an image, a video or a combined visual and audio stimulus. The item will remain on the screen until either of the triggers (KEYBOARD or TIMER) is activated.

If required, an optional follow-up question can be added by dragging in the appropriate nodes. |

Figure 3.5 Sample layout for Block 3 – 'Trial' – and Block 4 – 'Recording' – within the overall EyeLink structure.

advance. For any study requiring an audio track to be played concurrently with either text (e.g. a reading-while-listening study) or images (e.g. a visual-world study), the 'Synchronize Audio' tickbox should be checked within the Properties list for the DISPLAY SCREEN node. This will enable us to select an audio file from the Experiment Builder library to play alongside the visual stimulus.

Video stimuli are added using the Video Resource tool. Supported formats are AVI and XVID. To ensure good video timing, it is recommended that video files are converted to the required format (XVID or VFW) using the Split Avi application provided with the Experiment Builder software package. Since this separates the video and audio streams, both must be added to the library. The 'Synchronize Audio' tickbox will need to be enabled for any video resource to allow us to choose the requisite audio stream to play alongside it. For any experiment requiring visual and auditory stimuli to be accurately synchronised (including a video-based study), specific drivers should be activated and used (detailed in Section 7.9.13, Playing Sound, in the Experiment Builder manual).

Experiment Builder does not directly support inclusion of some of the more dynamic stimuli discussed so far, such as webpages or external software applications. We can use webpages as stimuli by taking screenshots and adding them as image files. Alternatively, SR Research provide a Screen Recorder tool that allows us to record eye-movements during other activities, such as surfing the web or using other pieces of software. More information on these is available via the SR Research support forum. For studies requiring a 'think-aloud' recording, Experiment Builder does support the recording of a participant's voice while viewing a stimulus. This may be useful if we want participants to describe an image they are viewing (e.g. a screenshot of a webpage).

If we don't have many stimuli (e.g. in a video-based study where we only want to show one or two videos), we can add them directly into the structure. In the majority of cases, this is probably not how we would add items. Most applied linguistics studies will require multiple stimuli, and adding 150 individual stimulus sentences in this way would be time-consuming and inefficient. The solution in Experiment Builder is to add a 'data source', which operates like a spreadsheet and which can be populated manually or by importing data from a text file. To do this we first need to create a prototypical trial (like the one in Figure 3.5), then link this to the data source containing our individual stimulus items. This is done at the level of the 'Trial' block in Figure 3.4 and is described in detail in Section 9 of the Experiment Builder manual.

Within the data source, each row represents one trial. If required, multiple items can be included in each trial by adding extra columns, and as many columns can be added as we need to specify additional variables, item groupings, etc. For example, having a column that specifies the 'Condition' for each trial (e.g. Experimental vs Control vs Filler) will make it easy to remove the fillers and compare the conditions of interest when we come to analyse our results. Text-based stimuli can be typed into the data source directly. If we want to add comprehension questions, we just need to add a column and type in the question that corresponds to each stimulus item, as in Figure 3.6.

Image, audio and video stimuli can be added to the data source by specifying the filename of an item that we have added to the library. Additional properties (e.g. if different images need to appear in different locations) can be specified by adding columns as needed. By default, Experiment Builder will present items in the order specified in the data source. If required, items can be randomised or pseudo-randomised in advance in the input file. Alternatively, Experiment Builder provides methods for internal and external randomisation, blocking and counterbalancing of stimuli. Section 9.6 of the Experiment Builder manual provides more information on how to randomise data sources.

The Experiment Builder user manual includes a worked example (Section 14, Creating EyeLink Experiments: The First Example) and a very useful project checklist to ensure that the relevant steps have been completed for a successful experiment. We can use this, alongside the Test Mode available in Experiment Builder, to troubleshoot our experiment prior to collecting data. EyeLink experiments need to be deployed as a stand-alone .exe file (or .app for Mac users) before they can be used with participants, and once this has been done no changes can be made. If we do need to make any changes after this point, we would do this by amending our original Experiment Builder file and re-deploying the experiment.

Tobii Pro Studio (Tobii)

Tobii Pro Studio uses a hierarchical structure organised on three levels. The topmost level (Project) contains one or more Tests, with each Test defining a sequence of stimulus items. Within a Test, when a Recording is performed the eye-movement data is recorded and associated with the relevant participant and stimulus information. Section 3 of the Tobii Pro Studio user manual explains this organisation in more detail.

Item	Condition	Stimulus	Question
1	Literal	The violence had even begun to affect normally 'safe' areas.	Was the city very peaceful?
2	Metaphorical	After all the rain the sunlight was bursting through the clouds.	Had the weather been pleasant?
3	Filler	The men had been chasing the dogs for several hours now.	Were the dogs in a cage?

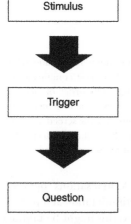

The columns above correspond to 'Stimulus' and 'Question' DISPLAY SCREEN nodes that we would include in our prototypical trial. We now need to tell Experiment Builder which information to display by 'referencing' the required column in the data source.

To do this, we select the text resource that has been added within the DISPLAY SCREEN node, then in the 'Text' field of the 'Properties' list double-click to openthe Attribute Editor. Within the Node Selection structure, we select Trial > DataSource > then the column name that corresponds to what we want to display (Stimulus or Question).

An explanation and example of this is provided in Section 10.1, Using References, in the Experiment Builder manual.

Figure 3.6 Sample data source in Experiment Builder (top panel). Text stimuli can be typed in directly and will appear according to the parameters we set in the 'Text Resource' that we added to our prototypical trial. Other columns such as 'Item' and 'Condition' are useful for sorting our data once it has been collected and is ready for analysis. Once we have added a data source we need to 'reference' the required columns at the appropriate point in our experimental structure (bottom panel).

Creating a Test in Tobii Pro Studio involves dragging the required media element into place on a presentation timeline, then editing its properties. The simple drag-and-drop interface means that items can be reordered easily until all stimuli and any filler items have been included. Tobii Pro Studio supports a wide range of media elements, including instruction screens, images, movies, websites, screen recordings, questionnaires and PDF documents. Other options for external video recordings (where video from another source such as a webcam would be recorded) can be used, but these require external equipment. Figure 3.7 shows a sample layout in Tobii Pro Studio.

A text-based study can be constructed in Tobii Pro Studio in a number of ways. One is to use the Instruction element, which enables us to type in and format our own text. The example in Figure 3.7 uses an Instruction element both for the instructions and Text 1. If

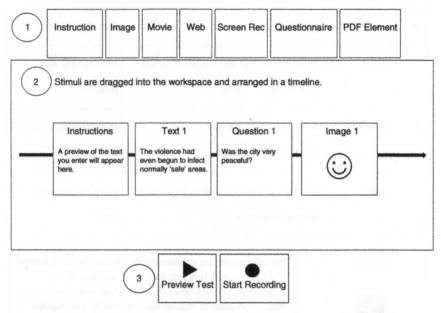

Figure 3.7 Schematic of a sample layout in Tobii Pro Studio. Stimulus items are added by dragging an icon along the top of the display (1) onto the workspace (2). This Test contains an instruction screen, a text stimulus, a comprehension question and an image. The order of elements can be changed by dragging to the required point on the timeline. Properties of each element are edited by double-clicking to open the media set-up dialogue box. At the bottom of the screen, the Preview Test button can be used to preview the experiment, and the Start Recording button will initiate a recording (3). NB: diagram is not to scale and some non-relevant icons are omitted.

we do this, we need to make sure that the 'Enable for Visualisations' option is ticked otherwise gaze data will not be recorded. Each of our stimuli (and each page if we are using multi-page texts) will require a separate element, so this might be impractical for studies with large numbers of stimuli. Alternatively, we can create images or PDFs for each of our items in advance and add these. For a text-based study where we want participants to read an extract over several pages, creating a multi-page PDF may be a good way to achieve this. If comprehension questions are required, these can be added using the Questionnaire element (multiple-choice questions only – no text input functionality is possible). A typical text-based study might therefore consist of Instruction element (stimulus) followed by a Questionnaire element (comprehension question), repeated as many times as required until all of our stimuli have been presented. The trigger for the stimulus element (to move the display on to the next element in the sequence) would be for the participant to press any key, then he/she would use the mouse to answer a multiple-choice comprehension question.

To add image or video stimuli, we drag the required icon into place on the timeline. Double-clicking the element will allow us to open the element's properties, from where we can browse to and add the required file, then edit other properties for the stimulus presentation. There is no dedicated audio stimulus media element, so this means that if we want to combine audio and visual stimuli we will need to prepare these in advance. For example, to create a reading-while-listening stimulus, we could create an image of our text, then use this as the background while we record the audio over the top using any video-editing software. The resulting video file could then be added to the timeline. The same principle could be used for a visual-world study, where we would prepare our images in advance, then add the prepared audio (edited in advance) over the still image to create a video file.

Tobii Pro Studio supports a range of dynamic options, so adding in web stimuli (allowing the participant to browse the web freely while his/her eye-movements are recorded) or a screen recorder (to enable us to ask participants to use another piece of software) is also just a case of dragging the required element into place and specifying the URL or identifying the location of the software that should be launched.

Various properties can be defined for each of the stimuli by double-clicking the element on the timeline. These include how each element will end (keyboard, mouse press or timed trigger), as well as things such as the size of images and the appearance of text. Tobii Pro Studio provides either an in-built counterbalancing option to vary the order of stimuli randomly across participants, or allows us to define and specify different Presentation Sequences if specific presentation orders of the test are required. Section 4.1 of the Tobii Pro Studio user manual provides in-depth information on how to add and edit the different media elements, and how to include counterbalancing or Presentation Sequences in our experiment.

The Preview Test option in Tobii Pro Studio allows us to review our stimuli and amend as required. Data can be collected from within Tobii Pro Studio as soon as all stimuli have been added and we are happy that the experiment is complete.

Experiment Center (SMI)

The basic functionality of Experiment Center provides a simple way to create a range of studies. Additional modules can be purchased for specific purposes. For example, the Reading Analysis module supports the creation and analysis of text-based studies, and the Observation module enables the recording of concurrent or retrospective think-aloud data from participants. The Experiment Center manual provides more information on the expanded functionality that can be added.

The Application Window interface in Experiment Center provides an easy way to build our study. Rather than having to create our own structure, we add each stimulus item individually to a master list. Items can be reordered by dragging them into the required position in the list. Figure 3.8 shows a schematic of a typical layout in Experiment Center.

Experiment Center supports a wide range of stimulus types. All stimuli are added by selecting the required icon from the toolbar, which will create a new item in the stimulus list. The properties that can be edited for each stimulus are the type (text, image, video, etc.) and the name of each item; whether it should have a timed or manual trigger; whether it should be sized to fit the screen; whether eye-movement data should be recorded or not (for some items such as instructions we may not require data to be recorded); what task it should be assigned to (so that we can create multiple blocks or different versions of our experiment); and what randomisation group it belongs to (to enable us to randomise our stimuli in various configurations). A mix of different stimulus types can be included in one list, so we can easily create a study asking participants to do different things.

Text-based studies can be created either by using the Text element, or by preparing our stimuli in advance as image or PDF files. Selecting a Text element will open a text editor, so each item can be typed in and the font, size, position, etc. can be specified. A Question element can be added, either as a way of asking comprehension questions, or as a way of

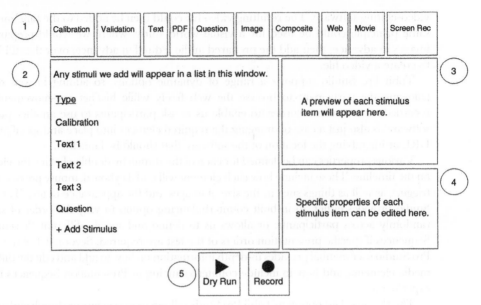

Figure 3.8 Schematic of the Application Window layout in Experiment Center. Stimuli are added using the icons along the top of the screen (1) and appear in a list in the left-hand panel (2). A preview of each item is provided in the top-right panel (3) and specific properties can be edited in the bottom-right panel (4). At the bottom of the screen, the Dry Run button can be used to preview the experiment, and the Record button will initiate a recording (5). NB: diagram is not to scale and some non-relevant icons are omitted.

collecting background data from participants. The answers can then be used to filter our participants during subsequent data analysis.

Image and video stimuli are added by selecting the required icon and then selecting a pre-prepared file on our computer. When adding images, if multiple files are selected each will be added as a separate item in the stimulus list. If we want to combine visual and audio stimuli (in reading-while-listening or visual-world studies), audio files can be easily added to most stimulus types as one of the fields available in the lower right-hand panel of the Application Window. Once we select the audio file that goes with the text or image, playback will begin once the stimulus is displayed. If a video stimulus is added it will be automatically encoded into an optimised format for playback. The Composite icon allows us to create a combined text/image/video stimulus, for example by uploading an image and then superimposing text over the top. If we have not prepared our items in advance, this would be an alternative way to create combined text and image stimuli (for storybook studies) or stimuli with multiple images (for visual-world studies), or to add keywords to a video.

If we have multiple stimuli, rather than adding them one by one we can upload a Stimulus List. Items can be prepared in a spreadsheet and uploaded together, which will be useful for a study involving a long list of items. Text, images and videos can be added like this, provided the required files are saved in the same folder as the spreadsheet. The spreadsheet must be prepared in a specific way, and Part VI Section 3 of the Experiment Center user manual provides details of how to do this for each stimulus type.

Once added, stimuli can be assigned to a specific Task. This provides an easy way for us to present different stimulus lists to different participants: all items can be added to the overall project, then assigned to different Tasks to allow us to show our different counter-balanced lists (i.e. Task 1 would be items from List A and Task 2 would be items from List B). Both the order and duration of stimuli can be randomised from within Experiment Center using the 'Randomization Groups' option. If 'Task' and 'Randomization Groups' are left blank, items will be displayed in the order they appear in the stimulus list.

A calibration sequence is automatically included at the start of any experiment built in Experiment Center. If a validation is also required, we will need to add this in using the appropriate icon on the Application Window toolbar. Additional calibrations and validations can be inserted at any point in the stimulus list if required. For longer studies, regular recalibrations are recommended as this will help to maintain a high level of accuracy. (See Section 3.4.2 for more on calibrating and validating experiments.) The Dry Run mode in Experiment Center can be used to preview our experimental sequence and troubleshoot the experiment as we build it. Once we have finished adding stimuli, the project can be used to record data immediately.

3.1.4 Defining Regions of Interest

Regions of interest (ROIs; also called areas of interest or AOIs) are the parts of the display that we are interested in measuring and analysing. In text-based studies this is likely to be a word, sequence of words or part of a sentence, but might also be larger areas, for example if we are interested in time spent looking at the whole text versus time spent looking at images in a study combining visual inputs. In image-based experiments ROIs can be a specific area of the display, such as the individual images for any given trial displayed in a visual-world study. For studies that combine text and images – such as a storybook experiment – we might be interested in both specific words and images as our ROIs. For any experiment where the stimulus will unfold over time (multimodal studies where an audio stimulus is combined with text or images, or video-based studies), our ROIs will be defined as specific areas of the display at specific time points or during fixed time windows. In most studies, having a clear idea of what we want to analyse is a key part of creating balanced and controlled stimuli. It follows that our ROIs will generally be decided in advance for each stimulus item. However, for certain types of dynamic stimuli – for example writing or translation tasks where we are interested in the output produced by participants – we may not know what our ROIs will be in advance since the output will be generated by each specific individual. Examples like these are discussed in Chapter 6.

ROIs in Text-Based Studies

For text-based studies, it is particularly important to define our ROIs carefully to ensure that we obtain the most appropriate data, but also to ensure that we aren't swamped with data that we don't need. Both EyeLink and SMI systems can identify each word in a text-based study as a separate ROI. (In SMI this is only the case if the Reading Analysis module is licensed. If so, it will identify separate ROIs for each paragraph, sentence, word and character in our study.) While this can be very useful in some studies (e.g. as a way of measuring global reading behaviour such as the average fixation duration or saccade length throughout the text), it can be less useful for the kind of manipulation we are often interested in. For example, in our text-based study looking at literal and metaphorical sentences, we are primarily interested in the reading times for our critical word: 'affect' versus 'infect'. We might also be interested in other areas of the sentence, such as the pre-critical and spillover regions, giving us three ROIs. If we allow the eye-tracking software to automatically treat each word as an ROI, analysis of these ROIs becomes less straightforward, as in Example 3.4.

Example 3.4 We can either identify our own ROIs in advance (a) or allow the software to identify each word as a separate ROI (b).

(a) The violence had <u>even begun to</u> infect <u>normally</u> 'safe' areas.
(b) <u>The</u> violence <u>had</u> <u>even</u> begun <u>to</u> infect <u>normally</u> 'safe' areas.

If we treat each word as a separate ROI, we have three potential issues. The first is that our pre-critical and spillover regions are segmented into separate words. This means that in order to analyse the whole region we would need to apply some kind of formula in the exported data to combine these into the ROIs we want. In comparison, in (a) we can easily identify the fixations on the pre-critical and spillover regions. The second problem is that by segmenting every word, we are producing much more data than we actually require. In this example, we have three data points in (a) but ten in (b). If we scale this up to include all of our stimuli (ten metaphorical sentences, ten literal sentences, twenty fillers) and participants (ten participants per stimulus list = twenty overall), we would end up with 8000 data points in the auto-segmented version, compared to 2400 in the version where we added our own ROIs. It is not hard to imagine how this would quickly become unmanageable in a study that included longer texts, such as paragraph or whole-page reading, where there might be perhaps 150 words per page.

The third reason to identify our ROIs carefully is that they are important for identifying regression patterns in the text. We will talk more about regressions in the following section (Section 3.2), but one thing we might be interested in is whether reading 'infect' in our text caused participants to return to the earlier word 'violence' to ensure that it had been correctly recognised and understood (see Example 3.5).

Example 3.5 Sequential numbering of ROIs is important for certain measures like regressions. In this example 'violence' would be ROI 1, and 'infect' ROI 2.

The <u>violence</u> had even begun to <u>infect</u> normally 'safe' areas.

Eye-tracking software calculates a 'regression' as a fixation on a previous ROI once the eye gaze has entered a later ROI (e.g. in Example 3.5, where 'infect' comes later than 'violence'). This means that for us to be able to analyse specifically whether 'infect' prompted more regressions to 'violence' than 'affect', these need to be clearly and sequentially identified as our ROIs. If we segmented each word into an individual ROI, the software would consider any regression to 'violence' from a word further on in the sentence, and any regression from 'infect' to a word earlier in the sentence. We might therefore not be able to tell whether it was specifically once 'infect' had been read that readers went back to read 'violence' again.

The ROIs we define will be determined by the nature of our research question. For text-based studies, whether we define single words as ROIs, or whether we want to identify phrases, clauses or even longer stretches will depend on what we are investigating. Longer stretches of text might be of interest in studies concerned with syntactic or discourse-level processes. We consider reading measures in more detail in Section 3.2 and in Chapter 4.

ROIs with Visual and Audio Input, Video and Other Types of Stimuli

For image-based studies we are likely to identify specific parts of the display as our ROIs. As we have noted, most applied linguistics studies are likely to combine a visual display with some kind of audio input, for example in the visual-world paradigm. In such studies, we are interested not just in where the participant looks, but also how eye-movements change over time. Similarly, in a video, we are likely to be interested in specific aspects of the display that are on the screen at certain times of the video.

In a visual-world study, we would identify separate ROIs for each of the images that make up the display. In the Chambers and Cooke (2009) example, this means a separate ROI for the four images at the north, south, east and west positions. We will therefore be able to see the number and duration of fixations for each ROI throughout the trial. However, as we discuss in more detail in Chapter 5, visual-world studies are generally concerned with looking patterns at specific points in time. For example, Holsinger (2013) defined two windows of 400 ms each: an 'Early Window' (starting 180 ms after the onset of the critical word and ending at 580 ms) and a 'Late Window' (starting at 580 ms and extending to 980 ms). If we want to do the same, we have two ways to do this. The first is simply to draw each ROI and collect data for the whole trial, then afterward manually divide our results into any fixations that occurred between 180 and 580 ms, and any that occurred between 580 and 980 ms. Alternatively, we can set our ROIs to only be 'active' during certain points in the trial. As we discuss in the following sections, the three pieces of software we have considered allow us to define start and end points for our ROIs. This means that we could draw ROIs around the images on our display, then tell the eye-tracking software when they should start and stop collecting data. When we export our results, fixations would automatically be divided up into ROIs by location on the screen and by the time window in which they occurred.

For videos we are also likely to want to define ROIs that are only 'active' at specific points (i.e. they will only include fixations during a certain time window). For example, Bisson et al. (2014) looked at how much attention participants paid to subtitles while watching a DVD. They defined two broad areas corresponding to the subtitle region (roughly the bottom third of the screen) and the image region (roughly the top two-thirds of the screen). They then used the subtitle timing information to determine whether fixations occurred in the subtitle region while a set of subtitles was actually present on the screen. Data was only analysed for those time windows when subtitles were visible, allowing Bisson et al. to determine the relative amount of attention paid to the subtitles in each of their conditions (for a full discussion of this study and the conditions they manipulated, see Section 5.4.1). As with the visual-world example, we could conduct a study like this and set multiple ROIs to be 'active' during specific time windows (e.g. the start and end point of each set of subtitles). We could go further and identify specific words in the audio input that we were interested in, then define our ROIs to collect data only when those words or phrases occurred during the video, for example if we wanted to look at how well participants learned unknown vocabulary from watching the video and reading the subtitles. In this case we could define ROIs for the specific words, then relate overall reading times for these to subsequent scores on a vocabulary test. Figure 3.9 demonstrates the different ways in which we could analyse looking patterns to subtitles.

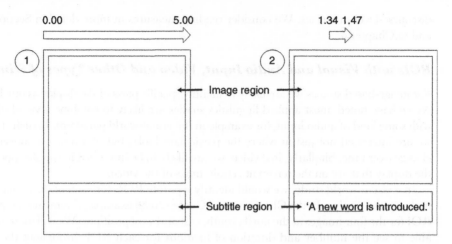

Figure 3.9 Example ROIs on a video with subtitles. In (1), two broad ROIs are defined for the image and subtitle regions. Fixation data will be collected throughout the video. The timing information can be used to filter our results into periods when subtitles are on the screen (as in Bisson et al., 2014). In (2), a time-locked ROI is defined that will only be 'active' from 1:34 to 1:47 – the period in the video when a specific set of subtitles appears on screen. Multiple ROIs with start and end points would be defined for each set of subtitles that we wanted to analyse. If we wanted to go further and look at a specific 'new word', we could create an ROI around its specific location in the subtitles to see how long participants spent reading it.

In videos and other dynamic stimuli, we may need to set ROIs that follow moving elements of the display. This is easiest if the motion is fairly smooth and linear, and we probably wouldn't want to try to define a dynamic ROI that tracked a complicated set of movements over an extended period of time. Although it is unlikely that we would need to track moving stimuli like this in the types of studies we consider here, we do briefly address the ways in which moving ROIs in each eye-tracking system can be created in the following section.

For some types of stimuli it may not be possible to define ROIs in advance. This is likely to be the case for software applications or webpages where the participants have a relatively free choice of what they can look at, in which case we do not have a predefined image to draw our ROIs onto before data has been collected. A good example would be someone using a chat window, where the text that appears will vary from person to person (see Chapter 6 for further discussion of this). In such instances, it would be necessary to wait until after data has been collected before we could identify and add ROIs. We should still have a broad idea of what we are looking for in advance, as this will help to ensure that our study design is robust and not simply a 'fishing expedition'.

Creating ROIs in the Three Eye-Tracking Systems

Here we provide a brief overview of how to create ROIs in the three systems we have considered so far. For clarity, we use the terminology adopted by each system: interest areas (IAs) in Experiment Builder/SR Research EyeLink systems, and areas of interest (AOIs) in both Tobii and SMI systems.

In Experiment Builder, IAs can be created either in advance when building the study, or following data collection using the dedicated SR Research analysis software Data

Viewer. For text-based experiments, each word can be identified as a separate IA by enabling the Runtime Segmentation option in Experiment Builder, or once the data has been collected by auto-segmenting trials in Data Viewer. As we pointed out, this may not be the optimal approach depending on the focus of our research, and may be most beneficial for obtaining global measures, or for longer reading studies with authentic texts where we are not able to create and control specific manipulations. In many cases it will be better to identify specific words and phrases in advance and draw in the IAs ourselves (see earlier discussion about Example 3.4). Other types of stimulus can also be 'auto-segmented', where Data Viewer will automatically create a grid of IAs for us, for example over an image. Often this will not be specific enough for our purposes, so we would again want to define our own IAs for analysis.

Adding IAs in advance can only really be done where we have very few stimuli, or for studies where the position of our critical elements will be the same for all items. For text-based studies where words will vary in their length and position in the sentence, this will be tricky. One solution is therefore to deploy our experiment and run through the final version ourselves to collect 'live' data. We can then draw in all the IAs we require in Data Viewer by selecting one of the Interest Area Shape icons and using the mouse to drag a box around the region we want to define as the IA. These Interest Area files (text files stating the name of each IA and the x and y coordinates on the screen) can be saved within the Experiment Builder project directory in the Library → Interest Area Set folder. We can then add a column to our data source to specify which IAs should go with which stimulus items. Re-deploying the experiment will mean that these IAs are automatically created in Data Viewer for any new data that we collect. This process can be a little confusing, but the Help menu within Data Viewer provides more information and an example. An Interest Area file can also be created whereby the ID, shape and location (x and y coordinates) of all of the IAs we require for our study are specified in a text file. This can be added to Experiment Builder prior to deploying our experiment, or to Data Viewer to add IAs once data have been collected.

Both time-locked and moving IAs can be created, and Data Viewer refers to these as 'dynamic' IAs. To create dynamic IAs, we need to deploy and run through our study once, then in Data Viewer we draw the required IAs onto each of our stimuli. Drawing static and dynamic IAs is done in the same way, but for dynamic IAs the 'Dynamic IA' tickbox needs to be checked. Dynamic IAs by default require us to specify a start and end time, which defines when it will be active during each trial. Moving IAs that track part of a video stimulus can be created in a number of ways, but one option is to use the Mouse Creation tool. In this, we create an initial IA, then during playback of the video we can click on the display at consecutive time points to follow the element we are interested in and create any subsequent IAs that are required in different locations. Slowing the playback speed or pausing the video at short intervals will help here, especially if we are following something that moves quickly or non-linearly in the display. Section 8.3, Interest Areas of the Experiment Builder user manual and Section 5.9 of the Data Viewer user manual (version 2.4.1, SR Research, 2015a) provide further information on how to create and add IAs in EyeLink experiments.

In Tobii Pro Studio, AOIs can be drawn manually for each stimulus item before or after data has been collected using the dedicated Areas of Interest tab. For 'non-interactive' elements (Instructions, Images, Video), once we have added our stimuli to the timeline they will be available to add AOIs, and any that we draw in will be listed on the left-hand pane. For 'interactive' media elements (Websites, Screen Recordings and PDFs),[6] the element will not be available for us to define AOIs until after data has been recorded for one participant. Each AOI we add can be set to be 'active' or 'inactive' at specific time points. We simply select the AOI we want to edit, then use the time indicator slider underneath the display to set the time points where we want it to start and stop. AOIs can be set to track an aspect of the display by selecting the starting time point and drawing in the required AOI. If we then move to a later time point and move (by dragging) or resize the AOI, Tobii Pro Studio will automatically calculate the intervening frames to ensure that the display is tracked in a continuous fashion. (NB: this interpolation is linear so will assume that the movement is in a straight line and at a constant speed. Any exceptions to this will need to be corrected manually on a frame-by-frame basis.) AOIs can also be 'grouped' so that data from a larger area can be considered, e.g. to combine text that is located on different parts of the screen for an overall analysis. Defining and editing AOIs is dealt with in more detail in Section 8 of the Tobii Pro Studio user manual.

In SMI systems, AOIs are created after data has been collected using the AOI Editor in the analysis software BeGaze. Once we have added AOIs to our stimuli, these will apply for all subsequently collected data. It is therefore possible to collect data from one participant then add in AOIs, and these will be applied to any participants we test from that point on. For text-based studies, the Reading Analysis module will automatically add AOIs for paragraphs, sentences, words and characters, but as before, this may not be ideal depending on our research question. We can draw in specific AOIs as required, and the process is the same for all stimulus types. We select the trial where we want to add an AOI, then choose the type of AOI (rectangle, ellipse, polygon) and use the mouse to draw it onto the display. For Composite stimulus elements, AOIs are automatically included for each of the text and image components we included when creating the item.

For all stimuli, once data has been recorded a video file of the whole trial will be available in BeGaze. Time-locked or moving AOIs can be created by selecting the frame at the appropriate time point and drawing the AOI that we require. We can edit the properties of each AOI to define the start and end point of the time window when it will be applied during the trial. If we add an AOI at a specific point then add a second AOI to a later frame in a different position on the display, BeGaze can automatically calculate the movement between the two and add the appropriate AOIs to intervening frames. See Part VI, Section 7 of the BeGaze user manual (SMI, 2016a) for more information on creating AOIs for a range of stimuli.

3.2   What Are the Different Eye-Tracking Measures?

Once we have prepared our stimuli, built our study and identified the ROIs we want to analyse, we need to think about what eye-movement measures will allow us to address our research question. Eye-tracking allows us to collect and analyse data for a wide range of different measures of eye-movements and relate these to language processing and perception more generally. While we do not need to decide on the appropriate measures in advance (at least, not in terms of building them into our experiment), we should consider which ones will allow us to best address our research question when we create our stimuli.

---

[6] While PDFs can be static and just display a single static page, Tobii Pro Studio does treat them as dynamic (since they can be multi-page and allow a user to scroll through them), and therefore AOIs cannot be added until data has been collected.

We discuss here the most commonly used measures in reading and visual processing studies, but other, more specialised measures may be appropriate in different contexts. For example, eye-tracking can also furnish a measure of pupil dilation, which can provide an indication of certain kinds of emotional response when reading (Laeng, Siriosi and Gredebäck, 2012). Emotions such as fear, arousal, anticipation, risk, novelty, surprise and conflict can all cause pupil dilation to increase, hence this may be of interest in studies investigating such responses.

3.2.1 Reading Measures

The literature on eye-movements during reading is well established and sizeable. We deal with reading in more detail in Chapter 4; see also Rayner (2009) for a detailed overview. We concentrate here on an overview of the measures most likely to be of use in applied linguistics studies. As stated in Chapter 1, our underlying assumption when we come to analyse eye-movements during reading is the 'eye–mind hypothesis' (Just and Carpenter, 1980). This means that what is being looked at is what is being processed, and the duration of any fixation or group of fixations is a reflection of the effort required to process what is being looked at (Staub and Rayner, 2007). Broadly, this means that in reading we assume that words that are fixated for longer require more cognitive processing, while words with shorter fixations are easier to process. Fixation times are usually measured in milliseconds (ms), although Tobii Pro Studio reports measures in seconds, and it is essential to remember that the comparisons we make are relative. In other words, longer/shorter fixations or greater/less processing effort must be in comparison to something. In our text-based study, we would be interested in the difference in the relative time spent reading the critical words 'infect' and 'affect' in our two conditions. As we suggested in Section 3.1.4, we might also be interested in the pattern of eye-movements, so do readers return to the earlier word 'violence' more in the metaphorical condition? Figure 3.10 shows both fixation and regression measures of potential interest in our example study.

As introduced in Chapter 1, eye-movement data is divided into fixations and saccades, with a complete sequence of the two being referred to as a scan path. Fixations are any

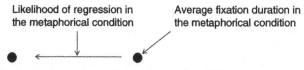

The violence had even begun to infect normally 'safe' areas.

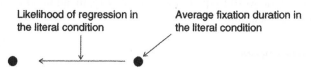

The violence had even begun to affect normally 'safe' areas.

Figure 3.10 Eye-tracking measures of interest in our reading example might be whether the average fixation time on our critical word ('infect' vs 'affect') varies between conditions, and whether there is a difference in the pattern of regressions to earlier parts of the sentence.

point where the eye is stationary on a target, and saccades are movements from one location to another. Since fixations (and specifically the duration of fixations) are more sensitive to linguistic factors than saccades (Staub and Rayner, 2007), these tend to be the measures we are most interested in for text-based studies. Saccades are important for us if we want to look at regression patterns, since longer backward saccades tend to be used to return to a prior part of a sentence in order to resolve comprehension difficulty or ambiguity. Fixation measures are classed as either 'early' or 'late' and are understood to reflect different stages of reading processing. Early measures are seen primarily as a reflection of highly automatic word recognition and lexical access processes, while later measures tend to reflect more conscious, controlled, strategic processes (Altarriba et al., 1996; Inhoff, 1984; Paterson, Liversedge and Underwood, 1999; Staub and Rayner, 2007). In broad terms, this maps onto 'first pass' measures (location and duration of fixations during the first reading of a piece of text) and 'total' measures (location and duration of all fixations, including any re-reading that is required).

Early Measures

Skipping rate is used to determine the proportion of words that receive no fixation during first pass reading and is the result of both visual factors and linguistic information. Skipped words are assumed to have been processed in the parafovea during the fixation on the previous word (Rayner, 2009, and see Section 4.1 for a discussion). Length, frequency, lexical status (function vs content words) and predictability are all determiners of whether a word is likely to be skipped. Skipping rate is reported as a probability (or percentage) and calculated as:

Total number of trials where word was skipped during first pass reading ÷ Total number of trials (× 100 to give a percentage)

First fixation duration refers to the length of the first fixation made on a word or ROI. It is most relevant where the ROI is a single word. A similar measure that is sometimes used is *single fixation duration*, which considers only those trials where one (and only one) fixation was made on a critical word or ROI. A comparable measure that considers all fixations made on a word or ROI before the gaze exits (to the left or right) is *gaze duration*, which is also sometimes called *first pass reading time*. This provides a useful way of applying an early measure to ROIs consisting of longer words or sequences of more than one word that are likely to receive multiple fixations.

Each of the above measures can be seen as an index of lexical access, or how easily the word is recognised and retrieved from the mental lexicon. These are also the earliest points at which we might expect to see an effect of the variable being manipulated (Liversedge, Paterson and Pickering, 1998). Factors known to affect the duration of early fixation measures include word frequency and familiarity, meaning ambiguity, predictability and semantic association.

Intermediate Measures

Regression path duration, also known as *go past time*, is a measure of the time spent on the word itself and any prior parts of the sentence before the reader moves past the critical word to the right. The regression pattern can also be considered in terms of *regressions out* of an ROI (how many times a regression from the critical word to the preceding text was made – also known as *first pass regressions out*) and sometimes also *regressions in* (how many times a regression from a later part of the sentence was made back into the critical ROI). These can either be measured in terms of number of regressions or as a percentage, i.e. how many trials had a regression out of or into the ROI. Regressions are hard to classify as either early or late since they can be indicative of difficulty when first encountering an item, and the subsequent time taken to overcome that difficulty (Clifton, Staub and Rayner, 2007).

Late Measures

Total reading time is the sum total of all fixations made on a word or ROI during a trial. It includes both first fixation/gaze durations and any subsequent re-reading. It is taken as a measure of the initial retrieval and subsequent integration of a word, and is likely to be affected by contextual and discourse-level factors as well as by the lexical factors already discussed. *Re-reading time* and *second pass reading time* are sometimes also reported. These measures are slightly different and have variable definitions in the literature. We define re-reading time as the regression path duration minus the first pass reading time, whereas second pass reading is the sum of all subsequent fixations on the ROI after it has been exited for the first time. (See Figure 3.11 for an example of each of these.) As well as the duration of any fixations, the total number of fixations (*fixation count*) can be measured and provides an alternative way of considering the attention paid to an ROI during the whole trial.

Later measures may not reflect purely lexical factors, and may be more influenced by contextual, syntactic or discourse-level properties of what is being read. For example, syntactic ambiguity can lead to longer fixations on a critical word or region, as well as more regressions to the prior context as the reader is forced to re-evaluate the initial analysis (Frazier and Rayner, 1982). Staub and Rayner (2007) conclude that lexical variables are the primary influence on early fixation times, while higher-level (contextual, sentence or discourse) variables are likely to show an influence later on, via re-reading and regressions and via increased overall fixation times. A crucial point to remember is that the measures are not independent: first fixation duration is a part of first pass reading time, which is a part of total reading time. Similarly, total reading time and total fixation count will generally be highly correlated. Analysing a range of measures to investigate the overall pattern should therefore be the aim, and if an effect only emerges in one of our measures, this should be interpreted with caution.

The principal reading measures are demonstrated in Figure 3.11. A range of other measures are available, and depending on our research question it might be worthwhile analysing them. For more on reading measures see Pickering et al. (2004) and Conklin and Pellicer-Sánchez (2016).

It is important to note that some of the terminology used both in the literature and in the three eye-tracking systems is not always consistent. Particularly for the different pieces of eye-tracking software, it is essential that we look at how the measures are defined in order to decide which are appropriate for our study.

3.2.2 Measures in Visual Scene Perception and Visual Search

As Holmqvist et al. (2011) point out, the sequential nature of reading does not apply to other stimuli, hence many of the measures applicable to reading behaviour are not as meaningful in the context of, for example, image- or video-based studies. Tanenhaus (2007a) makes an important distinction that in reading, longer durations are generally

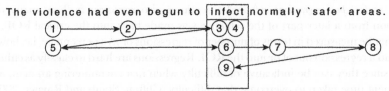

The violence had even begun to [infect] normally 'safe' areas.

Processing stage and measures	Definition and depiction on figure
Early measures	
Likelihood of skipping	Number of first pass fixation durations of 0 ÷ total number of trials.
	There is a fixation during first pass [3] so in this trial the critical word was not skipped. This contributes to the total number of trials (the denominator), but not the number of skipped trials (the numerator).
First fixation duration	The duration of the first, and only the first, fixation on an ROI: [3].
Single fixation duration	Since this trial has two fixations [3, 4] on the critical word, it would not be included in single fixation duration analysis.
First pass reading time/ gaze duration	The sum of all fixations on an ROI before exiting to the right or left: [3 + 4].
Intermediate measures	
Regression path duration/ go-past time	Sum of all fixations on the ROI and any regressions to earlier parts of the sentence before moving past the right-hand boundary of the ROI: [3 + 4 + 5 + 6].
Regression rate	Number of trials with a regression ÷ total number of trials.
(or regressions out)	This example has a regression [5], which contributes to both the numerator and denominator.
Late measures	
Total reading time	Sum duration of all fixations on the ROI during a trial: [3 + 4 + 6 + 9].
Re-reading	Regression path duration for the ROI minus first pass reading time: [3 + 4 + 5 + 6] - [3 + 4] = [5 + 6].
Second pass reading time	Sum of fixations on an ROI after it has been exited for the first time: [6 + 9].
Fixation count	Total number of fixations on ROI: [3, 4, 6, 9] = 4 fixations.

Figure 3.11 Example sentence with the ROI around 'infect' indicated by a box. An illustrative eye-movement pattern is depicted below the sentence, with fixations indicated by circles and the number indicating their order. The eye-movement pattern depicted in the sentence is related to eye-tracking measures in the table below. First, the processing stage is classified as 'early' or 'late'. Second, the eye-tracking measure is given with a description of how it is calculated, as well as relating it to the fixation numbers in the example.

equated with greater processing difficulty, while in visual-world and video studies, the measures of interest relate more to the when and where of fixations as the stimulus unfolds. Rayner (2009) provides a discussion of the differences between reading and other types of eye-tracking, such as perception of a visual scene or visual search, and concludes that there are 'obviously many differences between reading, scene perception and visual search … [but also] some important generalisations that can be made' (p. 1485). The difficulty of the stimuli and the nature of the task itself will determine both when and where eyes move, with more difficult stimuli leading to longer fixations and shorter saccades.

In simple image-based studies, it is a logical assumption that more looks to a specific area indicate that there is something salient or appealing about it, or that something has caused the participant to consider one part of a scene more than others. Visual-world tasks involve aspects of visual input and aural language processing, and there is a systematic relationship between what a participant hears and where (and when) the eyes move (Rayner, 2009). The same is true for video stimuli, where the participant will see what is on screen while listening to the audio track.

Visual tasks use measures such as *proportion of fixations* on various ROIs on the screen, as well as more general measures such as *total fixation times* and *fixation counts*, often time-locked to the onset of a critical stimulus. This means that we are specifically interested in how many fixations were made on a specific ROI, and how long each fixation was, during a specific time window. Measures are generally calculated relative to other parts of the display. For example, in our visual-world study with images at the four cardinal points, it is not particularly meaningful to know that there were ten fixations on the target image if we don't know how many fixations were made overall (there may have been twenty fixations on each of the other images). More useful is to compare the number or proportion of fixations for each of the four images on the screen, generally during a particular time window. The underlying assumption is that the image that is being processed when the participant hears the critical part of audio track will receive significantly more and significantly longer fixations than any of the others. A more detailed discussion of measuring eye-movements to visual scenes is provided in Section 5.1.

For dynamic stimuli the same principles apply. We would be interested in identifying how many fixations were made to specific areas of the display at specific time points in the video, or over the course of the whole video. For example, Bisson et al. (2014) measured total fixation duration, number of fixations and average fixation duration on the subtitle and image regions of the video in their study. For other studies, it is the time of the first fixation to a critical part of the stimulus that is important. Altmann and Kamide (1999) used a variant of this (*onset of first saccade*) to show that participants looked at a compatible item ('cake') earlier when they heard a biasing verb ('eat') than when they heard a non-biasing verb ('move'). Measures such as *time to first fixation* and *average fixation duration* are also of great use when we want to explore how participants' eye-movements unfold over time.

3.2.3 Selecting the Right Measures

An important part of any study is determining which measures are the most appropriate. In studies concerned with reading behaviour, a range of early and late measures are generally used, and multiple ROIs may be informative, as we have seen. The early measures described in Section 3.2.1 are most appropriate for studies concerned with lexical effects, particularly at the level of a single word. The later measures are also important for analysing lexical effects, in particular how a specific word is integrated into the surrounding text, and are also useful for a study that is interested in the effects of context, or in a study that requires participants to read a longer text for comprehension. For example, if we are interested in how well language learners process newly learned or previously unknown words that we introduce in a reading task, we can use both an early measure such as first fixation duration to evaluate how easily the participant was able to recognise the word when he/she first encountered it, and a measure such as total reading time to infer how well each word was understood. Regressions to the context preceding the word might also be informative, and participants who had more trouble under-standing a given word may return to the prior context more in an attempt to work out the likely meaning. If we also used a complementary measure such as a comprehension or vocabulary test, we could compare online behaviour (eye-tracking measures) with offline behaviour (test scores) as a way of further enriching our analysis.

The length of our ROIs will also determine the measures of interest. For regions longer than a single word, skipping rate or first fixation duration are of limited use. For multi-word units, such as idioms, the choice of both ROIs and measures might not be straight-forward. For example, analysing each individual word of an idiom might mask any 'whole phrase' effects, but only considering the phrase as a whole might also not tell us the whole story. Defining an ROI that encompasses the whole sequence, as well as ones for the component words, and using appropriate measures for each may allow a more complete picture of processing to emerge (for a discussion see Carrol and Conklin, 2014).

For image or video studies (or other dynamic stimuli), the number and duration of fixations are important, but there are different ways for us to analyse looking beha-viour. We can compare raw results such as average fixation durations, overall fixation time or fixation counts, or use an alternative, like mean number of saccades, as our dependent variable (which is what Chambers and Cooke (2009) used). Other studies calculate the relative number of fixations or the relative amount of time spent fixating each ROI. For example, Holsinger (2013) compared the proportion of fixations for each of the ROIs in his study and used this as his dependent variable for analysis. It is important to understand that different variables will require different approaches to analysis, so this is something we should consider carefully in advance (see Section 7.2 for more on this).

3.3 Selecting Participants

In Chapter 1, we noted that eye-movements tend to be fairly resistant to individual differences in monolingual adults. However, the same is not true of other populations, in particular for many of the groups that are likely to be of interest in applied linguistics: children, language learners, bilinguals, and people with language impairments. General proficiency, language background, reading skill and education level will vary among participants. We therefore need to consider how to control and/or measure relevant differences when recruiting people to take part in our study (unless any of these are participant-level factors that we might want to manipulate).

If our participants are children, we need to be careful to match our sample in terms of factors like chronological age, years of schooling, reading age and language background. Children are in general less likely to sit still and concentrate for long periods, so the duration of the study is an important concern. If possible, arranging to take our equipment into a school would be preferable to asking children and their parents to come to our laboratory, and would be likely to lead to more successful data collection. It is important to keep in mind that if we are dealing with children, the ethics procedures are likely to be stricter than if we are collecting data from adults.

Second language speakers will vary widely in terms of their language proficiency. We will see differences according to whether they are EFL (English as a first language) or ESL (English as a second language) learners, balanced or late bilinguals, and according to their individual experience of learning the L2 (second language). Jiang (2012) suggests that the three most influential factors in choosing participants for second language studies are general L2 proficiency, what their L1 (first language) is, and what the age of onset of L2 learning was. As well as these, we should consider specifically L2 reading and listening ability (depending on the topic of the study), and perhaps even cognitive differences like executive control,[7] which is known to be important for some of the processes of reading in a second language (Pivneva, Mercier and Titone, 2014; Whitford and Titone, 2012). Often it will be difficult, or even impossible, to find a group of participants who are matched on all of these variables. We should therefore aim to test as homogenous a group as possible (e.g. all from the same class, all with the same L1 background, all with comparable proficiency scores), then account for other individual differences in our analysis. In Section 7.2 we discuss how we might use techniques such as linear mixed effects modelling in order to do this.

Investigation of language-impaired populations is another area of applied linguistics where eye-tracking could provide a valuable tool. Such studies can be challenging since we are often targeting a fairly specific group of participants (e.g. patients with one particular type of aphasia), and sample sizes tend to be small as a result. The nature of impairments also means that our participants are likely to be quite varied, both in terms of the specific characteristics of the impairment itself, and in terms of us finding participants who all come from the same background. We should nevertheless try to match our participants on as many factors as we can. For example, if we want to use eye-tracking to investigate reading patterns in participants with dyslexia, we should aim to compare a dyslexic and control group who are matched on features like non-verbal intelligence, education level, etc.

When recruiting participants, we might also need to consider whether there are any physical or cognitive challenges that might limit their ability to take part, or which might limit their ability to provide informed consent. For some areas of study – such as dyslexia or hearing impairment – this is unlikely to be an issue. For others – people suffering from language difficulties following a stroke, for example, or older participants with degenerative conditions – we should carefully consider both the feasibility and the appropriateness of them taking part. For example, it might not be fitting to ask someone with limited mobility to come to our laboratory and sit in front of a screen for an extended period of time. It might also be the case that a person who has suffered a stroke has some degree of visual neglect that would prevent him/her from being able to view our stimuli as we intended. As with any other participant populations we are interested in, once we have recruited people who are willing and able to take part, we should do our best to account for the individual differences that are likely to exist.

---

[7] Executive control covers a range of functions that are necessary for the cognitive control of language and behaviour. These include things like attentional control, working memory, inhibitory control and cognitive flexibility. See Linck et al. (2014) for a meta-analysis of the role of working memory in second language processing.

3.3.1 How Many Participants Are Needed?

This question has no simple answer, since the nature of our study will determine the type of data being collected and the amount of it that we will need. One of the main aims of most language studies is to make claims that are in theory generalisable to a larger population, for instance if we test a set of children at a certain stage of development, we would like to generalise our findings to all children at this stage of development (who are similar on other relevant factors, like years of schooling). It is therefore important to ensure that in any study we have enough participants to eliminate person-specific 'noise' or idiosyncratic behaviour (Dörnyei, 2007). Further, when deciding how many participants might be needed questions like the following are important ones to consider.

Is the study quantitative or qualitative? A qualitative study might require fewer participants but more time per person. If the aim is to investigate individual behaviour, then a small but intensive sample might be appropriate. This might be the case in studies using a think-aloud protocol combined with eye-tracking. If the aim is to conduct quantitative analysis using inferential statistics that will allow us to make claims about a participant population as a whole, then larger groups will be required to ensure that our sample is typical of that population.

How many factors will we be manipulating? We discussed this in relation to preparing our stimuli, but it is also relevant if different groups of participants are being studied. For example, we might want to compare how 'older' versus 'younger' children understand a text, or we might compare the patterns of eye-movements for adult patients with left- and right-hemisphere damage to see how this affects reading and text integration. We should bear in mind that each participant factor we introduce will effectively halve our sample size, i.e. if we have a sample of twenty children, dividing them into 'older' and 'younger' readers means we will only have ten participants per group. Remember too that in a between-subjects design with more than one presentation list, we are effectively dividing our sample size by the number of lists we have (i.e. twenty participants in a two-list study will mean only ten per list). In a two-list study with two different groups of participants, we would therefore need forty people if we want to ensure that we have ten participants per condition (ten for group 1, list A; ten for group 1, list B; ten for group 2, list A; and ten for group 2, list B).

There is no consensus on the required number of participants in an eye-tracking study, and ultimately the answer will be 'the more, the better', since the standard error for our data will be reduced as our sample size increases. As with other aspects of our study, consulting published research on a similar topic will help us to decide what an appropriate sample size might be. We should also bear in mind that some level of data loss is inevitable in any study. This can be due to technical issues such as poor calibration or computer failure, or other factors such as participants not turning up to appointments, showing highly abnormal reading patterns, etc. Planning for more participants than we actually need will allow us to mitigate some of these issues.

3.3.2 Considerations about the Participants

Video-based eye-trackers do not actually touch the eye and are safe for anyone to use (Raney et al., 2014). There are no particular risk factors that will exclude people from an eye-tracking study, although it may be necessary to identify individuals with certain conditions – such as photosensitive epilepsy or migraines – and establish whether prolonged exposure to a computer screen normally has any effect on them, especially if we intend to show stimuli that contain flashing images. A rigorous screening procedure and close supervision during the experiment itself will help guard against any risk to participants.

Exclusion criteria for a study are more likely to be on the grounds of specific reading or visual disorders. Assuming we are not specifically investigating something like dyslexia, we would normally want to exclude any individuals who show 'abnormal' reading because of language or visual impairments (such as strabismus). Participants with vision that is corrected to normal with glasses or contact lenses are not normally problematic (see Section 3.4 on setting up an eye-tracker for more details), but if participants are required to attend more than one session they should not change, e.g. wear glasses to one session but contact lenses to another. Patterned or coloured contact lenses may cause problems and participants should be discouraged from wearing them to a study, and it will also help to ask participants to avoid wearing eye make-up since this can sometimes cause additional set-up difficulties. Keeping make-up remover wipes in the lab is also a good idea.

All of these considerations should be addressed when we first contact participants, to avoid anyone turning up to take part in our study who turns out to be unsuitable. Appointments should be arranged at a time when participants will be awake and alert – a drowsy participant may be both difficult to track and particularly unmotivated. As we discussed previously, for children or individuals with some kinds of impairment, taking the equipment to them may be much more fruitful and appropriate than expecting them to come to us.

3.4   Setting Up an Eye-Tracker

The physical set-up of an eye-tracker is an essential part of ensuring a high-quality dataset. Correct set-up, calibration and monitoring can ensure that our data is of good quality throughout, and minimises the risk of data loss. A large part of this comes from practice, and gaining experience as an operator of the equipment is the best way to become skilful and confident, and to learn how to deal with any problems that may arise. It is therefore a good idea to practise on a few people before starting to collect data for the first time.

Note that what we consider next are primarily eye-tracking set-ups where a participant will be invited to a laboratory to take part in our study, since these will comprise the majority of applied linguistics studies. We have mentioned some situations (such as when collecting data from children) where taking the equipment to our participants might be preferable. All three systems can be used to gather data in non-laboratory settings (see Section 2.2). We do not consider these options in detail here, but the eye-tracker user manuals provide more information. Once we have learned how to set up a stationary eye-tracker in a laboratory, adapting to a remote set-up should pose few problems.

3.4.1   Physical Set-Up of the Eye-Tracker and Participants

The physical set-up will depend on the make and model of our eye-tracker and the particular configuration chosen, but the basic procedure will be the same in most cases. The eye-tracker should be situated in a dedicated space where the conditions can remain constant for the duration of a study (i.e. for all of the participants that we will want to collect data from). Consideration should therefore be given to whether a space can be found where the eye-tracker can be left set up at all times, rather than having to be cleared away or moved on a regular basis. The location should also be quiet and ideally soundproof to minimise any outside noise that could create a distraction. The space should be well lit, but not in such a way that sunlight or artificial light causes a reflection on the computer monitor or eye-tracker, with the ability to control the temperature and ventilation if possible to ensure that participants will be comfortable.

Whichever eye-tracking system we are using, a set-up guide will be provided that will help with the basics of plugging the system in, getting started, installing software, etc. The user manuals contain important information about the recommended configuration, especially the distance between participants and the monitor, which must be carefully controlled to ensure that data can be accurately recorded. All eye-trackers will have limits on the amount of head movement that can be tolerated and the size of visual angle that the equipment can record, i.e. the distance left or right that a participant can look on the screen. As a rough guide, the distance between participant and monitor should be around 1.75 times the width of the monitor to ensure that data will be accurately recorded. In practice, this means that there should be a distance of around 40–70 cm between the participant and the monitor, depending on our system and set-up. In many cases set-up and calibration issues can be resolved by adjusting the distance between participant and monitor, or by using a smaller monitor. Specific requirements and tracking limits will vary and will be detailed in the documentation received with the eye-tracking system.

The participant should be seated in front of the display screen with no distractions, hence the operator should be seated either to the side or behind the participant. In some cases, especially if the tracker is located in a small space, a partition may be useful to ensure that the participant is not distracted by what the operator is doing. The participant should be seated at a comfortable height, so a height-adjustable chair is essential. To minimise movement during a study, a non-wheeled chair is preferable. In any case, participants should be reminded to stay as still as possible during the study, with their feet flat on the floor to discourage movement. A height-adjustable desk is also very useful since this will enable us to maintain a constant set-up for the camera, screen and any chin-rest or head support. This means that once the participant is seated comfortably the entire desk can be raised or lowered as required. The participant should be seated so that his/her eyes line up around two-thirds of the way up the screen. If a chin-rest is being used, the participant's chin should be flat on the chin-rest with his/her forehead against the forehead rest. Participants should sit forward so that the forehead makes contact with the forehead rest as this will mean that the head is positioned upright relative to the monitor. Once the participant is seated and the chair and desk adjusted, we need to ensure that the eye-tracker can successfully track the eye and record the eye gaze.

In EyeLink 1000 and 1000 Plus systems we need to position and focus the camera so that the participant's face appears clearly in the centre of the display window. Once the eye is detected a green box and crosshairs will appear over the centre, and we can toggle between a view of the whole face and the eye using the left and right cursor keys. The aim is to obtain a clear image of the pupil, which will appear in blue on the display. The camera should be focused so that the corneal reflection (indicated by a turquoise circle) is as small and as sharply focused as possible. The infra-red threshold value (the sensitivity of the camera) can be adjusted up or down to ensure that the pupil can be accurately tracked. This can be set automatically, but manual adjustments may be required, for example to reduce the threshold if a participant is wearing mascara or to increase it if the pupil cannot be found by the camera. Once the pupil has been found, the Search Limits option can be activated to prevent the tracker from searching elsewhere for the pupil. Various other settings (sampling rate, eye to be tracked, monocular vs binocular recording) can also be changed as required.

In both Tobii and SMI systems the set-up procedure is much more automatic. In Tobii systems, the operator does not have any control over the set-up of the camera since it is built into the monitor. The participant is seated in front of the display monitor and the eye-tracker will automatically detect and verify the participant's position and locate the eye. White circles appear on the screen to indicate that the eyes can be successfully tracked. A Track Status box helps to indicate whether the participant is seated appropriately, and again on-screen instructions help to indicate whether the position needs to be adjusted. In SMI systems, on-screen arrows indicate whether the participant is too close/too far away, and whether he/she is correctly centred in front of the display, so the position can be adjusted as required until the software indicates that the participant is sitting correctly. With both systems, once an optimal position has been obtained the participant should be encouraged to sit as still as possible throughout the experiment.

3.4.2 Calibrating the Eye-Tracker for Participants

All eye-trackers must be calibrated to each individual participant to optimise data recording. In Tobii Pro Studio and Experiment Center a calibration sequence is automatically included in each experiment, and in Experiment Builder the EL SETUP node should be included before any Trial block to incorporate the set-up and calibration sequence. Before calibrating, any major problems can be detected by asking the participant to look at the corners of the screen – if the tracking is lost at the extremities then some minor adjustments will be necessary.

The calibration itself consists of the tracker displaying a series of points on screen, which a participant must fixate in turn. The number of points used can be adjusted as required, and for studies requiring greater accuracy (e.g. full-screen reading), more points should be used. The default number of points varies in the three systems, but for most studies a nine-point calibration is standard. The calibration procedure is automatic in all three systems (i.e. the system proceeds once a stable fixation for each point has been detected) but a manual mode where the operator must accept each fixation can be used if desired. This is useful if, for example, a participant begins to anticipate the movement of the fixation points, and therefore moves to another point prior to a stable fixation being registered. The level of calibration accuracy will be reported on the operator's screen following completion, and the calibration process can be repeated as required until a high level of accuracy is obtained. All three eye-trackers include the option to replace the calibration point with an image or animation file. This can be very useful if we are working with children as it makes it much easier to attract and keep their attention to, for example, a clown or elephant than a black dot as a calibration point.

EyeLink and SMI systems also allow the operator to validate the calibration as a further check on the accuracy level of the eye-tracker. In EyeLink this is included automatically in the set-up procedure; in SMI, if a validation is needed then it must be added into the experimental structure. Since validations help confirm accuracy, it is recommended to include them whenever possible. The validation procedure repeats either the whole sequence or a subset of the fixation points and calculates the deviation of the participant's gaze from the values recorded during calibration. It will report the deviation in terms of degree of visual angle. If the error for any point exceeds 0.5°, we should recalibrate and revalidate the participant (Raney et al., 2014). In Tobii Pro Studio there is no validation option, but the accuracy of the calibration can be visually checked and verified prior to recording, and repeated if necessary. Tobii also run regular webinars on the topic of verifying data quality, and offer scripts to help with pre-study calibration that can be useful for later analysis. Once we have successfully calibrated and validated the eye-tracker, our study can begin.

3.5 Running Experiments

The process of running an experiment involves the collection of the data for each participant. This will generally include asking each person to sign a consent form in advance, setting up and calibrating the tracker, explaining any instructions, running the experiment, and collecting any demographic or language background/proficiency data that we require. Having a printed checklist prepared detailing all of the necessary steps will help to ensure that the procedure is the same for all participants and that nothing is forgotten. This is especially important if we will not be collecting all of the data ourselves.

3.5.1 Monitoring Trials

Before a study the operator should be prepared to answer any questions that participants may have about what they will be asked to do. During the study, the operator should monitor the tracker and perform any adjustments or recalibrations that may be required to ensure the integrity of the data. It is also a good idea to take notes, to keep a record of any trials that were problematic (e.g. if a participant sneezes or rubs his/her eyes during a particular trial), especially if the person monitoring the study is not the same person who will be analysing the data. This will ensure that any problematic trials can be checked and, if necessary, removed prior to data analysis. The participant should be asked to turn off any electronic devices such as mobile phones, and instructed that movement and talking should be kept to a minimum except during any breaks that may be built in to the study. Following the experiment, the operator should be prepared to debrief the participant and answer any questions.

3.5.2 Correcting for Eye-Drift

It is often a good idea to build in regular checks or recalibrations to ensure accuracy throughout our experiment. Experiment Builder also allows us to build in a trial-by-trial drift checking procedure (see the DRIFT CORRECT node that we included in our experimental structure in Figure 3.5).[8] This will display a fixation point before each trial, allowing the operator to check that the accuracy of the calibration has not changed for any reason. Once the participant has fixated on the fixation point, the system will report the visual error in the same way as during the validation procedure. If this exceeds the maximum error it will not allow a trial to begin, and will require the participant to re-fixate the point accurately before proceeding. It is up to the operator to monitor the accuracy of the drift correction point to decide if and when a recalibration may be

---

[8] Drift check merely checks and reports the level of accuracy, and is the default setting in EyeLink 1000/1000 Plus and Portable Duo systems. A drift correction – where the system continuously adjusts the calibration – is disabled by default on EyeLink 1000/1000 Plus and Portable Duo systems but is active by default for the EyeLink II.

required. Recalibrations can be performed at any time, provided we have inserted the EL SETUP node at the appropriate point in the experimental structure (see the section on building studies in Experiment Builder in Section 3.1.3). Participants naturally tend to relax their position over the course of a study so small adjustments may be required over time, and a recalibration and validation should be performed after any adjustments to the set-up or after any breaks.

Tobii Pro Studio and Experiment Center do not allow for either drift correct or unplanned recalibrations, but we can build additional calibrations into the structure if required. If our study consists of multiple blocks, it is a good idea to allow participants to take a short break after each one, then for the tracker to be recalibrated prior to starting again. In Tobii Pro Studio, an experiment requiring several blocks can be constructed as separate Tests within the same Project. Each will therefore be run independently and include a calibration at the beginning by default, and the operator will need to initiate each Test separately during an experimental session. Additional calibrations can be built into the experimental sequence in Experiment Center at any point by adding Calibration and Validation elements to the stimulus list.

3.5.3 Saving Data

Following completion of the study the eye-tracking software should save the data automatically. In EyeLink the results will be saved within our deployed project folder as .edf files. In Tobii, all data is saved directly within Tobii Pro Studio and subsequent analysis will take place there. In SMI the data will be saved as .idf files inside the Results directory of the program installation directory. Ensure that all files have been saved or been successfully copied from the host to the display computer prior to shutting down either machine. If there are offline data collection aspects of our study (e.g. a background questionnaire), we should make sure that these are numbered to match the filename of our saved eye-tracking data in order to make it easy to associate the two.

In all three systems an experiment can be aborted early if required. In EyeLink experiments this is only possible during a trial, when the Abort Experiment button will be available to the operator. Tobii and SMI experiments can be stopped early using the F12 and escape keys, respectively (alternatives can be set up as required). In all cases, aborting a study will mean that any data recorded up until this point will still be recorded to the relevant participant file, but may be of limited use depending on how many items have been seen.

3.6 Conclusions and Final Checklist

We have seen in this chapter that designing, building and running an eye-tracking study involves many of the same considerations as any language experiment. As such, careful planning can help to make the process easier, and becoming confident with the system you will be using will help to make your experiment a success. We discuss ways in which eye-tracking studies can be used to address a range of research questions in Chapters 4, 5 and 6, and consider what to do with the data you have collected in Chapter 7.

	Final checklist
• What kind of study will you be running?	⇨ Decide whether you will be using visual stimuli (text or images) or a combination of visual and auditory stimuli.
	⇨ For visual stimuli, decide whether you are primarily interested in fine-grained reading behaviour (text) or broader looking patterns (visual search).
	⇨ For combined visual and auditory stimuli, decide whether you will use images and spoken language (visual-world paradigm) or more authentic materials (videos).
	⇨ Your research question will normally inform the methods you choose, but having a clear idea of the stimuli you will need to create will help you to plan out the rest of your study.
• What properties of the stimuli should you consider for reading (text-based) studies?	⇨ Critical words should be matched between conditions and if necessary counterbalanced between presentation lists. Features such as length, frequency and predictability will all affect reading patterns.
	⇨ Critical words should not appear at the start or end of lines or sentences, wherever possible. For longer passages, critical words or sentences should not appear at the start or end of a paragraph.
	⇨ The appearance of the text is important. Font size, spacing and position on the screen should all be considered. A font like Courier New (or a different monospaced font) at a minimum of 14 pt and double line spacing is recommended in most cases.
• What properties of the stimuli should you consider for image studies?	⇨ Images should be matched for size and visual salience. In visual-world studies you should consider the properties of the 'target' and 'competitor' items carefully.
	⇨ Images should be positioned appropriately on the screen. The position of images should be counterbalanced so that the target image does not always appear in the same place.
	⇨ Images can be created in advance or, if using authentic stimuli, you can choose specific aspects of the image.
• What properties should you consider for combined visual/audio, video and dynamic stimuli?	⇨ If recording your own audio, make sure you don't introduce any confounding variables such as prosodic cues. Audio needs to be time-locked to the stimuli to allow for accurate analysis.
	⇨ Video and other types of dynamic stimuli such as webpages are likely to be authentic, so you need to choose carefully which ones to use.
• How many stimuli and participants will you need?	⇨ Methodological decisions (within-subject or between-subject design) and the nature of the study will determine this. Make sure you have enough 'power' in your study to allow you to draw clear conclusions from the analysis.

(cont.)

	Final checklist
• How do you build your study?	⇨ Work through the user manual and sample files provided with your eye-tracking software. Prepare your stimuli in advance then add them to the experiment. Test the experiment thoroughly before you use it to collect 'live' data.
• How do you know what to analyse?	⇨ Identify the ROIs that you will want to analyse in advance. ROIs can be added to stimuli at the build stage or added in afterward.
	⇨ For reading studies, ROIs will generally be words, phrases or even whole sentences or paragraphs.
	⇨ For any image- or video-based study ROIs are likely to be specific areas of the display.
	⇨ ROIs can be static or dynamic. Dynamic ROIs can be set to record data only at certain points, or track an aspect of the stimulus as it moves on the screen.
• How will you know what measurements to choose?	⇨ Reading studies have a detailed literature to help you decide which measures to use. A combination of early and late measures are often chosen to allow for detailed consideration of the data.
	⇨ For other types of stimuli the measures are more likely to relate to which parts of the display are fixated, or which images receive more attention over the course of a trial.
• What will you need to consider when setting up and running an experiment?	⇨ The tracker should be carefully set up to maximise accuracy. A quiet, stable location should be chosen where possible.
	⇨ Calibrating and validating the tracker well will help to make sure that the data you obtain is accurate. Practice is the best way to become a competent operator.
	⇨ The operator should monitor the experiment and perform any adjustments or recalibrations that he/she thinks are required.

Chapter 4

Researching Reading

4.1 Introduction

Reading is a relatively recent development in human history, existing for only a few thousand years (Immordino-Yang and Deacon, 2007). However, it has become an essential life skill in modern society, one that is developed over many years of exposure, formal instruction and practice. Good reading skill underpins academic achievement (for a discussion see Renandya, 2007), and for second language learners, reading is a gateway to learning new vocabulary, more colloquial language and new grammatical constructions (Wilkinson, 2012). As Huey summarised over a hundred years ago, and which is still as true today, gaining a complete understanding of reading – how we learn to read, how we become fluent readers, how to best teach reading, etc. – is an important aspiration.

And so to completely analyse what we do when we read would almost be the acme of a psychologist's dream for it would be to describe very many of the most intricate workings of the human mind, as well as to unravel the tangled story of the most remarkable performance that human civilization learned in all of its history. (Huey, 1908, p. 6)

We know that for readers the primary goal is to identify words, ascertain their meaning and integrate them into their unfolding understanding of a sentence and/or larger discourse. However, what exactly happens when we read? How do our eyes move? Do we look at every word when we read? Eye-tracking has allowed us to gain a fairly comprehensive understanding of what happens during reading and the factors that impact it, which will be an important focus in this chapter. As we will see more explicitly in Sections 4.3–4.6, a good understanding of both of these is fundamental to our ability to create well-designed studies.

As we saw in Chapter 1, reading involves a series of ballistic eye-movements (*saccades*), brief pauses (*fixations*) and movements back to previous parts of a text (*regressions*). Saccades occur largely due to the limitations of the visual system. More precisely, vision is 'clear' around a fixation, but clarity decreases moving away from it. This situation is depicted in Figure 4.1. In example (a) when the eyes fixate 'reader', this word is clear, making it easy to identify. Moving away from this point, vision becomes progressively less sharp. In order to clearly see further words, the eyes need to advance (perform a saccade). In (b) we see that when the eyes move forward from their position in (a) to fixate the word 'really', it brings this word and the surrounding ones into a region of good visual acuity.

The decreasing visual acuity from a fixation point outwards that is demonstrated in Figure 4.1 is due to the physiological structure of the eye (Balota and Rayner, 1991). More specifically, a line of text falling on the retina of the eye can be divided into three regions: the fovea, encompassing 1° of visual angle on each side of a fixation; the parafovea, extending to 5° of visual angle on each side of fixation; and the periphery, which includes

c) The very proficient reader saw a really long word.

Figure 4.1 Depiction of the decrease in visual acuity moving away from a fixation point (depicted by the eye) in (a) and (b), while (c) presents an unmodified version of the same sentence.

anything beyond 5° of visual angle (Rayner, Balota and Pollatsek, 1986). The fovea is specialised for maximum visual acuity. Moving away from the fovea, visual acuity decreases. Words appearing in the parafoveal region that are closer to the fovea will be clearer than those that are further away.

In reading it makes sense to talk about visual acuity in terms of letters and spaces (referred to as 'letter spaces') instead of talking about degrees of visual angle. Although it depends on the size of the print, in reading, three to four letter spaces are roughly equivalent to 1° of visual angle (Balota and Rayner, 1991). If we apply this to Figure 4.2 and say that three letter spaces equals 1°, then in the example in (a) when fixating on 'A', the fovea would include the three letters 'B', 'C' and 'D' on both sides of the fixation. The parafovea would encompass the following twelve letter spaces, stretching from 'E' to 'P' on either side of the fixation. Finally, the periphery would include anything from the first 'X' onwards. Importantly, really good visual acuity only encompasses the fovea and 'near parafovea' (the parafoveal region closest to the fovea), which generally corresponds to the currently fixated word and the next one (although the subsequent two to three words will be clear if they are both/all very short). This helps explain why saccades in silent reading are usually seven to nine letter spaces (see Table 1.1 in Chapter 1). Normally, this saccade length corresponds to what is needed to bring the word that occurs two words after the one that is being fixated into focus.[1]

Importantly, example (a) in Figure 4.2 *only* demonstrates the constraints on visual acuity due to the structure of the eye. The area from which readers actually extract useful information is in fact asymmetric. For readers of alphabetic languages like English that are read from left to right, the effective visual field only extends three to four letters to the left of fixation and does not extend beyond the boundary of the currently fixated word, regardless of the number of letters (Rayner, Well and Pollatsek, 1980). This is the situation depicted in example (b) in Figure 4.2. The fixation is on the 'a' in the word 'reader', but useful information is only extracted as far as the onset of 'reader' and not before the word boundary. In contrast, to the right of the fixation, useful information is extracted from the fovea and parafoveal regions. In (b) this encompasses the three final letters in the word 'reader' (foveal region) and subsequent twelve letter spaces (parafoveal region) which is up to the second 'l' in 'really'. Because visual acuity decreases moving away from the foveal

---

[1] In the literature it is common to see the notation *n*, *n*+1 and *n*+2, where *n* indicates the word being fixated, *n*+1 the word after the fixated one, and *n*+2 the word after that. In Figures 4.1 (a) and 4.2 (b), *n* = 'reader', *n*+1 = 'saw', *n*+2 = 'a'. Saccades often go from *n* to *n*+2.

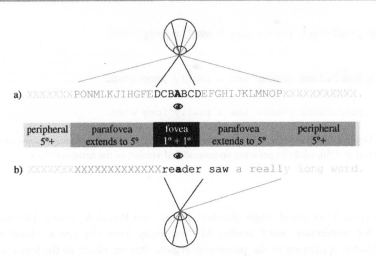

a) XXXXXXXX PONMLKJIHGFE**DCBABCD**EFGHIJKLMNOP XXXXXXXXXXXX

peripheral 5°+	parafovea extends to 5°	fovea 1° + 1°	parafovea extends to 5°	peripheral 5°+

b) XXXXXXXXXXXXXXXXXXXXXX**reader saw** a really long word

Figure 4.2 Illustration of a line of text falling on the foveal, parafoveal and peripheral regions of the retina. Example (a) shows these regions on a line of letters, while (b) demonstrates the asymmetric nature of visual acuity in reading.

region, the word 'saw' will be clearer than 'really' because it is closer to the fovea. It is important to note that visual acuity in reading is asymmetric in the direction of reading (Pollatsek et al., 1981). This means that in a language like Hebrew, where reading is right to left, parafoveal view extends to the left and not the right. Similarly, when Japanese is read vertically, the visual span is also asymmetric in the direction of reading – in this case downwards (Osaka, 2003). Thus in reading, there is asymmetric extraction of information in the direction of upcoming words (Clifton et al., 2016).

So why do we need this somewhat technical discussion about the distinction between words in the fovea and parafovea? The next few paragraphs will look at why these distinctions are important in reading, as well as their implications for designing research studies. As Figure 4.1 demonstrates, when the eyes land on the word 'reader' (in foveal view), it is seen clearly. During the fixation, the reader needs to use the visual, orthographic, phonological and potentially morphological information to identify the word and activate the lexical representation that contains information about its meaning, grammatical role, etc. The reader needs to keep track of all of this information and integrate it with similar information from preceding words.

Given all the processing work being done on the fixated word that is in foveal view (n), it seems plausible that readers might not have enough cognitive resources left to identify the next word that is in parafoveal view ($n+1$) – a word that is actually seen less clearly. However, evidence indicates that there is some processing of $n+1$ words that are in parafoveal view (for a fuller discussion see Hyönä, 2011; Rayner, 2009). Table 4.1 provides a summary of the processing effects that are evident for the word being fixated (in foveal view), as well as for the next word (in parafoveal view). As we can see from the table, letters and their corresponding phonemes are activated (orthographic and phonological decoding) for both the word in foveal view and the next one that is in parafoveal view. Morphological decoding of morphologically complex words occurs primarily in the

Table 4.1 Factors that have been investigated with regard to their ability to influence processing when words are in foveal (*n*) and parafoveal view (*n*+1), with 'yes' indicating that it affects processing, 'mixed' that the evidence is contradictory and '?' that it has not been reported (based on Hyönä, 2011; Rayner, 2009).

	Foveal processing	Parafoveal processing
Orthographic and phonological decoding Identifying letters and activating corresponding phonemes	Yes	Yes
Morphological decoding Identifying a word's morphemes	Yes	Mixed
Word length Longer words = more processing	Yes	Yes
Word frequency Words encountered less frequently = more processing	Yes	Mixed
Neighbourhood size	Yes	Mixed
Predictability More predictable word is in context = less processing	Yes	Mixed
Number of word meanings Words with more meanings = more processing	Yes	Mixed
Age of acquisition (AoA) Later learned words = more processing	Yes	?
Familiarity Less familiar words = more processing	Yes	?

fovea; evidence is mixed about whether it occurs for word *n*+1, and this may vary across languages. The length of words in foveal and parafoveal view influences looking times, with longer words leading to more and longer fixation times. Further, readers are able to judge the word length of upcoming words to around fifteen letter spaces to the right of a fixation. Information about upcoming word length, as well as context, may narrow down 'choices' about lexical candidates for words in parafoveal view, which can influence the length of saccades and fixation times. Put more simply, if word length and context allow a reader to make a good 'guess' about the next word, fixation time on it may be shorter because little effort may be needed to confirm the guess. In some cases the next word might be skipped altogether, thus a saccade will go to *n*+2 instead of *n*+1. This means that information about a non-fixated word can influence saccades and fixations to the words around it. Additionally, word frequency, age of acquisition (AoA; the age at which a word was learned), neighbourhood size,[2] predictability (how predictable a word is, given the prior context) and number of word meanings all affect the processing of the word in foveal

---

[2] Orthographic or phonological neighbours are words that differ from one another by only one letter or sound respectively. For example, the word 'hint' has the neighbours 'hilt', 'hind', 'hunt', 'mint', 'tint', 'flint', 'lint', 'pint', etc. The processing of a word has been shown to be influenced by the number of neighbours (neighbourhood size) and sometimes the frequency of its neighbours (Perea and Rosa, 2000), as well as the regularity of the grapheme-to-phoneme correspondence of a word and its neighbours, e.g. 'hint' and 'pint' (Sereno and Rayner, 2000).

view (*n*). There are mixed findings about whether words in parafoveal view (*n*+1) that differ along these dimensions influence the processing of the fixated word.

Overall, Table 4.1 demonstrates that a word in foveal view and the subsequent word, which is in parafoveal view, are both decoded in terms of their orthographic and phonological form. There is clear evidence that the specific word properties of the word being fixated (e.g. frequency) influence the number and duration of fixations to it. What is debated is whether or not, and the extent to which, *parafoveal-on-foveal effects* exist. More precisely, do the characteristics (e.g. frequency) of the word to the right of fixation influence the duration of the fixation to the currently fixated word? This question has important implications for models of reading and eye-movement control that often make claims about whether reading is serial (one word at a time) or parallel (more than one word at a time). For example, if the frequency or the ambiguity (multiple meanings) of the next word lengthen fixations to the current word, this would provide evidence of parallel processing.

What might the debated parafoveal-on-foveal effects mean in more practical terms? Let's say we are interested in looking at how readers process new words, so we invent some words and embed them in a context, like the one in Example 4.1. We define two regions of interest (ROIs), which are the known verb 'spoke' and novel verb 'woused'. Both occur in a similar structure, and so are well matched in that regard: pronoun + verb (word vs new word) + adverb + prepositional phrase. If we find longer and more fixations associated with 'woused' compared to 'spoke', this might lead us to conclude that new words require more processing effort. However, the increased fixations on 'woused' could be due to the low frequency of the following word 'vituperatively'. There is in fact (mixed) evidence indicating that if the word after a fixated word is low frequency, reading times on the fixated word increase (for a discussion of parafoveal-on-foveal frequency effects see, Hyönä, 2011). Thus, the long reading times on 'woused' could at least in part be due to a parafoveal-on-foveal effect, which would call into question our conclusion. Ideally, when comparing ROIs, the surrounding context should be identical or extremely well matched so that an upcoming word does not 'contaminate' the fixation times for our ROI (see Chapter 3 for more on preparing stimuli).

Example 4.1 An example passage to compare processing effort (reading times) for the known word 'spoke' and the non-word 'woused', which are the ROIs (indicated with smooth underlining). The adverbs following the ROIs (indicated with wavy underlining) are not well matched in word frequency.[3]

```
Lisa worked for an employment agency developing advice for job
seekers. She spoke extensively about her own experiences and
she woused vituperatively about her previous boss.
```

Using the word 'vituperatively' in Example 4.1 is a bit extreme. However, it highlights an important concern in experimental design. The words next to our ROI may influence the number and duration of fixations to it. Therefore, we need to ensure that all of the factors outlined in Table 4.1, which might lead to parafoveal-on-foveal effects, are accounted for. This can be achieved in different ways. We can make sure that our ROIs are embedded in identical contexts. As we discussed in Chapter 3, this is generally achieved by creating counterbalanced 'lists' of the different versions of our stimuli. For the current question about

---

[3] The ROIs, which are clearly demarcated in all of the examples, would not generally be visible to participants.

the processing of a new word like 'woused', it would mean that a sentence like 'She spoke extensively about her own experiences' would appear on one list and 'She woused extensively about her own experiences' would appear on another list. This way 'spoke' and 'wouse' occur in identical contexts, and fixation times to them should not be 'contaminated' by other factors. Alternatively, we can design contexts such that the words surrounding our ROIs are as well matched as possible on the properties listed in Table 4.1. In Example 4.1, this means that the words that occur after 'spoke' and 'woused' should be as similar as possible in terms of frequency, length, etc. Even if the words that occur after 'spoke' and 'woused' are well matched, they will not be identical, which could cause differences in fixations to our ROIs. Thus, analyses, like mixed effects modelling, that allow us to account for such differences should be considered (we discuss this further in Chapter 7).

Finally, we may want to look at reading of authentic texts like novels, newspapers, graded readers, etc. In such cases we will not be able to control factors as we normally would in a study. In these instances, analyses like mixed effects modelling that allow us to consider the potential influence of the word properties of an upcoming word will most likely need to be used. In Section 4.3 we will look at some studies examining the reading of an Agatha Christie novel, and we will consider in detail some of the methodological concerns associated with the use of authentic texts and ways to address them.

The discussion of parafoveal-on-foveal effects has demonstrated that the word to the right of a fixated word is processed, at least to some extent. Logically, if a word has been identified via parafoveal view, then the eyes do not need to fixate on it and the word can be 'skipped'. The eye-tracking record provides evidence that the processing of a skipped word takes place when a reader is fixated on the previous word: when a word is skipped, the fixation on the immediately preceding one is longer than when it is not skipped (Kliegl and Engbert, 2005). It turns out that readers only directly fixate about 70 per cent of the words in a text and skip the other 30 per cent (Schotter, Angele and Rayner, 2012). Different factors seem to lead to skipping, which Rayner (2009) provides a very thorough overview of. Content words are fixated about 85 per cent of the time, while function words are only fixated about 35 per cent of the time. The strongest predictor of skipping is word length. Words that are two to three letters long are fixated about 25 per cent of the time, while words that have eight letters or more are almost always fixated. Further, when two or three short words occur after a fixated word they might all be skipped. Words that are highly predictable from the previous context are often skipped, even when the word is long. If a high-frequency word occurs to the right of a fixated word, this can also lead to skipping. Finally, skipping may sometimes be due to oculomotor error, in other words a mislocated fixation (for an example of an oculomotor error see the example of 'overshooting' in Figure 1.1).

Why might skipping be relevant to applied linguists? We could have a research question that involves an ROI containing a word that is short, highly predictable, frequent and/or a function word. This would make our ROI susceptible to skipping. Looking at Example 4.2, we might be interested in how proficient and less proficient readers (i.e. children, low-proficiency second language learners, etc.) resolve pronouns in different contexts. As the previous discussion demonstrates, if the eyes land on the word 'because' or 'since' in any of the sentences in Example 4.2, the following pronoun 'he'/'she' is likely to be skipped because it is a function word (and short). If we simply set 'he'/'she' as our ROI, 35 per cent of our cells are likely to be missing data, which could skew our results. Further, our analysis would not reflect the processing effort for 'he'/'she' that occurred on the previous word 'because'. Thus, in cases like this one, the ROI generally includes our actual word of interest, as well as the one that precedes it.

Example 4.2 Sentences to explore how readers process pronouns in contexts making 'he'/'she' more or less ambiguous. The word of interest is a short function word that will often be processed during fixations to the previous word; thus, the ROI (underlined) should include the word that precedes it. Sentences would generally be presented across two experimental lists (L1 = list 1; L2 = list 2).

L1(a) Jill threw the ball to Sara <u>since she</u> liked to play catch.
L2(a) Tom threw the ball to Sara <u>since he</u> liked to play catch.
L1(b) Bill sold the bike to Sally <u>because he</u> needed the money.
L2(b) Jill sold the bike to Sally <u>because she</u> needed the money.

Something else that should be considered when looking at processing in sentences like those in Example 4.2 is that our critical ROIs differ in length. The sentences with 'she' are one character longer than those with 'he'. Because word length influences processing, this length difference makes our comparison and any conclusions we draw from it problematic. We can make character length corrections, to deal with the difference – dividing a reading time measure by the number of characters. This kind of transformation is questionable when there are only small differences in length, as in this example. In such cases, it is preferable to use a residual reading time, which is a way of comparing the raw reading times for each target word to the average reading time on a per-participant basis (for a discussion as well as an explanation of calculating residual reading times see Trueswell, Tanenhaus and Garnsey, 1994).

Example 4.2 looks for an effect of the pronoun on reading times, which may only be visible on the preceding word. Here it makes sense to have a longer ROI that includes the pronoun and the word right before it. In other cases, it may be the skipping behaviour itself that is of interest. For example, we may want to investigate how predictability influences reading patterns in skilled and less skilled readers. Consequently, we may need to look at parafoveal-on-foveal processing, as well as skipping rates. Therefore, we would set two ROIs – one that only includes the word of interest, and another that includes the preceding word(s). In Example 4.3, we might hypothesise that the word 'wolf' in the idiomatic expression 'to cry wolf' (meaning to raise a false alarm) is predictable in this context. To test this, we would look at fixation times and skipping rates to the word 'wolf' in both List 1 and 2. Because predictability can influence processing on the previous word, it would be important to set 'cried' and 'read' as another ROI. Finally, when skipping rates are high, particularly in one condition and not another, it is important to consider how 'empty cells' (cells with no data because there is no fixation time) might influence the pattern of results. This is a topic that will be taken up in Chapter 7 when we discuss data analysis in more detail.

Example 4.3 Sentences exploring the influence of predictability. The hypothesised predictable word (smooth underlining) and the preceding word (wavy underlining) are the ROIs. These would generally be presented across counterbalanced experimental lists (List 1/List 2).

List 1 Joey repeatedly called the police for no reason.
    He had <u>cried wolf</u> too many times for his accusations
    to be taken seriously.
List 2 Joey repeatedly practised the sight vocabulary words.
    He had <u>read wolf</u> too many times for him to get it wrong
    on tomorrow's reading test.

Thus far, we have had a brief overview of the mechanics of reading and what this means for eye-tracking research. The next section will provide a short summary of what eye-tracking has told us about reading. We will then turn to some methodological considerations when designing studies to investigate different phenomena in reading: known words, new words, multi-word units and syntactic integration.

4.2 What Do We Know about Reading from Eye-Tracking?

As we saw in the previous section, when we read our eyes move along a line of text, fixate a word and move to fixate another word. Broadly speaking, during fixations readers need to 'recognise' a word and 'integrate' this word into a larger sentence or context (Clifton et al., 2007). The distinction between word recognition and integration is helpful for our discussion because it can roughly be mapped onto the classification of 'early' and 'late' eye-tracking measures discussed in Chapter 3. However, it is important to recognise that not every element of reading can be classified neatly as recognition or integration. For example, a predictable word is easier to identify, but the predictability of a word relies on comprehending a context greater than this single word. That being said, by and large effects of recognition are seen in early eye-tracking measures and effects of integration are seen in late measures.

There is an extensive literature making use of eye-tracking to look at both word identification and integration. About ten years ago, Clifton et al. (2007) identified one hundred articles that just looked at word integration, focusing on the effects of syntactic, semantic and pragmatic factors on sentence comprehension. The eye-tracking literature on word recognition is at least as large. Clearly, it is impossible to comprehensively review such an extensive literature in a short space. In what follows, we will simply look at some of the key findings about word recognition and integration in reading, as well as considering how and why the findings might be important for designing studies.

4.2.1 What Do We Know about Word Recognition in Reading?

As we saw in Table 4.1, there are a number of factors that influence word recognition. More precisely, these characteristics impact the cognitive effort required to recognise a word and their effects are evident in the most commonly reported eye-tracking measures, like: *first fixation duration* – the duration of the first fixation on a word, provided that the word wasn't skipped; *single fixation duration* – the duration on a word when only one fixation is made on the word; and *gaze duration* – the sum of all fixations on a word prior to moving to another word (Clifton et al., 2007). Notably, these measures are all 'early'. Chapter 3 provides a more comprehensive discussion of eye-tracking measures and their classification as 'early' or 'late'. In what follows, we will briefly look at some of the main characteristics that have been shown to impact word recognition and examine how they influence eye-movement patterns. We will also consider some additional factors that may be important in more applied reading contexts.

The amount of time spent fixating a word is influenced by its frequency, which is established using corpora like the British National Corpus (BNC) or the SUBTLEX (Brysbaert and New, 2009). Readers look longer at infrequent than frequent words (Rayner and Duffy, 1986). However, differences between high- and low-frequency words disappear after three repetitions in a text (Rayner et al., 1995). It is important to note that corpus-derived frequency measures do not tell us how often a specific person has encountered a word. Thus, there can be high-frequency words that a particular reader may not have encountered very many times, as well as low-frequency words that he/she has come across a lot. To find out how familiar particular words are to individuals, we generally ask them to rate a word's familiarity on a Likert scale. When frequency is accounted for, there is still an effect of familiarity, such that less familiar words elicit more looking (Juhasz and Rayner, 2003; Williams and Morris, 2004). Further, words differ in their age of acquisition (AoA). AoA can be determined using large databases (corpora) that were created by asking people to indicate when they think they learned a word; alternatively a researcher can get these ratings for his/her particular stimuli. When frequency is accounted for, there is nevertheless an effect of AoA, with later-learned words increasing fixation times (Juhasz and Rayner, 2003, 2006).

For morphologically complex words like compounds ('backpack'), we need to consider the potential influence of the frequency of the compound as a whole, as well as that of the constituent morphemes ('back' and 'pack'). Evidence for frequency effects for each of these elements is somewhat mixed, but in general frequency effects for the different elements are found at different points in the eye-movement record, with the first morpheme having an earlier effect than the second morpheme and the whole compound (for a discussion see Hyönä, 2015; Juhasz, 2007). Another factor to consider if working with compounds is their transparency – whether we can determine the meaning of the whole based on the parts (e.g. 'backpack' vs 'hogwash'). There is limited evidence for an influence of transparency, which has only appeared in gaze duration (Hyönä, 2015; Juhasz, 2007). Significantly, as Hyönä (2015) points out, most of the research to date on multi-morphemic words has focused on compounds and has been done on a very limited set of languages (Finish, English, German and Dutch). Considerable work needs to be done to investigate the role of morphology in word identification for derived and inflected words, as well as in a wider range of languages.

Word identification effects that depend on more than the word that is currently being fixated are related to predictability and plausibility. Predictability can be conceived of in two ways. It can be a word-to-word contingency that is established using a corpus, which is often referred to as the 'transitional probability'. For example, the BNC can be used to determine how likely 'on' is following 'rely'. Alternatively, predictability of a word is related to a sentence's contextual constraint or bias. This is established via a cloze task.[4] For both types of predictability, more predictable words have decreased first fixation duration or gaze duration, and highly predictable words are often skipped altogether (Ehrlich and Rayner, 1981; McDonald and Shillcock, 2003b).

Plausibility has to do with how reasonable a word is in a particular context, which often makes use of our real-world knowledge. For example, how reasonable is it to cut carrots with a knife, axe or table? The plausibility of each of these instruments for cutting carrots would be established using ratings. Both implausible and anomalous words increase fixation times; however, an anomalous word has an immediate effect on fixations, while the effect of implausibility is evident somewhat later (Rayner et al., 2004).

A prominent factor affecting word recognition is lexical ambiguity, or the number of meanings that a word has (e.g. 'bank' – a place where you keep money; and 'bank' – the side of a river). The frequency of meanings can be balanced (relatively equal) or

---

[4] In a cloze task, word(s) are missing and participants are asked to provide them, e.g. 'He made many accusations, but had cried _____' versus 'He practised all of his vocabulary, and had read _____.' The percentage of 'wolf' completions in both sentences would serve as a measure of its predictability in each context.

unbalanced (one meaning is more frequent). The frequency of the two meanings *and* the strength of the (biasing) context influence eye-movement patterns and lead to what has been termed the 'subordinate-bias effect' (Duffy, Morris and Rayner, 1988; Sereno, O'Donnell and Rayner, 2006). The basic finding is that when frequency-balanced ambiguous words occur in neutral contexts, readers look at them longer than unambiguous control words matched on length and frequency. However, if they occur in a context biased towards one of their meanings, there is no difference in looking times between frequency-balanced ambiguous words and matched control words. In contrast, there is no difference in fixation times for frequency-imbalanced ambiguous and matched control words in a neutral context. If a context biases a less-frequent meaning, fixations are longer for the ambiguous word than the control. The effect on reading times resulting from having multiple meanings seems to be true of words that share orthography and phonology ('bank'), share orthography but differ in phonology ('tear'), and share phonology but differ in orthography (e.g. 'boar'/'bore'; Carpenter and Daneman, 1981; Folk, 1999). If the ambiguous words have different parts of speech (e.g. 'duck' as a noun and 'duck' as a verb), and the subordinate meaning is the only syntactically permissible continuation of a sentence, then there appears to be no subordinate meaning 'cost' on fixations (Folk and Morris, 2003).

Words can also share lexical properties across languages. Thus, just as 'bank' has two meanings, the word 'coin' has two meanings for someone who speaks English and French. It just so happens that the two meanings come from different languages – 'coin' in English is a 'piece of metal used as money' while in French it is a 'corner'. Words like 'coin' are referred to as interlingual homographs, and share orthography (and often have similar phonologies) but have distinct meanings. Interlingual homophones share their phonology, but not their orthography and semantics. These are words like 'pool'/'poule' in English and French respectively, which we saw illustrated in the visual-world paradigm in Chapters 1 and 3. Words can also share their form in terms of phonology and/or orthography, and have more or less the same meaning across languages. These are words like 'table' in English, 'table' in French and 'テーブル' ('teburu') in Japanese,[5] and are referred to as cognates. Interlingual homographs and homophones, as well as cognates, have been used extensively to investigate whether speakers of two languages selectively activate a single language or non-selectively activate both when reading in one language. For example, if a speaker of English and French reads, 'Jen found a coin while walking', 'coin' would only lead to longer fixations than a matched control word (much like 'bank') if the meanings from both languages are activated.

In reading, the influence of shared lexical properties across languages has predominantly been studied using interlingual homographs and cognates (for a review see Whitford, Pivneva and Titone, 2016). In such studies, participants are speakers of two languages, and their processing time for interlingual homographs and cognates is compared to that of language-unique matched control words. In general, cognates have shorter fixations than control words (Balling, 2013; Cop et al., 2017b; Libben and Titone, 2009; Van Assche et al., 2011). However, this does not appear to be the case

---

[5] In linguistic terms, Japanese words like 'テーブル' ('teburu') 'table' are 'loanwords' because they have been borrowed into the language. Importantly, it is the overlap in form and meaning that underpins the processing advantage for cognates and *not* their linguistic origins. Because loanwords share form and meaning, they are treated as cognates in the processing literature.

when orthography is not shared across languages (Allen and Conklin, 2017). In contrast, interlingual homographs have longer fixations than control words (Libben and Titone, 2009). For both types of words, these differences are evident in early measures of reading, but can persist through the late measures. These effects are modulated by the amount of orthographic overlap between the words in the two languages and can be influenced by the biasing strength of the sentence context (Whitford et al., 2016).

The research investigating eye-movements during reading has provided us with a good understanding of how readers identify words and how specific lexical characteristics contribute to processing effort, as well as the eye-tracking measures that are most likely to reflect this. The literature reviewed in this section has primarily focused on studies done with skilled, adult monolingual readers because reading research thus far has primarily examined this population. However, as the final part of the discussion indicates, research is beginning to look at other types of readers and situations – for example, reading in a second language. When working with and researching different populations, it is important to first have a good understanding of what 'typical' reading behaviour looks like. This allows us to see, for example, whether reading in a second language demonstrates similar effects for properties like frequency, length, etc. We could explore questions about AoA for a set of participants that learned the word 'dog' at age one but the word 'chien' in French at school at age twelve. Will 'chien' demonstrate AoA effects commensurate with words learned at twelve or one? Researchers are beginning to explore questions like these, and many others, with diverse populations of readers.

4.2.2 What Do We Know about Word Integration in Reading?

As we just saw, word identification processes are largely indexed by early eye-tracking measures. Some effects may persist and be evident in later measures as well. However, the picture is not so clear-cut for word integration and syntactic processing. Difficulties can show up at various points in the eye-tracking record (Clifton and Staub, 2011). Effects are seldom apparent in the earliest eye-tracking measures, and therefore first fixation time is rarely reported; however, they are occasionally found there (e.g. Staub, 2007). Effects can show up as increases in first pass reading times. Sometimes effects of syntactic processes may only show up as an increase in the frequency of regressions, increased go-past times and second pass reading times, or as increased times in the following region (what is called a 'spillover' effect; for a discussion see Section 3.1.2). Because effects can be found almost anywhere, it is worth inspecting data for a wide range of measures. The following provides a list of the commonly reported measures for word integration and syntactic processing (based on Clifton et al., 2007):

- first pass reading time
- go-past or regression path duration
- regressions out
- second pass reading time
- total reading time
- first fixation duration (sometimes reported, but the region should be short, often for spillover effects on an ROI of a single following word).

Why are effects found in such a wide range of measures when exploring word integration and syntactic processing? This may be in part due to experimental design. In studies of word recognition, ROIs are for the most part single words. In contrast, studies of syntactic processing may have ROIs that are two to four words long, and sometimes even longer. This greater variability in the length of ROIs leads to more variability in where and when an effect will appear in the eye-tracking record (Clifton et al., 2007). Looking at the sentences in Example 4.4, if we wanted to investigate word recognition for known and unknown (in this case invented) words, we would define 'copudamets' and 'binoculars' as our ROIs in (a) and (b), and compare the processing of the two. If we were interested in how the with-phrase is integrated into the sentence in (c), we would likely define the two words 'with binoculars' as our ROI.

Example 4.4 ROIs (underlined) for word recognition (a and b) and integration (c).

(a) John feared the man with <u>copudamets</u> hiding in the bush.
(b) John saw the man with <u>binoculars</u> hiding in the bush.
(c) John saw the man <u>with binoculars</u> hiding in the bush.

Another reason for the variability in where effects are found is that there are more options for readers when processing difficulties that arise due to (im)plausibility, complexity or syntactic misanalysis compared to when a word is difficult to recognise (Clifton et al., 2007). In the sentences in Example 4.4, when the eyes arrive at 'with binoculars' in (b) and (c), the sentence is ambiguous because the phrase could modify two things. It may be that 'John saw the man by using binoculars himself' or 'John saw the man who had binoculars.' The eyes can go back in the text to consider these two possibilities, they can stay where they are to work out the ambiguity, or they can move ahead hoping that upcoming information will resolve the issue or that it will turn out that it doesn't matter. In (a), when the eyes arrive at the unknown 'copudamets', there is nothing in the sentence to go back to that will help resolve the difficulty. The eyes can simply stay where they are and try to puzzle out the word, or they can move forward hoping the meaning becomes clear or that it doesn't matter.

Additionally, a wider range of factors contributes to word integration in sentence processing than in word recognition. As Clifton et al. (2007) say, 'We are far from understanding how these factors are coordinated and whether their coordination is modulated by differences in a reader's abilities and strategies' (p. 367). They go on to say that 'the greater flexibility in dealing with sentence comprehension difficulty and the wide range of factors that affect it could mean that high-level processing shows up in the eye-movement record in a variety of different ways, with any one effect appearing only occasionally' (p. 367). Furthermore, word integration and sentence comprehension may be impacted more by task demands and the goals of the reader than word recognition, which would also lead to greater variability in where effects are found. Again, this means that when exploring issues of morpho-syntactic processing, we may need to explore a range of different eye-tracking measures to find effects.

Thus far in this chapter, we have explored some basic properties of the visual system and how they impact reading. We have also discussed some of the main factors known to influence reading. More particularly, we have considered two elements of reading – word recognition and integration – and looked at where and when their effects might show up in the eye-movement record. As we have seen, there is a long history of reading research using eye-tracking. In what follows we will look in greater detail at some specific examples from the literature that demonstrate how we can implement eye-tracking to investigate the reading of words and meaning (Section 4.3); new words (Section 4.4); multi-word units (Section 4.5); and sentences and morpho-syntax (Section 4.6). In each section we will also focus on a different experimental paradigm and consider some methodological concerns for each: authentic texts (Section 4.3); created texts (Section 4.4); the boundary paradigm (Section 4.5); and matched and counterbalanced sentences (Section 4.6). Finally, we will look in more detail at two examples of matching participants from specific populations: second language readers (Section 4.3) and participants with an autism spectrum disorder (Section 4.6).

4.3 Words and Meaning

In this section we will consider a set of studies by Cop and her colleagues that primarily explored word recognition in monolingual English speakers and non-natives in their L1 (first language) Dutch and L2 (second language) English. Participants were asked to read the entire Agatha Christie novel *The Mysterious Affair at Styles* (Dutch title: *De zaak Styles*) while their eye-movements were monitored. Although the use of authentic materials, like a novel, adds an element of authenticity to any study, it leads to other important methodological considerations, which will be the primary focus of the discussion in this section. Authentic materials also provide a wealth of data that can be examined for a variety of things. Thus, across a series of papers, Cop and her colleagues have been able to explore a number of things like word frequency effects and the influence of cognates on reading, as well as sentence reading patterns. Cop and colleagues' four publications based on this dataset will form the basis of the discussion in this section: Cop et al. (2015a), Cop et al. (2015b), Cop et al. (2017a), Cop et al. (2017b).

4.3.1 Contextualising an Example Study: Reading an Authentic Novel

As we saw in the opening sections of this chapter, we know a considerable amount about what influences reading in well-educated, adult readers with no history of language impairments when they read in their L1. Table 4.1 listed a set of factors that have been shown to influence fixations when a word is in foveal and parafoveal view. However, considerable work remains to determine how these factors might impact reading in a much more diverse population of readers. The research by Cop and her colleagues begins to address this gap. They had monolinguals and non-native speakers read the same novel, which has allowed them to explore whether non-native speakers show similar effects in their L1 and L2, as well as being able to compare monolinguals and non-natives in their L1. With their large dataset, Cop and colleagues may eventually be able to explore many of the factors listed in Table 4.1, although more explicit manipulation may be required to explore some of them. It is important to note that the data reported in the four papers listed above all come from the 'same' reading study. For us, this means that the overview of the participants and materials is largely identical across their papers, and the discussion that follows draws on information from all of the papers.

In Cop et al.'s study, each participant read the entire Agatha Christie novel in four sessions of an hour and a half each. In the first session participants read Chapters 1 to 4, in the second 5 to 7, in the third 8 to 10 and in the fourth 11 to 13. The monolinguals read the book entirely in English, while the non-native participants read Chapters 1 to 7 in one language and 8 to 13 in the other. The order of the two languages was counterbalanced, such that half of the participants started reading the novel in Dutch and finished reading in

English and the other half started reading in English and finished in Dutch. Participants read the novel silently while their eye-movements were monitored. They were given multiple-choice comprehension questions to answer at the end of each chapter.

4.3.2 Matching Second Language Participants

For most eye-tracking research, whether we are investigating reading, listening, writing or any combination of these, if we are looking at the performance of a particular group, we need to show that the group itself is made up of a set of participants that are similar. The factors we match on will depend somewhat on the focus of the study. For example, it will be more important to match reading ability for a reading study and listening ability in a listening study. If a group is not well matched, this could influence eye-movement patterns and consequently our findings. For example, let's say we want to look at reading by non-native speakers. If we examine the performance of twenty participants, but do not assess and establish their proficiency, we may end up with a group with highly variable behaviour. This will make it hard to find significant results, and we may draw conclusions about non-natives more generally, when our results were driven by a subset of the participants. Thus, we need to convincingly demonstrate that our group is similar (i.e. has a similar proficiency and exposure to the L2). It is important to note that when we investigate reading by educated, adult native speakers with no history of language impairments, we generally assume (maybe incorrectly) that the group is made up of individuals who have similar reading skills. Importantly, if we want to compare groups of participants, we need to show that the two groups are the same and only differ on our manipulated factor. This means that if we want to compare high- and low-proficiency non-native speakers, the only characteristic that the groups should differ on is their proficiency. The groups should have the same number of participants, a similar gender composition, years/level of education, etc.

The studies by Cop et al. provide a very good example of matching participants. They monitored the eye-movements of fourteen English monolingual speakers and nineteen unbalanced Dutch(L1)–English(L2) bilinguals.[6] None of the participants in either group had a history of language or reading impairments. The two groups were matched in age (monolinguals M = 21.8, SD = 5.6; bilinguals M = 21.2, SD = 2.2).[7] They also had a similar level of education, as all participants were enrolled in a bachelor's or master's programme in psychology. The monolingual group had six male and seven female participants, while the bilingual group had two male and seventeen female participants. All of the bilinguals were intermediate to advanced L2 learners with a relatively late L2 age of acquisition (M = 11, SD = 2.46). Both groups of participants in the study completed a battery of language proficiency tasks, which were used to ensure that they were well matched and/or differences could be included as a factor in analyses. These tasks are outlined below:

---

[6] Cop et al. refer to their participants as bilinguals. It is common in the psycholinguistic literature to refer to any group of non-native speakers as 'bilinguals' and then to simply specify whether they are balanced/unbalanced, early/late, etc. bilinguals. It is important to note that because Cop et al.'s participants were recruited in Belgium it is likely that many, if not all, of them were actually multilinguals. Knowledge of additional languages could influence processing. Thus, ideally information about proficiency should be obtained for all of the languages known to participants.

[7] M means 'mean' and SD means 'standard deviation'.

- Spelling test
  - Because there is no standardised cross-lingual spelling test, English spelling was assessed using the WRAT 4 (Wilkinson and Robertson, 2006) and Dutch spelling with the GLETSHER (Depessemier and Andries, 2009).
  - The monolinguals were tested in English, while bilinguals were tested in English and Dutch.
- Vocabulary test – LexTALE (Lemhöfer and Broersma, 2012)
  - This is an unspeeded lexical decision task (decision whether a stimulus is a word or not) that can be administered in English, Dutch and/or German. It contains a high proportion of words with a low corpus frequency. It was developed as a vocabulary test and has been validated as a measure of general proficiency for the three languages.
  - The monolinguals were tested in English, while bilinguals were tested in English and Dutch.
- Speeded lexical decision task
  - Participants were asked to classify letter strings as words or non-words as fast as possible.
  - The monolinguals were tested in English, while bilinguals were tested in English and Dutch.
- Self-report language questionnaire – based on the LEAP-Q (Marian, Blumenfeld and Kaushanskaya, 2007)
  - The questionnaire contained questions about language-switching frequency/skill, age of L2 acquisition, frequency of L2 use and reading/auditory comprehension/speaking skills in L1 and L2.
  - Completed by both the monolinguals and bilinguals.

These tests, and the analyses of them, demonstrated that the monolinguals and the bilinguals were equally proficient in their L1, but the bilinguals had relatively less exposure to their L1 than the monolinguals had to their only language. The L2 (English) proficiency of the participants was lower than their L1 (Dutch) proficiency as assessed in all tasks. Further, the tasks showed that bilinguals varied in their L2 proficiency. For example, based on the norms reported in Lemhöfer and Broersma (2012), two bilinguals could be classified as lower intermediate L2 language users, ten as upper intermediate L2 language users and seven as advanced L2 language users. Proficiency differences were therefore an important factor to consider in analyses of the data.

4.3.3 Using Authentic Materials

When selecting authentic reading materials, it is important to consider a number of things. For one, research should be replicable. To achieve this, other researchers should be able to access the materials used in a study. When making our own materials this is straightforward; they can be made available in an appendix or upon request. When using published materials, like a book or novel, there may be copyright issues. While one researcher may receive permission to use a particular text for research purposes, this does not guarantee that others would be granted the same access. Therefore, others may not be able to replicate and/or extend the research with other populations. Ideally, when using authentic materials, we should use ones that are freely available or which can be made widely available to others. Cop et al. used a novel that is accessible as part of Project Gutenberg (www.gutenberg.org), which offers over 50,000 free books in various languages. Additionally, because Cop et al. wanted to investigate Dutch–English bilingual readers, an important consideration was selecting a novel that had been translated into Dutch. Further, their chosen novel is available in other languages, which means that future research can extend Cop et al.'s work by investigating reading of the same text in other languages.

When we create materials, we can design them to fit a set of particular constraints. In contrast, when using authentic materials, we need to select a text that meets whatever criteria we feel are important for our study. For example, Cop and her colleagues wanted to use a novel that could be read within four hours. If an average adult usually reads 250–300 words per minute, or 15,000–18,000 words per hour, this means that they could consider texts that have 60,000–72,000 words. Keeping in mind that this is a very general estimate, and there will be readers who are slower than average, particularly in the L2, choosing a book that comes in under the lower limit would probably be advisable.

After coming up with a set of books that met the length criterion, they checked them for difficulty in a number of ways. First, they wanted a book in which the frequency distribution of the words in the text was as similar to natural language as possible (as established by the SUBTLEX database). They used the Kullback-Leibler test (Cover and Thomas, 1991), which measures the difference between two probability distributions, to establish the divergence between potential texts and the database. Second, they looked at the number of hapax words (words that occur only once in the SUBTLEX database), and chose a novel that had a low number of hapax words. Finally, they calculated two readability scores: the Flesch Reading Ease (Kincaid et al., 1975), which returns a score between 0 and 100 (closer to 100 is easier to read); and the SMOG grade (McLaughlin, 1969), which indicates how many years of education are needed to understand a text. The Flesch Reading Ease for the novel was 81.3, and the SMOG was 7.4.

Because the bilinguals would read part of the novel in Dutch and part in English, Cop et al. compared the novel's translations on a number of characteristics: number of words; number of word types; number of nouns; number of noun types; number of sentences; number of words per sentence; number of characters (letters) per sentence; number of content words per sentence; average word frequency; average content word frequency; and average word length. In cases where *t*-tests revealed differences in these characteristics, and Cop et al. felt that the difference was important for their research question, they included the characteristic as a variable in their analysis.

In the study, the novel was presented in black 14 pt Courier New font on a light grey background. The text appeared in paragraphs and the lines were triple spaced. A maximum of 145 words appeared on a screen, spread over a maximum of ten lines. When readers came to the end of the screen they pressed a button to move onto the next one. Calibration was done at the outset and every ten minutes, or more frequently if the experimenter deemed it necessary.

4.3.4 Data Analysis and Results

Usually when we design a reading study, we try to ensure that our ROIs do not occur at the beginning and the end of a line, or right before or after punctuation. Studies using authentic texts usually exclude fixations that occur in these positions. Thus, generally we would remove the first fixation on every line, as well as any regressive fixations immediately following this fixation, as they are most likely corrective saccades triggered when the return sweep falls short of the beginning of the line (Hofmeister, Heller and Radach, 1999). All data associated with words preceded or followed by punctuation, as well as the first and last word of every line of text, should be excluded from analyses. After this, normal data cleaning procedures can be implemented, for example removing cases of track loss or other irregularities (see Chapter 7 for more on data cleaning). In addition to these procedures, Cop and colleagues removed fixations shorter than 100 ms. In their three studies focusing on individual word processing, for the most part, single fixations that differed by more than 2.5 standard deviations from the subject means per language were excluded from the dataset prior to any analyses.

Furthermore, Cop et al. constrained their datasets in certain ways to make them more manageable and to ensure that they were making relatively well-matched comparisons. When looking at individual word processing, Cop et al. usually excluded words that were identical cognates. Because cognates are known to speed processing, including them could skew the findings. Ideally, non-identical cognates should be removed as well. However, these are harder to identify through an automated process, which probably explains why they were retained in the dataset. Many of their analyses also excluded words that were not fixated and that were fixated more than once. While this helps restrict a very large dataset, the theoretical motivations for doing so should be made clear.

While not directly relevant to the focus of this section on word processing, when looking at sentence processing, Cop et al. did a number of things to match their items, and thereby restrict their dataset. As a result only 4.2 per cent of the original sentences were retained in the analyses, although the set of data still encompassed 210 sentences per participant – and were considered to be the set of optimally matched stimuli by the researchers. The following summarises their main inclusion/exclusion criteria for their study on sentence processing.

- Sentences were removed if they had
  - more than thirty-five words
  - an average word length of more than 7.4 characters
  - an average content word frequency lower than 1.56.
- Matched materials on semantic context:
  - each sentence was manually checked for translation equivalence
  - sentences that did not match were excluded from analyses.
- The final dataset only included Dutch–English sentence pairs that were matched on
  - average word length
  - number of words per sentence.

The measures that Cop and her colleagues used to analyse their data varied depending on whether individual words or whole sentences were the focus of the investigation. Although this differed slightly across studies, for investigations of word processing, Cop et al. examined the following measures: first fixation duration, single fixation duration, gaze duration, total reading time, go-past time and average skipping probability or skipping rate. When looking at the reading of the entire sentence, they explored: whole-sentence reading time including fixations and re-fixations, total number of fixations in one sentence, average fixation duration of the fixations in one sentence, average rightward saccade length per sentence, probability of making an inter-word regression towards or within a sentence, and probability of first pass skipping. For both words and sentences, the eye-tracking measures that Cop et al. used are ones that are commonly reported.

Unsurprisingly, across a series set of studies, Cop and her colleagues had a number of interesting findings. Here we simply sum up some of their main ones. They demonstrated that monolinguals and bilinguals in their L1 have similarly sized frequency effects. However, in their L2, bilinguals exhibit a considerably larger frequency effect. A cognate processing advantage showed up in different places in the eye-tracking record, depending on language (L1/L2), whether the cognates were identical or not, and word length. For sentences, monolinguals reading in their only language and bilinguals reading in their L1 did not differ in any key ways. However, in their L2, bilinguals had longer sentence reading times, more fixations, shorter saccades and less word skipping.

Importantly for our discussion of methodology, the Cop et al. studies demonstrate the kinds of things that we need to do (e.g. appropriate line spacing and font size) to ensure that we get good data that is not contaminated by various factors (excluding the word before punctuation to remove potential sentence wrap-up effects, etc.) when using authentic materials. Their research highlights different ways we can achieve a level of experimental control for stimuli that we have not specifically designed for a study. However, doing this means that much of the data that we collect will not actually be analysed. While we will have reading time measures for all of the words in a text (except for those that are skipped), only a subset of these will be included in any analyses. Furthermore, we will almost certainly need to use statistical analyses, like mixed-effects modelling, that allow us to account for the range of variables that influence reading patterns.

4.4   New Words

The opening sections of this chapter described word recognition and integration in reading and the factors that influence them. While the discussion focused on known words, children in their L1 and people reading in their L2 will often encounter unknown or 'new' words. By definition, new words have zero frequency for the reader, are completely unfamiliar and are certainly not predictable – all factors that are known to influence processing. Since their meaning is also unknown, integrating a new word into a reader's unfolding understanding of a sentence should also be challenging. However, little research has been done to track eye-movements to new words. Thus, important questions remain about what happens when people read new words, and how the reading patterns elicited by new words relate to performance on other tasks.

If we would like to study the processing of new words, we can embed unknown and known words in counterbalanced sentences (or longer stretches of discourse) that appear in different lists, or we could present them in a single text in different but well-matched contexts and compare the processing of the two. For such a study, we could use a methodology similar to the one we will see in Section 4.6. Alternatively, we could present unknown words in an authentic text. We would simply replace some of the known words in the text with unknown or non-words, and the methodological considerations would largely be the same as those outlined in Section 4.3. In addition, it would be advisable to assess the informativeness of the context: in other words, how much the context tells the reader about the meaning of each of the unknown words, as this will likely influence looking patterns. Instead of using authentic texts, we could design texts that have particular properties. Crucially, such texts may still feel authentic to readers. By designing our own texts, we can ensure that they are suitable for our target readers, for example, by only using vocabulary that is at an appropriate level. We can also manipulate and control how informative the context is for the unknown words.

Another consideration in such a study are the unknown words themselves. We could use actual but unknown words, or non-words. If we used unknown words, we would need to ensure that they were indeed unknown to the participants. This would usually be verified in a pre-test. However, by including the words in a pre-test, we would expose participants to them, as well as potentially drawing their attention to them, which could influence behaviour on the main task. Alternatively, we could use very 'word-like' non-words. In this case, we would be drawing conclusions about reading behaviour for new words when the input is not actually words. As with many experimental design decisions, there are advantages and disadvantages with our choices – we simply need to be aware of them and consider them when we draw conclusions from our data.

4.4.1   Contextualising an Example Study: Reading a Constructed Text

We will consider a study by Pellicer-Sánchez (2016) that looked at what L1 and L2 readers learn about new words when they encounter them in a constructed text. More specifically, Pellicer-Sánchez was interested in the incidental learning of new vocabulary from reading, as well as how the eye-movement pattern to new words changed over a number of occurrences. To investigate this, she compared the processing of non-words and matched known words embedded in a story. She used a set of offline vocabulary tests to look at what participants learned about the new words and examined how this related to their reading behaviour.

4.4.2   Matching Participants

Pellicer-Sánchez monitored the eye-movements of thirty-seven L2 speakers of English from various language backgrounds and thirty-six L1 speakers of English. Due to cases of drift (i.e. imprecise eye-movements indicating a deterioration of the calibration over time) in the ROIs, data from fourteen L2 participants and eleven L1 participants was discarded and not included in the analyses, leaving twenty-three and twenty-five participants in each group respectively. This is very high rate of exclusion and is *not* typical of reading studies of this nature, but was the result of particular methodological decisions (see the paper for further details). None of the participants in either group had a history of language or reading impairments. The two groups were fairly well matched in terms of age. Both cohorts were well educated, with the L1 participants being drawn from an undergraduate student population and the L2 participants were postgraduate and postdoctoral students. The L2 group had ten males and thirteen females, while L1 group had one male and twenty-four females.

The non-native speaker participants in Pellicer-Sánchez's study were much more diverse than those in the Cop et al. studies reviewed above. Here, the participants came from eleven different language backgrounds that used different scripts (alphabetic languages; logographic languages; syllabic languages or abugidas). When examining performance by participants from same- and different-script languages, it is important to consider how this might impact speed of reading and reading patterns. This can be done by comparing global reading measures to see if same- and different-script readers perform in a similar fashion. All of the non-native speakers had spent a minimum of twelve months and a maximum of six years living in an English-speaking environment ($M = 2.4$, $SD = 1.7$). They were advanced learners who had met a university entry requirement of English proficiency (6.0 or above on the International English Language Testing System [IELTS] or equivalent examination). At the beginning of the experiment L2 participants completed a self-rating questionnaire of proficiency (on a scale from one to ten, with ten being native-like). The mean values for all skills (reading, writing, listening and speaking) were all above seven and crucially all participants rated their reading skills at seven or above.

The discussion in Section 4.3.2 goes into more detail about matching and assessing participants who are non-native speakers, and presents the battery of language proficiency tasks that Cop and her colleagues used in their research to demonstrate that the non-native participants were well matched and/or to provide proficiency metrics that could be used as variables in analyses. Ideally researchers should use some of these tasks, or other similar ones, when conducting research with non-native participants.

4.4.3 Using Constructed Materials

When we create our own text, we can ensure that it addresses our research questions while at the same time making sure that it is appropriate for the target group of participants. For her study, Pellicer-Sánchez wrote a 2,300-word story. She carefully controlled the vocabulary in the story to help ensure that the acquisition of the unknown words would not be hindered by lack of knowledge of the remaining words in the text. Thus, 97 per cent of the words in the story belonged to the 3,000 most frequent words of the British National Corpus (BNC; determined by Compleat Lexical Tutor; www.lextutor.ca). Only four words (0.17%) were from the 5,000 to 9,000 frequency bands. These were considered adequate percentages to assure participants' comprehension.

Embedded in the story were six non-words and six control words (real known words), all of which were repeated eight times. This meant that forty-eight words in the text were unknown (2%), while the remaining were known (98%). The non-words were evenly spread throughout the text to make sure that there was a balanced distribution of unknown items throughout the story. To ensure that the new words would be unknown to all participants, non-words (i.e. invented letter strings that look like real words in English) were used. Non-words came from the Compleat Lexical Tutor (Cobb, n.d.), and modified to suit the required length (two syllables, six letters). They all replaced high-frequency (1,000–3,000 frequency band from the BNC), concrete nouns in the story. Further, Pellicer-Sánchez wanted to compare reading behaviour for the new and known words, and she wanted to make certain that any observed effect for the non-words was not simply a practice or repetition effect. Thus, she included six known words, also repeated eight times in the story, that had the same characteristics as the non-words (nouns, six letters and two syllables) and were from the same high-frequency band.

While the text was designed to make sure that the non-words were equally guessable from context, Pellicer-Sánchez wanted to confirm that this was indeed the case. She conducted a separate norming study with eighty-seven native speakers of English divided across eight groups. Group 1 read the first context in which each of the non-words appeared (including the non-word sentence, the previous sentence and the following sentence), Group 2 read contexts one and two, Group 3 read contexts one through three and so forth. Participants were asked to read the context and guess the meaning of the non-words. The results showed that the vast majority of participants provided the same guesses for the non-words (93%–98% agreement for each non-word), indicating that the context was equally informative for all of the unknown words.

The story was presented using 18 pt Courier New font with double line spacing. The text was divided over twenty-five screens, all of which were eight lines long and contained 82–103 words. A screen contained a maximum of two non-words. The position of non-words and known words was carefully controlled so that none of them appeared in initial or final position in a line or sentence. Following the story, there was a short, twelve-question true/false task to check that participants had read for comprehension. None of the questions contained a non-word. Before beginning the main study, to familiarise them with the task, participants read a short 423-word story, which also contained unknown words, and which was followed by comprehension questions. Calibration was done before and after the practice story and halfway through the experiment.

Pellicer-Sánchez's study also involved a set of three vocabulary tests: form recognition, meaning recall and meaning recognition. These were carried out after the reading task. The first vocabulary test assessed participants' ability to recognise the correct form of the non-words. A multiple-choice task presented four different options, and participants were asked to select the correct spelling of the target item. The second test measured participants' ability to recall the meaning of the non-words. Participants were shown items one by one and were asked to say everything they knew about the meaning of the item. A third measure of the form–meaning link (i.e. meaning recognition) was included to capture knowledge below the level of meaning recall. For each non-word, participants were given four possible meanings to choose from, as well as an 'I don't know' option. Careful attention was given to the design of distractors, which were all semantically related to the content of the story (otherwise their discrimination would have been too easy) and were all of the same word class. For all three tasks, participants had to indicate on a scale from one to four (one = very uncertain, four = very certain) how certain they were of their responses. Example 4.5 shows a sample of the created story with two non-words, as well as examples of the vocabulary knowledge tasks.

Example 4.5 The stimuli from the Pellicer-Sánchez (2016) study. Part A shows an example screen containing the two new words, 'holter' and 'soters', which were ROIs (underlined). Parts B and C show the form and meaning recognition task for these two items. Note that the meaning recall task is not depicted here as it allowed participants to provide unconstrained responses.

Part A
Hugo grew up in the <u>holter</u> with the other boys. It was not a very nice place for children. Nobody would like to grow up there. It was a very old place and not very comfortable. The boys never received any care at all. They never had enough warm <u>soters</u> or food. Life there was hard, but living alone in the outside world would be even harder. But living there was not free. Having a place to sleep and a bit of food to eat had a price. They had to work hard if they wanted to stay there.

Part B
Choose the right spelling for the following six words that have appeared in the story (only one is correct) and indicate in the scale on the right how certain you are of your response (1 = very uncertain, 4 = very certain).

1.   a) hotler b) holter c) houter d) houler **1 2 3 4**
2.   a) solers b) soters c) sorels d) sorets **1 2 3 4**

Part C
Select one of the five options. Only one is the correct definition. If you don't know the meaning of the word, please select option 'e'. Indicate on the scale on the right how certain you are of your response (1 = very uncertain, 4 = very certain)

1.   holter   **1   2   3   4**
       a) basement
       b) workhouse
       c) prison
       d) food hall
       e) I don't know.

2.   soters   **1   2   3   4**
       a) shoes
       b) clothes
       c) dishes
       d) tools
       e) I don't know.

4.4.4 Data Analysis and Results

Pellicer-Sánchez began by cleaning her data. Single fixation durations shorter than 100 ms and longer than 800 ms were discarded. (Note that for ROIs with more than one word, an 800 ms cut-off may be too short and overly conservative. For known, single words it is the standard cut-off.) Fixation counts greater than or equal to ten for an ROI were also discarded. This resulted in the loss of 5 per cent of the L2 data (218 fixations out of the total 3,824 fixations) and 6.5 per cent of the L1 data (227 fixations out of the total 3,262 fixations). Pellicer-Sánchez then examined the reading behaviour for the new and known words using the following eye-tracking measures: first fixation duration, gaze duration, number of fixations and total reading time. She explored the eye-tracking data for both the L1 and L2 participants, examining the influence of word/non-word status and number of occurrences. She also analysed the results of the vocabulary post-tests and explored the relationship between reading time measures and vocabulary knowledge.

Results of the study showed that both L1 and L2 participants learned new words from reading. For both groups, non-word reading got faster as the number of encounters increased, and non-word reading looked like that of already known words by the eighth occurrence. It also demonstrated that spending more time reading the non-words led to better meaning recall.

Importantly, the discussion of the Pellicer-Sánchez study highlights some of the methodological considerations when investigating the processing of unknown words, as well as a number of things we should consider when designing our own texts for eye-tracking (e.g. placement of critical words on the page, font size, line spacing).

4.5 Multi-Word Units

Eye-tracking while reading can be used to explore the processing of sequences of words, which are referred to in the literature by a number of names, such as 'formulaic sequences', 'multi-word units', 'multi-word expressions', etc. Eye-tracking has been used successfully to investigate idioms ('kick the bucket'), compounds ('teddy bear'), collocations ('strong coffee'), binomials ('fish and chips') and lexical bundles ('I don't want to'). Carrol and Conklin (2014) provide a detailed discussion of some of the challenges posed by ROIs that span multiple words. The main difficulty comes from the fact that such sequences are made up of individual words that at the same time form a unit. This is clearest in the case of idioms like 'kick the bucket', where 'kick' + 'the' + 'bucket' = 'die', while none of the words on their own mean 'die'. To reflect the fact that both the individual words and the whole sequence can contribute to processing, it is advisable to establish ROIs that allow us to analyse the processing of both. There are also some additional variables that should be considered when investigating multi-word units, which we will talk about in the next section.

4.5.1 ROIs and Additional Variables for Multi-Word Units

Two eye-tracking studies on idioms demonstrate different ways of achieving a balance between an exploration of the parts and the whole of multi-word sequences. In an investigation of the processing of three-word idioms by native and non-native speakers, Carrol, Conklin and Gyllstad (2016) defined two ROIs: the whole idiom, and the final word of the idiom. Because the final word may be predictable, and therefore elicit shorter fixations and more skipping, it was thought to be important to consider it by itself. For the whole idiom, Carrol et al. looked at first pass reading time, total reading time and fixation count, while for the final word they analysed likelihood of skipping, first fixation duration, gaze duration, total reading time and regression path duration. In a study on longer idioms, Siyanova-Chanturia, Conklin and Schmitt (2011) used a cloze task to determine the recognition point of idioms – the place where an idiom becomes recognisable. For example, if a native speaker encounters 'the straw that broke' they will recognise the idiom having seen the initial four words. Thus, the words up to and including 'broke' occur before the recognition point, while 'the camel's back' occur after the recognition point. Siyanova-Chanturia et al. defined three ROIs: the whole idiom; words up to the recognition point; and the words after the recognition point. For all three ROIs they analysed first pass reading time, total reading time and fixation count. Because all of their ROIs were made up of multiple words, the same eye-tracking measures were suitable for all of them. In contrast, because one of Carrol et al.'s ROIs was a single word, different measures were appropriate when looking at it.

In addition to considerations about what would be the best ROIs for multi-word sequences, there are some additional variables that may need to be considered when designing materials and/or in the analysis:

- Frequencies of the individual words and of the whole sequence
  These are established with a corpus.

- Cloze probability and/or recognition point
  Both are established with a cloze task and tell us how predictable a final word(s) might be and where the sequence is recognised.

- Transitional probability (forward and backward)
  This is established with a corpus and tells us how likely it is to see one word in the context of another. Forward transitional probability calculates the likelihood of one word following another (how likely is 'on' after 'rely'), while backward transitional probability calculates the likelihood of a preceding word (how likely that the word is 'rely' given the following word 'on').

- Association strength
  This tells us how strongly words are associated in memory and is established with databases such as the Edinburgh Associative Thesaurus (http://konect.uni-koblenz.de/networks/eat) and the University of South Florida Free Association Norms (w3.usf.edu/FreeAssociation). Association strength is mainly considered as a variable in investigations of collocations and binomials.

- Transparency and/or compositionality
  This tells us whether a sequence's meaning is computable from its parts. For example, 'kick the bucket' is not transparent, while 'fish and chips' is. Transparency and compositionality are generally established using rating and norming studies, and are assessed when the experimental materials contain items for which the meaning is not fully transparent, with idioms being the quintessential case.

- Mutual information score (MI score)
  The MI score shows the relationship between how many times a particular word combination appears in a corpus, relative to the expected frequency of co-occurrence by chance based on the individual word frequencies and the size of the corpus. MI scores are mainly considered as a factor in studies on collocations.

In general, studies of multi-word sequences have the same design and methodological considerations as studies investigating the processing of single words and morpho-syntax. Thus, a study on multi-word sequences would be very similar to those considered in the other sections in this chapter. In other words, we can present multi-word sequences in matched sentence pairs (similar to Section 4.6), we can embed them in a longer constructed reading context (like in Section 4.4), or we can study them as they occur in natural texts (as in Section 4.3). Because these experimental methods are presented in other sections, here we will consider a different experimental technique – the boundary paradigm.

4.5.2 Contextualising an Example Study: Using the Boundary Paradigm

A study by Cutter, Drieghe and Liversedge (2014) explored whether spaced compounds are processed like a large lexical unit during reading. To do this they used the boundary paradigm. The boundary paradigm involves a 'gaze-contingent display' (see Chapter 3 where we discuss types of triggers in eye-tracking studies), such that the stimulus that is being presented is updated as a function of where a participant is fixating. It allows researchers to control the input that the processing system receives to determine how different kinds of information are used. More specifically, there is a display that is triggered to change when the eyes cross a boundary that is invisible to participants. This means that what is viewed via parafoveal preview can be different from what will appear after the eyes cross the boundary. The previewed stimuli can be a number of different things, like a nonsense word in the Cutter et al. study, which is illustrated in Example 4.6. The paradigm allows us to compare how different types of preview affect the fixations on a target, which in turn allows us to establish how much is understood when a word appears in the parafovea and periphery. If having the 'wrong' information doesn't influence fixations relative to when the information is 'correct', then the information in the parafovea or periphery was not processed. In contrast, if a change in the stimulus changes patterns of fixations, it indicates that information in the parafovea affects processing.

Example 4.6 Stimuli from Cutter et al. (2014) making use of the boundary paradigm. The vertical black line represents the position of the invisible boundary. In the study there were four different types of preview. In all cases, when the eye crossed the boundary, the preview was replaced with the correct version of the spaced compound ('teddy bear'). Their three regions of analysis were: n, $n+1$ and $n+2$.

ROIs	n	$n+1$	$n+2$
(a) The small child gently cuddled his	fluffy	teddy	bear while ...
(b) The small child gently cuddled his	fluffy	teddy	hocu while ...
(c) The small child gently cuddled his	fluffy	fohbg	bear while ...
(d) The small child gently cuddled his	fluffy	fohbg	hocu while ...

In the example from Cutter and colleagues, there is a boundary after the word 'fluffy', which directly precedes the compound. Before participants' eyes crossed this, they had a preview of one of four different types of stimuli: (a) both words of the compound; (b) unmodified first word and modified second word; (c) modified first word and unmodified second word; and (d) both words modified. In all cases, once the boundary was crossed the compound 'teddy bear' appeared. Their ROIs were the word right before the boundary (n = 'fluffy'), the two words of the compound ($n+1$ = 'teddy', $n+2$ = 'bear') and the whole compound ('teddy bear'). They were particularly interested in a processing advantage for $n+1$ and $n+2$, which would provide an indication that compounds are processed as a lexical unit during reading.

4.5.3 Matching Participants and Controlling Materials

All of the participants in the study were adult, native English speakers with no history of language impairments, and were therefore assumed to have a similar reading skill. (For discussions of matching participants in populations where reading skill is assumed to vary see Sections 4.3.2 and 4.6.2). Cutter et al. tested sixty-one participants, but only analysed the data for forty-four of them. The data from the other seventeen partici-pants was removed before any analyses were carried out because these participants had noticed the changes in the display. Typically, participants who notice changes in boundary paradigm studies are excluded, and the rate of exclusion in this study is not unusual.

The study made use of forty spaced compounds, which were matched on a number of characteristics. Words occurring in the pre-boundary position (n) were matched for length and frequency, as were the words occurring in the first position of the compound ($n+1$), in the second position ($n+2$), as well as the whole compound. The mean forward transitional probability of the compounds was 0.42 in the BNC, which means that the first constituent appeared as part of the spaced compound 42 per cent of the time within the corpus. Cutter and his colleagues performed a cloze task on a similar set of participants to verify that the compounds were equally predictable. When participants were given the sentence up to the word n, the compound was produced 33 per cent of the time, and when they were given up to the word $n+1$, they produced the second word of the compound 97 per cent of the time. This indicates that the compound as a whole was not overly predictable, but the second word of the compound was after having seen the first one.

The non-words for the preview condition were generated using an algorithm that replaced letters in the actual words with other letters, thereby preserving the word shape of the original words. In the sentences themselves, the compounds were placed at least two words from the end of the sentence. Crucially, the cloze task showed that the sentences were equivalent in 'predicting' the compound. In the study, the forty experimental stimuli were interspersed among sixty-nine filler items. One-third of the trials had a yes/no question to ensure that the participants were reading for comprehension. Although it is not explicitly stated in the paper, it is assumed that the items were presented across four counterbalanced lists, such that a participant saw ten items in each of the four conditions (unchanged preview, modified first word, modified second word, modified both words).

4.5.4 Data Analysis and Results

As in other studies, Cutter et al. started by cleaning their data. They removed trials where the boundary change happened early and when the boundary change finished more than 10 ms after fixation onset. Trials in which participants blinked during a critical region were removed. Finally, they only analysed trials in which there was a fixation on word n. Together, their exclusions account for 44 per cent of the original data. It is important to note that this is considerably more data loss than we see with other paradigms, but is in-line with studies using the boundary paradigm.

Cutter and colleagues had four ROIs: n, $n+1$, $n+2$ and the whole compound. Thus, their analysis considered the parts of the compound and the compound as a whole. For all of the ROIs they looked at gaze duration, go-past time and single fixation duration. They also considered first fixation duration for n, $n+1$ and $n+2$, but not for the whole compound because this measure is only appropriate for short (single-word) regions. Finally, they only looked at skipping probability for $n+1$, $n+2$, as skipping is irrelevant before the compound occurs. Cutter et al. found that readers spent less time looking at $n+1$ when they had seen 'bear' in a preview condition. This processing advantage was evident when the word 'teddy' was present, but not its matched non-word 'fohbg' had been visible. This was taken as an indication that the second word of a spaced compound is processed as part of a larger lexical unit during natural reading. However, this only occurs when the first constituent is visible and indicates that a compound is present.

The Cutter et al. study introduces a paradigm that may be somewhat unfamiliar. It has been used extensively by Rayner and many of his colleagues to look at effects of parafoveal processing and how expectancies for upcoming words influence processing. Generally in such studies ROIs only include n and $n+1$. Because the Cutter et al. study was interested in the processing of compounds, $n+2$ was also an important region of analysis. Further, the discussion in this section highlights a range of variables relating to the individual words that make up the unit, as well as ones that relate to the whole, that we should consider when investigating multi-word units. Importantly, we should establish ROIs that consider the parts as well as the whole of the multi-word unit. Finally, we have seen that different eye-tracking measures are appropriate for ROIs of single versus multiple words.

4.6 Sentences and Morpho-Syntax

Thus far, we have focused on studies looking at word processing. In this section, we are going to turn to a study by Howard, Liversedge and Benson (2017) on syntactic processing. Notably, the study investigated readers who were on the autism spectrum and compared them to typically developed readers. While the main points of interest in this section concern how the participants and materials were matched, we will also consider other methodological aspects of the study.

4.6.1 Contextualising an Example Study: Counterbalanced Materials

As we saw in Example 4.4, a sentence like 'John saw the man with binoculars hiding in the bush' is ambiguous. The prepositional with-phrase can modify how the seeing was done 'with binoculars', or it can modify the man, 'the one with the binoculars'. In the literature on syntax this is called an attachment ambiguity. In other words, a modifier can attach to a higher node in a syntactic tree (referred to as high attachment) or to a lower node in the tree (referred to as low attachment). In our example, the 'seeing' interpretation reflects high attachment, while the 'man' interpretation reflects low attachment. Additionally, it is thought that verbs can have an attachment preference (i.e. a verb may be more likely to have high attachment). Further, real-world knowledge can play a role in attachment ambiguity. More specifically, 'with binoculars' is ambiguous because binoculars can be used for seeing and they are something a person can have. In contrast, in a sentence like 'John feared the man with binoculars', real-world knowledge tells us that the prepositional phrase cannot modify how the fearing was done; thus it can only refer to the man.

The Howard et al. (2017) study looked at how participants with and without an autism spectrum disorder read sentences containing an ambiguous prepositional phrase using verbs that had a high-attachment preference when there was and was not real-world knowledge to help disambiguate the sentence. Howard and her colleagues were trying to determine (1) whether the syntactic preferences (high attachment) held by typically developing readers are true of participants with an autism spectrum disorder, and if the time course of any disruption due to ambiguity is the same for both groups of readers; and (2) whether readers with an autism spectrum disorder use real-world knowledge during reading.

4.6.2 Matching Participants from a Special Population

As we discussed in Section 4.3.2, when we are studying a particular group of participants whose language and reading skills may vary, we need measures that show that the group itself is made up of a set of participants who are similar and/or that allow us to account for any participant differences in our analyses. An excellent example of the care that should be taken when comparing two groups comes from the Howard et al. study. First, they ensured that the group of autism spectrum disorder participants was similar. They did this by means of a standardised test – module 4 of the Autism Diagnostic Observation Schedule (ADOS-2; Lord et al., 2012). Using this test, they showed that all but four of their participants met the autism spectrum cut-off criteria. When these four participants

Table 4.2 Summary of the ways in which Howard and colleagues (2017) showed that their typically developed participants and those with an autism spectrum disorder only varied on the factor of autism. The first five characteristics demonstrate that the groups were the same, while the sixth shows that they differed on autism spectrum traits.

Participants with an autism spectrum disorder	Typically developed participants
Group composition to demonstrate that they have a similar size and gender make-up.	
19 adults (3 females)	18 adults (4 females)
Comparison of age to show that the groups are the same, $t(35) = 0.94$, $p = 0.354$.	
ages 18–52; M = 31.37 years SD = 10.45	ages 20–52; M = 28.33 years SD = 9.18
Comparison of various IQ measures from a standardised test, the Wechsler Abbreviated Scale of Intelligence (Wechsler, 1999) to show that the groups did not differ in IQ.	
verbal IQ $t(35) = 0.58$, $p = 0.621$	
M = 118.32 SD = 11.06	M = 116.50 SD = 11.07
performance IQ $t(34) = 0.99$, $p = 0.331$	
M = 116.21 SD = 14.75	M = 111.94 SD = 11.45
full-scale IQ $t(35) = 0.87$, $p = 0.389$	
M = 119.42 SD = 11.89	M = 116.17 SD = 10.79
Comparison of expressive language ability using the Clinical Evaluation of Language Fundamentals II (Semel, Wiig and Secord, 2003), showing the groups did not differ, $t(35) = 0.53$, $p = 0.599$.	
M = 86.95 SD = 6.22	M = 88.00 SD = 5.87
Comparison of general reading ability with the York Assessment of Reading Comprehension (Stothard et al., 2010), demonstrating that the groups did not differ in single-word reading or reading a passage for comprehension	
single-word reading $t(33) = 0.51$, $p = 0.614$	
M = 68.17 SD = 2.12	M = 67.74 SD = 2.96
passage comprehension $t(34) = 0.35$, $p = 0.727$	
M = 8.97 SD = 2.03	M = 9.19 SD = 1.77
Comparison of autism spectrum traits using the standardised Autism-Spectrum Quotient (Baron-Cohen et al., 2001), to show that the groups differed, $t(32) = 9.24$, $p = 0.001$.	
M = 37.37 SD = 6.10	M = 15.61 SD = 8.03

were excluded from the analyses, the pattern of results did not change. Further, Howard et al. established that their participant groups were essentially the same and only differed on whether they had an autism spectrum disorder or not. All of their participants were English native speakers with normal or corrected to normal vision. Table 4.2 shows that the groups were well matched on the number of participants, age and gender. A set of standardised tests was used to establish that the groups were the same, as well as demonstrating their critical differences. It is important to note that the groups' characteristics were compared using *t*-tests; thus differences or the lack of them were attested statistically.

4.6.3 Matching and Controlling Materials

The Howard et al. study employed a standard experimental design in which everything was held constant, while a particular factor was manipulated and compared (see

Example 4.7). First, they ensured that all of their verbs had a high-attachment preference – in other words that the preference was for the prepositional phrase to modify how the action was done. To test this, they asked a set of participants who were from a similar population as their typically developed participants to complete a cloze task: 'Charlie demolished the dilapidated house with _____.' Ninety-eight per cent of the completions modified how the demolishing was done rather than house, confirming that the sentences had a high-attachment preference.

Example 4.7 Experimental sentences from Howard et al. (2017). The lines delineating the main regions of interest (pre-target, target, post-target) would not have been visible to participants. The target region contains the word that was manipulated for real-world knowledge and would encourage a high attachment interpretation as in (a) or a low attachment interpretation as in (b).[8]

	pre-target	target	post-target	
(a) Charlie demolished the dilapidated house with	a huge	fence	last	year.
(b) Charlie demolished the dilapidated house with	a huge	crane	last	year.

Using the SUBTLEX database (Brysbaert and New, 2009), Howard et al. ensured that the nouns appearing in the target region were matched on a number of properties that have been shown to influence reading time: length, frequency, number of orthographic neighbours, mean bigram frequency, number of morphemes and number of syllables (a bigram is a sequence of two adjacent elements and typically refers to adjacent letters, syllables or words). They used t-tests to statistically demonstrate that there was no difference in the target nouns in the two conditions (e.g. 'crane' and 'fence' in Example 4.7). To make sure that two conditions did not differ in plausibility, Howard et al. carried out a plausibility rating task with a set of participants from a similar population to their typically developed participants, but who did not take part in the previous cloze task or the main study. They asked the participants to rate how likely it was that an event described in a sentence would occur. To prevent the low attachment of the prepositional phrase acting as a confounding variable, which could cause participants to rate these sentences as less likely, they reformulated the sentences to be an unambiguous description of the events depicted in the sentences: 'that a crane would be used to demolish a huge, dilapidated house' and 'that a huge, dilapidated house that has a fence, would be demolished'. Their rating study showed that the events described in the two conditions did not differ in plausibility.

At the end of their norming procedure, Howard and colleagues had forty-four sentence pairs like those in Example 4.7. The sentences were presented across counterbalanced lists such that each list contained only one version of a pair. All participants saw eighty-eight sentences; of these, forty-four contained an ambiguous prepositional phrase (22 high attachment, 22 low attachment). In addition, ten practice sentences appeared before the

---

[8] Howard et al. (2017) had additional regions of interest, but here we consider the three that were the main focus of the investigation.

experimental sentences. The stimuli were presented in a random order, with 50 per cent of them having a following yes/no comprehension question.

4.6.4 Data Analysis and Results

Howard and colleagues used fairly standard data cleaning procedures. They removed fixations of less than 80 ms and more than 800 ms (less than 1% of the original fixation data). Trials with a blink or other disruption were removed (7.95% of the data). Data points that were more than 2.5 standard deviations away from the mean, which was computed individually for each participant per condition, were excluded (less than 3% of the data from each fixation measure). The fixation measures were log transformed and linear mixed effects modelling was used to analyse the data. For skipping and regression rate, logistic linear effects models were computed.

To determine whether there were any basic differences between the two groups when reading syntactically ambiguous sentences, Howard et al. conducted an analysis of global reading measures using mean fixation duration, mean fixation count and total sentence reading time. They then analysed the pre-target region, the target region and the post-target region using the following eye-tracking measures: skipping rate, first fixation duration, single fixation duration, gaze duration, total time, second pass time, regressions in and first pass regressions out.

Howard and colleagues found that both groups of readers demonstrated a comparable reading disruption for low-attachment sentences. This suggests that the participants with an autism spectrum disorder have a syntactic preference for high-attachment sentences that is similar to that of the typically developed participants. Their similar performance also shows that the two groups make use of real-world knowledge in similar ways during reading. However, the participants with an autism spectrum disorder skipped target words less often and took longer to read sentences in second pass reading time, suggesting that they adopt a more cautious reading strategy and take longer to evaluate their sentence interpretation.

Even though this study looked at sentence-level processes, the same methodological concerns apply here as elsewhere. We need to consider whether our stimuli are well matched and designed so that any effects are not contaminated by variables that have nothing to do with our research questions. We also need to ensure that if we are looking at different populations of participants, they are well matched on all of variables except the one that is being manipulated. The Howard et al. study provides us with an example of good practice on all of these counts.

4.7 Conclusions and Final Checklist

There are a number of factors that have been shown to impact word recognition and integration in reading. When designing stimuli for a study or selecting an authentic text we need to carefully consider these variables. In other words, one of the most important aspects in designing a reading study is 'matching' our ROIs and the material that appears around them, and/or having good measures for word and sentence character-istics, so that they can be accounted for in our analyses. Equally important is the 'matching' of our participants. Thus, we need to have appropriate tasks to establish that a cohort of participants is similar, and/or that provide measures that can be used as a variable in an analysis. In this chapter, we considered a variety of different kinds of texts and tasks that we can use to explore reading: authentic texts (Section 4.3); created texts (Section 4.4); the boundary paradigm (Section 4.5); and matched and counterbalanced sentences (Section 4.6). In Chapter 6, we will consider eye-tracking in a wide range of reading contexts: language testing (Section 6.2), writing (Section 6.3), corpus linguistics (Section 6.4), translation (Section 6.5), computer-mediated communication (Section 6.6) and literary linguistics (Section 6.7).

Finally, we opened this chapter with a quote from Huey's (1908) influential chapter on 'The mysteries and problems of reading', so it seems only appropriate to close with another. As Huey says, the average reader does not understand how we read. However, hopefully this chapter has given us, as researchers, valuable insight into reading and provided us with the means to uncover more of the 'miracle' of reading.

Real reading is still the noblest of the arts, the medium by which there still come to us the loftiest inspirations, the highest ideals, the purest feelings that have been allowed mankind,—a God-gift indeed, this written word and the power to interpret it. And reading itself, as a psycho-physiological process, is almost as good as a miracle. To the average reader the process by which he gets his pages read is not understood... (Huey, 1908, p. 5)

<table>
<tr><td colspan="2" align="center">Final checklist</td></tr>
<tr><td>

• What is the focus of your research?
  • word recognition
    • for individual words
    • for multi-word sequences
  • word integration (morpho-syntactic processing)
• What variables should be considered when designing stimuli?
  • Stimuli need to be well matched and/or differences in stimuli characteristics should be accounted for in analyses.

• What eye-tracking measures should be considered?

• What do you need to do to 'match' participants?

</td><td>

⇨ The answer to this will dictate the kind of matching that needs to be done for the materials, as well as the eye-tracking measures that should be considered.

⇨ For individual words, consider the variables from Table 4.1.
⇨ For multi-word sequences, consider the variables listed in Section 4.5.1.
⇨ For word integration, matching will vary depending on the research focus.
⇨ For individual words, typical measures are: first fixation duration, single fixation duration and gaze duration.
⇨ For multi-word sequences, establish ROIs that encompass the individual words and the whole sequence. Different measures will be appropriate depending on the size of the ROI.
⇨ For word integration, effects could show up in a range of measures, so output data for a variety of them.
⇨ This varies depending on the target population. Look at the tasks other researchers have used for guidance. For an example of matching non-native speakers see Section 4.3.2 and those with an autism spectrum disorder Section 4.6.2.

</td></tr>
</table>

(cont.)

Final checklist

• What paradigm is most appropriate for your research question, and what do you need to consider for each design?

⇒ There are a range of techniques to consider, each having a set of methodological concerns. For a discussion of a few of them, see the following:
  • authentic texts, see Section 4.3
  • creating texts, see Section 4.4
  • boundary paradigm, see Section 4.5
  • matched, counterbalanced items, see Section 4.6.

Chapter 5

Researching Listening and Multimodal Input

5.1   Introduction

It's clear that reading is a visual task, so it is fairly obvious why eye-tracking is an appropriate methodology to study it. But how (and why) might we use eye-tracking to study listening?

When listening, most of us tend to look at something. In experimental contexts, we can manipulate what participants see so that the visual input has various relationships to what is heard and then explore how these relationships influence looking patterns. In many authentic contexts the auditory and the visual input also have a close connection to each other. In audio storybooks for children, the pictures correspond to the story that children hear. In other situations, like watching a film, the correspondence between the auditory and the visual input might seem less clear – what characters talk about doesn't necessarily relate to the visual environment. Nevertheless, eye-tracking can be informative in a number of ways. For instance, if listeners generally look at someone who is speaking, what happens when subtitles are present on the screen? Eye-tracking can address this question, as well as many others in the context of listening and multimodal input, which will be the focus of this chapter.

The discussion of reading in Chapter 4 showed that there are limits on the eyes' visual acuity. Vision is sharp around the fovea but decreases moving outwards. The eyes move (*saccade*) three to four times a second, with brief pauses (*fixations*), to bring new regions into an area of good visual acuity. The constraints on the visual system apply to viewing static and moving images, just as they did to reading, which means that the basic pattern of saccades and fixations is observed across a wide range of tasks. Importantly, eye-movements in both reading and viewing are thought to be under cognitive control (Luke and Henderson, 2016; Rayner, 2009; but see Vitu, 2003, for an alternative viewpoint). This means that the cognitive processes related to perception, memory and language influence the 'where and when' of eye-movements (Luke and Henderson, 2016). For applied linguists, what is important is that the eyes move quickly in response to the linguistic input and the perceptual features of what is being looked at.

There are some other basic similarities in eye-movement patterns for reading and for viewing images, scenes, etc. (for a discussion see Rayner, 2009). In both, the difficulty of the stimulus influences eye-movements. In reading, when the text becomes more difficult, fixations get longer and saccades get shorter. Equally, in viewing tasks, when a scene is more crowded, cluttered and/or dense, fixations get longer and saccades get shorter. Also in both, the difficulty of the task impacts eye-movements. Thus, there are fewer and shorter fixations in reading for gist compared to reading for comprehension. Similarly, there are fewer and shorter fixations in a visual search task (looking for an item on the screen) than when looking at a scene for a subsequent memory task. Furthermore, just as the eyes don't fixate every word in reading, viewers don't fixate every part of a scene, with fixations primarily landing on informative parts. Importantly, in scene perception the majority of fixations are centred on or are very close to objects and entities rather than on empty space or background (Henderson, 2003). This 'close to' or 'direct' fixation is needed to perceive, identify and encode objects and entities into memory.

There are also striking differences between reading and viewing. In reading, effects of word recognition and integration are evident in clearly defined eye-tracking measures (for a discussion see Sections 3.2 and 4.2). During listening, the influences of a word's characteristics (length, frequency, predictability, etc.) are apparent, but how this is measured is very different. We measure the location and timing of fixations to visual entities and objects relative to audio input. For example, if a spider appears on the screen, we assess whether participants look at it upon hearing it mentioned, and if so, how quickly. Additionally, in reading, words are fairly easy to identify, making it straightforward to explore their processing. In listening, objects and entities are the units of processing (what we measure looks to), but they are not as clearly differentiated as words and they often overlap (Luke and Henderson, 2016), so their properties are not as easily defined or quantified. This can make studying language in conjunction with viewing challenging. Further, in reading the decision of where to look is straightforward: in English we start at the top left-hand corner of a page. When looking at visual input, there is no obvious, clearly defined starting position for the eyes to go to. However, viewers appear to extract the 'gist' of the scene in as little as 40 ms (Castelhano and Henderson, 2008; De Graef, 2005), which helps determine what the informative regions of the scene might be for upcoming fixations. Finally, fixation durations and saccade length are significantly shorter in reading than when looking at images and scenes (Henderson and Hollingworth, 1998; Rayner, 2009).

In viewing while listening, the link between eye-movement patterns and the activation of lexical representations and their semantics was demonstrated in a groundbreaking experiment by Cooper (1974). He combined the presentation of visual images with spoken language. He showed participants a set of objects, such as a tree, dog, lion, zebra, etc. while hearing a story like the following: 'While on a photographic safari in Africa, I managed to get a number of breathtaking shots of the wild terrain . . . when suddenly I noticed a hungry lion slowly moving through the tall grass towards a herd of grazing zebra.' When participants heard the words 'lion' and 'zebra', they were more likely to fixate the corresponding images than other ones. Furthermore, when they heard 'Africa', they were more likely to look at the pictures of a zebra and a lion than a dog. Importantly, fixations were often generated before the end of the word. Thus, Cooper's pioneering research showed that participants initiated saccades to pictures that were named in his stories, as well as to pictures associated with words in the story (e.g. hearing 'Africa' elicits looks to lions and zebras, but not dogs).

Remarkably, it took almost twenty years before this technique was used again in psychology and psycholinguistics. In a set of influential studies in the mid-1990s, Tanenhaus and his colleagues demonstrated the value of a 'look while listening' methodology by replicating patterns of results found with other paradigms and by using it to investigate a wide range of linguistic phenomena (Altmann, 2011a). We will consider some of their key findings in Section 5.2. Tanenhaus and colleagues called the new technique the 'visual-world paradigm', which is how it is commonly referred to in psychology and psycholinguistics. It is important to note that the term is applied to a wide range of tasks where images are presented concurrently with aurally presented language input.

The visual input in these tasks can vary from a limited set of objects/entities to a realistic scene. Objects and entities may move on the screen, be highlighted in certain ways, or even disappear. However, the term is not generally applied to tasks involving the presentation of completely dynamic video material.

The Cooper (1974) study highlights the basic premise of the visual-world paradigm, namely that language can be linked to referents in the real world – or more accurately to situations or images depicted on a screen in experimental situations. In other words, looking behaviour provides an indication of our referential decisions. If we take as an example six-month-old children, who aren't saying words yet, we can show them a display with images of a cat, dog, cow and horse and play them the word 'doggie'. Their eye-movement pattern will tell us what they think the word 'doggie' refers to. If their eyes move to the picture of the dog upon hearing 'doggie', this will tell us that they know that the word refers to the dog and not the cat, cow or horse, even though they cannot verbalise this yet.

In fact, eye-tracking has been used successfully with infants. Tincoff and Jusczyk (1999) showed six-month-olds videos of their mother, father and unfamiliar men and women. When they heard the word 'mommy', they looked at a video of their mother more than at one of their father or an unfamiliar woman; and similarly for the word 'daddy' they looked more at a video of him than of their mother or an unfamiliar man. Thus, eye-tracking demonstrated that pre-verbal infants associate people with a name. In other words, 'mommy' refers to one particular person and 'daddy' to another particular person. However, each of these words has a one-to-one association, meaning that there is a single referent for the word. An important question has been whether six-month-olds also recognise words for referents that they experience as a category of objects. More specifically, do they realise that the word 'feet' refers to their feet, their mother's feet, their father's feet and a stranger's feet, which are all somewhat different? To answer this question, Tincoff and Jusczyk (2012) showed six-month-olds a video of a stranger's feet or hands. The infants looked more at the video of the feet when they heard the word 'feet' and more at the one of the hand when hearing 'hand'.

The two Tincoff and Jusczyk studies demonstrate that eye-tracking provides an indication of our referential decisions – we look at what we think a word refers to. The link between eye-movements and referential decisions is underpinned by a set of assumptions. To understand these assumptions, we first need to look at how eye-tracking while viewing works. In viewing tasks, we measure saccades and fixations to regions of interest (ROIs), which are objects or entities on the screen. In Figure 5.1,

◀ 'Look at the cross. Now click on the spider.'

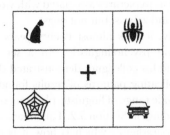

Figure 5.1 Examples of a visual-world paradigm task presented while participants hear linguistic input (◀). In Version A one image is larger than the others while in B the images are well matched on size.

we see examples of the visual-world paradigm, making use of a fairly standard format in which a fixation cross is presented in the centre of the screen and is surrounded by a set of images, which will be our ROIs. Participants could be asked to look at the cross at the beginning of the trial and then would receive the critical linguistic input. They might hear something like 'Look at the cross. Now click on the spider.' If participants fixate the spider upon hearing it named, this indicates that they think the word 'spider' refers to 🕷 and not 🕸, 🔑 or 🚗.

There is a set of assumptions that allow us to conclude that eye-movement patterns indicate something about our referential decisions (discussed in detail in Trueswell, 2008). These assumptions are:

1 Attention is driven by real-world knowledge, the input (images and language), and the goals of the participant (Sections 5.1.1 and 5.1.2).
2 Visual attention is an indication of referential decisions, which means that participants look at what they think is being referred to (Section 5.1.3).
3 In cases where morpho-syntactic processing is important for establishing a referent, referential decisions can tell us about parsing (Section 5.1.4).

5.1.1 Properties of the Stimuli and Real-World Knowledge Attract Visual Attention

Eye-movements provide an overt behavioural manifestation of the allocation of attention in a scene (Henderson, 2003). In basic terms, what we are looking at is what we are attending to. Visual attention is said to be driven by a number of factors, such as saliency, informativeness, interest, unusualness and emotion. Salience is typically defined in terms of visual properties such as contrast, colour, intensity, brightness, spatial frequency, movement, etc. (Rayner, 2009). If we consider this in terms of A and B in Figure 5.1, we see that in A, the picture of the spider is bigger than the other images. Attention could be drawn to it by virtue of its size and not the linguistic input. In B, the images are all the same size, thus attention to the spider upon hearing the word 'spider' could more convincingly be attributed to the linguistic input. When creating visual stimuli, care should be taken to match images on salience, making them equally likely to attract attention. Alternatively, salience may need to be considered as a variable in analyses (for a discussion of including stimuli variables as a covariate in analyses see Section 7.2).

Some research has demonstrated that participants have longer and more fixations to informative, interesting and unusual ROIs in a scene (for a discussion see Hollingworth and Henderson, 2000).[1] We can empirically establish which areas of an image are informative, interesting or unusual in a number of ways. For example, Rensink, O'Regan and Clark (1997) asked participants to describe a series of visual scenes. ROIs that were frequently mentioned were classified 'high interest' and ones that were rarely mentioned or were rarely listed were 'low interest'. Antes (1974) had participants rate regions of a scene for the degree to which they contributed to the overall information carried by the scene. Finally, Hollingworth and Henderson (2000) operationalised informativeness as the semantic consistency/inconsistency of an ROI in a scene (e.g. a fire

---

[1] As Hollingworth and Henderson (2000) point out, the term 'informativeness' is used in different ways in the literature. Some conceptualise it as the extent to which a region contributes to the overall meaning of the scene, while others see it as the level of constancy of a particular ROI in a scene, in other words the 'unusualness'.

hydrant pictured in a living room is incongruent or inconsistent). For our purposes, we need to be aware that such factors can influence eye-movement patterns and we should consider them when designing materials. Thus, we need to ensure that our ROIs are well matched on being informative, interesting and unusual; alternatively, we may need to consider these as factors in our analyses. On the other hand, these might be valuable factors to manipulate. For example, we could look at how 'unusualness' impacts vocabulary learning in children or second language learners. In a scene, since attention would be drawn to the abnormal fire hydrant in a living room, giving it a name might facilitate learning the word compared to when it is in a normal street scene and the object doesn't 'pop out'.

It is not just the unusualness of the objects/entities that drives attention. As was mentioned in Section 1.1, in visual search tasks, where participants are asked to find a particular object in a scene, attention is driven by real-world knowledge (Neider and Zelinksy, 2006). Thus, if participants are presented with a scene containing a sky and a road, when they are asked to look for a jeep their fixations are largely constrained to the road. Similarly, if they are asked to locate a hot air balloon they primarily look in the sky. Thus, when designing visual material, it is important to consider whether particular objects are depicted in their typical location, as this influences looking patterns.

A somewhat controversial view is that attention is quickly drawn to emotional stimuli. This is underpinned by the belief that being able to quickly identify objects/entities with high emotional value, like a 'scary' potentially poisonous snake, is important for survival (for a discussion see Acunzo and Henderson, 2011). Depending on the task and materials, some researchers have found increased early fixations, as well as longer overall fixations, to emotional stimuli (Nummenmaa, Hyönä and Calvo, 2006, 2009). In contrast, others have not found a difference in the first fixation time for emotional compared to neutral images, while they have found overall longer fixations to emotional stimuli (Acunzo and Henderson, 2011). Much like the other variables discussed in this section, it is important to keep in mind that emotional images may attract attention. Thus, it is another variable that may need to be controlled or considered in an analysis, or it could also serve as an interesting variable to manipulate.

We can see that it is important to take into account the visual properties of the individual elements presented on a screen. Another element of the visual environment is the display as a whole, which was discussed in more detail in Chapter 3. In brief, we tend to scan a screen with images from left to right (for languages where reading is from left to right), so it is important to counterbalance the location of a 'target' object. Further, we need to ensure that target objects appear in different locations on the screen.

Another important property of the display is the number of objects and entities it contains. For example, in Figure 5.1 the visual input only contains four objects. Clearly, this presents a much more restricted visual environment than an actual physical location or space. This is referred to as the 'close set problem' (Tanenhaus and Trueswell, 2006). Having a small set of visual alternatives results in different eye-movement patterns from when there is a large set. Because our visual array in Figure 5.1 only has four objects, locating the spider upon hearing the word 'spider' is quite easy. What if we had a scene with 100 objects? Finding the spider among all of the objects would be much more challenging. What typically happens is that the eyes fixate areas where we think that spiders might be located (webs, dusty corners, etc.), although they may not land on the spider itself. Thus, relevant ROIs would good 'spidery' locations, as well as the spider itself.

If the visual-world paradigm does not reflect a natural physical environment, we might ask ourselves if it has any value to applied linguistics research. Importantly, there are a number of good defences of the use of limited visual arrays. Altmann (2011a) points out that most people restrict themselves to talking about a few entities in their surroundings. Similarly, most people only look at a limited number of objects in their visual environment. This means that while the real world has many more objects/entities than a screen in an experiment, most of the time we only attend and refer to a limited number of them. Thus, the visual-world paradigm may be more natural than it appears. Furthermore, applied linguists are likely to use authentic materials. For example, we might present children with audiobooks, which have an audio recording of the text, as well as images. Pictures in storybooks are very unlikely to contain lots of objects and entities; more likely they will depict a few that are relevant to the storyline. This means that we do encounter situations that have limited sets of images with concurrent linguistic input.

5.1.2 The Goals of the Task Guide Visual Attention

Language mediation of eye-movements in listening is unconscious in the same way that it is in reading (Altmann, 2011a). More precisely, in Figure 5.1 the movement of our eyes to the picture of the spider upon hearing 'spider' is not under our conscious control. However, just because eye-movements are unconscious does not mean that participants are not 'strategic'. As the second part of the first linking assumption tells us, attention is in part driven by a participant's goals. This means that the task we set for our participants can influence their eye-movement patterns, making it important to consider how different tasks might generalise to various real-world communicative situations.

Experiments making use of the visual-world paradigm often require participants to click on objects (Altmann, 2011a). The task could be like the one depicted in Figure 5.1, in which participants are overtly told to click on a particular object. Alternatively, there might be a global task which involves clicking on certain types of images. In such cases, what needs to be clicked on is not explicitly spelled out in the language input for individual trials. At the outset of a study, participants could be told something along the lines of 'You will hear a set of sentences in which an object is being acted upon by someone or something else. Click on the object that is being acted upon.' Then they would hear linguistic input like 'The spider sat on the web.' Participants should click on the web because it is the object that is being acted upon by the spider. This method allows us to present listeners with more 'natural' sentences than studies where participants are directly told to click on one thing or another. Sometimes in addition to clicking on objects, participants might be asked to move them. Thus, in the context of Figure 5.1, a participant might be asked to 'Pick up the spider and move it to the web.'

Notably, some of the earliest eye-tracking studies involved monitoring eye-movements to actual physical objects that were placed in front of participants. This technique is still used with small children. Here participants are asked to grab and/or move actual objects. Crucially, in all of these paradigms, the eye-movements help participants achieve the clicking, moving or grabbing task; to accurately perform the task, participants need to decide what they are being asked to click on – in other words, determine the referent.

Another common paradigm is the sentence–picture verification task. In this type of study, participants are shown a scene while they listen to linguistic input and are asked to indicate whether the picture and the sentence 'match'. For example, participants would be shown either a picture of a spider on a web or of a spider on a window while hearing the sentence 'The spider was waiting on the web to catch an unsuspecting insect.' If they had seen a picture of a spider on a web, they would respond 'yes', that the picture and the sentence matched; if they saw a spider on a window, they would say 'no'. This type of task does not involve targeted mouse clicks or hand movements, but it does require a visual search of the pictured objects and entities. In all of these kinds of studies, the likelihood of fixating the target objects is very high (Altmann, 2011a). However, we cannot be sure that the same eye-movement patterns would occur without the need to verify a sentence–picture match, or to click on, move or grab something. Thus, there is a concern that these tasks do not reflect natural language comprehension.

To allay such fears, we can also make use of 'look-and-listen' or 'passive-listening' tasks. Here participants are simply given occasional comprehension questions that relate to the images they see and/or the sentences they hear. Because in our everyday lives we don't generally click on or touch entities and objects when we hear about them, look-and-listen and passive-listening tasks are much more natural. The disadvantage of such tasks is that the likelihood of fixating the various images on the screen can be quite low, and fixation patterns may dynamically rise and fall as various objects compete for attention (Altmann, 2011a). Importantly, as Altmann (2011a) points out, all tasks, even the more natural ones, have a strategic element to them. Thus, looking patterns can vary from participant to participant, or even for a single participant over the course of an experiment. At one extreme we might have participants who try to memorise each scene and its corresponding linguistic input, while at the other extreme we might have participants who simply maintain a central fixation without looking at the images on the screen and without trying to establish a relationship between them and the linguistic input. Despite this potentially highly variable behaviour, consistent eye-movement patterns are found across a range of tasks that are more and less natural.

A final paradigm that is worth mentioning is the 'blank-screen' task. Here participants are shown visual input like that depicted in Figure 5.1. The images are then removed and replaced by a blank screen. Once the blank screen appears participants might hear something like 'The spider is poisonous.' Even though the screen is blank, the eyes move to where the mentioned object had appeared (Altmann, 2004). In another version of the paradigm, participants could be presented with a sentence like the following during the blank-screen phase: 'The spider crawled onto its web.' They would hear a subsequent sentence along the lines of 'The spider lay in wait for its next meal.' In this case, the eyes don't go to where the spider had appeared in the image, but to where the language tell us it is now – on the web. This indicates that our attention is not simply drawn to the objects and the locations where we saw them appear, but to where we actually understand them to be (Altmann and Kamide, 2009).

In sum, paradigms that require participants to click on, grab or move objects force them to make referential decisions. Similarly, for sentence–picture verification, participants need to engage with the visual input and establish reference to complete the task. It is unsurprising that with such paradigms we see more looks to referents than when they are mentioned in look-and-listen and passive-listening tasks. Crucially, this means that in more passive tasks, we may need more items and participants to find statistically significant results.

5.1.3 Visual Attention Indicates Referential Decisions

We have discussed some of the visual properties and task demands that influence attention. Now we will consider in more detail the second part of the linking assumption – namely that listeners attend to what they think the linguistic input refers to. This means that word recognition and integration causes participants to shift their attention to particular objects and entities depicted on the screen. More specifically, the name of a picture determines the probability that a participant will shift attention to that picture, and therefore make a saccade to it (Tanenhaus and Trueswell, 2006). To assess attention in viewing, we measure when listeners launch a saccade and where they fixate as an utterance unfolds.

While the nature of a task and other variables can influence how long it takes to plan and launch a saccade, most researchers assume that eye-movements that were launched within 200 ms of a word's onset have been influenced by that word (Altmann, 2011a). In practical terms, this means that when participants hear instructions such as 'click on the spider', we expect them to launch eye-movements to the spider within 200 ms of the start of the word 'spider'. We consider the critical word's onset to be time point zero, and then at successive time points or intervals we can calculate the percentage of fixations to the various ROIs. Looking at Figure 5.1, we could calculate the percentage of looks to the spider, the web, the cat and the car at 50 ms intervals after the start of the word. We would expect to see an effect emerge at around 200 ms, such that there should begin to be more looks to the spider than the web, the car or the cat. Importantly, for each experimental item we need to establish the precise onset of this critical word. Thus, if 'spider' occurs at 3 sec 42 ms into the sound file, this would be where we start calculating percentage of looks. However, for another item the critical word might begin at 3 sec 35 ms, and therefore this should be time point zero for it.

In most cases, the onset of a word is where the critical region of analysis begins; however, see Section 7.2.4 for some additional considerations. For some research questions it might be reasonable to establish something else as our starting point. For example, if our screen contains a cat and a caterpillar and listeners hear instructions like 'click on the caterpillar', it might be interesting to look at what happens at the point that the words 'cat' and 'caterpillar' sound different. Thus, our time point zero could be when the /ə/ occurs. Studies on word recognition normally use the word onset, a word uniqueness point (e.g. the /ə/ in 'caterpillar') or the word offset as the starting point of analysis and then look at the fixations and/or saccades at certain intervals after that point. In studies on sentence processing, the time interval of interest is driven by predictions about what part of the sentence is of theoretical relevance.

Unlike in reading where there is widespread agreement about what eye-tracking measures to look at and where effects are likely to show up, the situation for analysing looking patterns to images is much more complex. Figure 5.2 exemplifies two ways of presenting and analysing data – one based on fixations (A) and the other on saccades (B). While it is fairly standard to look at percentage of fixations, as in A, not everyone agrees with this practice. Some researchers don't analyse fixations but instead measure the onset of a saccade towards an ROI, or they calculate the percentage of trials in which a saccade to the ROIs was launched within a specified time interval, as in B. In Figure 5.2, we see that participants were fairly equally likely to fixate each of the ROIs (spider, web, cat and car) when they heard 'click on the . . .', and they were more likely to fixate the spider upon hearing the word 'spider'. Importantly, what we see in A is that the increase in looks to the spider emerges at around 200 ms of the onset of the word. It is important to note that both

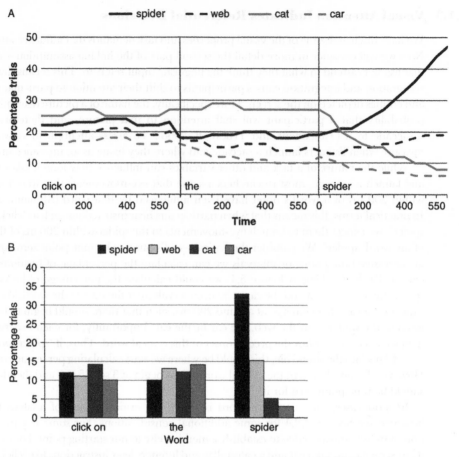

Figure 5.2 Two ways of representing eye-tracking data for visual ROIs. Example A presents the percentage of trials with *fixations* to the ROIs across time, which is resynchronised at the onset of each word. Example B shows the percentage of trials with *saccades* launched during each word towards the ROIs. Note that generally, these will not add up to 100 per cent, as participants will sometimes look to regions of the screen that have not been set as ROIs.

A and B are illustrations of the data. To establish that fixations and/or saccades are different for the different objects we would need to assess this statistically (see Section 7.2 for a discussion of this). Furthermore, there are a variety of different ways to depict and analyse data, such as calculating percentage of fixations or saccades, log likelihood or odds ratios, growth curves, etc. Altmann (2011a) provides a good overview of various ways of examining eye-movements to visual input and discusses the advantages and disadvantages of them.

Unfortunately, it is not just the eye-tracking measures that are controversial when analysing looks to visual scenes. There are also questions about how precise the spatial regions of analysis should be. When a scene is presented concurrently with linguistic input, the majority of fixations will land within the external boundary of the object (Altmann, 2011a). Thus, we can set the ROI's boundary as the object's actual boundary, as in A in Figure 5.3. Other researchers draw a rectangle around the object to demarcate the ROI, as in B, simply because this is easier to do using the software available with eye-tracking

A
B

Figure 5.3 Depiction of boundaries for visual ROIs (in grey), with a precise boundary that matches the external boundary of the object in A and a larger boundary that extends beyond the bounds of the object in B.

systems. Defining an ROI that extends beyond the exact boundary of the object will change the absolute number of fixations that 'count' as landing on the object; however, the overall pattern across conditions will essentially be unchanged (Altmann, 2011a). Even in the blank-screen paradigm, drawing rectangles around the ROIs, rather than defining precise ROIs, increases the number of looks that count as falling within the ROI, but does not change the overall pattern of results (Altmann, 2011a).

To sum up, hearing language with concurrent visual input (or just after a scene has been removed) can tell us about people's referential decisions. More precisely, people look at what they think a word refers to. However, there are a number of different considerations in terms of how we define ROIs and then analyse looking patterns to them. These concerns aside, this paradigm can serve as a valuable tool for applied linguists. For example, infants and children learning their first language, learners of a second language, anomic aphasic patients, etc. may not be able to use the word 'spider' or label an image of one. This might lead us to conclude that they do not 'know' the word. Importantly, if they have increased looks to the spider upon hearing its name, their eye-movements would indicate that while they cannot 'use' the word, they have an idea of what it refers to. Indeed, Tanenhaus (2007b) highlights how important the paradigm has been in studying language processing in pre-literate children.

5.1.4 Referential Decisions Can Tell Us about Parsing

As we have seen thus far, fixations give us insight into listeners' current interpretation of the speech input. Thus far, the discussion has focused on what eye-movement patterns tell us about what people think a word refers to. They can also tell us about a participant's syntactic parsing decisions. This can most easily be understood in terms of the example in Figure 5.4, which is loosely based on a study by Spivey and colleagues (2002). In both Versions A and B there are four objects: A = circle, cat, spider on a circle and a web; and B = circle, spider on a triangle, spider on a circle and a web. Participants would listen to a sentence like 'Put the spider on the circle on the web'. In A, where there is only one spider, upon hearing the word 'spider' there are more looks to it than the other objects. In B, which has two spiders, hearing 'spider' leads to equivalent fixations to the two spiders, and more to both of them than to the circle or the web. Crucially, at the point in the sentence where participants have heard 'put the spider on the circle', the phrase can be interpreted in different ways. First, 'the circle' could modify the spider – so the one that's on the circle. Alternatively, it could be a goal, such that participants should put the spider onto the circle. Interestingly, we see that how participants interpret 'the circle' changes depending on the visual context. In A, which only has one spider, they treat 'the circle' as a goal, and upon hearing the word 'circle' fixate the empty circle more. In B, where there are two spiders, 'the circle' is interpreted as a modifier telling them which spider needs to

◀ 'Put the spider on the circle on the web.'

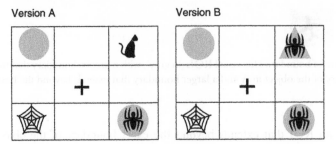

Version A   Version B

Figure 5.4 Example of audio (◀) and visual stimuli to examine syntactic parsing choices.

be 'put', as evidenced by increased looks to the spider that's on the circle compared to the empty circle or the spider on the triangle.

The example in Figure 5.4 shows us that eye-tracking with concurrent visual and spoken input can tell us about how participants syntactically parse a sentence. This is important because syntactic processing has primarily been studied with reading tasks, which will not be suitable for some populations. The kind of study we have discussed here is particularly useful for research with pre-literate children or various adult populations for whom reading may be more laborious.

5.2   What Has Been Studied?

In the first two sections of Chapter 4 we saw that tracking eye-movements while reading has told us a lot about the factors that influence word recognition and integration (e.g. frequency, length, predictability). Many of these same factors have been explored in relation to spoken language comprehension by monitoring eye-movements to images with concurrent auditory input. Much as with reading, there is a large literature on this; our discussion will only briefly touch upon some key findings. There are some excellent review chapters that provide a detailed overview of eye-tracking with spoken language (see Altmann, 2011a; Tanenhaus, 2007b; Tanenhaus and Trueswell, 2006).

In Chapter 4, we saw that for reading there are very early effects of orthographic and phonological decoding, word frequency and neighbourhood size (the number of words that differ in only one letter or sound). Spoken word comprehension has also demonstrated a sensitivity to these factors. First, eye-movements are closely time-locked to the unfolding acoustic signal and are influenced by the phonetic, phonological and prosodic properties of what we hear (Magnuson et al., 2003; McMurray, Tanenhaus and Aslin, 2002; Salverda, Dahan and McQueen, 2003; Salverda et al., 2007). For example, if listeners hear 'click on the /k/ . . .' in the context of Figure 5.1, they will look more at the cat and the car than the spider and the web, because the former both start with the /k/ sound. However, looks to the cat and car will quickly diverge based on coarticulation information of the subsequent vowel on the preceding consonant. More precisely, the /k/ in 'cat' and 'car' do not sound identical, and this information is used to direct looks to the appropriate referent very quickly. Second, there are more and longer fixations to images depicting high-frequency words than low-frequency ones (Dahan, Magnuson and Tanenhaus, 2001). Third, neighbourhood size (whether a word has many or few words that differ in one sound) influences word activation and therefore eye-movement patterns to its referent depicted on the screen (Magnuson et al., 2007). Thus, frequency and neighbourhood size speed activation of a word that has been heard, such that eye-movements to its referent appear sooner in the eye-tracking record.

Semantics, or word meaning, also influences eye-movements, such that hearing a word increases looks to that word, but also to words that are related to it. For example, hearing the word 'lock' leads to increased looks to a picture of a lock and also to a picture of the related word 'key' (Yee and Sedivy, 2001). This means that in Figure 5.1, when listeners hear the word 'spider', we would expect increased fixations to the depicted spider, but also to the pictured web because webs are semantically related to spiders. This is what we see in our hypothetical dataset depicted in Figure 5.2 – upon hearing 'spider' there is an increase in fixations on it and saccades to it, but we also see a rise in fixations and saccades to the web. Interestingly, the degree of conceptual overlap (assessed by ratings) but not the degree of shape overlap (also assessed by ratings) seems to drive this effect. In other words, the more semantically related the unmentioned object is to the mentioned one, the more looks there are to it (Huettig and Altmann, 2005). More specifically, there is increased attention to conceptually related items that is proportional to the degree of conceptual overlap. This could potentially provide a powerful tool for assessing semantic relations in populations like children and non-native speakers, as their eye-movements would provide us with an online measure of what items they find semantically related and potentially how strong the relationship is (at least relative to other semantic relationships presented in the study).

In Chapter 4, we saw that the debate about semantic activation in reading largely surrounds words that have multiple meanings (e.g. 'bat'). The visual-world paradigm has also been used to explore meaning activation for such words. Research has demonstrated that hearing the word 'bat' increases looks to both a picture of the winged animal and to a baseball bat (Meyer et al., 2007). Further, in the discussion of reading we saw that fixation times were dependent on the frequency of the two meanings of the ambiguous word and on how biasing the context was. A fairly similar pattern of results has been found for words like 'bat' in listening studies, such that there were increased looks to a picture depicting a high-frequency meaning compared to a low-frequency one (Chen and Boland, 2008). Interestingly, Chen and Boland (2008) also found that a context biasing the less frequent meaning increased looks to a picture related to it and decreased looks to a picture related to the more dominant meaning, which does not mirror the findings from reading.

Furthermore, in our discussion of reading we saw that predictability has a strong influence on eye-movements. In general, reading more predictable words (with predictability calculated in various ways) leads to shorter fixation times and more skipping. In listening, predictability has been studied in regard to a number of phenomena and here we look at a few examples of this. We have already seen one example of the effect of predictability in the introduction to the visual-world paradigm in Section 1.2, which we will consider again here. Altmann and Kamide (1999) presented participants with a picture of a boy and four objects, only one of which was edible (ball, car, train set and cake; Figure 5.5). Participants heard a sentence like 'The boy will eat ...'. Upon hearing 'eat' participants looked more at the edible object, the cake, than the other objects on the screen. In other words, they predicted that the upcoming word would be 'cake'. In a similar study, Sussman and Sedivy (2003) showed participants a visual array containing a milk carton, a girl eating cereal, a spider and a shoe while they played them sentences like 'What did Jodie squash the spider with?' They found that at the verb 'squash' participants anticipated the object on the screen that was 'squashable', and there were

◀ 'The boy will eat the cake.'

Figure 5.5 Example of the visual-world paradigm manipulating the predictability of objects. One of the objects, in this case the cake, was more predictable based on the auditory input.

more looks to the spider. Importantly, at the noun 'spider', eye-movements revealed that participants anticipated that a shoe had done the squashing and there were increased looks to it. Taken together, studies like these show that listeners predict upcoming words, which is revealed by their eye-movements.

In a similar vein, participants make predictions about what syntactic structure might be used based on what has recently occurred, which is often called 'syntactic priming' in the psycholinguistic literature. An example of this comes from a verb like 'give', which can take a double object or a prepositional object. We can say 'the boy will give the girl the doll' (double object) or 'the boy will give the doll to the girl' (prepositional object). Eye-tracking shows us that if someone has just heard a double object construction, they anticipate that the structure will be reused. Thus, when we show participants a scene containing a boy, a girl, a doll and a car, and play them a narrative like 'The boy and the girl are both generous. The boy will give the girl the doll. And the girl will give . . .', after the second occurrence of 'give', participants could expect either 'boy' or 'car' to come next. However, because they just heard a double object construction, there are increased looks to the boy. Thus, listeners' eye-movement patterns show us that they anticipated one syntactic construction over another (Arai, van Gompel and Scheepers, 2007; Thothathiri and Snedeker, 2008).

As the previous examples indicate, eye-tracking can tell us about syntactic parsing of auditory sentences and the kinds of syntactic predictions listeners make. Thinking back to our discussion of Figure 5.4, we saw that eye-tracking can also tell us about how listeners interpret syntactically ambiguous sentences. Thus, in a sentence like 'Put the spider on the circle on the web,' does 'the circle' modify which spider (the one on the circle vs the one on the triangle) or specify a location where the spider should be put? By monitoring participants' eye-movements we can assess their interpretation of this syntactically ambiguous phrase. In addition, eye-tracking has also been used to investigate how listeners resolve pronouns. For example, Arnold and colleagues (2000) showed participants a scene containing Donald Duck carrying a mailbag and either Mickey Mouse or Minnie Mouse on the opposite side of a screen while they heard sentences like 'Donald is bringing some mail to Mickey/Minnie while a violent storm is beginning. He's carrying an umbrella.' When Minnie is the second entity in the picture, it is clear that the 'he' carrying the umbrella is Donald, as he is the only male referent depicted on the screen and therefore the only antecedent for the male pronoun. In these cases, there are more looks to Donald. In the instances where Mickey is in the image, 'he' is ambiguous between Donald and Mickey, as they are both potential male referents for the male pronoun. Because Donald was mentioned first, he appears to be the most accessible referent and there are more fixations to him than to Mickey. In this way, eye-tracking can tell us something about how listeners assign referents to pronouns.

It is important to note that researchers have carried out a number of studies similar to those considered above with children (for a discussion see Trueswell, 2008). As mentioned previously in this chapter, tracking eye-movements to images with concurrent linguistic input is ideal for children. It can tell us a lot about processing in a population that for the most part cannot take part in reading experiments and that does not have the metalinguistic skills to reflect on their performance in the same way that adults can. In addition, there is a considerable literature using the visual-world paradigm to study auditory comprehension in non-native speakers (for a discussion see van Hell and Tanner, 2012). The studies investigating non-natives explore many of the same issues that have been discussed in this section. In Chapters 1 and 3, we looked at one such study. We saw that Chambers and Cooke (2009) analysed the looking patterns of native English speakers who were proficient in French to pictures of a chicken, a pool and two distractors (strawberry, boot) when they heard sentences like 'Marie va décrire/nourir la poule' [Marie will describe/feed the chicken], which contained a homophone (French 'poule' [chicken] sounds like the English word 'pool'). In the unbiased context ('describe the chicken'), there were increased looks to the picture of the pool that were all but eliminated in the biased context ('feed the chicken'). Thus, much like monolinguals in one language, we see that bilinguals activate all the words that correspond to the auditory input, even when they come from the language that is not currently being used. However, this activation is mediated by the biasing context.

Further, the visual-world paradigm is increasingly being used for studies with clinical populations. This is largely because it is fairly undemanding task-wise and does not require metalinguistic reflection or decision-making, and at the same time it taps into language skills that listeners use every day (Farris-Trimble and McMurray, 2013). Moreover, as the discussion in this section demonstrates, it is sensitive to subtle linguistic phenomena. Importantly, a study by Farris-Trimble and McMurray (2013) demonstrates that the visual-world paradigm is sensitive enough to measure group differences, as well as being stable enough to serve as a measure of individual differences. Thus, with appropriate benchmarking, certain aspects of fixation and saccade patterns could be related to differences in language ability, which may be relevant for clinical diagnostics. Crucially, this would also be true for populations such as children and non-native speakers.

Notably, the visual-world paradigm has been used to study more than listening; it has been employed in language production and dialogue tasks, as well as being used to investigate perspective-taking (for a discussion see Altmann, 2011a; Griffin, 2004). While we will not go into such studies here, in general they involve presenting participants with a visual scene and concurrent linguistic input, and require them to produce linguistic output themselves. All of this is done while their eye-movements are monitored. Many of these studies have a structure that is similar to the ones discussed here. For example, we could look at language production and syntactic priming for verbs that accept double and prepositional object alternations. Thus, participants would see a scene with a boy, a girl, a doll and a car. They would hear 'The boy and the girl are both generous. The boy will give the girl the doll.' They would then be given the prompt 'girl' and be asked to produce a sentence about her. We would be interested in whether participants produced 'The girl will give the boy the car,' which would be consistent in structure with what was just heard, or instead produced the other structure, 'The girl will give the car to the boy.' Of particular interest would be eye-movements to the car and the boy and how looking patterns might tell us something about what structure is being planned and ultimately produced.

5.2.1 Factors to Consider When Designing Visual Stimuli

Having briefly looked at some of the factors that have been shown to influence auditory comprehension, in order to find effects like those outlined above, we need to carefully consider the design of our stimuli. In Section 5.1 we discussed some of the properties that we should take into account when designing images (e.g. their salience, unusualness). However, there are a number of other things to bear in mind. A more specific example will help illustrate this. At the beginning of this section we saw that when listeners hear 'click on the /k/ ...' in the context of Figure 5.1, they would mainly fixate the picture of the cat and the car because they both begin with the sound /k/. Similarly, we would expect that when listeners hear 'click on the /ple^j/ ...' while looking at Figure 5.6 they would look at the picture of the plate and the plane, because both start with the sound /ple^j/; however, this would only be the prediction if listeners actually call the image in the upper left-hand corner a 'plane'. If instead they call it an 'aeroplane', upon hearing /ple^j/..., most of the fixations will be to the plate. Thus, our prediction might not be borne out simply because people do not refer to the stimuli in the way that we think they do. Similarly, in Figure 5.6, in the row below the fixation cross, would people call the first image a 'phone' or 'telephone'? The second image is clearly a phone-like

Figure 5.6 Depiction of two issues to consider for visual stimuli: (1) agreement about what images are called (e.g. plane/aeroplane, phone/telephone/mobile phone/cell phone); and (2) how easily identifiable the images are (e.g. images in the column to the left of the fixation cross).

device, but is it a phone/telephone/mobile phone/cell phone? Finally, looking at the column to the left of the fixation cross, are we even sure about what is being depicted? Is the top image supposed to be a train, a subway, a tunnel, etc.? The bottom picture looks like a train, but is it? And what would participants call these pictures? It is important to keep in mind when designing stimuli that when an object is named in the auditory input, fixations occur earlier when pictures are more easily recognisable than when pictures are less easily recognised. Thus, it is important to make sure that the critical objects and entities in our visual scenes can be recognised equally well, and that there is agreement about what they are called.

As the discussion of Figure 5.6 highlights, generally studies depend on participants being able to identify the objects – in other words, they are unambiguously one thing (e.g. a tunnel and not a subway). Also, many studies hinge on participants calling the identifiable object by a particular name. When we are designing our own stimuli, we can ensure that these two criteria are met in different ways. We can use pictures that have been extensively normed – in other words, tested or rated by participants for various factors, like name agreement and familiarity. For example, the Snodgrass and Vanderwart (1980) images are a set of black and white line drawings that have been normed for a number of properties.[2] Rossion and Pourtois (2004) updated these images by adding texture, surface details and colour, and renormed them. For each picture, they provide information about name agreement, or how many people called an image by a particular name (e.g. what percentage of people called an image a 'plane' vs 'aeroplane'). They also measured how quickly people could initiate saying the word (referred to as naming latency). Further, each of the images was rated for familiarity (how usual or unusual the object is in your realm of experience), visual complexity (the amount of detail or intricacy in the picture), agreement between pictures and mental images (participants were shown the name of the object, asked to imagine it, then shown the drawing and asked to rate how well the picture agreed with their mental image), and colour diagnosticity (on a scale ranging from the object could be in any other colour equally well, to the object appears only in the depicted colour in real life). Recently, a new database has been developed, MultiPic (www.bcbl.eu/databases/multipic), which provides a freely available set of 750 coloured pictures of concrete concepts. The pictures have been normed for name agreement and visual complexity in six different European languages (British English, Spanish, French, Dutch, Italian and German).

Alternatively, we can create or draw our own stimuli. Importantly, if we make our stimuli we will want to do some norming to ensure that they are well designed. At a minimum, we will want to make sure that our images are recognisable and referred to by the same word by participants using a picture naming task. Depending on any additional concerns, we may want to conduct other norming studies, along the lines of what Rossion and Pourtois (2004) did. When we use existing stimuli like audio storybooks or videos, we do not have the luxury of selecting or creating images that are equally identifiable, have an agreed name, are equally visually salient, etc. However, much like when we draw our own stimuli, we can norm images from a storybook page or images from different frames of a video. Again, minimally, we may need to evaluate whether our ROIs are recognisable and referred to by the same word by participants using a naming task.

---

[2] The Snodgrass and Vandewart pictures are copyright-protected. In order to use them in a study and/or in a publication, it is necessary to obtain a license. Even clip-art freely available on the web may be copyright-protected and therefore we may require permission to use and/or publish it.

We can conduct other norming studies if there are additional concerns about any of the visual images. We then can use this data as a variable in subsequent analysis of our ROIs.

5.2.2 Factors to Consider When Designing Audio Stimuli

Another important concern regarding the creation of stimuli is the audio files that participants hear (see Section 3.1.2). Unless we are interested in the influence of background noise, recordings should be made in a quiet environment. Many experimenters use a soundproof booth or room for recording, but generally a quiet room will suffice. When making recordings, we should try to speak at the same volume and maintain a fixed distance to the microphone, as movements will make stimuli sound louder or softer. Audio editing software (e.g. Praat, freely available from www.praat.org; Boersma and Weenink, 2016) can be used to normalise volume across stimuli. In general, intonation should have a broad focus so that there is no emphasis on any specific word. In particular, we should avoid emphasis on critical experimental words and on the words around them, unless we can ensure that this emphasis is the same across all stimuli. Because the person doing the recording may unintentionally add focus, audio files can be edited to remove intonational cues. As journals may require the sampling rate of recordings to be reported (e.g. 48 kHz, 16 kHz), it is important to note what the sampling rate is for our stimuli. In many cases the duration of a certain part of the stimuli will need to be edited for length. For example, in instructions like 'click on the . . .', we may want to ensure that 'the' is the same length in all of the audio files. Alternatively, we may want to use a single version of the phrase 'click on the' and simply splice in the target word for each of the items. Editing software will allow us to do both of these.

For pre-existing videos, there is less concern about the quality of the recordings themselves, as during production they will already have been edited. For example, volume would generally already be normalised. However, for such materials we cannot control whether certain critical words have intonational focus while others do not. We can use audio software to analyse various acoustic properties of the speech stream and add them as a variable in our analysis. Thus, we could assess whether particular words in a video receive intonational focus and then determine whether they are more likely to be learned by children or non-native speakers than words that do not have intonational focus. Additionally, we cannot control the linguistic input for videos we have not created ourselves – for example the level of difficulty of words in a film. Therefore, we will need to carefully consider potential videos before deciding to use them. It would be advisable to check the frequency of the words and evaluate whether they are likely to be at an appropriate level for our participants.

5.3 Visual-World Paradigm with Objects and Scenes

We have seen examples of the visual-world paradigm with sets of objects when they have been placed on a grid and when they have appeared in more 'natural' scenes. Importantly, the visual presentation in such studies can be modified in a number of ways. In the examples we have considered, when objects did not appear in a scene, they were presented on a grid. However, in some studies there is no visible grid. For example, participants might be presented with objects in different positions on the screen (e.g. right- and left-hand sides) without any visible division of the objects.

Most of the studies we have looked at have presented fairly 'static' images. However, in some cases the pictured objects could be 'picked up' and moved on the screen. For example, in Figure 5.1 participants could be asked to 'put the spider on the web'. Importantly, in the visual-world paradigm the objects and entities depicted on the screen can also be more 'dynamic' during the actual audio presentation, such as by flashing or receiving highlighting or even moving across the screen. These kinds of dynamic elements will help to capture participants' attention. For example, in the Tincoff and Jusczyk (2012) study discussed at the beginning of this chapter, infants were shown short (10 sec) video clips. In the clips a single hand or two feet slowly moved across a dark background. Importantly, the use of video clips, instead of static images, may better capture and maintain the infants' attention.

Shukla, White and Aslin (2011) showed six-month-olds an image with a set of three objects. One of the objects (e.g. a ball) pulsed on the screen to grab the infants' attention. It then changed size and rolled across the screen. During this period the infants heard a nonsense word like /mu.ra/ embedded in a longer string of speech. Finally, all three objects pulsed on the screen to capture the infants' attention. The researchers then played the nonsense word and monitored the infants' looks to the three objects to see if they looked more at the 'correct' object (which the infants did) – in this case the ball that had pulsed and rolled. These studies provide a few examples of attention-grabbing devices that can be used in conjunction with the presentation of otherwise fairly static images. Other kinds of manipulations are possible and can be considered when designing stimuli.

In sum, the visual-world paradigm can make use of static, or somewhat dynamic, images that appear with/without a grid, that appear in more naturalistic scenes, or that occur in short video clips. When creating these kinds of stimuli, there are two major concerns: (1) controlling and matching the images in the display; and (2) controlling and matching the audio input. This will be the primary focus of the following discussion.

5.3.1 Contextualising an Example Visual-World Study

In this section, we are going to look at a study by Morales and colleagues (2016) that explored how the grammatical gender (nouns being classed as male or female) influenced looking patterns in non-native speakers. Of particular interest was how and when having a different gender in the first language influenced processing in a second language. To explore this question, Morales et al. presented participants with pairs of pictures that either had the same or different genders in their two languages, and asked them to click on one of the two objects.

In two experiments, Morales et al. monitored the eye-movements of native Italian speakers who were proficient in Spanish to two pictured objects on a screen. (They also carried out a third experiment on native Spanish speakers as a control study. We will not discuss that here.) Participants heard the Spanish instructions 'encuentra el/la ...' (find the ...) and were asked to click on the named object via a mouse press. The critical manipulation in the study was the grammatical gender of the pictured objects. The three conditions in their second experiment are depicted in Table 5.1: (a) both members of the pair had the same gender in both Spanish and Italian; (b) both members of the pair had the same gender in Spanish, but different ones in Italian, meaning one word had a mismatching gender across the two languages; or (c) both members of the pair had different genders in both languages, but the genders were the same across Spanish and Italian.

In Spanish, the article ('el'/'la') needs to match in gender with the following noun. In Conditions A and B, because the gender of the objects is the same in Spanish, the article does not point to one potential referent over another. In terms of the examples in the table,

Table 5.1 Illustration of the grammatical gender manipulation in Experiment 2 in Morales et al. (2016). Of particular interest is the potential difference in eye-movements for Condition B where one of the nouns does not have the same gender in the first (Italian) and second (Spanish) languages.

	Condition A Same genders in Italian Same genders in Spanish		Condition B Different genders in Italian Same genders in Spanish		Condition C Different genders in Italian Different genders in Spanish	
Picture of:	*pot*	*butterfly*	*pillow*	*sheep*	*ladle*	*scarf*
Italian	pentola	farfalle	cuscino	pecora	mestolo	sciarpa
	(fem)	(fem)	(masc)	(fem)	(masc)	(fem)
Spanish	olla	mariposa	almohada	oveja	cazo	bufanda
	(fem)	(fem)	(fem)	(fem)	(masc)	(fem)

all would be preceded by 'encuentra la . . .', which could equally well be followed by 'olla/mariposa/almohada/oveja'. In contrast, in Condition C, the article clearly distinguishes which of the pictured objects will be mentioned. Thus, if listeners hear 'encuentra el . . .', the article is masculine and must be followed by a masculine noun, which is 'cazo'. Alternatively, hearing 'encuentra la . . .' provides a clear signal that the noun will be feminine, in other words it can only be 'bufanda'. Morales et al. expected that when the article gave a clear gender cue about the upcoming referent there would be more and earlier looks to the gender-matching referent (el-cazo; la-bufanda). In Condition A, they predicted no difference in looks to the pot and butterfly upon hearing the article, because it does not differentiate between the referents. In Condition B, while the feminine article does not predict one object over the other, if the participants are influenced by gender information from Italian, there will be fewer looks to the pillow, which would not follow a feminine article in Italian.

Morales and his colleagues monitored the eye-movements of thirty-two Italian–Spanish speakers in their Experiment 1 and twenty-six in Experiment 2. The two groups were well matched on a number of factors: age; the number of years they had used Spanish; and the number of years they had lived in Spain. Their Spanish proficiency was assessed using a self-rating questionnaire on a ten-point scale, and the two participant groups were similar across the four skills (production, comprehension, writing and reading). While the participants in Morales et al.'s study appear to be similar, if there are any concerns about the matching of participants' proficiency level, a wider range of tasks might be necessary to establish this. The discussion in Section 4.3.2 goes into great detail about matching and assessing participants who are non-native speakers and looks at a battery of language proficiency tasks. Performance on such tasks can be used to demonstrate that non-native participants are well matched and/or to provide proficiency metrics that can be used as variables in analyses. It is advisable to use some of these tasks, or other similar ones, when doing research with non-native participants.

5.3.2 Matching and Controlling Visual and Audio Input

Images

In Experiment 1, Morales and his colleagues used forty-eight black and white drawings from Lotto, Dell'Acqua and Job (2001). These are a set of images that have been normed in Italian on a number of factors: number of letters, number of syllables, word frequency, age of acquisition, name agreement, naming time, typicality and familiarity. Morales et al. presented participants with twelve pairs of twenty-four nouns in each of their conditions, as well as twelve filler pairs of pictures. They ensured that all of the nouns were controlled for frequency and number of letters across Spanish and Italian, and used *t*-tests to demonstrate that there were no statistical differences for the items in the different conditions. To establish that there were no cognates in the experiment, they considered the amount of phonological overlap between the names of each picture in the two languages by counting the shared number of letters. Additionally, the location of the picture that needed to be clicked on was counterbalanced across participants and presentation order was randomised for each participant.

In Experiment 2, Morales et al. used fifty-six black and white drawings from Snodgrass and Vanderwart (1980), which had been normed for name agreement, image agreement, familiarity and visual complexity. In this experiment they presented participants with fourteen pairs of twenty-eight nouns in each of their conditions, and included twenty-eight filler trials. They again matched their items for frequency and number of letters. Morales and colleagues say that care was taken to avoid items that were cognates; however, unlike in Experiment 1, they did not provide a measure to establish this. They simply ensured that pictures did not share the same initial phoneme in Spanish and Italian. Once again their materials were counterbalanced and the order of the stimuli was randomised.

In Experiment 1, before taking part in the main study, participants were shown the line drawings and asked to name them aloud in Spanish along with the corresponding definite article. This was done to ensure that the participants knew the name of each object in Spanish, as well as its gender. They were provided with the correct response if an error was made. Importantly, any pictures that were not named correctly in this phase of the experiment were excluded from the analysis of that participant's eye-movement data. In Experiment 2, this procedure was not carried out.

Audio

The audio instructions always had the same structure, 'encuentra' + definite article 'el' or 'la', and were followed by the target noun. In both experiments, the recordings were produced such that the sentences had broad focus, in other words with no emphasis put on the target noun phrase. Morales et al. controlled the duration of the instructions using the Praat software package. The word 'encuentra' was edited so that it always had a duration of 800 ms in Experiment 1 and 730 ms in Experiment 2. They controlled the duration of the definite article such that it was 147 ms in Experiment 1 and 200 ms in Experiment 2, and was always followed by 50 ms of silence. In this way they could be certain that the acoustic information about grammatical gender prior to the onset of the target noun was identical across all items in an experiment.

5.3.3 Data Analysis and Results

As with most types of studies, data analysis begins by removing problematic items and errors. Morales et al. removed blinks from their data. They also excluded trials where participants clicked on the wrong object (Exp. 1 = 0.26% of trials, Exp. 2 = 1.65%). They created ROIs by drawing 'boxes' around each of the pictures (as in Figure 5.3, B). Fixations were classified as falling into one of the ROIs (target or distractor) or outside of them (somewhere else on the screen). They carried out two types of analyses on their data. First, they looked at the proportion of fixations to the two images in a time window from article onset (Exp. 1 200–900 ms, Exp. 2. 200–550 ms). In both experiments, they used ANOVAs to compare fixation patterns, and found significantly more looks to target pictures when they had the same gender in the two languages than when they differed. Importantly, they were concerned that overlap in the feminine definite articles in the two languages could have driven their results (feminine definite article is 'la' in both Spanish and Italian, while the masculine is 'el' in Spanish and 'il' in Italian). To rule out this possibility, they did another analysis that included both gender (masculine vs feminine) and condition (congruent vs incongruent). They found no interaction between the two factors, which they took as an indication that the similarity between the feminine definite articles was not responsible for their pattern of results.

In their second analysis, Morales and colleagues wanted to look at *when* the grammatical gender of the definite article influenced looking patterns, in other words the gradual activation of target pictures' nouns across the conditions. To do this they conducted what are referred to as 'running *t*-tests' or 'time-step *t*-tests'. Because the sampling rate of their eye-tracking system was 500 Hz, they obtained information about the position of fixations every 2 ms. Thus, every 2 ms they knew whether someone was looking at the target, distractor or elsewhere. They performed successive one-tailed *t*-tests on the proportions of fixations to the target and distractor at each point (one data point = 2 ms) from 400 to 900 ms after pronoun onset (Exp. 1) and 200 to 550 ms after pronoun onset (Exp. 2).

Due to the large number of data points that are tested by this kind of analysis, it can lead to Type I errors (false positive errors). Guthrie and Buchwald (1991) spell out a formula to calculate the number of consecutive *t*-tests that need to be significant in order for there to be a reliable pattern. It is based on the number of participants, the sampling interval length and the temporal autocorrelation. Based on Guthrie and Buchwald's calculation, Morales et al. adopted a criterion to determine when differences between conditions were reliable (Exp. 1 twelve significant consecutive *t*-tests (24 ms); Exp. 2 eleven significant consecutive *t*-tests (22 ms)).

In Experiment 1, the analysis indicated that the first time point where the two conditions differed from each other was at 498 ms after article onset, and that this difference remained significant until the end of the time window. In other words, the influence of the grammatical gender in the native language impacted spoken-word recognition from 498 ms onwards. In Experiment 2 the difference between Conditions A and B became significant at 360 ms after article onset and remained significant until 462 ms. The fact that there is a smaller proportion of fixations to a target that has a different gender in Italian shows that gender information from a first language is activated while listening in a second language. Importantly, the running *t*-tests tell us something about the temporal dynamics of grammatical gender processing in a second language.

5.4 Using Authentic Material

As we have touched upon, when we use authentic materials like audio storybooks and videos we cannot control the visual or the audio input or create materials that are suitable for a particular set of participants. Instead, we need to ensure that what we select is appropriate for the group that will be tested. Further, if there are elements in the audio or visual stimuli that are important for our research question, we need to make sure that they are appropriately evaluated and considered in any analysis of the data.

One way that we might use authentic materials is if we want to look at children's word learning from watching television. There are shows that are specifically designed to help children learn new vocabulary, and we may want to test if they actually learn words by watching an episode. For example, *Martha Speaks* (based on the children's book of the same name by Susan Meddaugh) focuses on presenting children with vocabulary and synonyms, with each episode featuring a set of words that are 'explicit' because they are defined by one of the characters, or 'implicit' because they appear but are not defined.

Before beginning our study, we would need to identify the appropriate age group to test. We could use something like the Flesch Reading Ease Test and/or the Flesch–Kincaid Grade Level Test to look at the overall level of the language in an episode (Kincaid et al., 1975). Once we have identified an appropriate set of participants, we would need to assess whether they know the target words in terms of their form and meaning before and after the episode. If any images in the story are relevant to learning the words, we would need to evaluate whether they are recognisable and visually salient, and whether their concept and/or names are familiar to the participants. We would also need to consider whether there were particular acoustic cues, like intonation, which make certain words 'pop out' more, which could influence learning. Generally, evaluation of particular visual and audio characteristics would be done using a set of participants who are different to those in the main study, but are well matched with them. Finally, before testing begins, we would need to pinpoint when relevant images and language occur and identify appropriate ROIs at these spots in the video stream.

5.4.1 Contextualising an Example Video Study

Around the world, films are increasingly being imported from abroad and broadcast in the original foreign language with subtitles added in the native language. This is called 'standard subtitling', and it is often preferred to dubbing as it is cheaper and retains the original actors' voices, thus avoiding the issue of lip synchronicity. Advances in technology have made it possible to choose to add subtitles in a number of languages when we watch films or television programmes, and this can be done in a number of combinations: standard – foreign language soundtrack and native language subtitles; reversed – native language soundtrack and foreign language subtitles; or intralingual – the language of the soundtrack and the subtitles are the same. Intralingual subtitles are also referred to as 'captions', in particular when they are for the deaf and hard-of-hearing. These may contain information about the auditory input in general and not just the spoken discourse.

Importantly, when watching video with subtitles, a viewer has to process three sources of information – the soundtrack, the subtitles and the dynamic images in the film – as well as potentially dealing with linguistic input in both the foreign and native languages. Furthermore, the information coming from these different sources may be redundant, which could potentially render the reading of the subtitles less compelling. The study that we are going to look at investigated the extent to which people process subtitles under different subtitling conditions (standard, reversed and intralingual).

Eye-tracking provides an ideal methodology for examining how viewers make use of subtitles. More specifically, we can look at the number and duration of fixations in the subtitles and compare them under different linguistic conditions. In a study by Bisson, et al. (2014), native English speakers, with no knowledge of Dutch, were shown part of the film *The SpongeBob SquarePants Movie* (*De SpongeBob SquarePants Film*) under different Dutch–English subtitling conditions. They chose Dutch because it was a foreign language that their target participants were unlikely to have had contact with or know, which was also verified via a questionnaire. Because Dutch comes from the same Germanic language family as English, the two languages have many similarities, which could make reading more straightforward than in a language having an unfamiliar script.

Bisson et al. monitored the eye-movements of thirty-six participants. They were all asked to complete a questionnaire to verify their language background. On the basis of the information provided on the language questionnaire, data from some participants was excluded prior to any analysis because they had reading difficulties; were not monolingual; were not native English speakers; or had spent significant time in a Dutch-speaking country. The education level of the participants ranged from having completed secondary school to pursuing a postgraduate degree. Notably, some participants did not provide information about their educational background. This is an issue that can arise when asking people for demographic information; they may not wish to provide it. If we do not think that a particular variable is important to our study, we can include a participant's data even when we are not sure about it. If we believe that it is important, we may choose not to consider data from participants who have not provided information about it. Furthermore, if the variable is being used as a covariate or factor in an analysis, if a participant has not provided the relevant information, then generally his/her data would be excluded from any analysis.

Finally, it is important to note that Bisson et al. also looked at vocabulary acquisition for some of the Dutch words that occurred in the film. Because they did not find any significant results about word learning, we will not consider this element further.

5.4.2 Methodological Considerations for Video Stimuli

The Bisson et al. study had a between-subjects design, meaning that each participant saw the film in only one subtitling condition: (a) standard subtitling – Dutch audio with English subtitles; (b) reversed subtitling – English audio with Dutch subtitles; (c) intra-lingual subtitling – Dutch audio with Dutch subtitles; and (d) control condition – Dutch audio without subtitles. The control condition provided baseline information about how much time participants looked at the subtitle portion of the screen when subtitles were not present. This is important because in many cases, subtitles will appear over part of the image. Thus, participants may look to this part of the screen, not because of the subtitles, but because of the other visual information present there.

A further factor that needed to be considered was differences in the subtitles themselves. Dutch subtitles were present during 47 per cent of the movie extract compared to 50 per cent of the time for the English subtitles. Subtitles comprised either one or two lines of text that differed in length, both in terms of number of words and length of words, and were presented for an average of 3 seconds when written in Dutch and for 2.5 seconds when written in English.

In the study, participants were asked to watch an excerpt of the movie that lasted twenty-five minutes and consisted of four DVD chapters (two to five). The rationale for choosing an animated film was that the language of the soundtrack could easily be changed without affecting lip synchronicity. Four different versions of the movie were created and reformatted into AVI files so that they would be compatible with the Experiment Builder software. The control condition (Dutch audio with no subtitles) was created using the original movie chapters and audio in Dutch. The intralingual condition (Dutch audio with Dutch subtitles) was also created using the original movie chapters and audio in Dutch.

Bisson et al. adapted the Dutch subtitles in order to have a true word-for-word transcription of the audio instead of the abbreviated subtitles that came with the movie. The original subtitle timing information was added to the transcription using the subtitling program Submerge to ensure that the timing information (onset and offset of each subtitle) remained the same. The transcribed subtitles were added to the video and appeared where the original subtitles would have been on the screen. The standard condition (Dutch audio with English subtitles) was created using the original English subtitles. They were also reformatted using Submerge so that they matched the timing information in the intralingual condition. The reversed condition (English audio with Dutch subtitles) was made by adding the transcribed Dutch subtitles to the English soundtrack.

In the study, participants were informed that they would watch an animated film while their eye-movements were monitored. They were told that the film could be either in English or in a foreign language and that there might be subtitles. They were not told what the foreign language would be. They were asked to watch the film as they would normally do at home. Participants were not explicitly asked to read the subtitles nor were they told to pay attention to the foreign language. Furthermore, they were not told that there would be a vocabulary test after the film; however, they were told that they would be asked to answer some comprehension questions about the film. The movie chapters were presented in the same sequential order for all participants so that they could follow the storyline.

5.4.3 Data Analysis and Results

Bisson et al. started by splitting fixations according to whether they occurred in the image area or the subtitle area. The subtitle ROI was taken as an area of 1024 (whole width of screen) × 218 pixels that started 50 pixels from the bottom of the display screen. This was deliberately larger than the actual subtitle area to account for small vertical and horizontal inaccuracies in recording eye-movements. The image area included an area of 1024 × 450 pixels that started 50 pixels from the top of the display screen. Crucially, the subtitles' timing information was used to determine whether a fixation occurred during the presentation of a subtitle. Thus, if a fixation occurred in the subtitle region, when the timing information indicated that a subtitle was *not* present, then the fixation did *not* count as occurring in the subtitle ROI.

Data cleaning involved removing cases in which there was excessive vertical drift. In other words, instances where all fixations were shifted up or down were excluded from the analysis (6% of the data). Some subtitles had to be excluded because they occurred where there was already writing in English in the image or the subtitle area as part of the video display (10% of Dutch subtitles and 8% of English subtitles). Furthermore, the control condition (Dutch audio with no subtitles) was used to assess whether other visual aspects of the movie occurred in the subtitle ROI that drew viewers' attention. Where there were looks to this area in the control condition, subtitles occurring in these frames were not considered for analysis (24% of Dutch subtitles and 20% of English subtitles). In total, fixations occurring during 249 Dutch and 311 English subtitles were included in the final analysis, which represents 66 per cent and 71 per cent of the original subtitles respectively.

The total fixation duration, the number of fixations and the average fixation duration, as well as the proportion of non-fixated subtitles, were calculated for each individual subtitle and averaged for each participant. Each of these eye-tracking measures was subjected to a one-way ANOVA with subtitle condition as a between-subject factor with four levels (standard subtitling, reversed subtitling, intralingual subtitling and control condition). Tukey post hoc analyses were carried out to determine which conditions differed from each other. Importantly, Bisson et al. needed to take into account the fact that the duration of the subtitles' presentation differed between the conditions. Therefore, they normalised total fixation durations in the subtitle area by dividing the total fixation duration in the subtitle area by the duration of the presentation for each subtitle. Similarly, because of the unequal number of words in the subtitles, they were also normalised by dividing the number of fixations by the number of words for each subtitle. Finally, a normalised number of skipped subtitles was calculated by dividing the number of skipped subtitles by the total number of subtitles. All of the normalised data was subjected to one-way ANOVAs and Tukey post hoc analyses.

Because reading is made up of a set of consecutive fixations along lines of text (and not random jumping from one word to another across lines), Bisson et al. looked at consecutive fixations in the subtitle area to try to distinguish reading behaviour in the conditions with Dutch audio and either Dutch or English subtitles. Consecutive fixations were calculated for each participant for each subtitle (ranging from 2 to 20 consecutive fixations) for Chapter 4 of the DVD because it had the largest sample size and was the most closely matched in terms of average number of words per subtitle between the Dutch and English subtitling conditions. The proportion of consecutive fixations was calculated by adding up the number of consecutive fixations and dividing by the total number of fixations in the subtitle area, with independent samples t-test (two-tailed) showing no significant differences between the English and Dutch subtitles. Bisson and her colleagues hypothesised that one of the reasons why participants may have read Dutch subtitles was the presence of words that are orthographically identical and similar in Dutch and English (e.g. 'kind', meaning 'child' in Dutch, and 'promotie'/'promotion' which have the same meaning). To examine the effect of orthographic overlap, regardless of meaning overlap, the number of Dutch words that were either identical or similar to English words in each subtitle was calculated using the normalised Levenstein distance, which is a measure of orthographic similarity (Schepens, Dijkstra and Grootjen, 2012).

Overall, the analyses of the subtitles demonstrated that participants spent no more time reading the subtitles when they were in their native language than when they were in an unknown foreign language. The average fixation durations for the standard, intralingual and reversed subtitling conditions were 227, 240 and 243 ms respectively, which is in line with the average fixation duration for silent reading (Rayner, 2009). Furthermore, in both the standard and intralingual subtitling conditions, participants read most of the words in the subtitles, as indicated by the normalised number of fixations of about one per word. Reading behaviour in the standard and intralingual subtitling conditions was investigated further by looking at consecutive fixations and at the effect of orthographic overlap, with no significant differences between the two conditions. Bisson and colleagues took this as an indication that participants were not simply attracted to specific words in the subtitles, but that once their gaze moved to the subtitle area they read in a normal, uninterrupted fashion instead of alternating between the image and the subtitle areas, suggesting that reading behaviour was similar across the two conditions. This is surprising since participants in the intralingual condition had no prior knowledge of the language that appeared in the subtitles. It is possible that participants were simply trying to use the available information in the subtitles to understand the movie since they could not rely on the soundtrack for understanding. Crucially, participants in the reversed condition did not need the foreign subtitles to help them understand the film because their native language was present in the soundtrack. However, they still spent a considerable amount of time in the subtitle area.

Additionally, Bisson et al. explored looking patterns to the image ROI. They assessed total fixation duration, the number of fixations and the average fixation duration in the image area for the duration of every subtitle and averaged these for each participant. As with the subtitle ROI, each eye-tracking measure was subjected to a one-way ANOVA with subtitle condition as a between-subject factor with four levels. Similarly, Tukey post hoc analyses were carried out to determine whether the conditions differed from each other. They found that participants watching the film without subtitles spent more time fixating the image area than the participants with the English soundtrack and Dutch subtitles, and they in turn spent more time in the image area than participants with the Dutch soundtrack and Dutch subtitles. However, the latter still spent more time in the image area than participants with the Dutch soundtrack and English subtitles. Overall, analyses revealed that the average fixation duration in the image area was significantly longer for the condition without subtitles compared to the other conditions and that there were no significant differences between the conditions with subtitles. The findings in the study support the view that the reading of subtitles still allows for the processing of the images (Perego et al., 2010), instead of watching a video simply becoming a reading exercise (Jensema et al., 2000).

5.5 Conclusions and Final Checklist

In this chapter we have seen that we can use eye-tracking to shed light on listening comprehension. This is done by presenting participants with visual images and concurrent language input. Importantly, looking patterns are generally time-locked to specific elements (words, syntactic structures, appearance of subtitles, etc.) in the input. Notably, just as in reading, a number of factors have been shown to influence eye-movement behaviour. This means that when we design our stimuli, or when we select authentic material, we need to carefully consider a number of variables. These should be matched or controlled as well as possible, or accounted for in our analyses. Finally, as in any study, it is important to have in place appropriate tasks to establish that a cohort of participants is similar, as well as how they differ.

Final checklist	
• What is the task – active vs passive?	⇨ Passive tasks like 'look and listen' will require more participants and items than active tasks involving clicking on or moving objects.
• What properties of the visual stimuli should be considered?	⇨ This will depend on the type of visual input and the manipulation. • Ensure that the objects/entities in images or videos are easily identifiable and will be referred to by the same names by participants.

(cont.)

	Final checklist
	• Evaluate images or video frames for important characteristics (e.g. visual salience, unusualness).
	• If there are target images, ensure that they do not appear in one position on the screen more than in others.
• What properties of the linguistic input are important to consider?	⇒ This will depend on the manipulation.
	• When the focus is on words, consider word-level variables (length, frequency, etc.).
	• When the focus is on morpho-syntax, consider predictability, etc. and other relevant aspects of the sentence.
	• When working with particular populations, we need to ensure that the linguistic input is at an appropriate level.
• What properties of the audio input should you consider?	⇒ In the audio, you need to identify the precise time point a critical element in the stimuli occurs and time-lock ROIs to this.
	⇒ Evaluate sound files for important characteristics (e.g. loudness, intonation).
• What do you need to do to 'match' participants?	⇒ This varies depending on the target population. Look at the tasks other researchers have used for guidance.
	• For an example of matching non-native speakers see Section 4.3.2 and those with an autism spectrum disorder Section 4.6.2.
• What do you need to consider for analysis?	⇒ There are a range of ways of looking at and analysing looking patterns to visual input. Consider what might be the most appropriate for your particular research question. See Chapter 7 for a discussion.
	⇒ Consider what variables related to the linguistic and visual input, as well as the participants, should be included in the analysis.

Chapter 6

Using Eye-Tracking in Other Contexts

6.1 Introduction

We have remarked that eye-tracking has become widespread in psychology and psycho-linguistic research over the past thirty years – it has even been referred to as the 'gold standard' in research in these fields (Rayner, 2009, p. 1474). As we saw in Chapters 4 and 5, much of the focus in this literature has been on establishing the influence of word characteristics (e.g. frequency, length) on processing, as well as on how comprehenders integrate words into sentences and larger contexts. Traditionally, the research has been carried out in very well-controlled studies where factors are meticulously matched. Recently, there has been an increase in the number of studies that have attempted to mimic more authentic language situations and contexts, and/or make use of authentic materials like novels, movies, television episodes, etc. We have already seen some examples of this in Chapters 4 and 5, where we looked at one study in which participants were asked to read an entire Agatha Christie novel (Section 4.3) and another in which they watched part of the SpongeBob SquarePants movie (Section 5.4). These more 'authentic' studies bring up a whole host of methodological considerations that were only briefly touched upon in previous chapters.

Importantly, applied linguists' main interest is in looking at authentic language in various contexts. Eye-tracking technology is increasingly being used to study (more) authentic materials in the sub-disciplines within applied linguistics, such as language assessment, writing development, corpus linguistics, translation, computer-assisted language learning and literary linguistics. Because in many instances researchers are interested in the processing of visual input (written text, images, video, etc.) and/or auditory language input, the research has many of the same methodological considerations that we have discussed previously. However, many of their novel experimental designs raise many new methodological issues, which will be the focus of the discussion in this chapter.

As we will see as we go through the chapter, some of the sub-disciplines in applied linguistics have incorporated eye-tracking technology into their research in the last decade or so, while others have made some initial forays with the technology, and still others have not made use of it at all. By and large eye-tracking research is still in its infancy in applied linguistics. This means that while Chapters 4 and 5 dealt with long-standing research areas, and we were able to present clear and well-established patterns of results, the same is not true here. However, many of the findings reviewed in those chapters will be relevant to our current discussion. For example, a word's characteristics (e.g. frequency, length, predictability) influence how easily it is recognised and integrated into a larger context – both in visual and auditory comprehension – and thus is an important factor to consider when designing materials or choosing authentic ones.

Because Chapters 4 and 5 had a large and well-developed literature to draw on, our main focus was on presenting seminal papers that gave us a good starting point for our discussion of experimental design, as well as providing examples of good practice. However, because much of the discussion in the current chapter focuses on a very small (or non-existent) literature, we have taken a different approach. In this chapter we go through possible studies and designs in a more speculative way. We provide an overview of the topics and research questions that have been or could be investigated within different sub-disciplines, as well as discussing some of the key methodological considerations when conducting such studies. We also go through the design of an example study in each of these contexts that illustrates good research practice. Importantly, the aim of this chapter is not to provide a comprehensive review of the literature in the different sub-disciplines but to present key studies (where these exist) to illustrate the type of research that can be conducted in each area using eye-tracking.

It is important to note that no *single* reader is likely to be interested in all six of the fields we cover in this chapter. Most readers will be interested in eye-tracking research in one (or maybe two) of these disciplines. Thus, literary linguists would be interested in the section on this particular topic and potentially the one on translation research – maybe if they do research on translated texts. It is unlikely that they would also be interested in language testing, computer-mediated communication, etc. Therefore, we wanted each section to be self-contained, so that readers would not have to hunt through the chapter to find the information they need to design a study in their particular area. Alongside this, many of the general methodological concerns cross-discipline boundaries. For example, considerations for a written translation study are fairly similar to those for studying learners' written messages in synchronised computer-mediated communication. The competing demands of compartmentalisation and overlapping methodological concerns mean that anyone who reads all six sections will encounter some repeated themes.

Finally, the goal of this chapter is to reflect some of the latest developments in the application of eye-tracking technology to various sub-disciplines in applied linguistics. Because of technological advances, it is likely that eye-tracking will be used in new and exciting ways in the future. Importantly, the range of contexts and topics covered in this chapter, together with those covered in Chapters 4 and 5, should provide the methodological foundations necessary to inform future research.

6.2 Eye-Tracking in Language Testing

Language testing is one of the areas in applied linguistics that has recently witnessed a considerable increase in the number of studies that use eye-tracking. A key concern has been the validity of tests. An important aspect of test validation involves examining the extent to which tests tap into the set of cognitive processes that are employed by proficient language users in similar tasks in the real world (Field, 2013), which is often referred to as cognitive validity. Cognitive validity has mainly been examined by studying candidates' behaviour with verbal reports and with evidence-based models that attempt to link testing behaviour to underlying cognitive processes. However, there are issues with relying on the outcome of a task to tell us about processing during the task itself (O'Sullivan and Weir, 2011; Weir, 2005) and with using approaches that rely on test-takers' retrospective recall because of their veridicality risks (Brunfaut and McCray, 2015). Eye-tracking can potentially provide a technique that circumvents these issues, which has led language testers to make use of the technology to investigate test-takers' behaviour.

However, eye-tracking measures cannot be directly mapped onto specific cognitive processes in language tests. If we wanted to establish this relationship, we would need to identify a very specific aspect of a process and design a tightly controlled experiment that would only look at and manipulate this particular aspect, for example across lists, along the lines of what we discussed in Chapter 4 (e.g. a lower-level process like the recognition of specific lexical items in the text that are important to successfully answer a specific question). Even in such a carefully controlled study, linking the processing effort evident in a set of eye-tracking measures to a particular cognitive process should be regarded with caution. Thus, it is important to keep in mind that eye-tracking measures cognitive effort, which tells us a lot about performance on language tests, but it does not *directly* reflect specific cognitive processes in testing or in other domains.

6.2.1 What Can Be Measured?

Most high-stakes tests of linguistic proficiency are designed around the four main skills of reading, listening, writing and speaking, and important elements of these four processes can be examined using eye-tracking. We will look at each of these in what follows.

Testing Reading

School-age children and adults who are learning or know a second language will be very familiar with standardised tests. In some countries children start taking them as young as five years old. Second language learners often need to take standardised language tests to demonstrate proficiency for admittance to educational institutions, to gain citizenship, etc. Such tests generally have a reading component and most of them present test-takers with a reading passage and a set of comprehension questions.

Eye-tracking can be used to examine looking patterns to specific areas of the test (the whole passage area, the question area, specific sections of the passage or specific questions) and movements between the different areas. We can also measure how looking patterns are affected by readers' individual differences (e.g. level of proficiency of second language readers, age, grade level of first language readers), as well as by task-related properties such as the type of reading passage and type of comprehension questions used (e.g. direct questions, inferential questions). Eye-tracking can also be used to measure the relationship between looking patterns and test performance.

Some of these issues have recently started to be addressed by language testing researchers. Bax and Weir (2012) were interested in looking patterns to the questions, answer options and specific areas in the text when taking a computer-based CAE (Cambridge English: Advanced) reading test. Bax (2013) had a similar focus, but added an additional proficiency manipulation. He presented readers of different proficiencies with passages and test items from a computerised IELTS reading test. He examined the number and duration of visits (defined as the interval of time between the first fixation on a region of interest (ROI) and the next fixation outside the ROI) to the whole reading text, groups of sentences or individual sentences and phrases or words. These studies were the first ones to use eye-tracking to investigate test-takers' behaviour when reading tests and opened a new line of eye-tracking research. However, the lack of controlled and/or matched ROIs and the insufficient number of items to account for the low sampling rate of the eye-tracking system makes it difficult to draw conclusions from the data, particularly in relation to the processing of words and phrases.

Brunfaut and McCray (2015) used eye-tracking to examine potential differences in test-takers' eye-movement behaviour when completing tasks targeting different CEFR

(Common European Framework of Reference for languages) levels (A1–B2). They presented participants with eight reading tasks and fifty test items and looked at the number and duration of fixations and number and length of saccades and regressions to the text and response options in the different tasks. Although they modified the layout and presentation of the tasks and controlled for features like line spacing, the comparison of CEFR levels was between different types of tasks. As the authors acknowledge, differences in eye-movements could therefore be due to both CEFR level and task type, which makes conclusions about them problematic.

Importantly, all three of these studies are groundbreaking in their application of eye-tracking to investigate reading behaviour in actual language tests, and demonstrate the potential of the technology. They also highlight the importance of creating carefully designed studies so that our data will allow us to address our research questions.

Testing Listening

Listening is an important component of most tests of linguistic proficiency, both in children learning a first language and in children and adults learning a second language. It may seem counterintuitive to look at listening with eye-tracking technology; however, many listening tests are accompanied by some visual input (e.g. videos, a picture related to the audio). As we saw in Chapter 5, looking patterns to visual input can tell us quite a lot about listening comprehension. Thus, eye-tracking can be used to measure looking patterns to static images and videos during listening tests and to explore the relationship between this looking behaviour and performance on subsequent questions. As with reading tests, the effect of individual differences (e.g. level of proficiency of second language readers, age, grade level of first language readers) on looking patterns can also be examined.

Pioneering work in this area was recently done by Suvorov (2015), who used eye-tracking to investigate test-takers' looking patterns to two types of videos (context videos – visuals that provided information about the context of the spoken discourse; and content videos – visuals that provided information semantically relevant to the verbally presented information), as well as exploring the relationship between viewing behaviour and test performance. He presented participants with six video prompts and five multiple-choice questions and looked at fixation rate, dwell rate/gaze rate and total dwell time on the whole video area. The participants could take notes during the study, in other words look away from the screen where their eye-movements were being monitored. As the author points out, the note-taking behaviour, and therefore track loss (i.e. the pupil will not be tracked by the equipment while participants are writing a response) could have influenced the eye-movement data.

Testing Writing

Another important component of many standardised tests is writing. Writing clearly has a visual component to it, and we can measure looking patterns to different ROIs in writing tests: the prompt/instructions area (when visible on the screen), the writing area and movements between these two. We can also measure looking patterns to specific parts of the writing and prompt areas (specific words or phrases) while test-takers produce their text and/or pause to monitor their writing. The relationship between looking patterns and the quality of the text produced could also be examined (see Section 6.3 for a detailed discussion).

Révész, Michel and Lee (2016), for example, examined test-takers' eye-movements during 'pausing events' when writing. They categorised participants' eye-movements during pauses according to whether they remained on the word, clause, sentence or paragraph where the writing stopped. The relationship between the online looking behaviour and the quality of the output was also examined. Crucially, this study demonstrates the potential of eye-tracking to investigate processing during writing tests. Furthermore, in addition to analysing looking behaviour during pauses, we could select more specific ROIs in the stimuli – for example particular words in the prompts, as well as certain words, phrases or syntactic constructions in the written output. We could analyse the number and duration of fixations to these ROIs, providing a richer analysis of the online behaviour (see Section 6.3.2 for a discussion of methodological considerations).

Testing Speaking

As was touched upon in Chapter 5, eye-tracking has been used in language production studies. In these kinds of tasks, participants are shown a picture or image and asked to talk about it. We can examine how eye-movements to different parts of the visual input relate to what people say. Clearly, this kind of task can be extended to a testing situation by examining looking patterns to different sections of a visual prompt and exploring how eye-movement patterns relate to successful completion of the task. As with any test, we can also explore how individual differences and task-related factors influence looking patterns.

A study by Michel, Révész and Gilabert (under review) has taken exactly this kind of approach, although their focus was on task performance instead of the evaluation of a specific language test. They asked participants to complete six oral tasks (three types of tasks and two levels of complexity per task type) that involved the use of a visual prompt. They looked at the number of fixations, total fixation duration and median saccade length to the prompt ROIs. As the authors acknowledge, the specific task manipulations across the three task types were different, which makes it difficult to relate any changes in cognitive effort to specific task design features.

Evaluating the Evaluators

Clearly, for anyone taking a high-stakes test, a key concern is how their work is evaluated and ultimately their score. Also, testing companies want to understand more about how scores are given and ensure a high level of inter-rater reliability. Eye-tracking offers a new and innovative way to look at the raters' behaviour and assess how this relates to the score they give. We can use eye-tracking to measure evaluators' looking patterns to assessment rubrics while scoring tests. We can also examine how this looking behaviour relates to their score.

Winke and Lim (2015), for example, recorded raters' eye-movements to different sections of an on-screen analytic rubric (each of the sections defined as an ROI) while they rated forty essays. They examined five components of the rubric (controlling for the length of the descriptors) and looked at time to first fixation, total fixation duration and visit count to examine how much attention was paid to each of the sections in the rubric. Importantly, the task involved recurrent movements from the printed essays being marked to the on-screen rubric. This led to considerable head movement, and therefore track loss, which could have influenced the pattern of results.

From the brief review above it is clear that eye-tracking can be used to explore the performance of test-takers on tests of the four main linguistic skills. Undoubtedly, this has important benefits for the testing community, and results from studies in this area will certainly lead to a better understanding of the tests themselves, ultimately resulting in better tests and better measures of proficiency for non-native speakers and skill level for children learning their first language.

6.2.2 Methodological Considerations

The discussion thus far has drawn attention to some of the groundbreaking work in testing research that highlights the tremendous potential of eye-tracking technology to add to our understanding of the tests themselves and test-takers' performance, as well as the perfor-mance of those who evaluate the tests. However, as with all new and innovative methods, there are inevitable teething problems. In what follows we discuss some important methodological considerations for using eye-tracking in testing research.

For most research purposes, and certainly for those described in the previous section, it is not appropriate to present test-takers with a test in its actual format and expect to be able to make valid claims about the processing of very specific elements of the stimuli. We generally need to compromise certain elements of the 'authentic' testing experience in order to design a feasible study that provides data that will be analysable. Thus, we have to walk a fine line between creating a controlled study and one that at the same time preserves key characteristics of the test. The type and amount of adjustment that needs to be made varies according to the stimuli itself and the research questions.

Text with Questions

The typical format of a reading test consists of a text and a set of comprehension questions presented either at the bottom or to the side of the computer screen. If our aim is to examine the percentage of total time test-takers spend processing these two areas, the test could be presented in its original format. The text and the question areas can be defined as two separate ROIs (see Figure 6.1).[1] Looking at late processing measures (e.g. total reading time and total number of fixations) in each of the ROIs would show the amount and percentage of time readers spend on each input source. However, to compare the number and duration of fixations made in these ROIs, data would need to be normalised. As illustrated in Figure 6.1, the two ROIs have different sizes and different amounts of information. Since the text ROI contains more information, we would expect it to attract more fixations than the question ROI.

Since all ROIs in this example contain written verbal input, data could be normalised based on the length of the written stimuli. This normalisation could be done in a number of ways. A common normalisation procedure is to divide fixation counts and durations by the number of words in each of these ROIs. In this chapter we will refer to number of words as the normalisation procedure, but fixation data could also be divided by the number of syllables or characters. However, linear mixed effects (LME) modelling or multiple

---

[1] The boxes indicating ROIs in the figure would not be visible to participants in the current example or any subsequent ones in this chapter.

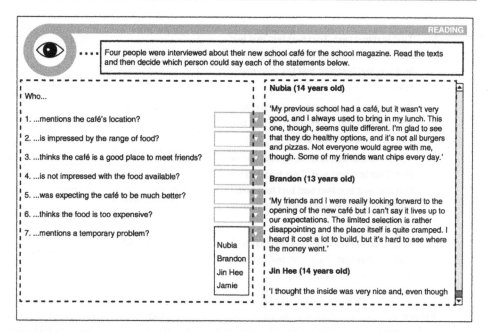

Figure 6.1 Example of stimuli for an eye-tracking study examining performance on an authentic reading test. The stimuli shown is Part 3 of the Aptis reading test (British Council). The two main ROIs (the question ROI and the text ROI) are indicated by boxes with dashed lines.

regression analyses would be more appropriate as they would allow researchers to account for a number of factors that could influence processing in the ROIs (e.g. number of words, word length, word frequency). With the layout depicted in Figure 6.1, we could make claims about the time test-takers spend processing each of the input sources. However, as illustrated in Chapter 3 (see Figure 3.1), the small font size and insufficient line spacing would make it impossible to make any claims about reading a specific word or section of the text or question.

If like Bax (2013) we want to examine more specific parts of the text (e.g. words or phrases) that participants attend to when processing each of the comprehension questions, important modifications would need to be made in the presentation of stimuli. We would need to use a task that, while resembling the format of the real test in terms of type and position of stimuli, is specifically designed for our study. Each of the questions/test items would need to be defined as separate ROIs, with at least double spacing in between the ROIs (see Figure 6.2). A measure like the time to first fixation would tell us the order in which each of the questions were read. Examining late measures would allow us to identify which questions elicit a greater number and longer fixations and therefore receive more attention and/or require more processing effort. As touched on in Chapter 3, we would want to ensure that the questions were well matched in length and other properties like syntactic complexity, or that appropriate analyses were used to account for any such differences. Further, analysing the pattern of regressions between the question ROIs and the text ROI would provide information about how test-takers make use of these two sources of information. In order to ascertain whether a precise part of the text (e.g. word or phrase) is read when answering a particular question, more fine-grained ROIs in the text area would need to be defined. To obtain good-quality data in these smaller ROIs, the text

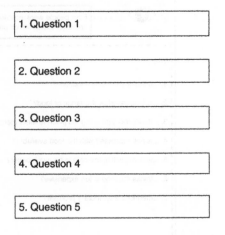

Figure 6.2 Representation of stimuli for an eye-tracking study examining the processing of the text and questions in a reading test. The text area and the questions are defined as ROIs with each question constituting a separate ROI. The ROIs are indicated by boxes.

would need to be formatted with a large enough font size and at least double line spacing (see example in Figure 6.2). We could then look at the time it takes test-takers to find and attend to the ROI (e.g. by looking at the time to first fixation in the ROI) and the time they spend fixating that ROI.

In the majority of cases we will have predefined ROIs. However, there might be some cases in which predefining ROIs might not be possible or desirable. For example, certain test items are designed to be more difficult, and we may want to assess where test-takers look for information when they encounter them. In such instances we may not have a single predefined ROI and we may have to look at a wide range of ROIs to be able to capture what words or sections of the text attract the most attention for these questions.

In some readings tests, such as the one depicted in Figure 6.1, test-takers need to scroll through the reading text to see all of it. Using a scrolled-down text would mean having ROIs that move with the text (see Chapter 3 for more on creating different kinds of ROI).

If, like Brunfaut and McCray (2015), we are comparing behaviour across different reading tasks, we need to make sure that the texts that are being used are comparable in terms of topic, length and level of difficulty, as all these factors affect test-takers' reading behaviour. If we do not control for factors like these, we will not know whether any differences in the eye-movement record are due to task differences or to other properties of the texts.

In other cases we might be interested in exploring participants' eye-movements while reading an on-screen passage and simultaneously completing a set of questions on a response sheet, or vice versa. This is similar to what Winke and Lim (2015) did with raters processing an on-screen test rubric while scoring printed essays. Notably, such a method will introduce head movements, and therefore variability in the data. With current eye-tracking systems, especially those that are less tolerant of head movement, any design that takes test-takers' eyes away from the screen while completing the task will lead to track loss, and the recurrent movements to and from the screen will lead to drift and loss of calibration which will affect the quality of the data. To help address this, drift correct and recalibrations would need to be included frequently in any such study, which will be done differently depending on the system used (see Chapter 3 for a more detailed discussion on the inclusion of drift correct and recalibrations).

Texts with Visual Input

In addition to written input, reading tests sometimes present non-verbal information such as graphs, figures or pictures. In this case we might want to explore test-takers' processing of the non-verbal information while completing the reading task. In Figure 6.3, the title, text and image areas are the three ROIs. A potentially interesting research question would be about the proportion of time test-takers spend fixating the text or the image/figure/ graph area and how that relates to test performance. For example, do test-takers who spend more time looking at the image/figure/graph perform better on particular types of questions? However, in other cases we might be interested in the direct comparison of reading times in the text and image areas. Late eye-tracking measures such as total reading time and total number of fixations will provide information about the relative time test-takers spend processing each of these sources of information during a reading task. If this is our aim, an important methodological concern is how to make valid comparisons of verbal and non-verbal information. One option would be to normalise the data based on the size of the ROIs, dividing the fixation counts and durations by the number of pixels in each ROI. This would give an approximation of fixations when size differences are accounted for. However, this only partially solves the problem and does not make the different ROIs fully comparable. As discussed in Chapter 1, images and text convey different types of

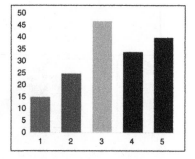

Figure 6.3 Representation of stimuli for an eye-tracking study exploring the processing of text and visual stimuli in a reading test. The title, text and graph are identified as the three ROIs and are indicated by boxes.

information and therefore have different degrees of saliency, leading to different patterns of eye-movements. Thus, even with ROIs of identical size (or when this has been normalised), the comparison of processing times would be problematic. This important limitation needs to be acknowledged when interpreting results of experimental studies using such a format.

Auditory and Visual Stimuli

In video-based listening tests, test-takers are sometimes presented with people or characters speaking on a computer screen, which is believed to provide a more realistic representation of the listening in spoken interactions. Generally this is accompanied by a set of comprehension questions about the audio and/or visual content. Much as with reading, we know when information critical to answering a particular question occurs in the input. Thus, an interesting aspect to look at is test-takers' eye-movement behaviour when hearing a specific word or segment of the audio and how those looking patterns at that time point relate to test-takers' ability to answer a particular question. To investigate this, different ROIs would need to be defined for each of the parts of the video stimulus.

An important ROI in this type of test would be the face of the speaker (see Figure 6.4), as we use visual cues to understand speech and a considerable proportion of fixations will likely be made in this area. Similarly, the hands of the speaker (which support the speaker's

Figure 6.4 Example of stimuli for an eye-tracking study exploring performance on a video-based listening test. Different areas of the visual display are defined as ROIs and are indicated by boxes.

linguistic codes) and the graph on the board (which is related to the content of the lecture) would also be interesting ROIs. Here, we would need a mix of ROIs. For any material on the board, we may want to define a single ROI for the duration of the video, or else define ROIs that would capture fixations only once certain information had been written. ROIs that move with the speaker would be required during particular time windows (see Chapter 3 for more on different types of ROI). Visualisations like heat maps (a simple colour-coded representation of how much attention different areas of the display receive) could be used here to identify any other potential ROIs to be defined and analysed (see Chapter 7 for a detailed discussion of different types of visualisation).

In Figure 6.4, the three ROIs have different sizes and would be more or less salient, and therefore would need to be normalised. While we can normalise for size based on number of pixels in the ROIs, accounting for factors like salience and information density is more problematic (see discussion in Chapter 5).

Other listening tasks may involve presenting test-takers with a set of questions on the screen while they listen to audio input. We could examine fixation counts and durations to each question/test item (defined as separate ROIs) – or even specific words or phrases in a question – while a specific part of the recording is being presented. Again, the auditory stimuli and eye-movements to the ROIs should be time-locked so that we know exactly where test-takers are looking when hearing a specific part of the auditory stimuli. For example, it would be interesting to see whether test-takers who shift their attention (perform a saccade) more quickly to the question that relates to the information in the audio file perform better than test-takers who shift their attention more slowly or not at all.

Written Text Production

Writing tasks often provide prompts like texts, pictures or graphs for test-takers to write about. Researchers can look at test-takers' eye-movements to these. If test-takers are presented with on-screen prompts and are asked to respond on a separate sheet, the recurrent head movements between the screen and response sheet would lead to track loss. Frequent drift correct and recalibration would need to be built into the study to help deal with this. In contrast, responses could be made directly on the screen. The text presenting the instructions or prompt and the response box would be defined as separate ROIs (see Figure 6.5). Analysing the fixation counts and durations in these ROIs would give us an indication of the time test-takers spend processing the instructions and monitoring their typing on the screen. Since the text in the topic/instruction ROI is static and the text in the response box ROI changes as the writing unfolds, the response ROI would need to be dynamic and normalised based on number of words at very specific time points (e.g. after 45 seconds ten words have been typed and after 90 seconds twenty-nine words), as well as on other relevant features to make the two ROIs comparable. Information about regressions to the topic/instruction area would indicate how much test-takers rely on the information provided here and when they utilise it. Similar to other designs, recalibration and drift correct would be necessary to account for recurrent head movements to and from the keyboard. Importantly, track loss will be greatly influenced by the typing skill of the participant, with touch typists having to look at the keyboard less, therefore having less track loss. For less proficient typists the onset of a typing event will likely correspond with looks to the keyboard and track loss. The timing of test-takers' typing should be recorded (e.g. using keystroke-logging), so that we know when track loss is due to looks to the keyboard. Understandably, there will

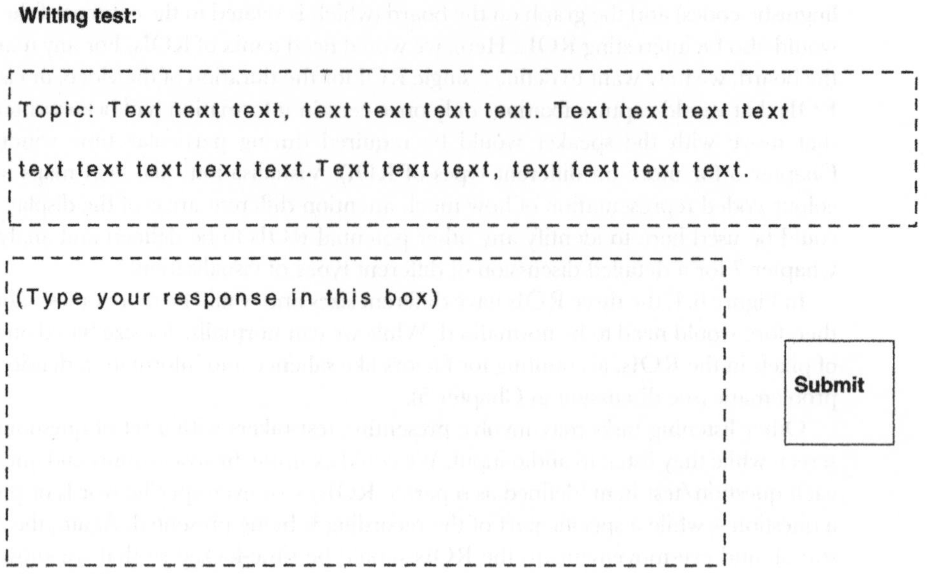

Writing test:

Topic: Text text text, text text text text. Text text text text text text text text text. Text text text, text text text text.

(Type your response in this box)

Submit

Figure 6.5 Representation of stimuli for an eye-tracking study examining performance on an online writing test. The topic/instruction area and the response box are defined as separate ROIs and are indicated by boxes with dashed lines. Importantly, the information in the response ROI will change moment-to-moment.

be a great deal of variability in how many data points are lost for individual participants, which would need to be acknowledged in the discussion of the data (see section 6.3 for a more detailed discussion of writing studies).

Spoken Production and Visual Stimuli

As we saw in the previous section and Chapter 5, eye-tracking has been used in language production studies. Thus, it can easily be extended to investigations of speaking tests, which is exactly the kind of approach taken by Michel et al. (under review). For example, we can explore test-takers' eye-movement behaviour to a map before and while they give spoken directions (see Figure 6.6). More specifically, we could examine test-takers' eye-movements while producing a particular utterance to determine whether it corresponded to what they were attending to. For example, when mentioning the 'Information point' from Figure 6.6, are participants looking at this part of the map? To determine this, relevant parts of the map would need to be established as ROIs and test-takers' productions would need to be time-locked to their looking behaviour. Depending on the nature of the research question, it might also be important to normalise the different ROIs. Looking patterns will not only depend on the size of the ROIs but also on the complexity of information. For example, in Figure 6.6, ROIs where a change in direction is needed will likely attract more looks. This would need to be considered in the discussion and interpretation of data.

As touched upon in Section 2.2, as technology advances, we might be able to conduct studies with portable eye-tracking glasses to examine test-takers' allocation of attention to the interlocutor's gestures, body movements or facial expressions during speaking tests.

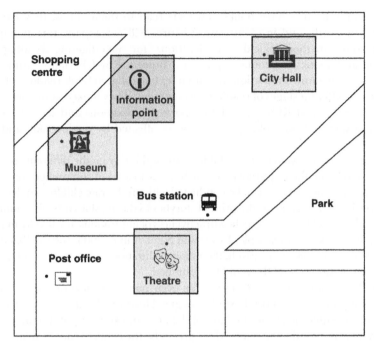

Figure 6.6 Example of stimuli for an eye-tracking study examining performance on a speaking test. The map is used as a prompt in the speaking test. Relevant parts of the map are defined as separate ROIs and are indicated by grey boxes.

Other Educational Applications

Educators and researchers who are interested in language skills in children and adults will not merely be interested in standardised tests. They will want to assess a variety of topics that will touch on the four skills (reading, writing, listening and speaking), as well as questions that go beyond them (e.g. the effectiveness of different input modes on learning grammar, vocabulary and comprehension; the effect of different text presentation modes on reading fluency; the effect of individual differences on how comprehenders process different sources of input). Much as with testing, eye-tracking can – and in some contexts is already starting to – be incorporated in new and exciting ways into learning and education research. While study designs might vary somewhat from what we have discussed in this section, the methodological considerations will largely be the same as those considered in this and previous chapters.

For example, let's say we want to look at how children or adult learners make use of glosses as they read, with the text taking up three-quarters of the left-hand side of the page and glosses running down the right-hand side of the page. We would likely set ROIs that consist of the sentences where the glossed words appear, the glossed words and their glosses. By setting these as ROIs we could see how different readers make use of glosses. If we included a set of comprehension and/or vocabulary questions, we could evaluate how gloss use relates to performance on any post-tasks. This is almost identical to the design we considered for reading tests; the question ROIs are simply swapped for gloss ROIs.

Further, children often have books and texts read to them. Thus, they can hear and see written words, and in many cases pictures will accompany this. (Chapter 5 considered some methodological considerations for investigating reading with a concurrent audiobook that contains pictures.) Indeed, Roy-Charland, Saint-Aubin and Evans (2007) examined attention to written text in a shared book-reading situation with children at different stages of reading development. They looked at the proportion of time spent on the text ROIs, and the proportion of fixations and saccades on the text ROIs to examine how looking patterns were affected by reading skill and book difficulty.

We may also want to evaluate how children use and integrate the different sources of information, and relate their eye-movement behaviour to a set of comprehension and/or vocabulary tasks. Similar studies can be conducted with pre-literate children to determine the extent to which they fixate on the print of storybooks during shared book reading and explore the influence of book design (the attractiveness of illustrations, the text format, etc.) on looking patterns (see, for example, Evans and Saint-Aubin, 2005; Justice, Skibbe and Canning, 2005). In this type of research, the number, duration and proportion of fixations to the print and illustration ROIs would be examined.

Importantly, a short section on testing, or even one on education more broadly, cannot cover the myriad of possible study designs. However, because of the technical restrictions of the equipment and the kind of data eye-trackers output, the methodological constraints are broadly the same. More precisely, the concerns about written input are the same regardless of whether they are specifically designed for a study, or taken from a standardised test, teaching materials, an actual book/novel, etc. Thus, we always need to think about what kind of ROIs we can establish if we present small text with no line spacing versus larger text with double or triple line spacing. The same goes for audio and other visual input (pictures, images or videos), as well as for combinations of the different kinds of input. Consequently, each input type and the task demands impose a broadly similar set of methodological considerations, which means that this chapter should give researchers a good idea about the relevant methodological considerations for almost any kind of study.

6.2.3 Example Study

The previous section has provided an overview of the key methodological issues that need to be considered when designing eye-tracking studies in language testing research in relation to each of the four main skills. This section will present some of those issues in relation to a particular study.

As in the study by Brunfaut and McCray (see Section 6.2.1), we might be interested in examining the cognitive processes implicated in a reading test. Let's suppose that, as language testers and test designers, we want to examine the functioning of the reading section of the TOEIC test (Test of English for International Communication, ETS). The TOEIC reading test has three parts in which test-takers have to read several texts and answer different types of comprehension questions. In particular, we want to focus on the first part of the reading section, 'Incomplete Sentences'. In this part test-takers are presented with a set of sentences that have a missing word or phrase and they have to choose which of the four provided options corresponds to the missing element. We could examine looking behaviour to the text, the sentence fragment and sentence completion options to establish when and how test-takers make use of the different sources of information and how this relates to successful and unsuccessful options. The following more specific questions could be addressed:

1 Which part of the item do test-takers read first, the sentence or the options?
2 Do they read all options?
3 Which options involve more cognitive effort (longer reading times)?
4 When and how many times do test-takers' eyes move between the options and the sentence?
5 How does the behaviour in (1), (2) and (3) relate to successful/unsuccessful performance, as well as to participant variables such as language proficiency?

Having decided on the topic and some research questions, the next step is to decide on the presentation of stimuli. We need to ensure that the stimuli are designed in such a way that the experiment provides data that can legitimately answer the research questions we have identified.

In a paper and pencil version of the test, the items are all presented on one sheet of paper. However, presenting all of the items on the same screen for an eye-tracking experiment would mean a font size that is too small and insufficient line spacing. Even using equipment with high accuracy and precision, data collected with 'authentic' stimuli presentation would not be of high enough quality to make any claims about the reading of specific parts of the sentences or specific options. In order to answer the research questions above, we could present a maximum of two or three items per screen (see Figure 6.7). Participants would press keys on a keyboard or button box to proceed to

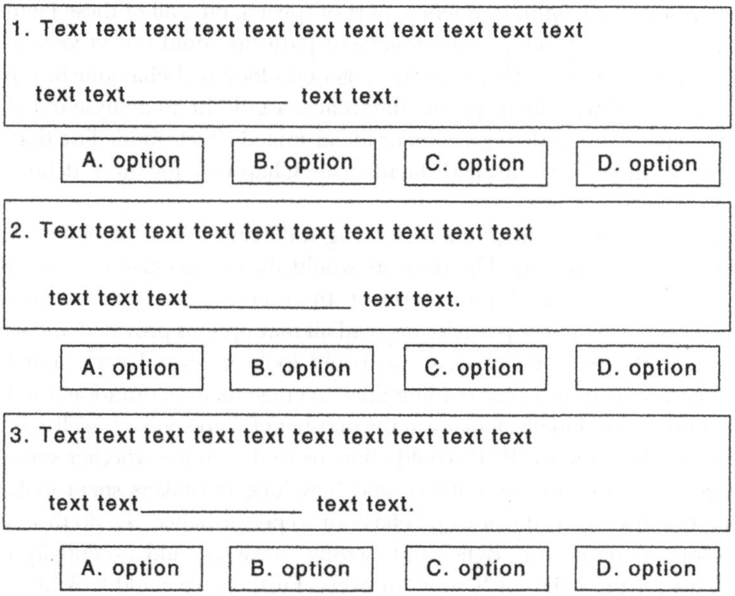

Figure 6.7 Representation of stimuli for an eye-tracking study exploring performance on a reading test with incomplete sentences. Test-takers are presented with a set of incomplete sentences and options to complete them. Each of the sentences and options are defined as separate ROIs and are indicated by boxes.

the next set of items. This might induce looks away from the screen, so (if possible) a drift correct would be inserted after each screen. If the system we are using does not allow us to insert drift correct, a recalibration should be built in after every few items. This design would provide the best data quality.

Notably, on a paper and pencil version of the test, test-takers could skip any item and come back to it. Designing an eye-tracking study where participants can go back and forth between different screens would be challenging due to the constraints of the software. Thus, the easiest study to design would be one in which participants answered all of the questions on a screen and then proceeded to the next, but could not return to the previous one, which is in fact a common scenario in many computer-administered tests.

In order to answer our research questions, the sentence and each of the four options would be defined as separate ROIs (see Figure 6.7). None of the research questions outlined above necessarily requires us to look at the reading of each word in the sentence. Therefore setting the whole sentence as an ROI should be enough. However, if we also wanted to find out which parts of the sentence participants attend to in order to identify the missing word/phrase, a separate ROI could be defined for each word.

With this design we have kept the content of the real test items while changing their visual presentation, as well as losing the flexibility to move forward and backward between screens with the various items. While this may raise questions about the ecological validity of our task, it means that we can acquire the data we need to answer our research questions. Another methodological concern is about the items themselves. We said that we would use items from the TOEIC, which means that our findings should be generalisable to the actual test. However, since we did not design the items ourselves we might have concerns about how well controlled the sentences and options are. Unless the test designers have carefully controlled the sentences for syntactic complexity, length, etc. and the options for length, frequency, part of speech, etc., all of these factors could impact looking behaviour. Thus, eye-movement patterns could reflect very particular item-specific characteristics rather than more general looking behaviour in this kind of task. One way to deal with item-specific differences would be to analyse our data with statistical tests such as multiple regression or linear mixed effects modelling that account for the role of all these 'uncontrolled' factors (see Chapter 7 for more details on data analysis).

Coming back to our research questions, looking at the time to first fixation in each of the ROIs would answer the first one. This measure would allow us to examine which ROI (the sentence or any of the options) is processed first. In order to answer the second and third research questions (i.e. whether participants read all four options provided and which one seems to require the most processing), we could look at several early and late eye-movement measures (e.g. first pass reading time, average fixation duration, total reading time and fixation count). Finally, looking at the number of regressions, as well as when test-takers regress, to the sentence ROI would allow us to determine whether some options induced more looks back to the sentence and how long test-takers spent looking at it. The fifth question tries to relate looking behaviour to performance. To do this, we would compare looking patterns for 'right' and 'wrong' answers, and potentially compare looking patterns for the different 'wrong' answers. Further, we could look at a range of participant-level variables (e.g. proficiency, years studying English, first language) to see how they relate to performance on the task and to looking behaviour.

As discussed in this section, the possibility of offering new insights into the cognitive effort of test-takers has made eye-tracking particularly attractive to language testing researchers. In combination with other traditional measures, such as stimulated recall, it can provide the richest account to date of test-takers' real-time processing. It is therefore of paramount importance to standardise the use of the technology and the reporting of data. The methodological considerations described in this section will facilitate standardisation and will help to ensure that we produce interpretable and meaningful findings.

6.3 Eye-Tracking in Writing Research

Section 6.2 demonstrated how eye-tracking can be used to examine processing specifically related to test-takers' performance on writing tests. Other writing-related questions are not necessarily concerned with assessment, but rather with the process of writing itself. Although a few studies have used eye-tracking to examine writing, we still know little about writers' eye-movements during text production.

Skilled writing is thought to involve the interaction of different processes. It consists of a series of writing and pausing events. More specifically, when composing their texts, writers pause to plan, edit (detect errors), review and evaluate the text they are producing – and of course they produce written output. These events have mainly been examined using think-aloud protocols, with a few studies monitoring writers' keystrokes and mouse movements (see Spelman et al., 2008, for a review) and others combining both think-aloud protocols and keystroke-logging (e.g. Stevenson, Schoonen and de Glopper, 2006). Importantly, eye-tracking allows researchers to examine writers' eye-movements during the different events in the text production process. For example, where do writers look on the screen when they plan? Do they look at all of their written text when they edit and evaluate?

6.3.1 What Can Be Measured?

During text production writers do not necessarily look at what they are producing on the screen. They might be looking at any number of things: a source document or visual stimulus that is used as prompt for a writing task; the text produced so far; the keyboard; or areas in the wider environment. Eye-tracking can be used to examine writers' eye-movements to these different locations during writing and pausing, as well as the effect of different factors on eye-movement patterns. Each of these topics is discussed in what follows.

Unfortunately, given the current technological constraints, eye-trackers can only provide accurate and precise data about fixations for ROIs on a screen. Thus, the vast majority of research is likely to investigate looking patterns for written output and input (prompts) that appear on the screen. Looks to things that appear off the screen, like a keyboard, a paper with a prompt or the wider environment, will likely all be recorded as track loss by most systems, as well as decreasing accuracy when participants look back to the screen. Eye-tracking systems that *can* track looks away from the screen have limited accuracy. Thus, they will be able to determine that a participant is looking in the vicinity of the keyboard, but would not be able to differentiate between looks to the keyboard itself and a pen a few centimetres away from it or to specific keys. Despite these constraints, some researchers are interested in evaluating looking patterns to and away from the screen. We will discuss the methodological concerns for this type of design.

Eye-Movements to the Screen

Most writing studies have investigated writers' eye-movements to the text being produced at different time points. During writing events, writers often look at the text being produced to monitor their writing. During pauses, writers are often re-reading what they have written (Kaufer, Hayes and Flower, 1986). This is likely done to assess the accuracy and appropriateness of what has been produced, as well as to plan the content and form of what will be written next (Torrance et al., 2016). Importantly, eye-tracking allows researchers to examine where writers attend during writing and during pauses, and for how long.

With eye-tracking we can monitor writers' reading of the whole text, which will vary in length depending on where the writer is in the task. More specifically, after writing for three minutes the 'whole text' might refer to 100 words, while at five minutes it might refer to 210 words. We can set the 'whole text' as an ROI, or as with other types of studies, we can define more specific ROIs. For example, Torrance et al. (2016) examined the amount of attention that competent writers paid to their own text during pauses. They looked at the proportion of reading time on the last word typed before pausing compared to other areas of the existing text. They also examined how writers' specific location in the text at the moment of pausing – whether they were mid-word, or were just about to start a word or a new sentence – influenced the probability of looking back to their text. In a somewhat less natural writing task, Van Waes, Leijten and Quinlan (2010) presented participants with an incomplete sentence containing an error and asked them to correct the embedded error and complete the sentence. They looked at fixations made in three ROIs: the incomplete sentence prompt, the error in the prompt and what the writers produced.

Very often in a writing task, participants are asked to compose a text based on sources or prompts (e.g. short text, quote, graph). As long as the prompt appears on the screen, eye-tracking can be used to examine writers' eye-movements to the prompt and typing areas during writing or pausing events, as well as any movements between these two areas. Alamargot et al. (2007), for example, examined writers' eye-movements to a source document and the text being produced.

Because pauses and writing events are important constituents of the text production process, we can investigate how looking patterns to the text and/or to the prompt during these events relate to the quality of the written output. We could therefore score the written outputs on a variety of measures of writing quality (e.g. structure and organisation, audience awareness, grammar, vocabulary, tone) and relate those scores to the total amount of re-reading of the text and/or prompt that is done during pausing or typing events. This would allow us to examine differences in looking patterns of skilled and less skilled writers.

Eye-Movements off the Screen

As stated above, during writing and pauses writers might look at the keyboard or elsewhere. In order to examine looking patterns away from the screen, we would need to use an eye-tracking system that allows us to set ROIs off the screen. However, as we have already said, with current technology, any eye-tracker that has the accuracy to pinpoint looks to an individual word on the screen cannot accurately track looks away from the screen or back to it without recalibrating the system. Thus, studies that want to compare

ROIs on and away from the monitor would be limited to large areas such as the whole screen or keyboard, rather than to smaller ROIs like specific words in the text or specific parts of the keyboard. A study by Johansson et al. (2010) examined writers' looks to the monitor and keyboard (defined as the two ROIs) while writing. Fixations to the monitor and the keyboard ROIs were examined using a head-mounted system with magnetic head-tracking, which tracks the head position more accurately. Importantly, as Johansson et al. explain, a main drawback of this set-up is the impossibility of determining with precision looks to the individual words that writers are reading at specific moments.

Factors Affecting Eye-Movements in Writing

Eye-movements in writing tasks are likely to be influenced by various writer-related and task-related variables, which means there is much to explore. For example, Nottbusch (2010) measured looks to pictures presented on screen, which were designed to elicit more or less complex syntactic structures, and to the written output that he asked participants to produce. He assessed the relationship between looking patterns to the two ROIs and the syntactic complexity of what the writers produced. Alamargot et al. (2007) looked at the effect of writing abilities on the number and duration of reading-while-writing events. In a similar vein, Alamargot et al. (2011) examined the effect of working memory capacity on eye-movements during pauses in writing by analysing eye-movements to three main ROIs (i.e. two different areas in a source document and the whole of the text produced at a specific time point).

6.3.2 Methodological Considerations

The examination of eye-movements during text production involves the analysis of fixations to a text that changes continuously and in unpredictable ways. This presents certain methodological challenges that do not arise when examining most of the other types of stimuli that we have considered in this chapter. In what follows we discuss some of the methodological considerations that are particular to writing.

Matching Eye-Movements to the Text Produced

Examining eye-movements in writing tasks generally involves the recording of both eye-movements and keystrokes. Software like ScriptLog (Strömqvist and Karlsson, 2002) and InputLog (Leijten and Van Waes, 2013) records all keyboard events and their temporal distribution. The log files generated by these programs can provide detailed information on typing statistics, pauses and edits. Importantly, the keystroke data can be integrated with eye-movement data. Notably, when typing, the text moves both horizontally and vertically, and matching fixations to the text as it develops cannot be done by associating words with static ROIs (Torrance et al., 2016). As Wengelin et al. (2009) explain, two approaches can be adopted to overcome this problem: 'One is to display synchronized keystroke and eye movement data in a form that makes it easy for the researcher to examine them together. Alternatively, knowledge about how the text is displayed on the screen can be used to reconstruct screen states as they changed during writing' (p. 339).

Specific programs that integrate eye-movement and keystroke data should be used, as doing this integration manually would be a laborious and complex task. The software TimeLine (Andersson, Dahl and Holmqvist, 2006), for example, allows us to synchronise data from ScriptLog and the eye-tracker. It generates a temporally ordered graphical representation of what the writer looked at and what keys he/she pressed during the text production process. EyeWrite (Simpson and Torrance, 2007) is an integrated editor and analysis system that identifies the words that the writer fixates and their location within the developing text. It can convert fixation locations specified as screen coordinates to text-relative location variables. This would allow us to extract fixation data during specific pausing or writing events, not only relative to their position on the screen but also to their relative location in the text (see Wengelin et al., 2009 for a discussion).

Identifying ROIs in Written Production

The software discussed above generates records containing synchronised eye-movement and keystroke data, which will allow us to identify ROIs in the text or visual stimuli during specific writing or pausing events. Only fixations made in the ROIs during the event under examination (writing or pausing) would be analysed.

If our aim is to examine eye-movements to the whole text being produced (and not specific parts of the text) and/or to the prompt or source document, the whole typing and/or prompt area would be defined as ROIs. Looking at measures such as number of fixations and total reading time in the typing and prompt ROIs will provide information about how much the text and the prompt have been processed during the writing or pausing events. We could also analyse the proportion of time spent in the text and prompt ROIs. Looking at the number of regressions to the prompt ROI and the timings of those regressions would provide further information about how writers make use of the information available there.

If, like Torrance et al. (2016) and Van Waes et al. (2010), we want to examine eye-movements during writing or pausing events to specific parts of a text, more fine-grained ROIs will need to be defined participant-by-participant. The synchronised eye-movement and keystroke data will allow us to identify where exactly writers look in the text while writing or pausing. As usual when examining smaller ROIs, the task needs to be set up with a big enough font size and enough line spacing to be able to obtain the required data. These ROIs will differ in terms of word-level features (e.g. length, frequency, word class) and these factors need to be accounted for in our data analysis. Looking at early and late eye-tracking measures would provide information about the processing of these ROIs and about which ones receive the most attention during pausing or typing events.

Examining Handwritten Production

The methodological considerations discussed above concern the production of typed texts. However, like Alamargot et al. (2007, 2011), we might be interested in the examination of eye-movements during the production of handwritten texts. Importantly, if we want to examine writing in children, we will need to do this with handwritten texts, as they are unlikely to know how to type – at least at the early stages of writing development. In these cases special devices that record handwriting activity are used. Eye and Pen (Chesnet and Alamargot, 2006), for example, makes a synchronous recording of handwriting activity (recorded on an A4-size, digitised tablet) and eye-movements. A sheet of paper containing source information and/or the space for the writing task is attached to the tablet surface and participants are asked to write with a special electromagnetic pen. Pen movements (coordinates and pressure) are sampled by the tablet at 200 Hz and eye-movements are sampled by an EyePuter head-mounted eye-tracker with a sampling frequency of 480 Hz. The recording of pen movements allows for the identification of pauses and the eye-tracker records fixations to the different areas of the tablet. As with typing, the handwriting activity and eye-movement data need to be synchronised. Most of the devices that track hand-writing do not have the features necessary to examine fixations to smaller areas of the stimuli and produce data of high enough quality. Thus, eye-movements to bigger ROIs, such as the whole prompt and text production areas in the tablet, are usually examined. However, as technology advances, this will likely change.

Controlling for Writing Ability

As touched upon above, data in writing studies are likely to be affected by participants' writing ability. Thus, we should either select participants of similar writing abilities, or account for differences in our analysis. Alternatively, we may want to manipulate writing ability – in other words study it as a factor in our study. Whether we match, account for or manipulate writing abilities, we need to establish the writing ability of our participants. Alamargot et al. (2007) provide a good set of measures for us to consider if we want to assess factors that may affect writers.

Also, as we've seen in other sections, writers differ in how much they need to look at the keyboard while typing. For example, Johansson et al. (2010) showed that touch typists can continually monitor their writing, while keyboard gazers will switch more often between the monitor and keyboard. Again, this is a factor that we can match across all of our participants, account for statistically or manipulate as a factor in our study. However, as Hvelplund (2014) notes, if we only investigate touch typists, this would place important limitations on our potential pool of candidates. Therefore, he recommends controlling for this statistically in the analysis of eye-movement data. Furthermore, keyboards vary depending on the writing system and language. Thus, if we are testing participants from different language backgrounds, this could increase the amount they need to look at the keyboard, and therefore lead to more track loss. Whenever we include participants who will need to make frequent looks to the keyboard, it is important that we also include frequent opportunities for drift correct and/or recalibration.

6.3.3 **Example Study**

As the previous discussion highlights, there are many potential avenues to explore in text production. In our example study, we will focus on pausing events. Let's imagine that we are interested in writers' eye-movement behaviour during pauses while producing a short text. The following research questions could be addressed:

1 Which parts of the text receive more attention during pauses?
2 Where are those areas located in relation to the pauses (in the last word being typed, in the previous sentence or in the previous paragraph)?
3 How much reading is done during all the pauses in the writing task?

The first thing to consider would be the design of the writing task. In this study, since we are not interested in the processing of the prompt, only the typing area will appear on the computer screen. Participants will be given the topic for the writing task before the start of the experiment. Since the first two research questions involve the analysis of specific words in the text produced, font size and line spacing are crucial methodological considerations. Because of the recurrent movements to and from the keyboard, it might be best to have triple line spacing and use 14 pt (or more) Courier New font. If our aim was to look at the overall reading of the text produced, we could have a smaller font size and line spacing, allowing for a longer text to fit in the typing area.

In this study participants would be asked to write a short text which will fit onto one screen and scrolling would not be necessary. Since this is a short task, only an initial calibration would be used. However, for longer tasks recalibrations and drift correct would need to be considered.

A keystroke-logging program like InputLog or ScriptLog and software like EyeWrite would be used to synchronise eye-movement and keystroke data. After data collection, keystroke logs would be inspected to identify pausing events. Two seconds seems to be a common threshold for identifying pauses in writing research (e.g. Johansson et al., 2010). The example in Figure 6.8 shows that there are two pauses longer than two seconds, one after the word 'sister' and one after 'sailing'. The synchronising software will produce an output file that reports the start time, duration and location (relative to the screen and to the text) of each fixation. The output file will also report times of key presses, the key that is pressed and initial cursor location (relative to the screen and to the text). With these data we will be able to analyse the number and duration of fixations made to the different areas of the text during pauses, answering the first research question. As explained in the previous section, software like EyeWrite would allow us to convert the fixation locations to text-relative location variables. We would therefore be able to extract fixation information about the words being fixated during pauses and their position in relation to each pause. Looking at the number and duration of fixations in the different types of ROI (i.e. ROIs located on the last word being typed, in the previous sentence and in the previous paragraph) would allow us to answer the second research question. In order to answer the third research question, the duration of all fixations made during all pausing events would be added together and a mean total reading time calculated per participant. This would give us a measure of the total time

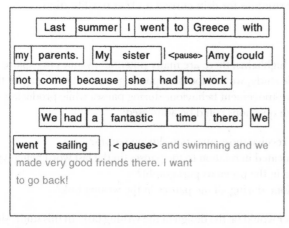

Figure 6.8 Example of output of a writing task showing the text produced and the pauses made. The words typed until the point at which the second pause occurred are defined as separate ROIs and are indicated by boxes.

participants have spent reading the text during pausing events. Since participants might produce texts of slightly different lengths, data would need to be normalised based on the number of words.

6.4 Eye-Tracking in Corpus Linguistics

Broadly speaking, corpus linguistics relies on computer software to count linguistic patterns (Biber, Conrad and Reppen, 1998). Thus, there are two important elements – the corpus data and the corpus tools used to analyse that data (Anthony, 2012). An important concern in corpus linguistics is users' interaction with the tools and with the corpus-generated data that they output. A few studies have used computer tracking software to gain a more direct record of participants' use of corpus tools (e.g. Chan and Liou, 2005; Gaskell and Cobb, 2004; Hafner and Candlin, 2007; Pérez-Paredes et al., 2011). The logs generated can provide information about participants' searches, the time and date they accessed the tool, the referring page, the search query, the number of times a word was looked up, etc. With eye-tracking we could investigate not only the number of search queries or the specific words that are searched, but also what learners are attending to while doing those searches and the amount of time they spend looking at specific areas of the screen. This would provide a much clearer understanding of how users interact with corpus tools.

Another important question is how people engage with the output produced by corpus tools, which often looks markedly different to standard written text (see for example Figure 6.10). Eye-tracking can provide information about looking patterns to the output, which will tell us where readers allocate their attention and how much processing effort is expended looking at various parts of the corpus-generated output. In this section we will consider looking patterns to both the tools and the output they produce.

6.4.1 What Can Be Measured?

Corpus linguistics is a large and vibrant field and eye-tracking could potentially be incorporated into corpus linguistics in various ways. Here, we will concentrate on two areas where we believe that eye-tracking could offer some useful insight: (1) the use of the output from corpora in language teaching; and (2) the development of corpus software.

The benefits of corpus linguistics to language teaching have long been acknowledged (Timmis, 2015). Corpora can contribute to language teaching, for example, by giving students corpus data. Alternatively, learners can be asked to use corpus tools and access data for themselves. Although a lot has been written about what can be done with corpora in the classroom, empirical evidence to validate the approach is still scarce. Evaluations of the use of corpora in the classroom have primarily relied on subjective observation or informal testing (Gilquin and Granger, 2010) and on indirect measures like questionnaires, interviews and reflective logs (e.g. Bernardini, 1998; Kennedy and Miceli, 2001; Varley, 2009). Eye-tracking offers a direct, online measurement of learners' attention to various aspects of corpora (or corpora-derived materials) and the possibility of relating their use to performance on language tasks.

Corpus tools output concordance lines (see example in Figure 6.10), which have been said to be a good way to ascertain and model authentic language use. While they can provide a comprehensive set of examples of 'real-life' language, they are often displayed in a format that people may find challenging to read. There are questions about the benefit of authentic examples when they are difficult to read, and researchers have yet to explore how readers engage with such concordance lines. Monitoring readers' eye-movements when they encounter concordance lines would allow researchers to begin to answer this question. We could find out, for example, which lines or parts of the lines are read, if there are looks between the different areas within a line and how much time is spent reading the lines.

A second area in corpus linguistics where eye-tracking could provide valuable insight is the development of corpus software. When developing tools to search and analyse corpora, the goal is to provide user-friendly interfaces that are suitable for users without extensive computer experience. Thus, an important concern is designing tools that users can easily and successfully use. Eye-tracking can provide a better understanding of how users engage with a particular tool and its different functions, which could inform further development. We could, for example, get information about how long it takes users to find and use a particular function and the time spent looking at different sections of the tool.

Information about users' viewing behaviour while reading a set of concordance lines or while making use of various functions in a corpus tool could also be related to other types of post-task data (e.g. questionnaires on users' attitudes, tests assessing their knowledge of specific lexical patterns searched in the corpus), allowing us to explore the relationship between people's interaction with the corpus resource and their linguistic performance or their attitudes towards the use of the tool.

6.4.2 Methodological Considerations

As with testing and writing, there are important methodological considerations when eye-tracking both corpus tools and corpus-generated output. In this section we go through some of the key methodological issues when looking at users' interaction with a corpus tool and particular functions of the tool. We will also discuss monitoring eye-movements when reading concordance lines.

Interacting with the Tool

Corpus linguists might be interested in examining how learners and other users interact with a specific corpus tool. For example, the Wikipedia corpus (Davies, 2015) has help files that support the use of different functions (e.g. list, collocates, compare words). We might be interested in finding out whether users read the help files when they use a particular function and at which points in their searches they read them. In this case, our main ROI would be the help area. Examining the number and duration of fixations in the help ROI would provide information about the time that users spend reading the help file while performing their searches. We could also set the search area as a separate ROI and examine the number of regressions, as well as when regressions from the search to the help ROIs occur. This would provide detailed information about the specific points during a search that users attend to the help area. Comparing users' eye-movement behaviour to the different help files would allow us to identify which ones are used the most frequently – and maybe conclude which are actually the most 'helpful'. For this comparison, eye-movement data would need to be normalised according to the number of words in each of the help ROIs. When comparing reading times in different ROIs, potential differences in size and in the type of input presented would need to be accounted for in the analysis of the data. Further, since we would be examining users' live interaction with the real tool, we would be dealing with a dynamic stimulus (see Chapter 3 for more on working with dynamic stimuli).

Reading Concordance Lines

As discussed in the previous section, a key emphasis in corpus linguistics is using the knowledge gained from corpora, as well as the corpus output itself (e.g. concordance lines), in the classroom. However, little is known about how people read concordance lines. To assess this, we could present the concordance lines exactly as they are outputted from a tool (Figure 6.9) or we could modify them (Figure 6.10), which would allow us to establish more precise ROIs. Thus, similar to a classroom-based task, we could give participants a handout with a set of questions about specific linguistic patterns and ask them to use a concordance tool to generate a set of concordance lines, or give them a set of modified concordance lines. Our ROIs would be the area where the concordances are displayed (pre- and post-keyword and the keyword itself) (see Figure 6.9), and we could look at total reading time and number of fixations to those ROIs. Eye-movement data would, at a minimum, need to be normalised for the number and frequency of the words in each of the ROIs. Further, some corpus tools display part of the output in the concordance lines in colour, which could make some of the ROIs more salient than the others and affect participants' eye-movement behaviour. If the general settings of the corpus tool allow us to

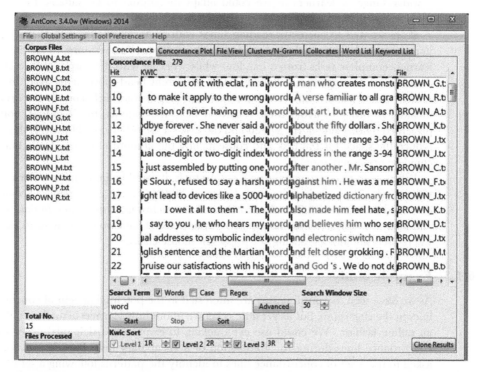

Figure 6.9 Example of stimuli for an eye-tracking study exploring users' engagement with the concordance tool from AntCont (Anthony, 2014). The keyword area, the preceding words and the following words in the lines are the three ROIs and are indicated by boxes with dashed lines.

change the font colour, the use of black font for all words would be preferred. If we use the coloured stimuli, this would need to be acknowledged as an important uncontrolled factor in the discussion and analysis of the data.

If our aim is to conduct a detailed analysis of the reading of specific parts of the concordance lines, the use of modified stimuli would be preferable. When we design our own stimuli so that we can have smaller, more precise ROIs, we will need to have a reasonable font size and at least double line spacing. This means that we will not be able to include as many concordance lines on the screen (see Figure 6.10). Therefore, we will need to carefully think about which lines are important to include in order to address our research question. This would compromise the 'authenticity' of the study as users will not be interacting with the real tool, but it will allow us to make valid claims about the reading of specific parts of concordance lines, which would otherwise be impossible.

Each of the modified concordance lines could be defined as a separate ROI (see Example A in Figure 6.10). We could also establish even smaller ROIs, like the keyword and the words right before and after it (see Example B in Figure 6.10). Given that the concordance lines vary in many ways, we would need to consider this in our analysis (e.g. normalise for frequency and length of the stimuli). Additionally, as we see in Figure 6.10, some of the concordance lines contain complete sentences while some do not, which could influence reading patterns. This is something that would need to be considered in our analysis. Importantly, the use of modified concordance lines would allow us to work with a wider range of learners as we could adapt the stimuli to be suitable for different proficiency levels.

If we wanted to correlate reading times with performance on a task, it would be important to design a task that we can easily evaluate. Furthermore, in studies where learners complete tasks from a handout while working with the corpus tool or concordance lines, the experiment would involve recurrent head movements away from the screen which would make recalibrations and (if possible) drift correct important to include. In order to avoid these recurrent head movements, the 'handout' could be presented on one side of the screen and the task on the other side. However, this would reduce the space for the task and consequently the amount of concordance lines that could be presented at once.

When asking users to engage with corpus tools, it could be informative to look at eye-movement data in conjunction with keystroke and/or mouse event data. The software described in Section 6.3.2 could also be used to synchronise these different data sources and analyse them in combination. These synchronised data would allow us to ascertain where users are looking during key presses or mouse clicks.

6.4.3 Example Study

As we have seen, corpus linguists are interested in the potential benefit of concordance lines in the classroom, but as yet little is known about how learners actually use them in an online fashion. We could use eye-tracking to examine participants' processing of concordance lines during the completion of a vocabulary task. Participants could be asked to use a set of concordance lines to identify the patterns following a set of target words, and their responses in the vocabulary task would show whether they have successfully identified the patterns. A set of research questions like the following could be addressed in a study like this:

Example A

and its weavers have the opportunity to sell them in Oaxaca
We have an ideal opportunity to balance these issues.
This presents an exciting opportunity to find ways to change it.
Students have ample opportunity to show their experience.
They lost a significant opportunity to enlist professional.
This creates an opportunity for critical self-analysis.
This provides an excellent opportunity for everyone.

Example B

and its weavers have the	opportunity	to sell them in Oaxaca
We have an ideal	opportunity	to balance these issues.
This presents an exciting	opportunity	to find ways to change it.
Students have ample	opportunity	to show their experience.
They lost a significant	opportunity	to enlist professional.
This creates an	opportunity	for critical self-analysis.
This provides an excellent	opportunity	for everyone.

Figure 6.10 Example of stimuli for an eye-tracking study exploring the processing of a set of concordance lines (concordance lines modified from the Corpus of Contemporary American English, Davies, 2008–). In Example A, each line is defined as a separate ROI. In Example B, the keyword, preceding and following context in each concordance line are defined as separate ROIs. ROIs are indicated by boxes.

1. Which parts of the concordance line (the pre-keyword, the keyword and the post-keyword regions) do learners pay more/less attention to?
2. Do participants read all of the concordance lines and give an equivalent amount of attention to each?
3. Is reading behaviour related to performance on the tasks?
4. How do participant variables (proficiency, reading skill, etc.) relate to reading patterns and task performance?

We would first select target words (the keywords), matched for length, part of speech and frequency. Participants would be presented with a set of concordance lines for each word and would be asked to identify any linguistic patterns around the keywords. Ideally, the concordance lines would be matched for factors like length, vocabulary level, word frequency, whether they present complete/incomplete sentences, etc. Because our research questions require examination of precise ROIs, we would use modified concordance lines with appropriate font size and line spacing. The area preceding the keyword, the keyword and the context following the keyword would be selected as separate ROIs (see Example B in Figure 6.10). Looking at the number and duration of fixations made on these three types of ROI would provide information about which receives more attention from learners. We might also want to set smaller ROIs that are more specific to the linguistic pattern, to see how much time participants spend looking at the pattern itself. In Figure 6.10 we see two patterns following the word 'opportunity', which we could also designate as ROIs: 'to' + verb; and 'for' + (adj) noun. Since each ROI has a different number of words that vary in frequency and length, analysis of the eye-movement data would need to take this into account. This procedure would be repeated for all of the keywords. An average value per eye-tracking measure would be calculated per participant so that each learner would have an average measure for the pre-keyword, the keyword and the post-keyword region, as well as for the 'pattern' ROIs if we established them.

Statistical analysis of each type of ROI for all participants in the experiment will provide an answer to the first research question. In order to answer the second research question, we could look at the effect of the order of appearance on the processing of the concordance lines (1st–7th in Figure 6.10). We might hypothesise that participants would read the first few lines and then realise that the noun 'opportunity' is usually followed by an infinitive verb clause, and they might not read the remaining lines to identify other patterns. We could look at the number and duration of fixations on all ROIs per line and explore whether there is an effect of position on reading times. We could also look at reading times to our 'pattern' ROIs to see if early examples of the pattern are attended to more than later ones.

In order to answer the third research question, we would calculate an average of the normalised total reading time per set of concordance lines per participant and correlate that average to their performance on each of the vocabulary tasks. This would allow us to find out whether there is a relationship between the time spent reading the concordance lines for a keyword and the successful completion of the task. Finally, we could examine any of the participant variables we have measured (e.g. proficiency, reading skill, language background) in relation to the reading patterns explored in the first three research questions.

6.5 Eye-Tracking in Translation Research

In all of the domains we have looked at thus far, researchers have been interested in understanding a particular behaviour (reading, writing, listening, speaking, etc.). In the past, our knowledge about these kinds of behaviours has generally come from observation and analysis of the output of the behaviours themselves. Translation is no exception to this, and an understanding of the mental processes implicated in translation has largely come from examining the utterances received and produced by the translator and the way he/ she uses them (Grucza, 2013), as well as being based on interviews, questionnaires and think-aloud protocols.

Recent advances in technology have opened up many possibilities to gain a better understanding of the processes involved in translation (Grucza, 2013). In the 1990s translation researchers began to make use of computer technology, video recording, screen recording and keystroke-logging to investigate the translation process, but it was not until after 2000 that eye-tracking was incorporated into translation research (Pluzyczka, 2013). Since then, eye-tracking has become a popular quantitative research tool in translation research (Hvelplund, 2014), used to examine the cognitive effort involved in different types of translation (Korpal, 2015). As Korpal (2015) claims, 'By means of eye-tracking experimenters may investigate moment-by-moment changes in the cognitive effort necessary to perform a given translation/interpreting task' (p. 199). Recent studies have used a combination of keystroke-logging and eye-tracking to gain a better insight into the comprehension and production processes in translation (Göpferich et al., 2011). In contrast to some of the fields discussed thus far where eye-tracking research has yet to really emerge, eye-tracking has been quite prominent in translation research for the past ten years.

6.5.1 What Can Be Measured?

Different areas of translation research have made use of eye-tracking technology: (1) written to written (*written translation*); (2) written to oral (*sight translation*); (3) visual to oral, i.e. when the source is an image and the target text has oral form (e.g. audio description); (4) oral to written (e.g. subtitles); and (5) development and evaluation of computer translation tools.

Although in translation studies the focus of investigation is usually on the cognitive effort expended by the translator in different tasks, the eye-movements of the recipient of the translation can also be monitored. As Zwierzchoń-Grabowska (2013) explains, research conducted on sight and written translation has typically focused on the translator's eye-movements, while research on audio description and subtitles has focused on analysing the recipient's eye-movements. In general, studies involving eye-tracking in translation have analysed the fixations, saccades and regressions of translators and recipients in a variety of contexts. In what follows we discuss each of the topics identified above.

Written to Written

Within the context of *written translation*, translation competence requires, as a minimum, reading and writing in two languages and the ability to coordinate and combine these skills (Dragsted, 2010). Translators need to construct meaning in the source text and represent meaning in the target text. Thus, we are dealing with two types of processes: the processing of the written source text for the specific purpose of being translated and the monitoring of their own translating and typing. Eye-tracking can therefore be used to examine the coordination and combination of these processes. In particular, eye-tracking can be used to examine translators' eye-movements to the source and target texts at different time

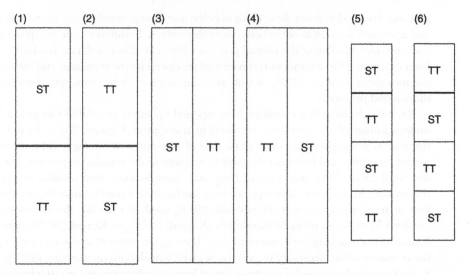

Figure 6.11 Possible locations of the source (ST) and target (TT) texts in eye-tracking-supported written translation studies (adapted from Zwierzchoń-Grabowska, 2013, p. 78). In configurations 1 and 2 the ST and TT are placed one above the other; in configurations 3 and 4 they are placed side by side; and in configurations 5 and 6 they are divided into shorter parts and presented in alternate order.

points in the translation process, as well as movements between these two areas. Similar to the writing projects described in Section 6.3.2, we could analyse translators' eye-movement behaviour during typing and pausing events. This would allow us to see whether during certain pauses or typing events, translators look at the source text or monitor the text they are writing. This will also help identify parts of the source and target text that require more or less processing effort.

In research on written translation, where both the source and target texts are displayed on the computer screen, the location and size of those areas is a very important concern. Zwierzchoń-Grabowska (2013) identified six different possible configurations (see Figure 6.11). Eye-tracking could be used to examine which of them leads to the most effective translation of the same text. More precisely, we can see which ones elicit more and longer fixations, which would tell us if a particular configuration is more difficult to process.

In written translation, translators are often presented with the source text and a machine-translated text and they are asked to edit the machine translation, as opposed to producing the target text from scratch. Eye-tracking can be used to investigate the post-editing of machine translations. As Hansen-Schirra and Rösener (2013) explain, eye-tracking can be used to identify which parts of the translated text make translators go back to the source text. From this we could infer elements of the translation that appear to be more problematic or which require a greater degree of consideration for the translators.

Written to Oral

Within the domain of *sight translation*, eye-tracking can be used to examine the translator's processing of the written source text while producing the oral target text. Sight translation is thought to involve a very special type of reading, as the translator is expected to reproduce the text almost immediately, leaving very little time for reading (Pluzyczka, 2013). An interesting question, then, is to compare the reading of the same text for translation and 'normal' reading purposes to establish the cognitive demands of the translation task.

Eye-tracking can be used in sight translation research to explore which parts of the on-screen source text are the most difficult for translators. For example, Pluzyczka (2013) recorded the eye-movements of participants who were training to be translators while sight translating three paragraphs that contained certain translation difficulties (e.g. abbreviations, specialised terms, collocations). Eye-movement patterns were used to identify places where the students had difficulties. Eye-tracking has also been used to compare the fixations made in a source text by professional translators and students (Pluzyczka, 2013). Looking at students' fixation patterns when processing texts of similar characteristics over the course of training can be used to examine the development of translation skills. This would provide an indication of when their skills begin to resemble those of skilled professionals. Eye-tracking has also been used to examine the differential effect of syntactic complexity on translators' cognitive effort in written translation and sight translation, providing a better understanding of the cognitive demands that characterise sight translation (e.g. Shreve, La Cruz and Angelone, 2010).

Visual to Oral

In certain situations translators produce oral texts from visual sources (images or videos). This type of audio-visual translation has been referred to as *audio description*. It provides an oral description of visual input and was originally developed for blind and partially sighted viewers (Szarkowska et al., 2013). These oral descriptions are used in a variety of contexts. In museums, for example, we often have oral descriptions of artwork for blind visitors. In educational contexts, audio descriptions are also used to support language development. Eye-tracking has been used to explore the applicability of audio description in a variety of contexts. Several studies have looked at differences in the listeners' processing of visual stimuli with or without audio description. For example, Szarkowska et al. (2013) showed sighted primary school children a film with and without audio description while their eye-movements were recorded. They analysed fixation count, fixation duration and saccade amplitude (i.e. the size of the saccade) to the video stimulus and examined differences in the two conditions. Similarly, Vilaró et al. (2012) examined whether the soundtrack influenced the perception of audio-visual texts. They tested four different soundtracks to the same clip and explored differences in eye-movements with the addition of sound.

Oral to Written

Subtitles have been identified as another type of translation, where oral words are 'translated' into written text. As stated earlier, the focus in this type of research is not the translator but the recipient – in other words, how the recipient processes the text. Szarkowska et al. (2013) used eye-tracking to examine potential differences in the processing of subtitles by deaf, hard of hearing and hearing participants. They recorded participants' eye-movements while watching twenty-three short clips and looked at time to first fixation to the subtitles and the time participants spent reading subtitles compared to the time spent watching the whole clip (see Section 5.4 for a discussion of a study examining the processing of subtitles).

Evaluation of Computer Translation Tools

Another area of translation research that has received considerable attention from researchers in the past ten years is the development and evaluation of computer translation tools. Several computer programs can be used during the translation process. Examining translators' interaction with those resources has become a crucial concern in translation research. With eye-tracking, we could look at the number and duration of fixations to the different windows of a tool: a source text window, a window with the evolving target text, a window with supporting information to help with the translation, etc. As Hansen-Schirra and Rösener (2013) showed, examining translators' eye-movements to the different areas of a tool interface provides information about which areas or windows are neglected during the translation process, which ones are attended to, and when in the translation process the different areas are looked at. As in Hansen-Schirra and Rösener, we could examine translators' attention to these areas in different systems in order to examine the usability and efficiency of different tools. Similar to what we saw in corpus linguistics, eye-tracking could be used to examine how translators interact with various tools and programs, which would inform and ultimately improve the development of these tools.

6.5.2 Methodological Considerations

Applying eye-tracking to translation research faces many of the same methodological challenges as other eye-tracking research, as well as others that are particularly relevant to translation studies. An important methodological consideration for all the translation topics discussed so far relates to the interpretation of eye-movement data. As discussed in Chapter 1, eye-tracking makes use of the eye–mind assumption, which holds that what we are looking at is what we are thinking about. As we saw in Chapter 4 there are some important caveats to this. Translation, due to the nature of the task itself, may provide another instance where we want to treat this assumption with caution. As Hvelplund (2014) explains:

> For translation, specifically, this means that although the translator is looking at the ST [source text], he may well be considering possible target language (TL) equivalents of that specific ST word, and when looking at the TT [target text], the translator may well be constructing meaning hypotheses based on ST content. In translation research, and other research disciplines as well, this problem of possible disagreement between visual focus and cognitive focus merits caution, and observations ought to be interpreted in the light of this potential weakness. (p. 210)

Importantly, Hvelplund (2014) recognises that there is a reasonable basis for assuming some sort of relationship between eye-movements and translation processing; however, we should always consider the simplifications that this assumption makes when interpreting our data. Hvelplund's quote highlights a general methodological concern in translation research. There are other issues that are more (or less) relevant to the different translation contexts discussed in the previous section. In what follows we will identify key methodological considerations for each.

Written to Written

As in the other research investigating writing, it is important to keep in mind that reading a source text and one that is currently being written are two very different types of reading that elicit different eye-movement patterns (Hvelplund, 2014). While keeping this caveat in mind, a common research question in written translation research is the amount of attention (processing effort) that is paid to what is being translated (source) and to what is being produced (target) when they are both presented on the computer screen (e.g. Carl and Kay, 2011; Dragsted, 2010). In this case, the main methodological concerns are very similar to those described in Sections 6.2.2 and 6.3.2. We would be dealing with two main processes, namely the reading of a provided written text and the production of a written one. We could examine the amount of overall reading in the source and target text ROIs (see Figure 6.5). Potential differences in the size of these ROIs would need to be accounted for. Examining regressions between the source and target ROIs would provide information about the transition between the reading and production modes. We could also look at eye-movements to specific parts of the source and target texts by defining smaller ROIs. Lexical and syntactical differences between ROIs would need to be taken into account.

Importantly, in translation we expect that a translator will read a section of text (a 'chunk of text') and then produce the corresponding text in the target language. We could examine the reading and writing processes for a particular chunk of text. To do this, we would need to identify what constitutes that chunk of text. In the translation literature this has been operationalised as a minimum of two consecutive fixations in the source text within a particular time interval and as a sequence of successive keystrokes that are not interrupted by a pause of a particular duration (Carl and Kay, 2011). These chunks would then constitute our ROIs.

As we have seen previously, in order to be able to examine precise ROIs on the screen, we will need to have a large enough font size and adequate line spacing. This means that we will likely have to present a text that would normally appear on a single typewritten page across a number of screens. Thus, we would divide the text into different parts, each constituting a trial in the eye-tracking experiment, and we would ask translators to translate each part, with a drift correct after each trial (if possible) or recalibrations after every few trials. These modifications of course come at a cost. As O'Brien (2009) explains, 'Translators normally work with larger chunks of text and, therefore, one could argue that we are not investigating "real scenarios" [when we give them smaller sections of text]. The validity of our research is, therefore, compromised' (p. 262).

In all of these cases, looking at the integration and combination of the reading of the source text and the production of the target text, a key methodological consideration is the synchronisation of eye-movement and keystroke data and the use of synchronised data to define our ROIs. Specialised software that integrates these sources of information should be used (e.g. Translog II; Carl, 2012). This synchronisation is crucial when analysing measures like the eye-key span, defined as the time between a fixation on a word in the source text and the first keystroke of its equivalent in the target text (Dragsted, 2010). These eye-key span values are calculated by deducting the timestamp in milliseconds of the onset of the source text fixation from the onset of the production of the equivalent target text word.

Finally, as with other writing research (see Sections 6.2.2 and 6.3.2), we might be interested in the examination of eye-movements during pausing and typing events. The same methodological considerations as in the writing projects would apply here. Additionally, an important methodological consideration in eye-tracking-supported translation studies is participants' writing capacities and ability to touch type (see Section 6.3.2).

Written to Oral

In sight translation research, we might be interested in examining the overall number and duration of fixations to the source text while producing the oral text. The whole source text area could be designated as our ROI. Examining the total number of fixations, the average fixation duration and the total reading time will provide an indication of how the source text is processed. If we are interested in the processing of specific parts of the source text, as in Pluzyczka (2013), different ROIs would be selected for each of these. In all cases, eye-movement data would need to be normalised according to the different features of those ROIs (e.g. length of each word, number of words) and analyses would need to account for other word-level and sentence-level features that were not controlled for.

Another interesting research question in sight translation research is to examine the processing of the source text while producing a specific part of the oral target text. To do this, the oral production would need to be recorded and the eye-movement data would need to be time-locked to it. This would allow us to investigate where exactly in the source text translators are fixating while producing a particular part of the oral output. Care should be taken to ensure that the audio is accurately synchronized with the eye-movement record, and if necessary specialised recording software should be used.

Researchers have also been interested in examining errors in the oral production. Investigating this with eye-tracking can be challenging as translators are not necessarily looking at the word they are producing, and instead may already be reading the upcoming words in the source text. Therefore, an analysis will need to involve not only the target word but the subsequent words as well. Pluzyczka (2013) found that translation studies students frequently did not show longer fixations at the moment errors were made, which she interpreted as them not being aware of making a mistake. However, longer fixations could have been made in subsequent words due to spillover effects. Because often what is being read and what is being said do not align, determining the appropriate ROI can be challenging. In this case, visualisations like heat maps might provide some insight and help inform what we designate as ROIs. As will be further explained in Chapter 7, such visualisations can be used to identify areas with more fixations, which can then be selected as ROIs. Reading times in the 'difficult' areas should be compared statistically to other ROIs of similar characteristics, so as to be able to make valid claims about the increased cognitive effort required by those potentially problematic areas.

Visual to Oral, Oral to Written and Evaluation of Computer Translation Tools

The last three types of translation largely face the same methodological concerns discussed elsewhere. For example, in the examination of translators' processing of an image in visual to oral translation, we would monitor looks to the different parts of the visual input, taking into consideration the methodological concerns highlighted in Chapter 5. We could relate looking patterns to the oral output produced by the translator. In the examination of visual to oral translation, time-locking the visual input and the oral production will be an important aspect of the design. Specialised software that allows for this synchronisation of eye-movement and oral data should be used.

As discussed in the previous section, research in oral to written translation has focused on an examination of the recipient's processing of subtitles. The methodological considerations discussed in Section 5.4 would apply to this context. Similarly, the key methodological considerations in the examination of translators' interaction with computer translation tools would be the same as those discussed in Section 6.4.2 on the examination of users' interaction with corpus tools.

6.5.3 Example Study

As we have seen in the discussion thus far, there is a rich and developed literature making use of eye-tracking to investigate translation. The example study we will consider here focuses on a translator's processing of a source text during written translation. Let's imagine that, as translation researchers, we are interested in examining how professional translators deal with the translation of a specific type of culturally based expressions in English, i.e. idioms, with no literal translation equivalents in the target language. The following research questions could be addressed:

1 How long do translators spend fixating the source and target texts? Is the amount of reading related to the quality of the output?
2 How do translators process the target expressions in comparison to matched control expressions?
3 How many times do translators go back to the source text while translating these source expressions?

The first thing we would need to decide is the layout of the task. Both the source text and what is being produced need to be visible on the computer screen. These two areas should be the same size to avoid having to account for size differences in our ROIs (see Figure 6.12). Since one of the aims of the study is to examine the processing of specific phrases in the source text, the texts need to be designed with a big enough font size and line spacing. This limits the amount of text that can be presented on the screen, and therefore stimuli would need to be designed such that they could be presented across screens. Participants would be asked to translate a set of short texts, each containing one or two target expressions (a greater density of such expressions might make the objective of the task apparent to participants). A set of idiomatic expressions with the same structure (verb + adj/article + noun) would be selected (e.g. 'to go cold turkey', 'to find your feet', 'to ring a bell', 'to face the music'). They would all be presented in the text in the same infinitive form. Differences in length, individual word frequency and whole idiom frequency would be accounted for in the analysis. The texts in which these expressions appear would be specifically designed for this experiment to ensure that no other low-frequency lexical items were included, that the target idioms appeared in the same position within the sentence, and that the contextual cues were equally informative (see Chapter 4 for more information on factors to control in the design of texts). A set of control texts, i.e. texts containing a literal paraphrase of the target expressions (e.g. 'to remind me of something' for 'to ring a bell') would also be created. Finally, a set of filler texts (i.e. texts of similar characteristics not containing idioms or any of the control expressions) would be included in the experiment. The presentation of these target, control and filler texts would be randomised to control for the possibility of an order effect.

Participants would be asked to translate each text and press 'Enter' to proceed to the next text. Because the task involves a typing component, most participants will look away from the screen towards the keyboard at certain points in the study and the amount of

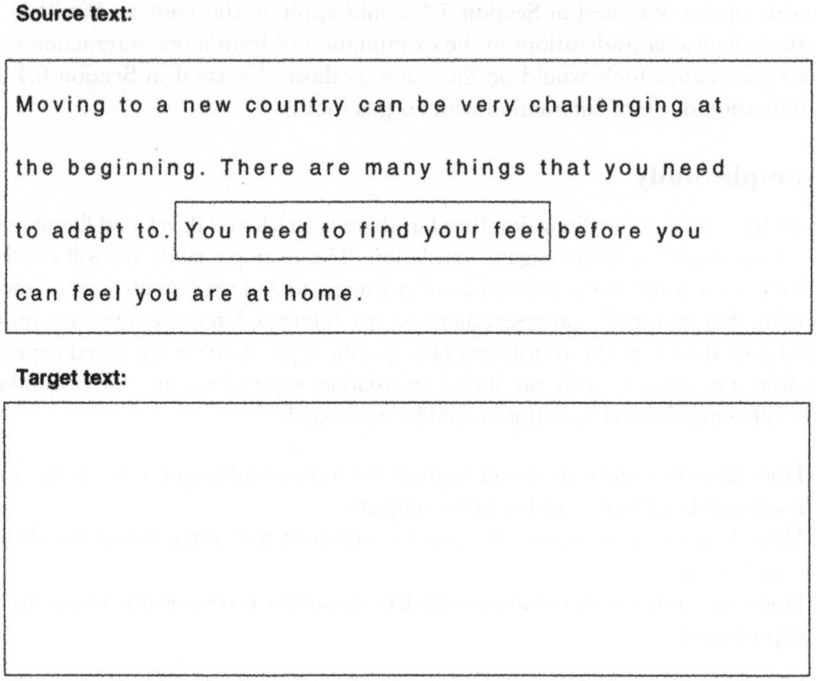

Source text:

Moving to a new country can be very challenging at the beginning. There are many things that you need to adapt to. You need to find your feet before you can feel you are at home.

Target text:

Figure 6.12 Example of stimuli for an eye-tracking study examining performance on a written translation task. The source text, target text and idiom areas are identified as ROIs and are indicated by boxes.

looks away will likely depend on typing skill. A drift correct should be added before the presentation of each text to account for possible drifts and track loss caused by the recurrent movements to and from the screen. If the system does not allow for drift correct, frequent recalibrations should be included.

In order to answer the first research question, the target and source text areas would be defined as ROIs. We would look at the number of fixations, total reading time and average fixation duration in each of these two ROIs for the duration of each item before proceeding to the next one. The translated texts would be scored on a range of measures (e.g. accuracy, organisation) by a different group of professional translators and these scores could be evaluated in relation to the average total reading time spent in the source and target text ROIs, answering the second part of the first research question.

Addressing the second research question would require the selection of more specific ROIs. In this case, each of the target and control expressions would be selected as separate ROIs (see Figure 6.12). An average value of each eye-tracking measure for target and control ROIs would be calculated and their means would be compared. To answer the third research question, we could look at the number of regressions to the source text ROI from the onset of the production of the translated target expression until the target expression had been completed. This would provide information about the number of times that participants need to go back to the source text while translating a given expression. This analysis would involve the identification of the production units that are equivalent to the source expression (the translator produces 'encontrar tu sitio' for 'find your feet'). The timestamps for the production event (typing 'encontrar tu sitio') would dictate when the ROI is active in the source text. More specifically, we would only measure eye-movements to the source text while its translation was being produced. We would use specialised software of the type described in Section 6.4.2 to integrate and analyse eye-movement and keystroke data.

In our example, we created a controlled study with very circumscribed conditions. This allows us to make specific claims about producing a very particular kind of translation. However, in the real world, translators would have tools at their disposal to help them translate such language. Thus, our study, while informative, does not represent an authentic translating situation for this kind of written materials. However, the inclusion of interactive resources like online dictionaries would affect the quality of the data recorded. This is an important methodological concern that would need to be considered in the interpretation and discussion of results.

6.6 Eye-Tracking in Computer-Mediated Communication in Language Learning

In many educational settings, researchers and educators are interested in the value of computer-assisted language learning. Thus, we can use computers to help children learning their first language and children and adults learning their second language, as well as certain populations with language difficulties. Because this is such a broad area, here we will focus on one prominent example of computer-assisted language learning, which involves computer-mediated communication. This is primarily of interest in the domain of second language learning because it requires the users to produce written language.

In the (second) language learning context, computer-mediated communication refers to any type of communication between student and student/teacher that is facilitated by computer applications. It can be synchronous (online chats and voice over internet protocol (VoIP) calls) or asynchronous (wikis, weblogs and emails). One type of computer-mediated communication that has attracted particular attention from second language acquisition researchers is synchronous computer-mediated communication (SCMC, i.e. written computer chats) in the form of web chat rooms and instant messenger programs. The belief is that such communication fosters attention to form, facilitating certain behaviours and attentional processes that in turn facilitate language learning (Smith, 2012).

Like many of the domains we have considered in this chapter, research in this area has mainly focused on the examination of the output (e.g. transcripts of chat sessions). However, a log of what someone typed provides a limited picture of his/her online processing. A few studies have examined users' behaviours using retrospective reports (e.g. Lee, 2004), keystroke logs (e.g. Pellettieri, 2000), video recording (e.g. Lai and Zhao, 2006) and video screen capture (Sauro and Smith, 2010). Unfortunately, these measures tell us very little about how attention is allocated to the input or output in SCMC, or about the cognitive effort that is expended on either one. Eye-tracking offers the means to explore this (Michel and Smith, 2017).

6.6.1 What Can Be Measured?

Eye-tracking can be used to investigate several aspects of SCMC, including learners' allocation of attention to the different areas of the computer interface, eye-movements to the input and output messages, and the processing of specific parts of the input and output. In what follows we discuss these in turn.

As with the corpus and translation projects discussed in Sections 6.4.2 and 6.5.2, during SCMC learners interact with a computer program, and eye-tracking can be used to examine learners' allocation of attention to different areas of it. Thus, we could present participants with a particular computer interface with different functions and we could monitor looks to the different sections of the tool. For example, Stickler and Shi (2015) examined learners' eye-movements while completing an online activity in which they had to communicate interactively with the tutor and other participants. Stickler and Shi used heat maps to identify areas on the screen that had increased activity, and these were then selected as the main ROIs for analysis. They analysed the number and duration of fixations to these different ROIs, allowing them to gain a better understanding of the areas of the online platform that received more attention by learners and those that were neglected.

Eye-tracking can also be used to examine learners' looking patterns to the output they produce in online chat interactions. As with the writing and translation projects described in Sections 6.3.2 and 6.5.2, we could look at learners' eye-movements to the output area displayed on the screen. Of more specific interest might be eye-movements during different time windows: for example, while learners are drafting their message (before sending it) and after sending it. Eye-tracking could be used to examine the processing of the utterances produced by the interlocutor, as well as the looks between what the interlocutor produces and what the participant produces.

If we would like to explore the relationship between the input and output, and, in particular, how the input informs the output, it might be informative to look at recasts. Recasts are a type of corrective feedback that 'correctly restate or rephrase (modify) all or part of a learner's utterance to be more target-like by changing one or more sentence components while still retaining its meaning' (Smith and Renaud, 2013, p. 147). Recasts are considered a beneficial and powerful form of corrective feedback. However, their effectiveness depends on learners' attending to and noticing them. Learners' attention to recasts has traditionally been examined by questionnaires and concurrent and retrospective recall. Eye-tracking can potentially provide a more direct measure of attention, and some researchers have begun to use the technology to explore attention to recasts (e.g. Smith, 2012; Smith and Renaud, 2013). We could take a transcript and log of a student–instructor chat to look for examples of recasts. We might see that the student typed, 'I wented to the movies over the weekend,' and the instructor responded with, 'So, you went to the movies. What did you see?' We would define our recast ('you went to the movies') and the original output ('I wented to the movies') as our ROIs, and we could look at learners' eye-movements to these two ROIs.

6.6.2 Methodological Considerations

As discussed in the previous section, eye-tracking can be used to examine learners' attention to the different sections of the online platforms used in SCMC activities. Although making use of a different type of interface, these projects would be very similar to those discussed in Sections 6.4.3 and 6.5.3 exploring users' interaction with corpus and translation tools. The same methodological issues would apply here (see Section 6.4.3 and Figure 6.9). In addition, because the type of SCMC that we have considered here has focused on reading and writing, many of the methodological considerations are similar to those we discussed in relation to testing, writing and translation. In what follows we will address concerns that are particularly important in the SCMC context.

A. Reading during drafting

B. Reading after sending

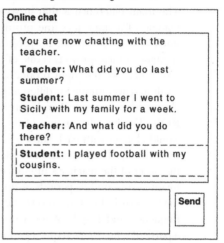

Figure 6.13 Example of stimuli for an eye-tracking study examining learners' processing of their own messages at different time points in a synchronous computer-mediated communication (SCMC) task. Two time points are represented (A: reading during drafting but before sending the message; B: reading after sending the message). The learner's message at time points A and B is defined as the ROI and is indicated by a box with dashed lines.

Eye-Movements to the Output

The examination of the processing of learners' own messages in online communication is very similar to what was described in the testing, writing and translation sections in this chapter. Crucially, as in these other domains, keystroke and eye-movement data need to be mapped and sorted by timestamp. Specific software of the type described in Section 6.3.2 could be used to synchronise and analyse keystroke and eye-movement data. The selection of ROIs would then depend on the time window we want to explore (see Figure 6.13). If we are looking at a student's reading of his/her message while drafting but before sending it, an important methodological consideration is the identification of 'drafting events'. O'Rourke (2012) explains that drafting events can be identified as 'those stretches of events and fixations occurring between an initial keypress and the pressing of the enter key, which publishes the draft' (p. 321). The keystroke data would allow us to identify this time period. The ROIs would be the typing area and they would be activated only during a drafting event (see Figure 6.13). When examining reading after sending the message, the ROIs would be the area corresponding to each sent utterance activated from the moment the message was sent until the next drafting event starts (see Figure 6.13). As with all writing research, the language that is produced in each of the ROIs will vary on a number of different factors, which would need to be accounted for in our analysis.

Eye-Movements to the Input

The projects described above involve the examination of the interlocutors' processing of their own utterances. However, we could also use eye-tracking to examine the processing of the messages produced by the other participant in the communicative exchange. This would be very similar to the processing of source documents in writing and translation projects. The main difference is that in writing and translation projects we were dealing with the reading of a static text (the prompt in writing studies and the source text in translation studies), whereas in SCMC projects all texts are interactive. The dynamic nature of the stimulus in these projects is one of the main methodological challenges (Michel and Smith, 2017). Because the input produced by the interlocutor could be almost anything, defining ROIs and accounting for differences between them statistically is challenging. In this case, as illustrated in Example A in Figure 6.14, the tutor's utterances would be defined as separate ROIs. The live chat nature of this experiment would mean that the position of the ROIs would change with each subsequent utterance. ROIs would therefore need to be defined dynamically. The fixations in the ROIs selected for analysis would be those corresponding to the onset of the teacher's utterance and the onset of the learner's written response, which might correspond to periods of track loss (because of the student possibly looking down to the keyboard). Fixation counts and durations would need to be normalised by the number, frequency and length of the words in each ROI, so that we could make claims about a particular utterance requiring more cognitive effort or attention by the learner. Otherwise, the more and longer fixations found in a particular utterance would not necessarily correspond to increased attention but to any of these uncontrolled features.

Eye-Movements to Smaller ROIs

In other cases we might be interested in the processing of specific parts of a given input or output message. For example, as in Smith and Renaud (2013), we might be interested in examining learners' attention to the different recasts provided by the tutor. In this case, we need to ensure that the task is designed such that it has a big enough font size and adequate line spacing so that we can accurately track eye-movements to smaller parts of a message. Crucially, to analyse looking patterns to recasts, we first need to identify them. This is done manually, by going through a transcript of the interactions. This is a time-consuming process and should be considered before embarking on the study. Further, if we were interested in looking behaviour due to different types of recasts (e.g. lexis, grammar, spelling) or their difficulty, this would need to be manually coded (for an example see Smith and Renaud, 2013).

Once recasts have been identified and coded, the keystroke log would tell us when the recasts have been produced. The synchronisation of keystroke and eye-movement data would allow us to define our recast ROIs. We would assess looks to and from the recast and the student's original output. Since the recast ROIs will have different lengths and sizes, data will need to be normalised. Greater than expected looking times to the recast would provide an indication that it had been attended to. However, as explained throughout the book, this 'increased attention' can only be determined by comparison to reading behaviour in a matched control condition, which would be difficult in this context. Better evidence that the recast had been attended to would be looks back to the student's original output upon seeing the recast.

Finally, like all of the studies that require typing by participants, looks to the keyboard will increase track loss, and this will vary depending on the typing skill of each individual. Furthermore, as we touched upon in our discussion of writing studies (see Section 6.3.2), keyboards vary depending on the writing system, and even for the same writing system, keyboards can be subtly different. Thus, for the second language learners who were the focus of discussion in this section, track loss due to looks to the keyboard will be a particular

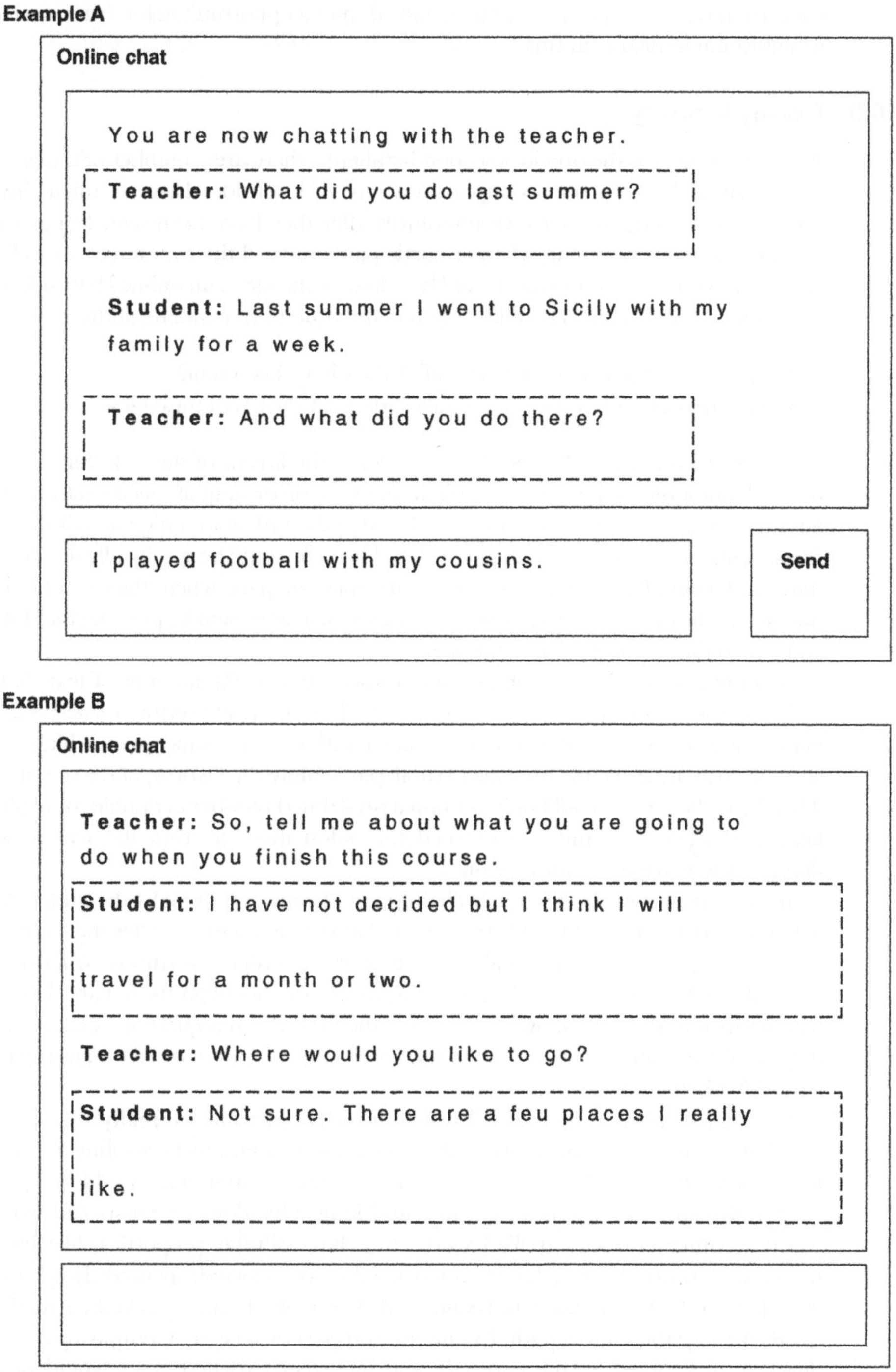

Example A

```
Online chat

    You are now chatting with the teacher.
    ┌─────────────────────────────────────────────┐
    ╎ Teacher: What did you do last summer?        ╎
    ╎                                              ╎
    └─────────────────────────────────────────────┘

    Student: Last summer I went to Sicily with my
    family for a week.

    ┌─────────────────────────────────────────────┐
    ╎ Teacher: And what did you do there?          ╎
    ╎                                              ╎
    └─────────────────────────────────────────────┘

    I played football with my cousins.        Send
```

Example B

```
Online chat

    Teacher: So, tell me about what you are going to
    do when you finish this course.
    ┌─────────────────────────────────────────────┐
    ╎Student: I have not decided but I think I will ╎
    ╎                                               ╎
    ╎travel for a month or two.                     ╎
    └─────────────────────────────────────────────┘

    Teacher: Where would you like to go?

    ┌─────────────────────────────────────────────┐
    ╎Student: Not sure. There are a feu places I really ╎
    ╎                                               ╎
    ╎like.                                          ╎
    └─────────────────────────────────────────────┘
```

Figure 6.14 Example of stimuli for an eye-tracking study examining learners' processing of messages in a synchronous computer-mediated communication (SCMC) task. In Example A, the teacher's utterances are defined as the ROIs, whereas in Example B, the student's own messages are defined as the ROIs. ROIs are indicated by boxes with dashed lines.

concern. It will be very important to include frequent opportunities for drift correct and/or recalibration to deal with this.

6.6.3 Example Study

As the discussion in the previous section highlights, there are a number of things we could look at in SCMC. In our example study, we will consider how we might investigate learners' processing of their own utterances after they have been sent. In particular, we are interested in examining whether participants re-read their messages, as well as their attention to errors. Participants would be asked to engage in an online chat with a tutor to talk about a given topic. The following research questions could be addressed:

1 Do learners review their messages after they have been sent?
2 Do learners attend to spelling mistakes made in their sent messages?

The first thing we would need to consider is the layout of the task. Since one of our research questions involves the examination of the processing of specific parts of learners' messages, as explained earlier, we would design the task with a big enough font size and line spacing (see Example B in Figure 6.14). The task would be specifically designed for the study and would have two main sections: the message pane where the sent utterances are shown and the drafting/typing pane. Utterances would be sent by pressing the 'Enter' key, and would then appear in the sent pane.

As in writing projects, an important consideration is the amount of text that will be visible on the screen during the interactive task. If we keep all previous messages in the sent pane, the text would need to become smaller with each utterance sent, which would not allow us to analyse eye-movements to small parts (individual words) of the sent utterances. Therefore, the screen would only contain a predefined number of double- or triple-spaced lines, and when the limit was reached the oldest message from the sent pane would disappear to leave space for new ones.

In order to answer the first research question, the messages sent by the student would be defined as ROIs and would only be activated after being sent, i.e. after the learner presses the 'Enter' key, until the next drafting event starts. In order to do this we will need to align keystroke and eye-movement data. Looking at the number of ROIs that are skipped (those with no fixations) would allow us to answer the first research question. This skipping rate data would also allow us to calculate the percentage of messages that a given participant reads after being sent.

In order to answer the second research question, what we really want to know is whether learners' eye-movements show increased attention to spelling mistakes they have made after they have been sent. This 'increased attention' would be operationalised in this study as significantly more and longer fixations on misspelled words compared to other correctly spelled words that have similar properties, like length and frequency. Another set of ROIs would need to be selected: incorrectly spelled words (e.g. 'feu' in the last message in Example B, Figure 6.14) and matched correctly spelled words (having the same length, frequency and part of speech). Comparing number and duration of fixations in the correctly and incorrectly spelled items would provide an answer to the second question. As in the case of recasts, the identification of spelling mistakes would need to be done by inspecting the transcript of the interaction. This would be a time-consuming part of the study and this needs to be considered when evaluating the feasibility of the research. In this study we are focusing on one type of errors; however, we might be interested in the processing of different types of errors. Since error type could affect patterns of eye-movements (see Section 4.1), we would need to code each error accordingly in order to include this as a factor in our analysis.

6.7   Eye-Tracking in Literary Linguistics

A recent development in the application of eye-tracking has been in the field of literary linguistics, where a small but growing number of studies have attempted to use this technology to shed more light on the reading experience. Literary linguistics – often also called stylistics – approaches the study of literature from a primarily linguistic perspective. Stockwell (2005) argues that at the heart of stylistic analysis is the combination of formal linguistic description and broader ideological interpretation. This means that key linguistic features at all levels – phonological, morphological, lexical, syntactic and pragmatic – are analysed, and literary linguistics considers how the rules of language are either observed or violated to create specific effects within a text (Simpson, 2004).

One aim of this kind of research is often to use close linguistic analysis to inform the 'reader experience', or to demonstrate how the linguistic choices relate to specific effects in the minds of readers (Gavins and Steen, 2001). The problem here is that often the analysis treats the 'reader' as an entirely abstract entity, making claims about the presumed effect that a feature or set of features has without actually being able to back this up with real data. When literary linguists do collect data from real readers, they tend to be of the 'think-aloud' type, whereby a participant is asked to describe his/her thought processes while reading a text. Corbett (1997) cautions against the 'easy equation between what readers say they are doing and the actual cognitive processes which are occurring as they read' (p. 199), but suggests that this kind of approach can still be beneficial as a way of connecting the text and the people experiencing it. Other approaches are to use surveys or questionnaires to elicit information from readers after they have read a text. This does provide empirical data, but is 'offline' in the sense that it is collected after the text has been read and processed, and again there is no guarantee that what readers say they were doing is what they actually were doing.

We can use eye-tracking to help us understand how features such as word choice, syntactic structures and other identifiable patterns affect the online processing of texts, i.e. how actual readers process the text in real time. This allows us to address questions of 'reader experience' in a more empirically grounded way, by recording and analysing global and local eye-movement behaviour. Consequently, much of what we would need to consider for a literary linguistics eye-tracking study is the same as for any reading study (see Chapter 4). We may be interested in individual words (Section 4.3), multi-word sequences (Section 4.5), or whole sentences (Section 4.6). The principal differences are that in general, we are concerned with longer stretches of text (longer extracts, as opposed to single sentences or short paragraphs), and that the texts we want to study will be authentic, as opposed to ones that we have created with a specific manipulation in mind. This would be more in line with the study discussed in Section 4.3 where readers were presented with an entire Agatha Christie novel.

6.7.1   What Can Be Measured?

As with any of the reading studies discussed in Chapter 4, what we can measure will depend on what aspect of the text we are interested in. The studies by Cop and colleagues discussed in detail in Section 4.3 provide an excellent example of how eye-tracking can be applied to a whole novel, and then the data used to answer a number of different research questions. Eye-tracking a whole novel is clearly time-consuming, and most studies are concerned with smaller samples of text and more specific research questions.

One example of this is a study by Guy et al. (2016), which addresses an argument that exists in the world of literature over the role of 'editorial completeness' in the publishing of different editions of a text. That is, many classic texts exist in multiple forms, with minor changes between editions, and the question of whether it is important to faithfully record every single alteration has been hotly debated. For example, in the 1846 edition of *Oliver Twist*, Dickens refers to Fagin as 'The Jew', while in a later edition (1867) he is referred to by name. Changes can be lexical (which are called 'substantive'), as well as involving a range of minor changes to punctuation ('accidental' changes), which may often simply be down to publishers' house style, or even typesetter errors. Carrol et al. (2015) used eye-tracking to test how many of these sorts of change were even noticed by readers. They presented pairs of extracts (no more than a few lines long) from Dickens (*Oliver Twist*) and James (*The Portrait of a Lady*) that contained either substantive variants, accidental variants or no change, and used the number and duration of fixations on the sentence as a whole and the location of the change to measure how much attention was paid to these ROIs.

Other research questions have targeted specific structures, such as poetic enjambment (i.e. sentences or clauses in a poem that continue over a line break). Koops van't Jagt et al. (2014) found differences in reading patterns (fixations and regressions) for poetry versus prose, poetry with and without enjambment and for different types of enjambment. Researchers have also used eye-tracking to look at specific textual and layout features of poetry, such as lineation, spacing and shape (Roberts et al., 2013; Schaffner et al., 2012). Roberts et al. (2013) combined visual inspection of eye-movement patterns with detailed comments from participants to show that the spacing of a poem can have an effect on how it is read. Schaffner et al. (2013) used visualisations of fixation patterns and specific measures (fixation duration, number of fixations and saccade size) to show that irregular visual poems can induce a number of specific effects in readers, and that these can be inferred from the pattern of eye-movements.

Another use of eye-tracking in this area is to substantiate claims about the 'cognitive validity' of linguistic patterns that have been identified by literary and/or corpus linguists. Importantly, when doing so we need to keep in mind that eye-tracking measures processing effort; thus, claims about eye-tracking providing evidence about specific cognitive processes or about how language is represented in the mind need to be treated with caution. For example, Mahlberg, Conklin and Bisson (2014) used eye-tracking to try to determine whether patterns previously identified in Dickens's texts using corpus stylistics (Mahlberg, 2013) had any psycholinguistic reality. That is, are corpus-derived patterns that occur with a high level of frequency registered as 'chunks' by readers? The authors showed participants a series of extracts from Dickens novels and tracked eye-movements to the chunks and passages as a whole (fixation durations and number of fixations), then combined this with data elicited during the study – questions about what the participants had noticed about some of the characters mentioned in the texts. This combination of online (eye-movement) and offline measures allows us to add a further level of detail to any analysis of how literary patterns create effects in the minds of readers.

With all of the studies discussed here, eye-tracking can be used both as a stand-alone measure of reading patterns or combined with other data (often data elicited from questionnaires or think-aloud studies). Data can be analysed both quantitatively and qualitatively to provide a rich picture of how real readers respond when presented with authentic literary texts. In general, the aim is to see whether linguistic patterns identified using other methods (corpus analysis, stylistic analysis, etc.) can be corroborated and supported with empirical data from real readers.

6.7.2 Methodological Considerations

Most of the methodological considerations for studies of literature or natural texts are the same as for any reading study (see Chapter 4), so here we consider anything additional that we might need to take into account.

The main challenge is likely to be the level of control we have over our stimuli. Unlike when we invent our own stimulus materials, if we are choosing authentic texts we have no control over aspects like word length or frequency, or broader features like syntactic complexity, sentence length and any pragmatic or discourse-level features. For example, Cop et al. (2015a, 2015b), who presented readers with an Agatha Christie novel, were interested in global measures of reading behaviour, averaged out across the course of a whole novel, but they were still careful to define an 'optimally' matched set of items for their analysis (see Section 4.3). If we are interested in a small subset of specific words or phrases from within a given text, we will need to be careful in how we choose these. We could select a set of words that we were particularly interested in, and then find comparable words matched for length and frequency. However, the context that each word appears in would not be controlled. We could try to account for this in a number of ways. For example, we might ask a separate set of participants to rate our texts for the informativeness of the context. In many cases (especially for whole texts or even whole novels) this might simply involve too many variables to be feasible. We might still consider aspects such as transitional probability for keywords (i.e. how likely is word y once word x has been seen) as a way of trying to account for some aspects of the context. One aspect that we can control is the layout, in terms of the font size and line spacing, but also in terms of ensuring that keywords or sentences do not appear at the start or end of a page.

Finding an appropriate way to analyse the data is another challenge. As we discussed in Chapter 3, most reading studies create a clear comparison between conditions. Our analysis is therefore straightforward, and we would compare the words or phrases in condition A with those in condition B. In authentic texts we either need to find something to compare our items of interest to, or come up with an alternative approach to analysis. For the first option, what we are measuring will be important. If we are interested in global reading measures for literary texts versus other kinds of text (such as newspaper reports), we might simply compare average fixation patterns, saccades and regressions for the two types of text. If we are interested in local measures such as reading patterns for specific words and phrases, we can approach this in a number of ways. As suggested in the previous paragraph, we could identify examples in the text of words that were matched with our target items for key variables like length and frequency, then compare fixation data for the two sets of words. While it would not be possible to balance these on all variables, it would provide a basic level of comparison, and with enough care and attention it should be possible to identify words that appear in similar syntactic structures, similar length sentences, etc.

In some cases, the items we want to compare will not be easy to analyse because of differences in length, frequency, etc. that we cannot control. For example, in the 'variants' study discussed in the previous section (Carrol et al., 2015), the items being compared were necessarily different, e.g. comparing 'Fagin' with 'the Jew'. In this case we could include features like length and frequency as covariates in our analysis (see Chapter 7 for more on this), as a way to try to account for the differences that they would cause. Alternatively, we could try to 'normalise' our units of analysis (as discussed for other studies in this chapter). That is, for each word or phrase we can divide reading time by length (normally in characters, but alternatively in syllables, depending on our research question) to calculate a measure of 'fixation duration per character' (Sanford and Filik, 2007). This gives us a way to compare units of different lengths, but may be relatively unsuitable for short words.

We may also need to consider how to analyse specific words or phrases in relation to the wider text. For example, in the variants study (Carrol et al., 2015) each sentence was seen twice, which means that in all likelihood the second reading will always be quicker than the first. The aim was to see whether the changed portion of the sentence (the ROI) received more attention on second reading, so the authors calculated the difference in reading rate (fixation duration per character) between the sentence as a whole and the ROI. The assumption was that there should be no difference between these two for the first reading of the sentence. On second reading, the sentence in general should be read more quickly, but if the ROI was 'noticed' as being different, its reading rate should be slower than the rest of the sentence.

The alternative to many of the issues discussed here is to adapt the texts in order to create stimuli that are easier to analyse and compare. For example, we could insert or change keywords, or rewrite sections of our authentic texts to ensure that we have a clear comparison between target and control words. The downside (as with many of the studies discussed in this chapter) is that manipulating our materials like this means that they are not strictly authentic any more, so we may need to be careful about the claims we make.

The Cop et al. (2015b) study demonstrates another consideration, which is the length of the experiment. If we want to ask participants to read an entire novel, we will need to plan to collect data over several sessions, as it would be unreasonable (and highly unrealistic) to ask participants to sit and read an entire book in one sitting. Cop et al. (2015b) conducted their study over four sessions of ninety minutes. Note that this exceeds the maximum length of one hour that we recommended in Chapter 3. For longer reading studies it will be up to the researcher to decide on an appropriate balance between the length of each session and how many sessions will be needed (and how many participants we can persuade to take part). For longer sessions we should ensure that breaks and regular recalibrations are included. If we are using extracts from novels or presenting abridged forms of the text, this can obviously make for shorter sessions but may require us to 'fill in the gaps' to explain to participants what has happened in the intervening pages. This will be especially important if we want to ask any questions about general understanding of the story, or to make any claims about continuity throughout the course of a novel.

If we are combining eye-tracking with questionnaires or surveys, we will need to decide whether to include these throughout the study or present them at the end. If we present them throughout, then regular head movements as participants look at the keyboard may lead to track loss and loss of accuracy. We should therefore aim to include regular recalibrations as a way of ensuring accurate tracking throughout. If we include all of our questions at the end, this mean that the participants move less so tracking is more accurate, but it may also mean that participants are less able to remember all of the details, especially if we have asked them to read long texts. Again, finding a balance is key here, for example by showing several pages of an extract then asking some questions, then recalibrating before the next set of pages is shown.

A final methodological consideration when it comes to authentic texts and literary interpretation is that some of our standard assumptions about the link between eye-movements and processing difficulty might not be as straightforward as they seem. For example, we generally assume (with good reason) that longer reading times are reflective of greater processing effort. When reading literature, however, there is an aesthetic dimension that we also need to consider. That is, readers might linger on a word or phrase because they enjoy it, or may pay more attention to a particular part of the text for other reasons. We might therefore need to treat the data in a more qualitative manner, and the specific way we do this will be determined by our research question.

6.7.3 Example Study

A prerequisite to any study using eye-tracking in a literary linguistic context would be a detailed stylistic analysis of the key features of a text or set of texts. In other words, eye-tracking is probably best used in this context to complement existing analyses, and to try to find empirical evidence from readers that supports (or refutes) an existing interpretation. With this in mind, we identify here an example from Stockwell (2005), concerning *The Inflatable Volunteer* by Steve Aylett (1999). This novel presents a first-person narrative from a character who is 'either set in a rich fantasy world or represents the hallucinatory imagination of the focalizer, Eddie' (Stockwell, 2005, p. 751). Stockwell goes on to highlight how some of the lexical choices help to establish a disorienting effect on the reader. He identifies three types of phrase that he thinks are important here: conventional idioms ('spanner in the works'), but also phrases that sound idiomatic ('slamming the frighteners') and entirely invented items ('a spider in the mouth'). He goes on to suggest that such invented phrases help to give the feel of 'a disconcerting defamiliarization of the world' (p. 752).

We could use eye-tracking to try to substantiate this analysis. The following research questions could be addressed:

1 Do readers show any difference in reading patterns for the three types of phrase?
2 Do the local and global reading patterns reflect the 'disorienting' feel of the passage?

Our first task would be to select some representative passages from the book that contained the key lexical items and phrases that we had previously identified. For example, we could select ten extracts where this kind of disorientation was particularly prominent, and ten where the prose was more straightforward and less disorienting. This would be based on our own stylistic analysis, but could be supplemented by asking some volunteers to 'rate' each passage for how disorienting they considered it to be. By doing this we could generate a numerical rating of how disorienting each of our passages was. Within these extracts, we could identify all examples of idioms and designate each as 'conventional', 'pseudo-idiomatic' or 'invented'. Each of these would then be identified as ROIs in our texts, as in Example 6.1.

Example 6.1 Example study using extracts from *The Inflatable Volunteer* (Aylett, 1999). Phrases and words that we had previously identified as contributing to the disorienting feel of the novel would be marked as ROIs (underlined here).

Bone midnight Eddie – the little red lizard curled up in a rose. Yeah there's nightmares and nightmares – you know what I'm saying. I've taken part in somewhere the curtains have caught fire off the devil's roll-up and the clueless bastard ghosts have barged in late and we were all of us shuffling apologies to the poor sod on whom we were meant to be <u>slamming the frighteners</u>. Torment's not what it was. Subjective bargaining and the belly flop of the old smarts flung <u>a spanner in the works</u> an age ago Eddie. That and lack of imagination. Nothing like <u>a spider in the mouth</u> to get you thinking.

In this example we would need to consider all of the features of reading studies identified in Chapters 3 and 4. Text is therefore in an appropriate font and size, lines are double-spaced, and the margins ensure that text is not too close to the edge of the screen.

Participants would be shown a total of twenty extracts. It might be necessary to provide a short introduction to explain what is going on, or we might want each extract to be read as a stand-alone piece. We could ask participants to identify any words that they felt were particularly odd or attention-grabbing, and then compare these responses to the eye-tracking data. We would need to decide whether to ask this after each extract (in which case participants might begin to anticipate this question when they read extracts later in the study), or to ask them at the end of the study (in which case participants might not remember some of the phrases that they read earlier on). In this example, we will ask participants a series of open questions after each extract:

1 How would you describe the extract you just read?
2 Were there any words or phrases that particularly made you think that?

One way to obtain these data would be to audio-record each session, and ask participants to articulate their answers. These data could be transcribed and analysed qualitatively, i.e. we could evaluate the answers provided to see how much they agreed with our stylistic interpretation. We would also have the rating data that we used when selecting the passages as another measure of how disorienting each passage was.

In order to address the first research question, we could use the eye-tracking data to compare reading times for each type of phrase. Since the items are all of different lengths, we could either 'normalise' the data by dividing the fixation times for each phrase by the phrase length, or else include phrase length and word length and frequency in our analysis (see Chapter 7). A logical hypothesis would be that the invented and pseudo-idioms might be more attention-grabbing, leading to more and longer fixations and more re-fixations, as well as more regressions as readers might use the surrounding context to try to work out what they mean.

To address the second research question we could use our eye-tracking data to assess the global reading patterns (sentence reading time, average fixation duration, average saccade length, regression rate) for passages that we have identified as 'disorienting' versus those that we consider to be more straightforward. We could relate this to the initial ratings we used to identify the different types of passage, to see whether overall more disorienting passages led to more and longer fixations, shorter saccades and more regressions. We could also relate the qualitative data we obtained from our participants – about the 'feel' of each passage and the words that they thought contributed to this – to the global and local eye-tracking data to see whether those items that were fixated for longer were also more likely to be identified by participants as contributing to the overall disorienting feel of the extracts.

By combining eye-tracking and a more qualitative analysis of the elicited data, we might therefore be able to obtain support for our previous stylistic analysis. Such an approach is necessarily somewhat subjective, but it would provide a way to use empirical data to substantiate the lexical patterns that we had identified as important.

6.8 Conclusions and Final Checklist

The topics and areas covered in this chapter are by no means exhaustive, but they should have provided a good overview of the kind of projects that can be conducted in these contexts. Hopefully, the discussion has provided researchers with the background necessary to conduct studies in these areas, as well as highlighting some of the key methodological considerations that need to be addressed. Importantly, the main aim of the research discussed in this chapter has been to look at the processing of authentic materials like tests, texts, online tools, etc. Throughout the discussion we have seen that it is often necessary to decide whether to maintain the authenticity of our stimuli or modify them so that we can gain insight into more precise ROIs, like single words or phrases. Thus, when designing our experiments, we need to keep in mind the limitations of the equipment, as well as thinking about aspects of experimental design covered in previous chapters (see Sections 2.5, 3.6, 4.7 and 5.5). This final checklist aims to help researchers evaluate methodological considerations for the kinds of studies discussed in this chapter.

Final checklist
• Consider your research questions. Do these research questions allow you to use real materials (e.g. a real test, a corpus tool, a translation program)?	⇒ If you are looking at the processing of bigger sections of the stimuli, e.g. the processing of the source and target text areas in a translation task, you might be able to use the real material. ⇒ If you are examining the processing of smaller areas of the input, e.g. parts of learners' utterances in synchronous computer-mediated communication, you will need to modify the real materials and create your own task.
• Think about the compromises you need to make with the design of materials. Would the study still accurately represent the processes you are interested in examining?	⇒ If you need to make considerable changes to the materials, they might no longer be a valid representation of what you are interested in examining.
• Consider the design and presentation of the task and stimuli. What is the best layout to accurately answer your research questions?	⇒ The size, position and characteristics of the stimuli are important methodological considerations in the design of tasks.

(cont.)

Final checklist

• How do data need to be coded in order to answer your research questions?	⇒ In some of the projects we have mentioned in this chapter, the research questions could only be addressed by a manual coding of the data, e.g. when identifying errors in online messages. Is this feasible within your study context?
	⇒ The coding can sometimes be done with the use of an add-on script that would make it more automatic and less time-consuming, but this would require researchers to have a programming background.
• What eye-tracking measures should be considered?	⇒ The measures you choose will depend on the type of ROI that you have in your study.
	⇒ For individual words a range of early and late measures should be used.
	⇒ For larger ROIs (e.g. the whole typing area of a writing task) several late measures should be analysed.
• Which factors (apart from those described in Chapters 3, 4 and 5) are affecting eye-movement data in your study (e.g. recurrent movements to and from the keyboard, ability to touch type)?	⇒ These factors would need to be controlled for in the design of the experiment or in the analysis of the data.
• For authentic texts, what additional considerations are added to your study?	⇒ Authentic texts are less controlled, so you may need to be more creative in how you approach the analysis if you do not want to compromise their authenticity. Qualitative analysis might also be required to combine eye-tracking with other types of data.

Chapter 7

Working with the Data

7.1 Making a Start with the Data

Eye-tracking studies generate a lot of data and it can be hard to know what to do with all of it. This chapter will address how to deal with the data from start to finish. We will begin with the process of spotting and removing problem trials, data 'cleaning' and exporting data for analysis. We will then turn to different methods of visualisation and analysis, and give some examples of how this can be done.

The data generated by the eye-tracker will contain all of the information collected during our experiment. This will include the events (fixations, saccades, blinks) that were recorded during each trial, as well as any responses we asked participants to make (key presses, etc.), and any demographic data, answers to questionnaires and so forth that we built into the experiment. We can visualise, analyse and export the data using the dedicated software provided with each system: Data Viewer (SR Research, www.sr-research.com), Tobii Pro Studio (Tobii, www.tobii.com) and BeGaze (SMI, www.smivision.com).[1] If we defined our regions of interest (ROIs) in advance, we can easily export the data we need to analyse for our experiment.[2]

Data Viewer allows us to import each individual results file into one composite file for analysis. This will create a master Data Viewer Session (.dvs) file where we can work on all of our results in one place. Data can be inspected and a number of visualisations produced, then exported for further analysis. Any operation performed on the Data Viewer Session file (cleaning, exporting data, etc.) can therefore be done on all trials at the same time. The Data Viewer Session file doesn't make any changes to the original EyeLink data files (.edf), so the raw data will still be available if we need it for any reason. Tobii Pro Studio deals with the building, recording and analysis of data in one place, so visualising data, defining ROIs and analysing data are done using the 'Visualizations', 'Areas of Interest' and 'Statistics' tabs, respectively. We can also export our data for further analysis using the 'Data Export' tab or export a video file using the 'Replay' tab. BeGaze can be launched from within the Experiment Center software or can be started independently. All data collected within a project are automatically available for analysis. Data can be visualised in a range of ways and the image or video files exported for use in papers or presentations. There are also a number of options for analysing and exporting the raw data as required.

---

[1] As noted elsewhere, SMI has been purchased by Apple. It is unclear how their systems and software will be updated and supported in the future.

[2] We can combine the output of the dedicated analysis software with specialised programs as required, for example software to log and analyse keystrokes in writing studies (see Section 6.3.2). As we mentioned in Chapter 3, a number of plug-ins and third-party software options can be used, but we do not consider them in detail here.

7.1.1 Checking the Data

Our first job should be to visually inspect the data to ensure that any unusable or clearly problematic trials are excluded. If the initial set-up and calibration were done carefully, problems should be minimal, but some level of data loss is likely in most studies for a variety of reasons. By visually inspecting the data we can spot any obvious problem trials and/or participants and eliminate them, then additional data can be collected if required. For example, if data from an individual participant is unusable because of poor calibration or other technical issues, we might want to remove it and collect data from another person, depending on our required sample size and whether we have the opportunity to collect more data.

More likely than a participant's data being entirely unusable is the case where individual trials need to be removed. This can be for any number of reasons, such as a participant accidentally initiating a trigger too soon, a participant sneezing or rubbing his/her eyes, because a participant blinked, or because a trial experienced track loss, where the pupil was temporarily lost by the eye-tracker. In text-based studies this is generally operationalised as a trial where two consecutive ROIs receive no fixations during first pass reading, i.e. where two content words in a row are skipped entirely. This is not always a straightforward decision, so it is up to the experimenter to review the data and decide what does/does not constitute usable data.

In image- or video-based studies, deciding whether the tracking has been lost might be trickier since the ROIs are not 'skipped' in the same way. Trials where fixation data is very sparse (markedly fewer fixations than on other trials) or where there are substantially more fixations than we would expect should be reviewed, and this is where the operator keeping notes is useful as this may help to explain why the data looks different for a specific trial (e.g. the participant sneezed during trial 12). There is no rule for what constitutes an acceptable level of data removal, but anything more than around 10 per cent would probably be considered quite high. (Note that in certain types of studies like the boundary paradigm, data loss may be higher – see Section 4.5.) We should also check whether the amount of data that we remove is comparable across conditions, to ensure that there is no one condition that is affected markedly more than any other. If it was, this might be an indication that our conditions weren't as balanced as we thought.

In some cases, the calibration during our data collection may have been imperfect, leading to minor location errors, i.e. fixations may be offset by a small margin. Careful monitoring and recalibration during the experiment should avoid this, but small offsets may be salvageable depending on the requirements of our study. In a single-line reading study, for example, data that is horizontally aligned but vertically misaligned might be okay, as in the example in Figure 7.1.

In Data Viewer we have the option to adjust individual fixations by manually moving the location for a single point. Drift correct can also be performed for a number of fixations at once using the Batch Drift Correct feature, which aligns them all so they appear in a straight line. For single-line reading where we can be confident that the fixations all

The violence had even begun to infect normally `safe´ areas.

Figure 7.1 Eye-movement data where the calibration was vertically misaligned. Each circle represents a fixation, with longer fixations indicated by larger circles.

belong to one line of text, some degree of vertical adjustment may be acceptable, but horizontal adjustments are substantially more subjective and should almost always be avoided. For multi-line text or image-based studies, such adjustments can be less clear-cut and should be approached with caution. Ultimately it is up to us as researchers to decide how much, if any, of this type of adjustment is acceptable, and it may be more reliable to simply remove trials where the calibration is problematic, if this does not lead to too much data being rejected.

Tobii Pro Studio does not offer the option for us to manually adjust fixation data, so it is important that we achieve accurate set-up and calibration from the start of the experiment. It is possible to export fixation data and apply a correction (assuming that the offset of the data was consistent throughout) using an external program such as Matlab.

BeGaze offers an option to adjust the entire dataset if there is a consistent offset compared to the original calibration (e.g. if a participant shifted position during the experiment). The Gaze Offset Correction option is available in certain data views by selecting the time point where the gaze data begins to look wrong. By right-clicking on the stimulus and selecting the Offset Correction option, we can drag the fixation data into the required position to correct any minor problems. Data from this point on will be corrected by the same amount, and the Offset Correction can be discontinued or altered at a later time point (if the participant shifted position again). In earlier versions of BeGaze this option appears as Calibrate, rather than Offset Correction.

7.1.2 Cleaning the Data

Once we have removed any items that are clearly unusable and made any vertical adjustments to fixations, we can begin *data cleaning*, which is the process of consolidating very short fixations and removing any outliers in the fixation data.

Before undertaking any data cleaning, it is useful to understand how the eye-trackers actually calculate fixation data. Each of the systems considered here apply slightly different algorithms to interpret the eye-movements that have been recorded (see the user manuals for details on this). In other words, some degree of processing has already been done by the software to determine what constitutes a fixation, to account for blinks, etc. In the majority of cases, the default settings will provide us with a very good dataset. Certain further options for data cleaning are available to us, depending on the specific requirements of our study. For text-based studies in particular, it is common for researchers to remove fixations that are above or below certain thresholds since these are likely to represent outliers. In reading, very short fixations tend to be removed or merged with nearby fixations. Often fixations below a certain threshold (e.g. 50 ms) are merged with any fixations occurring within a specified distance (e.g. 1° of visual angle). A threshold is also usually set for any remaining short fixations (i.e. those that are not close enough to another fixation to merge) to be removed, on the grounds that it is unlikely that any information could have been extracted during fixations of less than around 80 ms. Often very long fixations are also removed, and it is a common procedure for researchers to remove data points that are 2.5 standard deviations above or below the overall mean. However, we should consider both the task and the research question when making such decisions. In natural reading, we might choose to remove fixations longer than around 800 ms on the grounds that these tend to represent momentary losses in concentration by participants. If the focus of our study is unknown words and how well readers are able to learn them from the written input, we might expect much longer fixations as learners try either to remember a word or guess its meaning. In visual-world studies researchers may also choose to remove or merge very short fixations (e.g. Scheepers, Keller and Lapata, 2008), but we might expect to see longer individual fixations on a given ROI than in reading studies. We should therefore be careful about how we define any criteria for data removal, and base our decisions on established practices in similar published research.

Data Cleaning in the Different Eye-Tracking Systems

Data Viewer provides two in-built cleaning options. In the first (Fixation Filter), fixations below a certain user-defined duration threshold will be merged with fixations falling within a pre-set distance. In other words, if two very short fixations occur next to each other, Data Viewer will consider them to be one single fixation and merge them. The second option – specifically for reading data – is a four-stage cleaning process to merge and then delete fixations outside of specified thresholds. This can be performed on all participants and trials simultaneously by selecting the topmost folder in the file structure. This process cannot be reversed and the Data Viewer user manual stresses that this option is not appropriate for all users.

Tobii Pro Studio has a number of predefined Fixation Filters that allow us to amend the way that it calculates and cleans fixations. The different filters apply slightly different criteria in terms of removing very short fixations or merging adjacent fixations, so it is good idea to read the recommendations in Section 6 of the Tobii Pro Studio user manual and decide on the most appropriate setting for our specific study.

In BeGaze the default settings for how fixations and events are classified are determined by the sample rate of the study and in general will not need to be altered. We can use the Adjust Event Detection option, which will allow us to specify certain parameters such as excluding the first fixation from each trial if required, and also change the lower fixation duration threshold (by default set to 80 ms). Further information on this can be found in Part VII of the BeGaze user manual.

Neither Tobii Pro Studio nor BeGaze have a default setting for the removal of fixations above a certain upper limit. Very long fixations in our data can be removed manually in the data analysis stage if required, i.e. we can sort our data by fixation duration and delete any data points that exceed the threshold we have decided on.

Whatever data cleaning procedures we undertake, we should ensure that we are clear and transparent in reporting these when we write up our results. That is, we should report how much data has been removed and why, and precisely what data cleaning procedures and thresholds we used. Table 7.1 summarises the stages of checking and cleaning data.

7.1.3 Visualising the Data

Visualisations can be a useful way to get the 'big picture' of our data. Visualisations will present us with a summary of the eye-movement data for an individual trial or group of trials, either for one participant or averaged across all of our participants. This kind of summary may be of most use in studies that use image or video, as it means we can easily evaluate the relative attention paid to a specific portion of the display at a certain time point. For example, in the visual-world example from Chambers and Cooke (2009), visualising the data would quickly show us how much attention was paid to each of the

Table 7.1 Stages of checking and cleaning data in eye-tracking studies.

1   Visual inspection
     Checking the raw data should allow us to spot any obviously unusable trials. This will include
        those with a lot of missing data, where the calibration is poor, etc.
2   Data removal
     Data can be removed either for entire participants (if calibration was consistently poor) or on
        a trial-by-trial basis.
3   Fixation adjustment
     Some minor adjustments to the fixation data may help us to salvage trials where the
        calibration is not perfect. Generally this will apply to single-line text and we should only
        adjust the vertical position of fixations, never the horizontal.
4   Data cleaning
     Very short fixations (50–100 ms) are generally merged with neighbouring fixations and/or
        removed. Very long fixations may also be removed, either at this stage or when we export
        the data. The data cleaning procedures we choose should be justified by our research
        question and the type of data we are dealing with (reading, visual search, etc.).
5   Reporting
     We should keep a record of everything we do during this stage and report the amount of data
        removed, as well as the data cleaning procedures we undertook.

four images in any given trial, either for an individual participant or for all participants combined. For reading studies visualisations are generally of less use, although it might be helpful in some cases to get an idea of the order of fixations and any regressions that occurred for a particular trial.

All three eye-tracking systems provide a range of options for visualising the eye-movement data (see Chapter 2), but we should remember that this is not in itself a method of data analysis. Blaschek et al. (2014) suggest that visualisation is a primarily qualitative way of examining the data, and provides a way of generating hypotheses for further exploration with statistical analysis. Visualisations are also useful for demonstrating overall patterns in papers or presentations.

Visualisations can be still images or animations, and can relate to one subject or be aggregated over a number of participants and trials. Still images show an overview of the fixation and saccade data, either for a whole trial or during a specific time window. This can be useful for getting an idea of how much attention was paid to the various aspects of the display. For example, in a storybook study we could show the total number of fixations on the image and the text during a trial for two participants – one who subsequently did well on a post-reading comprehension test and one who did less well. In a reading study a still image would show us the location of fixations, the duration of fixations and the order, with arrows indicating the pattern of saccades. Animations are useful if we want to show how eye-movements unfold over time. For example, it might be useful to show a video of the reading patterns for one participant, to demonstrate 'typical' eye-movements. We could also use an animation to show how eye-movements unfold over the course of watching a video, or show how fixation patterns develop on a visual-world display once participants have heard the critical word. Visualisations therefore present a number of ways to present our data, and we briefly describe the main techniques available below.

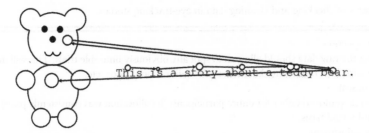

Figure 7.2 Example scan path data showing the fixation patterns for a specific trial. Each circle represents a fixation on the text ('This is a story about a teddy bear.') or image, with the size of the circle indicating the duration. Saccades are indicated by arrows. Data from multiple participants can appear for the same trial, and different participants would be represented by different colours (only one is shown here for clarity). The data can be exported as an image summarising the trial as a whole (as here) or as a video showing the fixations as they unfolded over the course of the trial.

Spatial Overlay / Scan Path / Gaze Plot

All three software packages provide a way to visualise the pattern of fixations and saccades during a given trial. This can be as a still image (showing all fixations that occurred during the trial) or an animation/video (showing the change in fixations over the course of the trial). In each case, the size of the circle representing a fixation gives an indication of its duration (bigger circles = longer fixations). Figure 7.2 gives an example of this. Data Viewer presents data in this way by default in its Spatial Overlay View, and fixations, saccades and other events can be toggled on or off as required. Version 2.3 onward of Data Viewer allows us to combine data from several participants using the Aggregate Mode. In BeGaze, the Scan Path option can be used to show data for one or more participants for a single trial. The Gaze Replay option shows the same data but for all trials in the experiment one after another. In Tobii Pro Studio, the Gaze Plot option can be selected to show data for a single participant for the whole session or for a range of participants within a specified time window. In all three systems the visualisation can be exported and saved as either an image or video file.

Bee Swarms

Bee swarms provide a way of visualising data for multiple participants for a given trial. They are similar to a gaze plot, but the location of fixations, rather than the duration, is the focus. In a bee swarm, fixations from all participants are represented with a different colour for each person, and all fixations are the same size regardless of their duration. This can give either a static view of the pattern of fixations at a specific time point (e.g. 200 ms after the critical word in a visual-world study, which image were participants looking at?), or a dynamic indication of how the location of fixations changes over time. Bee swarms can be exported as either images or animations. In Tobii Pro Studio, Bee Swarm is available as one of the Preset options within the Gaze Plot tab. In BeGaze, Bee Swarm is one of the dedicated visualisation options and is generated by selecting the appropriate icon along the top of the screen. Data Viewer does not provide an option to produce or export bee swarms, although the Aggregate Mode would allow us to combine scan path data for several participants to achieve something similar. From here we can easily export an animation to show how gaze position changes over time for multiple trials or participants.

Heat Maps

Heat maps are commonly used to show the relative attention paid to different areas of the display. The heat map provides a simple colour-coded way to interpret fixation data: areas that received relatively more attention (more and longer fixations) during the trial normally appear in red, and areas that received relatively less attention (fewer and shorter fixations) normally appear in green or blue. Heat maps can show data from a single participant or multiple participants for the same trial. In some systems (e.g. Tobii Pro Studio), if participants have seen different versions of a 'test' (i.e. different counterbalanced lists) it may only be possible to produce a visualisation for each version at a time, rather than across the experiment as a whole. As with the other visualisation types, data can be represented as a static image to show the pattern for the trial as a whole or as an animation showing changes over time. Figure 7.3 shows an example heat map.

In Data Viewer and Tobii Pro Studio heat maps can be customised to depict fixation count or duration. Heat maps in BeGaze are calculated based on the accumulated time spent looking at each part of the display over the course of a trial. BeGaze also offers the option of producing a Focus Map, which operates like a reverse heat map. Rather than superimposing a coloured overlay that obscures the view of the stimulus, the Focus Map alters the transparency of the display to show only those areas that are fixated. Fixated areas are therefore visible, while non-fixated areas are obscured. (Note that the same feature is called a Gaze Opacity Map in Tobii Pro Studio.)

Despite their usefulness in representing an overview of our data, heat maps (and in fact all of the visualisations discussed here) should be used cautiously. They are often used inappropriately, for the wrong reasons, and may do not include the information that is necessary to interpret them (Bojko, 2009). Holmqvist et al. (2011) point out that the intuitiveness and simplicity of heat maps is a benefit but also a potential problem, since it is tempting for the people looking at them to draw immediate conclusions that perhaps

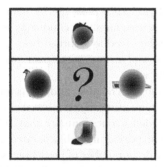

Figure 7.3 Example heat map showing the relative number of looks to each picture in a visual-world study (adapted from Chambers and Cooke, 2009). Areas with more fixations over the course of a trial are darker, with areas of fewer fixations appearing lighter. (NB: in most heat maps full colour would be used, with red indicating the 'warmest' areas, or those that received the most attention.) In this example, the target (the chicken – 'poule') is darkest, with the interlingual distractor ('pool') appearing lighter, and both of the other unrelated images appearing lighter still.

would not be supported by more detailed analysis. For example, the heat map in Figure 7.3 suggests that more attention was paid to the chicken than any of the other images. However, this is just summary data (albeit in graphical rather than numerical form), analogous to other summary data such as mean number of fixations or total fixation duration. The only way to know whether there really are significantly more or longer fixations to the chicken is by conducting statistical analysis (see Section 7.2.4). On the other hand, as Blaschek et al. (2014) suggest, heat maps can be very informative in identifying areas for further analysis, for example in highlighting areas that we may not have originally identified as potential ROIs, but which nonetheless received substantial attention during a trial. In this case, we could retrospectively add in ROIs and subject these areas to further analysis (although in general we should be cautious about this kind of post hoc analysis).

7.2 Analysing Data

While visualisations can be good for identifying broad patterns, in most cases statistical analysis will be required if we want to draw any firm conclusions from our experiment. The eye-tracking data will therefore need to be exported in numerical form in order for us to analyse them using a statistical package such as R or SPSS. In Data Viewer the eye-movement data must be exported before any analysis can be performed. Both Tobii Pro Studio and BeGaze provide some in-built statistical functions to perform a basic analysis of our data and obtain descriptive statistics. In most cases we will need to perform more rigorous analysis, so both also allow us to export the raw data for further investigation.

7.2.1 Exporting Data

In Data Viewer we can export a range of reports using the Analysis menu. These include Trial, Fixation and Saccade Reports that provide a summary of the data, but the option that we are most likely to need is the Interest Area Report. This will provide data for each ROI that we have specified in our study. A huge range of fixation and saccade information can be generated, but in most cases we will want to export only the measures that we have identified as being important for our research question. Other variables such as participant number, trial order and the name and ID of the ROIs, as well as those specific to our study (i.e. the columns we included in our data source such as item numbers, conditions, etc.) can also be included for export. Our exported data will be saved as a spreadsheet (.xls) file. Each row will represent the data for one ROI in one trial for one participant, hence it is important to have labelled our ROIs in a meaningful way.

Tobii Pro Studio provides descriptive statistics in the form of tables and charts using the Statistics tab. It also allows us to filter the results we require using any variables that we may have built in to the study, for example if we included a questionnaire that collected demographic data. For further analysis, data can be exported in a tab separated (.tsv) or spreadsheet (.xls) format. The Data Export tool provides a number of predefined settings for data export, or we can specify our own. The default option is to export all available data types or, to avoid having overly large datasets to work with, we can work through the options to select only the data that we require.

BeGaze allows us to observe lots of different information about our data prior to exporting it, but the functionality is dependent on what modules we have included in our license. For image- and video-based studies two very useful options are the Binning

Chart and Proportion of Looks functions, each of which allows us to compare the relative amount of time spent on different ROIs at specific time windows during a trial. If the Reading Package is installed, we will also be able to select a number of metrics for further analysis based on the measures we have identified as important for our study. For each of these specific analysis modules, as well as the more general Metrics Export wizard, we would simply select the participants, trials and measures that we require, then choose the appropriate format to export the data. Data can be exported and saved as tab separated data or exported to the clipboard and copied into spreadsheet programs such as Excel.

Note that when it comes to choosing the eye-tracking measures we want to export and analyse further, not all of the options discussed in Section 3.2 will be available in all of the systems. For example, fixation data but not regression data can be exported as standard within Tobii Pro Studio. This underlines the importance of thinking about what measures we want to look at in advance so that we can ensure that this will be possible in the system we are using.

Exporting Data for Specific Time Windows

As we have already discussed elsewhere, in some cases we may only want to export data for a specific time window. This is often the case for visual-world studies (e.g. Figure 7.4), where we want to look at the development of eye-movements over time, or video-based studies, where we are interested in the pattern of eye-movements during a specific part of the stimulus (e.g. each set of subtitles). As we outlined in Section 3.1.4, there are different ways we can achieve this. Often we may just choose to export all of our data, then divide it up manually when we begin our analysis. We can also set ROIs to be 'active' during certain time windows, hence the data would already be sub-divided when we export it.

Alternatively, we can set limits for which parts of the data we want to analyse, and all three systems allow us to specify the time period for which we want to export data. In Data Viewer we can set up specific Interest Periods, which can be based on timings or on events such as button presses. These can be used to specify time windows as in Figure 7.4, and we would set each Interest Period according to the start and end times required (relative to the overall start of the trial). More information on how to set Interest Periods is provided in Sections 6.3 and 6.4 of the Data Viewer user manual. In both Tobii Pro Studio and BeGaze we can specify the window we are interested in. In Tobii Pro Studio the option to select a time interval is available within the Statistics tab, and in BeGaze this is one of the

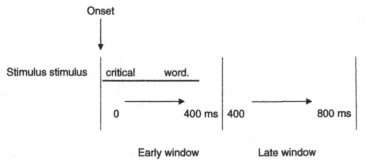

Figure 7.4 Early and late windows for analysing visual-world data. The first analysis would consider the 400 ms period immediately following the offset of the critical word in the audio stimulus. The late window would cover the period from 400 ms to 800 ms post-onset.

options that can be set during data export. In both cases this would involve setting the start and end times, then exporting the data for each time window in turn.

7.2.2 Preparing the Data for Analysis

Once we have exported our data, it will be ready to analyse in our chosen statistics package. Analysis is likely to be done with either SPSS or R, so we should make sure that we are familiar with the requirements of the software before importing our data. For example, R requires the data to be in a 'one data point per line' format, so if we have exported summarised or averaged data, this will not be acceptable.

In some cases, even after exporting our data, it may still require some tidying up before we can begin analysis. For example, in Section 3.1.4 we discussed how SR Research EyeLink and SMI experiments can automatically separate words into ROIs for further analysis. If we have used this option rather than defining our own ROIs, it may be helpful to remove any superfluous data (the words we are not interested in analysing). One way to do this would be to import our data into a spreadsheet application like Excel first. Sorting the data by ROI will allow us to order the items alphabetically, making it easy to identify those words that we were interested in and those that we could discard. Once we have filtered out any unwanted items, we can import our data into R or SPSS for further analysis.

We might also choose to 'transform' our data to normalise the distribution, for example by applying a logarithmic transformation (a 'log transform') to all of our duration measures (Box and Cox, 1964; Whelan, 2008 provides a discussion of this topic as it relates to reaction time data). This technique is used to reduce 'skewing' in the data, i.e. with duration measures we would typically expect a densely clustered series of data points from 100 to 500 ms, then an increasingly sparse rightward 'tail' of longer fixations. Converting the data by calculating the logarithm of each value will maintain the same pattern of results but reduce the size of this rightward 'skew'. This kind of procedure will not be appropriate for all types of data, and as with any of the data cleaning discussed previously, we should ensure that we (1) understand what we are doing (and why) before we do it, and (2) report any such procedures clearly when we present our results. In eye-tracking, fixation durations are often log transformed and other types of data are often subject to different procedures, which we deal with in the following sections.

7.2.3 Approaches to Analysis

The discussion in the following sections is intended simply as an introductory guide to the different statistical techniques that could be used to explore eye-tracking data. It should be supplemented with some of the many excellent guides to statistics that are available as a way of understanding the techniques more fully before we begin our analysis. Most researchers in applied linguistics will have at least some training in statistics and are likely to be familiar with the commonly used techniques such as correlation analysis, t-tests and ANOVAs. Another approach that has become increasingly popular (and increasingly requested by journals) is the use of linear mixed effects (LME) modelling as a way of analysing linguistic data. In particular for the type of data generated during an eye-tracking study, LME modelling may be a good choice, although it does require an additional investment of time to learn how to apply this method. While

LME models can be implemented in SPSS, a much more common approach is to use the lme4 package (Bates et al., 2015) within R, which is freely available.

There are a number of good reasons to use LME models rather than ANOVAs or *t*-tests. In these more traditional methods, data are averaged across trials and separate analyses are run to compare the average between conditions by subjects and by items. If both analyses return a significant result, researchers often conclude that there is a difference between conditions that can be generalised to other participants and other items.[3] In LME models, every data point is included in the analysis (there is no averaging), which gives the analysis more statistical power. LME models are also more efficient in handling missing data points. A big advantage is that there is no need to run separate item and subject analyses, since both are included as random variables in the analysis. This helps us to account for individual variation in our participants and the items we have chosen, both of which may be high in applied linguistics studies. Another major benefit is that a number of covariates (control variables) can be included in the analysis. This means that our analysis can account for item-level properties such as word length or frequency, and also participant properties such as age, amount of time learning a second language, and any proficiency data that we may have such as vocabulary test scores. A number of researchers (e.g. Baayen, Davidson and Bates, 2008; Barr et al., 2013) now advocate LME models as a viable and appropriate option for analysing many types of linguistic data.

7.2.4 Types of Data and How to Analyse Them

Deciding how to analyse our data appropriately is a vital part of producing robust, replicable results. Importantly, in eye-tracking we will be faced with different types of data depending on the measures we are looking at. Broadly, our data will be either continuous (where each value falls along a scale), discrete (where values exist at specified intervals, e.g. whole numbers) or categorical (where each value falls into one of a limited number of categories). Examples of continuous eye-tracking data are fixation durations or saccade length. Values here will fall somewhere on a scale from zero to whatever the upper limit of our data is. Discrete data are generally count data such as number of fixations or number of regressions, and must be analysed appropriately. Examples of categorical eye-tracking measures are likelihood of skipping (any given word is either 'skipped' or 'not skipped'), regression rate (whether there was a regression or not during a trial) or fixation location. Fixation location would be considered categorical because at any given point a participant is fixating one (and only one) of the ROIs. When it comes to analysis, it is common for researchers to convert categorical variables to make them easier to compare, for example, by expressing the percentage of trials that had a skip or regression, or comparing the proportion of fixations to the different images in a visual display (although see Jaeger, 2008, for the potential problems this can cause in analysis, and see the following sections for alternative approaches).

Reporting and Analysing Data in Reading Studies

The analysis in a reading study will be driven by the eye-tracking measures we have chosen to export. Our data is likely to be made up of continuous (e.g. fixation duration),

---

[3] See Clark (1973) and the 'language as fixed effect fallacy' for more on this.

discrete (e.g. fixation count) and categorical (e.g. skipping likelihood, regression rate) data, and we will need to adopt different analyses for each one. As we stressed in Chapter 3, eye-tracking measures are not independent, and only by finding a pattern that emerges across several measures can we claim that our results demonstrate a consistent effect.

As in any study, we should provide detailed descriptive statistics for each of the measures we intend to analyse. The first measure we can look at is skipping rate, which is likely to be of interest in studies concerned with single-word analysis. Since any skipped item by definition has a first fixation of 0 ms, including this in the calculation of means for duration measures or in any further analysis will be problematic. We should therefore consider this measure before we go on to look at any others. The eye-tracking software will have calculated whether each word or ROI was skipped during first pass reading and will normally assign a value of 1 if it was skipped, or 0 if it received any fixation at all. This can be used to calculate the overall percentage of trials that were skipped for each condition, which is normally reported as a percentage; e.g. if out of 1600 trials, 135 contained no fixation on the critical word during first pass reading, the overall skipping rate would be 135/1600 x 100 = 8.4 per cent. The same is true for any other 'rate' measures, such as proportion of regressions into or out of an ROI.

Subsequent duration measures should only be reported for those items that were not skipped during first pass reading, and it is common practice to exclude any skipped items from further analysis altogether. Alternatively, it may be of interest to exclude skipped items from analysis of early duration measures but retain them in order to examine patterns in later measures (including regressions). As with other methodological decisions we make, this should be reported clearly in the write-up of results.

Next, fixation and regression measures can be reported for each condition. This will involve calculating the mean and standard deviation/standard error values for each of our conditions for each measure of interest. Mean values are normally reported in milliseconds for duration measures and as raw figures for any count-based measures (such as fixation count or number of regressions). Like visualisations, descriptive statistics (or figures based on them) do not in themselves constitute a complete statistical analysis, but they are an important step in understanding our data and a useful way of depicting key patterns.

Subsequent analysis should be undertaken for each of the measures we are interested in. If we are using an ANOVA we would need to calculate the average for each measure by subjects and by items and run separate analyses, usually reported as F_1 and F_2. Duration measures – either as raw or log transformed values – can generally be handled in ANOVAs fairly easily. Both proportion of skipped words and fixation count are more problematic in ANOVAs since neither type of data has a normal distribution (which violates one of the assumptions of ANOVA). The data may therefore need to be transformed, or we may need to choose an alternative kind of analysis. Proportion data is often arcsine transformed prior to analysis, although Jaeger (2008) demonstrates that even after this transformation, ANOVAs can produce misleading results for categorical responses of this nature.

Using LME models therefore presents an appropriate alternative, and a number of very useful introductions to this type of analysis are available (e.g. Baayen, Davidson and Bates, 2008; Winter, 2013; Winter and Wieling, 2016). The different types of data can all be analysed in more or less the same way, although for skipping rates (and other similar measures) and count data we need to specify the distribution required:

'binomial' for skipping rates and 'poisson' for count data. To construct our model, we identify the dependent variable (e.g. first fixation duration), the independent variables (called 'fixed effects' in LME models; e.g. in our text-based study example from Chapters 1 and 3, our fixed effect would be the categorical variable 'Sentence Type' with values of 'Metaphorical' and 'Literal'). We also need to identify any covariates that may be of interest (e.g. word length), and we would include both our participants (subjects) and stimuli (items) as random effects. The resulting formula for our model would be:

FirstFixation Duration ~ SentenceType + WordLength + (1 | Subject) + (1 | Item)[4]

Constructing such models can be done in a number of ways. One is to include all of the possible variables of interest and then remove those that do not make a significant contribution to the 'fit' of the model. An alternative is to start with a basic model (including only the fixed effects of interest) and add variables one by one to see if they improve the fit. Such issues are discussed in the literature on LME modelling, and as before we should explain in full any decisions we make in our write-up.

Covariates

The ability to include covariates is a big advantage of LME models, especially in applied linguistics research where multiple item and participant characteristics are likely to be of interest. Word, phrase or sentence length are typically included, either in characters or words. Word frequency is also a covariate of potential interest. Raw corpus data should generally be log transformed to normalise the distribution and to ensure that variables are on comparable scales. An alternative is to use the Zipf scale (van Heuven et al., 2014), which plots relative frequency on a seven-point scale. Other covariates of potential interest could include the kind of variables considered in Chapter 4 such as familiarity and cloze probability, as well as the order in which items were shown to our participants (to account for experimental effects like participants either speeding up as they got used to the task or slowing down towards the end of a long experiment). Participant variables may include both continuous values (e.g. age of the participant) and categorical values (e.g. boys vs girls or native speakers vs language learners). Other variables can be included as either continuous or categorical. For example, a measure of proficiency could be included either as a score on a vocabulary test, or with participants divided into 'high' and 'low' groups.

Continuous predictors should generally be centred by subtracting the overall mean from each value, to facilitate interpretation of their effect (Schielzeth, 2010). For example, if we had collected 'familiarity' ratings for a set of words on a scale from 1 to 7, we would 'centre' this scale around zero and values would extend from −3.5 to +3.5. In R, categorical covariates (or fixed effects) are 'treatment-coded' by default so that one represents the 'baseline'; e.g. the variable 'native speaker status' might have 'native speaker' as the baseline to which 'language learners' would be compared.

---

[4] This formula only includes 'random intercepts' for subject and item, which may not be appropriate as it can have a very high Type I error rate. We should also check whether we need to include 'random slopes' for important effects. This is a key issue in LME models, and is one that we should ensure we understand before we begin our analysis. We do not discuss it in detail here, but see Barr et al. (2013) or Winter and Wieling (2016) for an introduction and rationale.

For studies looking at authentic texts, LME models represent a good option since they allow us to statistically 'control' for a range of predictors that vary in authentic materials (see the examples discussed in Section 4.3.3). Aspects such as sentence length and word length and frequency can therefore be included as covariates in our analysis, although wherever possible we should still try to 'balance' these in our stimuli. More specifically, we may only consider very specific words in an authentic text, which although they are not controlled, meet a very specific set of criteria (see, for example, the stringent criteria adopted by Cop et al., 2015b).

Reporting and Analysing Data in Visual Studies

For visual-world, video-based and other similar studies we should again begin by providing descriptive statistics for our variables of interest. In any study using visual stimuli we will generally focus on either the time spent looking at various aspects of the stimuli (in relation to other parts of the display) or the likelihood that participants fixated a specific ROI at various time points during a trial. Our possible dependent variables may therefore be total fixation duration, average fixation duration, or fixation or saccade counts for specific ROIs. We might also be interested in the time taken for participants to fixate a certain ROI (e.g. Altmann and Kamide, 1999, who used *time to first saccade* as the dependent variable). Many visual studies tend to use a proportionate measure to evaluate looking behaviour, i.e. of the total number of fixations/saccades during a specific time period, how many were to each of the images (e.g. Tanenhaus et al., 1995)? We should report means and standard deviations for any of the measures we are interested in, for each time window we have identified (see Section 7.3 for some ways that we can present our results visually).

The most common approach in visual-world and other image-based studies has been to identify separate time windows (e.g. an early and late window) and use an ANOVA or *t*-test to compare fixation or saccade patterns to each of the stimuli. There are a number of approaches that can be used, and Altmann (2011a) discusses techniques such as calculating the log likelihood or odds ratios and using growth curves, which we do not address in detail here. Analysis normally considers each time window separately (e.g. Hanna, Tanenhaus and Trueswell, 2003; Holsinger, 2013; Nadig and Sedivy, 2002), although we may also want to compare the different windows as a way of measuring the development over time. How many windows we want to define and how long they should be will depend on the aim of our study. In studies focused on how looking behaviour unfolds over time, we might choose to define multiple windows of 100 ms or even 50 ms each. As we saw in Chapter 5, in visual studies we are normally interested in how looking develops as soon as the critical word has been heard. A common technique is to delay the start of the first window to 150–200 ms following the onset of the critical word, on the grounds that this is the length of time normally required to initiate a saccade in response to a stimulus (Allopenna, Magnuson and Tanenhaus, 1998; Matin, Shao and Boff, 1993). Not all studies do this, however, and Altmann (2011b) suggests that language-mediated effects of saccadic movement can be observed as early as 100 ms after the critical word onset.

Although traditional analyses have proven to be a relatively robust way of dealing with visual-world data (Huettig, Rommers and Meyer, 2011), the objections raised previously about the use of ANOVAs to deal with categorical data still stand. As with reading studies, we should be aware of the need to treat proportional data appropriately, so we should consider the type of data we are analysing, any transformations that may be required and the most suitable method of analysis. Barr (2008) discusses some of these issues in more detail, and demonstrates how analysis of visual-world data using discrete time windows can obscure the true nature of any effects in the data, since it treats time as a categorical rather than a continuous variable. Use of LME modelling (with the appropriate transformation – see Barr, 2008) therefore again offers an alternative (see also Winter and Wieling, 2016, for an analysis of time-varying data using LME). In this case, instead of analysing a 'window' of 400 ms, we could instead include the time of each fixation (relative to when the critical word was heard) as a continuous variable as a way of modelling the fixation patterns over time. As well as giving us a much more detailed record of how behaviour unfolds over time, many of the benefits outlined for reading studies also apply: the ability to include subjects and items as random variables in a single analysis, the ability to include a number of covariates, etc.

Such an approach might also allow us to examine what Barr, Gann and Pierce (2011) call anticipatory baseline effects (ABEs), or the effect of what participants may have been looking at prior to the onset of a critical word. Barr et al. (2011) suggest that these effects are common in studies that provide either situational or linguistic context prior to a critical stimulus being heard. In most cases, good experimental design (ensuring that no unintended context is provided, careful counterbalancing of the position of your stimuli, etc. – see Chapter 3) will mean that ABEs should not be a problem.

For video-based studies we are again likely to be interested in what our participants were looking at during a specific time window or windows. For example, we could compare overall time spent reading each set of subtitles to see how these were utilised by language learners (as in Bisson et al., 2014, discussed in Section 5.4). Alternatively, we may be interested in relating the eye-tracking data to another measure such as attainment on a post-experiment test. In this case, we could analyse the eye-tracking data to see whether more and longer fixations on target words in the subtitles or other potentially relevant ROIs led to higher test scores, either on an overall basis or on an item-by-item basis (using fixation time on an individual word as a predictor of whether that word was correctly identified in the subsequent test). While correlation analysis could be used here, LME modelling again provides a more robust way to explore this and account for a range of other variables. We might also want to compare whether the type of video – for example 'context' versus 'content' videos, as in Suvorov, 2015, discussed in Section 6.2.1 – had an impact on looking behaviour, in which case we could include this as a categorical variable in our analysis.

Ultimately, the choice of analysis will be directly determined by the nature of our data and the specific research questions. Most types of eye-tracking data considered here can be analysed using traditional approaches such as ANOVA, although we should be careful when applying this to count and proportionate data. LME models are also appropriate, and journals are increasingly asking for this type of analysis to be applied. For applied linguistics research, the ability to include a number of covariates to account for item- and participant-specific properties makes this an attractive alternative to other methods.

7.3   Presentation of Results

We should present our results in a way that allows us to clearly demonstrate the main patterns in our data. Visualisations may be useful, but tables or figures to summarise the

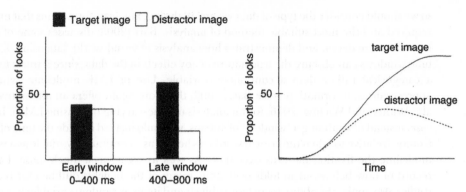

Figure 7.5 Hypothetical plots for visual-world data showing looking patterns over time to a target image and distractor. The left panel shows analysis where discrete early and late windows have been identified. The right panel shows the same data but with time plotted as a continuous variable. Note that total proportion will often not add up to 100 per cent because participants have the option to not look at either image.

descriptive statistics for our variables of interest should always be provided. In text-based studies it may be useful to present the means for multiple measures in a table, rather than providing a number of different figures. For visual-world or video data, a figure demonstrating the development of looking behaviour over time is a useful way of illustrating the main findings. This can be done by averaging data for discrete time windows or by plotting the proportions of looks to the different images over time as a continuous curve, as shown in Figure 7.5.

The results of any statistical analysis we undertake should be reported in full. For LME models, this would include the full outputs of any models we have created, and we should include a full description of the model fitting procedure to make clear which covariates we have included and what random effects structure we have used. Often including all of this information can take up a lot of space, so it may be more appropriate to summarise the results in the text and include all model outputs in an appendix or supplementary materials. Similarly, if we are using ANOVAs or *t*-tests, the results should be reported in full for all analyses.

While not strictly part of the results, we should also ensure that we clearly describe the parameters of our study, including aspects like the size and refresh rate of the screen, the experimental set-up, how long the study took, what data cleaning procedures were used, etc. Ensuring that we are clear and transparent in how we report our methodology and results is a key part of conducting and writing a good eye-tracking study.

7.4   Conclusions and Final Checklist

The discussion in this chapter should give researchers a clear idea of what will need to be done with eye-tracking data in order to produce sound analysis. A good grounding in statistics is essential, and consulting the respective user manuals will also help to get the most out of the data we have collected. As with many of the methodological issues that we have dealt with, comparing our study with similar published work is always a good guide when choosing the most appropriate approach to data analysis.

Final checklist	
• Inspect your data thoroughly once it has been collected.	⇨ Any clearly problematic trials should be removed. Some level of data adjustment may be possible to correct vertical misalignment in reading data.
	⇨ Data are generally cleaned to merge or remove very short fixations and remove very long ones.
• What type of visualisations will be helpful for your data?	⇨ Visualisations are a good way to demonstrate broad patterns or identify areas for further analysis, but should not be treated as analysis in and of themselves.
• Data should be exported for further analysis.	⇨ For reading studies you need to decide on which measures to analyse further. For image- or video-based studies, interest periods may be required if you need to analyse your data in discrete time windows.
	⇨ Descriptive statistics should be provided for all of the measures you choose for further analysis.
• What type of analysis will you need to use?	⇨ Traditional analyses like ANOVAs and *t*-tests are limited and may require transformations for certain types of data. Linear mixed effects modelling provides a more robust way to analyse data. This will also allow you to include a number of covariates that are likely to be of interest in applied linguistics research.
• Report results in a clear and comprehensive way.	⇨ Use tables and figures to help demonstrate the main patterns, and provide a full output of your analysis. Be transparent about all methodological choices you have made.

Chapter 8
Conclusions

In this book we have tried to present a beginners' guide to eye-tracking for anyone working in the field of applied linguistics. Given the increasing availability (and affordability) of this technology, it is becoming a popular choice for a wide range of topics that will be of interest to applied linguists. We have tried to condense thirty-plus years of eye-tracking literature to provide an overview of what eye-tracking has told us and what it can tell us, and tried to outline the principles that underpin this methodology. We have presented a practical guide to choosing the right equipment for your needs, provided a walkthrough of the process of designing and building a study using the main systems available, and offered some guidance on working with data. Throughout the seven chapters in this book we have outlined the main methodological issues that need to be considered when conducting eye-tracking research in a wide range of areas. As with any approach to research, the best way to learn is to dive in. Many of the methodological issues raised in the book will become much clearer once you start designing and building your own study, working with participants, and collecting and analysing data.

As we have shown in this book, eye-tracking is certainly a useful and important methodology, and a valuable tool for researchers from a variety of backgrounds with a range of interests. It provides a way to investigate online linguistic processing and behaviour in a relatively naturalistic way, and a whole host of important research topics have been enriched by well-designed, thoughtful eye-tracking studies. But it is not a panacea, and a number of misconceptions exist that may limit both the application of the methodology and the interpretation of eye-tracking data. A version of the following list of misconceptions was first proposed by Bojko and Adamczyk (2010) for eye-tracking in the field of user experience research, and restated by Grucza (2013) as it relates to translation processes. We have adapted the list to be more relevant to the field of applied linguistics, and address some common misconceptions below as a way of wrapping up the issues we have discussed throughout the book.

8.1 All Language Research Can Benefit from Eye-Tracking

Not all research topics will be suitable, and not all research environments will be conducive to the use of eye-tracking. As we stated in Chapter 3, the first question any researcher should ask is whether eye-tracking is even the right choice. Given the investment that will be required in terms of learning to use the equipment, preparing a study and collecting and analysing data, you should make sure that it is an appropriate method before you begin.

8.2 Eye-Tracking Results Are Easy to Interpret

Eye-tracking produces a large amount of data, and if you do not know what it is telling you, then it can be very difficult to make any meaningful interpretations. The literature on eye-movements in reading (Chapter 4) is long and detailed, so being able to make inferences about what is going on at each stage will require a good understanding of the different measures. Likewise, data from visual-world or other image-based or video studies is only meaningful if we are able to interpret it within an established framework (Chapters 5 and 6). The studies we have reviewed throughout this book will provide an excellent starting point so that you can get an idea of what an eye-tracking study might provide in terms of results.

8.3 Participants Don't Always Do What You Want Them to Do

There are really two key points to remember here. The first is that the task you employ will have a huge impact on how participants behave. Participants' viewing behaviour will vary according to what they are asked to do (read for comprehension, watch a video for enjoyment, locate an image in a visual array as quickly as possible, etc.), so this should be considered carefully when you put your study together. Second, all participants will be different. We know a lot about what eye-movements reflect *in general*, but every individual person you collect data from will behave in a unique way. This is why you should ensure that a large and representative sample of data is collected, and why we recommend a method of analysis (like linear mixed effects modelling) that accounts for random variation among both subjects and items.

8.4 Let's Track and See What Comes Out!

An exploratory approach like this is unlikely to ever be of much use in an applied linguistics study. A well-designed study should always have a clear research question and clearly defined variables (see the studies discussed throughout Chapters 4–6). Given the time and effort required to conduct eye-tracking studies, fishing expeditions are never going to be a productive way to conduct research (of any kind). A small-scale pilot study might be useful as a way of identifying broad areas for investigation or troubleshooting aspects of your study, but otherwise the more clearly defined your aims and research questions, the better your study will be.

8.5 There Is a Magic Sample Size for All Eye-Tracking Studies

As we discussed in Chapter 3, there is no 'right' number of participants for eye-tracking, just as there is no 'right' number of participants for any methodology. The choices you make in your study design will affect how many people you require (How many conditions do you have? How many presentation lists?), so the best approach is always to read widely and base your choice on comparable studies. Practical issues – such as how easy it is to recruit the people – will always be relevant as well. So if, for example, you want to investigate people with a certain kind of language impairment, be aware that it might be hard to find a large number of participants who meet your requirements.

8.6 Eye-Tracking Is All about Heat Maps

We have addressed this in Chapter 7, when we discussed visualising data. Visualisations such as heat maps provide a useful way to summarise data in a presentation or paper, but do not represent analysis in themselves. (In effect, they are the same as a table of mean values, just with the data presented in a graphical rather than numerical form.) The majority of papers that use eye-tracking to explore reading or listening will likely not produce any heat maps or other visualisations at all, and rigorous statistical analysis should always form the bedrock of your research.

8.7 Eye-Movement Analysis Can Be Done by Watching Gaze Videos in Real Time

Given the amount of data produced during any eye-tracking study, this would be no mean feat! Even if it were possible to reliably judge the fixation data for a single trial, the aim of any study is to aggregate data across trials and participants, so visual inspection is of little value other than for the purposes of data checking and cleaning, as outlined in Chapter 7. A visualisation of representative fixation data could be useful in demonstrating your study during a presentation, but otherwise statistical analysis is an essential aspect of this kind of research.

8.8 The Dot on the Screen or Output Indicates Exactly Where a Person Looked and What They Saw

Such an assumption may seem like a logical one to make given the 'eye–mind hypothesis' we discussed in Chapter 1. As we have seen, the reality is not this straightforward. In a well-calibrated system with a high enough sampling rate, we can be confident that the point of a fixation is indeed what the participant is looking at, but given the research on parafoveal processing and other late and early effects in reading behaviour that we discussed in Chapter 4, this does not tell the whole story. For systems with lower sampling rates, we are less able to make such precise claims about the location of fixations. Ultimately, eye-tracking research requires the researcher to analyse and interpret the data in a thoughtful and realistic way. Only if an experiment is appropriately designed and controlled can we make strong claims about specific aspects of language processing.

8.9 All Data Should Be Analysed

There is no reason to assume that all the data you collect must be used. Problems with set-up or calibration, participant issues and other technical problems may mean that some of your data are much better off discarded; a participant with atypical behaviour is by definition outside of the group you wish to make generalisable claims about; and as we discussed in Chapter 3, identifying every word in a reading study as an ROI can generate significantly more data than we need (and in general there is no point in analysing data from any 'fillers' that we included in the experiment). Given what we know about reading in particular, some degree of data cleaning and trimming is always desirable to eliminate outliers and make the data as representative as possible. Whatever data you do include should be analysed appropriately if you want to make meaningful and justifiable claims, and remember to be as clear as you can when describing the decisions you made.

8.10 Anyone Can Do Eye-Tracking

The affordability and usability of modern eye-trackers mean that more and more researchers can and should use them. After all, this is why we wrote this book! But good-quality research involves more than simply learning how to use the equipment and knowing which buttons to press to produce a heat map. All researchers should ensure that they understand the principles and practices of what makes for good research design in general (including things like statistical analysis of the data), and good eye-tracking design in particular. Knowledge of the theory and practice underlying eye-tracking takes time and effort. As we hope we've demonstrated, this can certainly be time and effort well spent, and can lead to extremely fruitful and enjoyable research.

We hope that the discussion provided in this book will enable both researchers and students to understand the eye-tracking studies they come across in journals or at conferences, and also to think about planning and conducting their own eye-tracking studies.

References

Acunzo, D. J. and Henderson, J. M. (2011). No emotional 'pop-out' effect in natural scene viewing. *Emotion*, 11(5), 1134–1143.

Alamargot, D., Caporossi, G., Chesnet, D. and Ros, C. (2011). What makes a skilled writer? Working memory and audience awareness during text composition. *Learning and Individual Differences*, 21, 505–516.

Alamargot, D., Dansac, C., Chesnet, D. and Fayol, M. (2007). Parallel processing before and after pauses: A combined analysis of graphomotor and eye movements during procedural text production. In M. Torrance, L. van Waes and D. Galbraith (eds.), *Writing and Cognition: Research and Applications* (pp. 13–29). Amsterdam: Elsevier.

Allbritton, D. W., McKoon, G. and Gerrig, R. J. (1995). Metaphor-based schemas and text representations: Making connections through conceptual metaphors. *Journal of Experimental Psychology: Learning, Memory, and Cognition*, 21(3), 612–625.

Allen, D. and Conklin, K. (2017). Naturalistic reading in the L2 and the impact of word frequency and cross-linguistic similarity. *Journal of the Ochanomizu University English Society*, 7, 41–57.

Allopenna, P. D., Magnuson, J. S. and Tanenhaus, M. K. (1998). Tracking the time course of spoken word recognition using eye movements: Evidence for continuous mapping models. *Journal of Memory and Language*, 38, 419–439.

Altarriba, J., Kroll, J., Sholl, A. and Rayner, K. (1996). The influence of lexical and conceptual constraints on reading mixed-language sentences: Evidence from eye fixations and naming times. *Memory and Cognition*, 24(4), 477–492.

Altmann, G. T. M. (2004). Language-mediated eye movements in the absence of a visual world: The 'blank screen paradigm'. *Cognition*, 93(2), B79–B87.

Altmann, G. T. M. (2011a). The mediation of eye movements by spoken language. In S. Liversedge, I. Gilchrist and S. Everling (eds.), *The Oxford Handbook of Eye Movements* (pp. 979–1004). Oxford: Oxford University Press.

Altmann, G. T. M. (2011b). Language can mediate eye movement control within 100 milliseconds, regardless of whether there is anything to move the eyes to. *Acta Psychologica*, 137(2), 190–200.

Altmann, G. T. M. and Kamide, Y. (1999). Incremental interpretation at verbs: Restricting the domain of subsequent reference. *Cognition*, 73(3), 247–264.

Altmann, G. T. M. and Kamide, Y. (2009). Discourse-mediation of the mapping between language and the visual world: Eye-movements and mental representation. *Cognition*, 111(1), 55–71.

Andersson, B., Dahl, J., Holmqvist, K. et al. (2006). Combining keystroke logging with eye tracking. In L. Van Waes, M. Leiten and C. M. Neuwirth (eds.), *Writing and Digital Media* (pp. 166–172). Amsterdam: Elsevier.

Andersson, R., Nyström, M. and Holmqvist, K. (2010). Sampling frequency and eye-tracking measures: How speed affects durations, latencies, and more. *Journal of Eye Movement Research*, 3(3), 1–12.

Antes, J. R. (1974). The time course of picture viewing. *Journal of Experimental Psychology*, 103(1), 62–70.

Anthony, L. (2012). A critical look at software tools in corpus linguistics. *Linguistic Research*, 30(2), 141–161.

Anthony, L. (2014). AntConc (Version 3.4.3) [Computer software]. Tokyo, Japan: Waseda University. Available from www.laurenceanthony.net

Arai, M., van Gompel, R. P. and Scheepers, C. (2007). Priming ditransitive structures in comprehension. *Cognitive Psychology*, 54(3), 218–250.

Arnold, J. E., Eisenband, J. G., Brown-Schmidt, S. and Trueswell, J. C. (2000). The rapid use of gender information: Evidence of the time course of pronoun resolution from eye tracking. *Cognition*, 76(1), B13–B26.

Aylett, S. (1999). *The Inflatable Volunteer*. London: Phoenix House.

Baayen, R. H. (2010). A real experiment is a factorial experiment? *The Mental Lexicon*, 5(1), 149–157.

Baayen, R. H., Davidson, D. J. and Bates, D. M. (2008). Mixed-effects modeling with crossed random effects for subjects and items. *Journal of Memory and Language*, 59, 390–412.

Balling, L. (2013). Reading authentic texts: What counts as cognate? *Bilingualism: Language and Cognition*, 16(3), 637–653.

Balota, D. A. and Rayner, K. (1991). Word recognition processes in foveal and parafoveal vision: The range of influence of lexical variables. In D. Besner and G. W. Humphreys (eds.), *Basic Processes in Reading: Visual Word Recognition* (pp. 198–232). London: Routledge.

Baron-Cohen, S., Wheelwright, S., Skinner, R., Martin, J. and Clubley, E. (2001). The autism-spectrum quotient (AQ): Evidence from Asperger syndrome/high-functioning autism, males and females, scientists and mathematicians. *Journal of Autism and Developmental Disorders*, 31(1), 5–17.

Barr, D. J. (2008) Analyzing 'visual world' eyetracking data using multilevel logistic regression. *Journal of Memory and Language*, 59, 457–474.

Barr, D. J., Gann, T. M. and Pierce, R. S. (2011). Anticipatory baseline effects and information integration in visual world studies. *Acta Psychologica*, 137, 201–207.

Barr, D. J., Levy, R., Scheepers, C. and Tilly, H. J. (2013). Random effects structure for confirmatory hypothesis testing: Keep it maximal. *Journal of Memory and Language*, 68, 255–278.

Bates, D., Maechler, M., Bolker, B. and Walker, S. (2015). Fitting linear mixed-effects models using lme4. *Journal of Statistical Software*, 67(1), 1–48.

Bax, S. (2013). The cognitive processes of candidates during reading tests: Evidence from eye-tracking. *Language Testing*, 30(4), 441–465.

Bax, S. and Weir, C. J. (2012). Investigating learners' cognitive processes during a computer-based CAE reading text. *Cambridge ESOL: Research Notes*, 47, 3–14.

Bernardini, S. (1998). Systematising serendipity: Proposals for large-corpora concordancing with language learners. *Proceedings of TALC98* (pp. 12–16). Oxford: Seacourt Press.

Biber, D., Conrad, S. and Reppen, R. (1998). *Corpus Linguistics*. Cambridge: Cambridge University Press.

Bisson, M.-J., van Heuven, W. J. B., Conklin, K. and Tunney, R. (2014). Processing of native and foreign language subtitles in films: An eye tracking study. *Applied Psycholinguistics*, 35(2), 399–418.

Blaschek, T., Kurzhals, K., Raschke, M., Burch, M., Weiskopf, D. and Ertl, T. (2014). State-of-the-art of visualization for eye tracking data. In R. Borgo, R. Maciejewski and I. Viola (eds.), *Eurographics Conference on Visualization (EuroVis'14) State of the Art Report*. Geneva: Eurographics Association.

Boersma, P. and Weenink, D. (2016). Praat (Version 6.0.33) [Computer software]. Available from www.fon.hum.uva.nl/praat

Bojko, A. (2009). Informative or misleading? Heatmaps deconstructed. In J. Jacko (ed.), *Human–Computer Interaction. New Trends* (pp. 30–39). Berlin/Heidelberg: Springer.

Bojko, A. and Adamczyk, K. (2010). More than just eye candy: Top ten misconceptions about eye tracking. *User Experience Magazine*, 9(3).

Box, G. E. P. and Cox, D. R. (1964). An analysis of transformations. *Journal of the Royal Statistical Society: Series B (Methodological)*, 26(2), 211–252.

Brown, A. C. (1895). *The Relation between the Movements of the Eyes and the Movements of the Head: Being the Fourth Robert Boyle Lecture Delivered before the Oxford University Junior Scientific Club*. London: Henry Frowde.

Brunfaut, T. and McCray, G. (2015). Looking into test-takers' cognitive processes while completing reading tasks: A mixed-method eye-tracking and stimulated recall study. *British Council Assessment Research Awards and Grants: Research Reports*, 1–55.

Brysbaert, M. and New, B. (2009). Moving beyond Kucera and Francis: A critical evaluation of current word frequency norms and the introduction of a new and improved word frequency measure for American English. *Behavior Research Methods, Instruments and Computers*, 41(4), 977–990.

Carl, M. (2012). Translog – II: A program for recording user activity data for empirical reading and writing research. *Proceedings of the Eight International Conference on Language Resources and Evaluation.* European Language Resources Association (ELRA), Istanbul, Turkey.

Carl, M. and Kay, M. (2011). Gazing and typing activities during translation: A comparative study of translation units of professional and student translators. *Meta: Translators' Journal*, 56(4), 952–975.

Carpenter, P. A. and Daneman, M. (1981). Lexical retrieval and error recovery in reading: A model based on eye fixations. *Journal of Verbal Learning and Verbal Behavior*, 20(2), 137–160.

Carrol, G. and Conklin, K. (2014). Eye-tracking multi-word units: Some methodological challenges. *Journal of Eye Movement Research*, 7(5), 1–11.

Carrol, G. and Conklin, K. (2017). Cross language priming extends to formulaic units: Evidence from eye-tracking suggests that this idea 'has legs'. *Bilingualism: Language and Cognition*, 20(2), 299–317.

Carrol, G., Conklin, K. and Gyllstad, H. (2016). Found in translation: The influence of L1 on the processing of idioms in L2. *Studies in Second Language Acquisition*, 38(3), 403–443.

Carrol, G., Conklin, K., Guy, J. and Scott, R. (2015). Processing punctuation and word changes in different editions of prose fiction. *Scientific Study of Literature*, 5(2), 200–228.

Castelhano, M. S. and Henderson, J. M. (2008). The influence of color on perception of scene gist. *Journal of Experimental Psychology: Human Perception and Performance*, 34(3), 660–675.

Castelhano, M. S. and Rayner, K. (2008). Eye movements during reading, visual search, and scene perception: An overview. In K. Rayner, D. Shen, X. Bai and G. Yan (eds.), *Cognitive and Cultural Influences on Eye Movements* (pp. 3–33). Tianjin: Tianjin People's Publishing House.

Chambers, C. G. and Cooke, H. (2009). Lexical competition during second-language listening: Sentence context, but not proficiency, constrains interference from the native lexicon. *Journal of Experimental Psychology: Learning, Memory, and Cognition*, 35(4), 1029–1040.

Chan, T. and Liou, H. (2005). Effects of web-based concordancing instruction on EFL students' learning of verb-noun collocations. *Computer Assisted Language Learning*, 18, 231–250.

Chen, L. and Boland, J. E. (2008). Dominance and context effects on activation of alternative homophone meanings. *Memory and Cognition*, 36(7), 1306–1323.

Chesnet, D. and Alamargot, D. (2006). Eye and Pen (Version 1.0) [Computer software]. Poitiers: Octares.

Clark, H. H. (1973). The language as-fixed-effect fallacy: A critique of language statistics in psychological research. *Journal of Verbal Learning and Verbal Behavior*, 12, 335–359.

Clifton, C. and Staub, A. (2011). Syntactic influences on eye movements in reading. In S. Liversedge, I. Gilchrist and S. Everling (eds.), *The Oxford Handbook of Eye Movements* (pp. 895–909). Oxford: Oxford University Press.

Clifton, C., Ferreira, F., Henderson, J. M., Inhoff, A. W., Liversedge, S. P., Reichle, E. D. and Schotter, E. R. (2016). Eye movements in reading and information processing: Keith Rayner's 40 year legacy. *Journal of Memory and Language*, 86, 1–19.

Clifton, C., Staub, A. and Rayner, K. (2007). Eye movements in reading words and sentences. In R. van Gompel, M. H. Fischer, W. S. Murray and R. L. Hill (eds.), *Eye Movements: A Window on Mind and Brain* (pp. 341–372). Amsterdam: Elsevier.

Cobb, T. (n.d.). Compleat Lexical Tutor (Version 8) [Online resource]. Available from www.lextutor.ca

Colantoni, L., Steele, J. and Escudero, P. (2015). *Second Language Speech: Theory and Practice.* Cambridge: Cambridge University Press.

Conklin, K. and Pellicer-Sánchez, A. (2016). Using eye-tracking in applied linguistics and second language research. *Second Language Research*, 32(3), 453–467.

Cooper, R. M. (1974). The control of eye fixation by the meaning of spoken language: A new methodology for the real-time investigation of speech perception, memory, and language processing. *Cognitive Psychology*, 6(1), 84–107.

Cop, U., Dirix, N., Drieghe, D. and Duyck, W. (2017a). Presenting GECO: An eyetracking corpus of monolingual and bilingual sentence reading. *Behavior Research Methods*, 49, 602–605.

Cop, U., Dirix, N., Van Assche, E., Drieghe, D. and Duyck, W. (2017b). Reading a book in one or two languages? An eye movement study of cognate facilitation in L1 and L2 reading. *Bilingualism: Language and Cognition*, 20(4), 747–769.

Cop, U., Drieghe, D. and Duyck, W. (2015a). Eye movement patterns in natural reading: A comparison of monolingual and bilingual reading of a novel. *PloS One*, 10(8), 1–38.

Cop, U., Keuleers, E., Drieghe, D. and Duyck, W. (2015b). Frequency effects in monolingual and bilingual natural reading. *Psychonomic Bulletin and Review*, 22(5), 1216–1234.

Corbett, J. (1997). *Language and Scottish Literature*. Edinburgh: Edinburgh University Press.

Cover, T. M. and Thomas, J. A. (1991). *Elements of Information Theory*. Wiley Series in Telecommunications. New York, NY: John Wiley & Sons.

Cutter, M. G., Drieghe, D. and Liversedge, S. P. (2014). Preview benefit in English spaced compounds. *Journal of Experimental Psychology: Learning, Memory, and Cognition*, 40(6), 1778–1786.

Dahan, D., Magnuson, J. S. and Tanenhaus, M. K. (2001). Time course of frequency effects in spoken-word recognition: Evidence from eye movements. *Cognitive Psychology*, 42(4), 317–367.

Davies, M., (2008–). *The Corpus of Contemporary American English: 520 Million Words, 1990-Present*. Available online at http://corpus.byu.edu/coca

Davies, M., (2015). *The Wikipedia Corpus: 4.6 Million Articles, 1.9 Billion Words*. Adapted from Wikipedia. Available online at http://corpus.byu.edu/wiki

Davis, M., Marslen-Wilson, W. and Gaskell, M. G. (2002). Leading up the lexical garden path: Segmentation and ambiguity in spoken word recognition. *Journal of Experimental Psychology: Human Perception and Performance*, 28(1), 218–244.

De Graef, P. (2005). Semantic effects on object selection in real-world scene perception. In G. Underwood (ed.), *Cognitive Processes in Eye Guidance* (pp. 189–211). Oxford: Oxford University Press.

Depessemier, P. and Andries, C. (2009). *GL&SCHR. Test voor Gevorderd Lezen & Schrijven*. Antwerp: Garant.

Dörnyei, Z. (2007). *Research Methods in Applied Linguistics: Quantitative, Qualitative and Mixed Methodologies*. Oxford: Oxford University Press.

Dragsted, B. (2010). Coordination of reading and writing processes in translation: an eye on uncharted territory. In G. M. Shreve and E. Angelone (eds.), *Translation and Cognition* (pp. 41–62). Amsterdam: John Benjamins.

Duchowski, A. (2007). *Eye Tracking Methodology: Theory and Practice*. London: Springer-Verlag.

Duffy, S. A., Morris, R. K. and Rayner, K. (1988). Lexical ambiguity and fixation times in reading. *Journal of Memory and Language*, 27(4), 429–446.

Ehrlich, K. and Rayner, K. (1983). Pronoun assignment and semantic integration during reading: Eye movements and immediacy of processing. *Journal of Verbal Learning and Verbal Behavior*, 22 (1), 75–87.

Ehrlich, S. F. and Rayner, K. (1981). Contextual effects on word perception and eye movements during reading. *Journal of Verbal Learning and Verbal Behavior*, 20(6), 641–655.

Evans, M. A. and Saint-Aubin, J. (2005). What children are looking at during shared storybook reading. *Psychological Science*, 16(11), 913–920.

Farris-Trimble, A. and McMurray, B. (2013). Test–retest reliability of eye tracking in the visual world paradigm for the study of real-time spoken word recognition. *Journal of Speech, Language, and Hearing Research*, 56(4), 1328–1345.

Field, J. (2013). Cognitive validity. In A. Geranpayeh and L. Taylor (eds.), *Examining Listening.* (pp. 77–152). Cambridge: Cambridge University Press.

Folk, J. R. (1999). Phonological codes are used to access the lexicon during silent reading. *Journal of Experimental Psychology: Learning, Memory, and Cognition,* 25(4), 892–906.

Folk, J. R. and Morris, R. K. (2003). Effects of syntactic category assignment on lexical ambiguity resolution in reading: An eye movement analysis. *Memory and Cognition,* 31(1), 87–99.

Frazier, L. and Rayner, K. (1982). Making and correcting errors during sentence comprehension: Eye movements in the analysis of structurally ambiguous sentences. *Cognitive Psychology,* 14, 178–210.

Gaskell, D. and Cobb, T. (2004). Can learners use concordance feedback for writing errors? *System,* 32(3), 301–319.

Gavins, J. and Steen, G. (eds.) (2003). *Cognitive Poetics in Practice.* London: Routledge.

Gilquin, G. and Granger, S. (2010). How can data-driven learning be used in language teaching? In A. O'Keffee and M. McCarthy (eds.), *The Routledge Handbook of Corpus Linguistics* (pp. 359–371). London: Routledge.

Göpferich, S., Bayer-Hohenwarter, G., Prassl, F. and Stadlober, J. (2011). Exploring translation competence acquisition: Criteria of analysis put to the test. In S. O'Brien (ed.), *Cognitive Explorations of Translation* (pp. 57–85). London: Continuum.

Griffin, Z. M. (2004). Why look? Reasons for eye movements related to language production. In J. M. Henderson and F. Ferreira (eds.), *The Integration of Language, Vision, and Action: Eye Movements and the Visual World* (pp. 213–247). New York: Psychology Press.

Grucza, S. (2013). Heat maps, gaze plots . . . and what next? The access to translation competences and translation processes. In S. Grucza, M. Pluzyczka and J. Zajac (eds.), *Translation Studies and Eye-Tracking Analysis* (pp. 15–31). Frankfurt am Main: Peter Lang.

Guthrie, D. and Buchwald, J. S. (1991). Significance testing of difference potentials. *Psychophysiology,* 28(2), 240–244.

Guy, J., Scott, R., Conklin, K. and Carrol, G. (2016). Challenges in editing late nineteenth- and early twentieth-century prose and fiction: What is editorial 'completeness'? *English Literature in Transition,* 59(4), 435–455.

Hafner, C. A. and Candlin, C. N. (2007). Corpus tools as an affordance to learning in professional legal education. *Journal of English for Academic Purposes,* 6, 303–318.

Hanna, J., Tanenhaus, M. K. and Trueswell, J. C. (2003). The effects of common ground and perspective on domains of referential interpretation. *Journal of Memory and Language,* 49, 43–61.

Hansen-Schirra, S. and Rösener, C. (2013). Proactive use of eye-tracking in the translational workflow. In S. Grucza, M. Pluzyczka and J. Zajac (eds.), *Translation Studies and Eye-Tracking Analysis* (pp. 139–151). Frankfurt am Main: Peter Lang.

Henderson, J. M. (1993). Eye movement control during visual object processing: Effects of initial fixation position and semantic constraint. *Canadian Journal of Experimental Psychology,* 47(1), 79–98.

Henderson, J. M. (2003). Human gaze control during real-world scene perception. *Trends in Cognitive Sciences,* 7(11), 498–504.

Henderson, J. M. and Hollingworth, A. (1998). Eye movements during scene viewing: An overview eye guidance in reading and scene perception. In G. Underwood (ed.), *Eye Guidance While Reading and While Watching Dynamic Scenes* (pp. 269–293). Oxford: Elsevier.

Henderson, J. M. and Hollingworth, A. (1999). High-level scene perception. *Annual Review of Psychology,* 50(1), 243–271.

Hofmeister, J., Heller, D. and Radach, R. (1999). The return sweep in reading. In W. Becker, H. Deubel and W. Mergner (eds.), *Current Oculomotor Research: Physiological and Psychological Aspects* (pp. 349–357). New York: Plenum Press.

Hollingworth, A. and Henderson, J. M. (2000). Semantic informativeness mediates the detection of changes in natural scenes. *Visual Cognition,* 7(1–3), 213–235.

Holmqvist, K., Nyström, M., Andersson, R., Dewhurst, R., Jarodzka, H. and Van de Weijer, J. (2011). *Eye Tracking: A Comprehensive Guide to Methods and Measures*. Oxford: Oxford University Press.

Holmqvist, K., Nyström, M. and Mulvey, F. (2012). Eye tracker data quality: What it is and how to measure it. In S. Spencer (ed.), *Proceedings of the Symposium on Eye Tracking Research and Applications: Santa Barbara, CA, March 28–30, 2012* (pp. 45–52). New York: Association for Computer Machinery.

Holsinger, E. (2013). Representing idioms: Syntactic and contextual effects on idiom processing. *Language and Speech*, 56(3), 373–394.

Howard, P. L., Liversedge, S. P. and Benson, V. (2017). Benchmark eye movement effects during natural reading in Autism Spectrum Disorder. *Journal of Experimental Psychology: Learning, Memory, and Cognition*, 43(1), 109–127.

Huettig, F. and Altmann, G. T. M. (2005). Word meaning and the control of eye fixation: Semantic competitor effects and the visual world paradigm. *Cognition*, 96(1), 23–32.

Huettig, F., Rommers, J. and Meyer, A. S. (2011). Using the visual world paradigm to study language processing: A review and critical evaluation. *Acta Psychologica*, 137, 151–171.

Huey, E. B. (1908). The mysteries and problems of reading. In *The Psychology and Pedagogy of Reading* (pp. 1–14). New York: Macmillan.

Hvelplund, K. T. (2014). Eye-tracking and the translation process: Reflections on the analysis and interpretation of eye-tracking data. *Minding Translation*, 1, 201–223.

Hyönä, J. (2011). Foveal and parafoveal processing during reading. In S. P. Liversedge, I. D. Gilchrist and S. Everling (eds.), *The Oxford Handbook of Eye Movements* (pp. 819–838). Oxford: Oxford University Press.

Hyönä, J. (2015). Are polymorphemic words processed differently from other words during reading? In A. Pollatsek and R. Treiman (eds.), *The Oxford Handbook of Reading* (pp. 114–128). Oxford: Oxford University Press.

IBM SPSS Statistics (Version 24.0) [Computer software]. (2016). Armonk, NY: IBM Corp. Available from www.ibm.com

Immordino-Yang, M. and Deacon, T. (2007). An evolutionary perspective on reading and reading disorders? In K. W. Fischer, J. H. Bernstein and M. H. Immordino-Yang (eds.), *Mind, Brain, and Education in Reading Disorders* (pp. 16–29). Cambridge: Cambridge University Press.

Inhoff, A. (1984). Two stages of word processing during eye fixations in the reading of prose. *Journal of Verbal Learning and Verbal Behavior*, 23, 612–624.

Irwin, D. E. (1998). Lexical processing during saccadic eye movements. *Cognitive Psychology*, 36(1), 1–27.

Irwin, D. E. and Carlson-Radvansky, L. A. (1996). Cognitive suppression during saccadic eye movements. *Psychological Science*, 7(2), 83–88.

Jaeger, T. F. (2008). Categorical data analysis: Away from ANOVAs (transformation or not) and towards logit mixed models. *Journal of Memory and Language*, 59, 434–446.

Jensema, C. J., El Sharkawy, S., Danturthi, R. S., Burch, R. and Hsu, D. (2000). Eye movement patterns of captioned television viewers. *American Annals of the Deaf*, 145(3), 275–285.

Jiang, N. (2012). *Conducting Reaction Time Research in Second Language Studies*. New York and Oxford: Routledge.

Johansson, R., Wengeling, A., Johnasson, V. and Holmqvist, K. (2010). Looking at the keyboard or the monitor: Relationship with text production processes. *Reading and Writing*, 23, 835–851.

Juhasz, B. J. (2007). The influence of semantic transparency on eye movements during English compound word recognition. In R. van Gompel, M. H. Fischer, W. S. Murray and R. L. Hill (eds.), *Eye Movements: A Window on Mind and Brain* (pp. 373–389). Amsterdam: Elsevier.

Juhasz, B. J. and Rayner, K. (2003). Investigating the effects of a set of intercorrelated variables on eye fixation durations in reading. *Journal of Experimental Psychology: Learning, Memory, and Cognition*, 29(6), 1312–1318.

Juhasz, B. J. and Rayner, K. (2006). The role of age-of-acquisition and word frequency in reading: Evidence from eye fixation durations. *Visual Cognition*, 13(7–8), 846–863.

Just, M. A. and Carpenter, P. A. (1980). A theory of reading: From eye fixations to comprehension. *Psychological Review*, 87(4), 329–354.

Justice, L. M., Skibbe, L. and Canning, A. (2005). Pre-schoolers, print and storybooks: An observational study using eye movement analysis. *Journal of Research in Reading*, 28(3), 229–243.

Kaufer, D. S., Hayes, J. R. and Flower, L. S. (1986). Composing written sentences. *Research in the Teaching of English*, 20, 121–140.

Kennedy, C. and Miceli, T. (2001). An evaluation of intermediate students' approaches to corpus investigation. *Language Learning and Technology*, 5(3), 77–90.

Kincaid, J. P., Fishburne, R. P., Rogers, R. L. and Chissom, B. S. (1975). *Derivation of New Readability Formulas (Automated Readability Index, Fog Count and Flesch Reading Ease Formula) for Navy Enlisted Personnel* (Research Branch Report 8–75). Millington, TN: Naval Technical Training, US Naval Air Station.

Kliegl, R. and Engbert, R. (2005). Fixation durations before word skipping in reading. *Psychonomic Bulletin and Review*, 12(1), 132–138.

Koops van't Jagt, R., Hoeks, J., Dorleijn, G. and Hendriks, P. (2014). Look before you leap: How enjambment affects the processing of poetry. *Scientific Study of Literature*, 4(1), 3–24.

Korpal, P. (2015). Eye-tracking in translation and interpreting studies: The growing popularity and methodological problems. In Ł. Bogucki and M. Deckert (eds.), *Accessing Audiovisual Translation* (pp. 199–212). Łódź: Peter Lang.

Laeng, B., Sirois, S. and Gredebäck, G. (2012). Pupillometry: a window to the preconscious? *Perspectives on Psychological Science*, 7(1), 18–27.

Lai, C. and Zhao, Y. (2006). Noticing and text-based chat. *Language Learning and Technology*, 10(3), 102–120.

Lee, L. (2004). Learners' perspectives on networked collaborative interaction with native speakers of Spanish in the US. *Language Learning and Technology*, 8(1), 83–100.

Leijten, M. and Van Waes, L. (2013). Keystroke logging in writing research: Using Inputlog to analyze and visualize writing processes. *Written Communication*, 30(3), 358–392.

Lemhöfer, K. and Broersma, M. (2012). Introducing LexTALE: A quick and valid lexical test for advanced learners of English. *Behavior Research Methods*, 44(2), 325–343.

Leow, R., Grey, S., Marijuan, S. and Moorman, C. (2014). Concurrent data elicitation procedures, processes, and the early stages of L2 learning: A critical overview. *Second Language Research*, 30 (2), 111–127.

Libben, M. R. and Titone, D. (2009). Bilingual lexical access in context: Evidence from eye movements during reading. *Journal of Experimental Psychology: Learning, Memory, and Cognition*, 35(2), 381–390.

Linck, J., Osthus, P., Koeth, J. and Bunting, M. (2014). Working memory and second language comprehension and production: A meta-analysis. *Psychonomic Bulletin and Review*, 21(4), 861–883.

Liversedge, S. P., Gilchrist, I. and Everling, S. (2011). *The Oxford Handbook of Eye Movements*. Oxford: Oxford University Press.

Liversedge, S. P., Paterson, K. B. and Pickering, M. (1998). Eye movements and measures of reading time. In G. Underwood (ed.), *Eye Guidance in Reading and Scene Perception* (pp. 55–75). Oxford: Elsevier Science.

Liversedge, S. P., White, S. J., Findlay, J. M. and Rayner, K. (2006). Binocular coordination of eye movements during reading. *Vision Research*, 46(15), 2363–2374.

Lord, C., Rutter, M., DiLavore, P. C., Risi, S., Gotham, K. and Bishop, S. (2012). *Autism Diagnostic Observation Schedule* (2nd edition). Torrance, CA: Western Psychological Services.

Lotto, L., Dell'Acqua, R. and Job, R. (2001). Le figure PD/DPSS. Misure di accordo sul nome, tipicità, familiarità, età di acquisizione e tempi di denominazione per 266 figure [PD/DPSS pictures: Name agreement, typicality, familiarity, age of acquisition norms and naming times of 266 pictures.]. *Giornale Italiano di Psicologia*, 28(1), 231–245.

Luke, S. G. and Henderson, J. M. (2016). The influence of content meaningfulness on eye movements across tasks: Evidence from scene viewing and reading. *Frontiers in Psychology*, 7, 1–10.

Mackworth, N. H. and Morandi, A. J. (1967). The gaze selects informative details within pictures. *Perception and Psychophysics*, 2(11), 547–552.

Magnuson, J. S., Dixon, J. A., Tanenhaus, M. K. and Aslin, R. N. (2007). The dynamics of lexical competition during spoken word recognition. *Cognitive Science*, 31(1), 133–156.

Magnuson, J. S., McMurray, B., Tanenhaus, M. K. and Aslin, R. N. (2003). Lexical effects on compensation for coarticulation: The ghost of Christmas past. *Cognitive Science*, 27(2), 285–298.

Mahlberg, M. (2013). *Corpus Stylistics and Dickens's Fiction*. New York and London: Routledge.

Mahlberg, M., Conklin, K. and Bisson, M.-J. (2014). Reading Dickens's characters: Employing psycholinguistic methods to investigate the cognitive reality of patterns in texts. *Language and Literature*, 23(4), 369–388.

Mannan, S. K., Ruddock, K. H. and Wooding, D. S. (1995). Automatic control of saccadic eye movements made in visual inspection of briefly presented 2-D images. *Spatial Vision*, 9(3), 363–386.

Mannan, S. K., Ruddock, K. H. and Wooding, D. S. (1996). The relationship between the locations of spatial features and those of fixation made during the visual examination of briefly presented images. *Spatial Vision*, 10(3), 165–188.

Marian, V., Blumenfeld, H. K. and Kaushanskaya, M. (2007). The Language Experience and Proficiency Questionnaire (LEAP-Q): Assessing language profiles in bilinguals and multilinguals. *Journal of Speech, Language, and Hearing Research*, 50(4), 940–967.

Matin, E., Shao, K. C. and Boff, K. R. (1993). Saccadic overhead: Information-processing time with and without saccades. *Perception and Psychophysics*, 53, 372–380.

McDonald, S. A. and Shillcock, R. C. (2003a). Low-level predictive inference in reading: The influence of transitional probabilities on eye movements. *Vision Research*, 43(16), 1735–1751.

McDonald, S. A. and Shillcock, R. C. (2003b). Eye movements reveal the on-line computation of lexical probabilities during reading. *Psychological Science*, 14(6), 648–652.

McLaughlin, G. H. (1969). SMOG grading: A new readability formula. *Journal of Reading*, 12(8), 639–646.

McMurray, B., Tanenhaus, M.K. and Aslin, R.N. (2002). Gradient effects of within-category phonetic variation on lexical access. *Cognition*, 86(2), B33–B42.

Meyer, A. S., Belke, E., Telling, A. L. and Humphreys, G. W. (2007). Early activation of object names in visual search. *Psychonomic Bulletin and Review*, 14(4), 710–716.

Michel, M., Révész, A. and Gilabert, R. (under review). Eye-tracking and stimulated recall as means of investigating cognitive load and processes during L2 task performance.

Michel, M. and Smith, B. (2017) Eye-tracking research in computer-mediated language learning. In S. May (ed.), *Language and Technology*. Encyclopedia of Language and Education (pp. 1–12). Cham: Springer International Publishing.

Miles, W. R. (1930). Ocular dominance in human adults. *Journal of General Psychology*, 3, 412–429.

Morales, L., Paolieri, D., Dussias, P. E., Kroff, J. R. V., Gerfen, C. and Bajo, M. T. (2016). The gender congruency effect during bilingual spoken-word recognition. *Bilingualism: Language and Cognition*, 19(2), 294–310.

Nadig, A. S. and Sedivy, J. C. (2002). Evidence of perspective taking constraints on children's on-line reference resolution. *Psychological Science*, 13, 329–336.

Neider, M. B. and Zelinsky, G. J. (2006). Scene context guides eye movements during search. *Vision Research*, 46(5), 614–621.

Nottbusch, G. (2010). Grammatical planning, execution, and control in written sentence production. *Reading and Writing*, 23, 777–801.

Nummenmaa, L., Hyönä, J. and Calvo, M. G. (2006). Eye movement assessment of selective attentional capture by emotional pictures. *Emotion*, 6(2), 257–268.

Nummenmaa, L., Hyönä, J. and Calvo, M. G. (2009). Emotional scene content drives the saccade generation system reflexively. *Journal of Experimental Psychology: Human Perception and Performance*, 35(2), 305–323.

O'Brien, S. (2009). Eye tracking in translation-process research: Methodological challenges and solutions. In I. M. Mees, F. Alves and S. Göpferich (eds.), *Methodology, Technology and Innovation in Translation Process Research* (pp. 251–266). Copenhagen: Samfundslitteratur.

O'Rourke, B. (2012). Using eye-tracking to investigate gaze behaviour in synchronous computer-mediated communication for language learning. In M. Dooly and R. O'Dowd (eds.), *Researching Online Foreign Language Interaction and Exchange: Theories, Methods, and Challenges.* Telecollaboration in Education (pp. 305–341). Bern: Peter Lang.

Osaka, N. (2003). Asymmetry of the effective visual field in vertical reading as measured with a moving window. In G. d'Ydewalle and J. Van Rensbergen (eds.), *Perception and Cognition: Advances in Eye Movement Research* (pp. 275–283). Amsterdam: North-Holland.

O'Sullivan, B. and Weir, C. J. (2011). Test development and validation. In B. O'Sullivan (ed.), *Language Testing Theories and Practices* (pp. 13–32). Basingstoke: Palgrave Macmillan.

Parkhurst, D. and Niebur, E. (2003). Scene context selected by active vision. *Spatial Vision*, 16(2), 125–154.

Paterson, K., Liversedge, S. and Underwood, G. (1999). The influence of focus operators on syntactic processing of short relative clause sentences. *Quarterly Journal of Experimental Psychology*, 52A, 717–737.

Pellettieri, J. (2000). Negotiation in cyberspace: The role of chatting in the development of grammatical competence. In M. Warschauer and R. Kern (eds.), *Network-Based Language Teaching: Concepts and Practice* (pp. 59–86). Cambridge: Cambridge University Press.

Pellicer-Sánchez, A. (2016). Incidental L2 vocabulary acquisition from and while reading. *Studies in Second Language Acquisition*, 38(1), 97–130.

Perea, M. and Rosa, E. (2000). The effects of orthographic neighborhood in reading and laboratory word identification tasks: A review. *Psicológica: Revista de metodología y psicología experimental*, 21(3), 327–340.

Perego, E., Del Missier, F., Porta, M. and Mosconi, M. (2010). The cognitive effectiveness of subtitle processing. *Media Psychology*, 13(3), 243–272.

Pérez-Paredes, P., Sánchez-Tornel, M., Alcaraz Calero, J. M. and Aguado-Jiménez, P. (2011). Tracking learners' actual uses of corpora: Guided vs. non-guided corpus consultation. *Computer Assisted Language Learning*, 24(3), 233–253.

Pickering, M., Frisson, S., McElree, B. and Traxler, M. (2004). Eye movements and semantic composition. In M. Carreiras and C. Clifton (eds.), *On-Line Study of Sentence Comprehension: Eye Tracking, ERPs and Beyond* (pp. 33–50). New York, NY: Psychology Press.

Pivneva, I., Mercier, J. and Titone, D. (2014). Executive control modulates cross-language lexical activation during L2 reading: Evidence from eye movements. *Journal of Experimental Psychology: Learning, Memory, and Cognition*, 40, 787–796.

Pluzyczka, M. (2013). Eye-tracking supported research into sight translation. Lapsological conclusions. In S. Grucza, M. Pluzyczka and J. Zajac (eds.), *Translation Studies and Eye-Tracking Analysis* (pp. 105–138). Frankfurt am Main: Peter Lang.

Pollatsek, A., Bolozky, S., Well, A. D. and Rayner, K. (1981). Asymmetries in the perceptual span for Israeli readers. *Brain and Language*, 14(1), 174–180.

R Development Core Team. (2016). *R: A language and environment for statistical computing*, version 3.3.1. R Foundation for Statistical Computing, Vienna, Austria. Available from www.r-project.org

Raney, G. E., Campbell, S. J. and Bovee, J. C. (2014). Using eye movements to evaluate the cognitive processes involved in text comprehension. *Journal of Visual Experimentation*, 83, e50780.

Rayner, K. (1978). Eye movements in reading and information processing. *Psychological Bulletin*, 85(3), 618–660.

Rayner, K. (1998). Eye movements in reading and information processing: 20 years of research. *Psychological Bulletin*, 124(3), 372–422.

Rayner, K. (2009). Eye movements and attention in reading, scene perception, and visual search. *Quarterly Journal of Experimental Psychology*, 62(8), 1457–1506.

Rayner, K. and Duffy, S. (1986). Lexical complexity and fixation times in reading: Effects of word frequency, verb complexity, and lexical ambiguity. *Memory and Cognition*, 14(3), 191–201.

Rayner, K. and Pollatsek, A. (1989). *The Psychology of Reading*. Englewood Cliffs, NJ: Prentice Hall.

Rayner, K., Balota, D. A. and Pollatsek, A. (1986). Against parafoveal semantic preprocessing during eye fixations in reading. *Canadian Journal of Psychology*, 40(4), 473–483.

Rayner, K., Pollatsek, A., Ashby, J. and Clifton, C. (2012). *The Psychology of Reading* (2nd edition). Hove: Psychology Press.

Rayner, K., Raney, G. and Pollatsek, A. (1995). Eye movements and discourse processing. In R. F. Lorch and E. J. O'Brien (eds.), *Sources of Coherence in Reading* (pp. 9–36). Hillsdale, NJ: Erlbaum.

Rayner, K., Warren, T., Juhasz, B. J. and Liversedge, S. P. (2004). The effect of plausibility on eye movements in reading. *Journal of Experimental Psychology: Learning, Memory, and Cognition*, 30(6), 1290–1301.

Rayner, K., Well, A. D. and Pollatsek, A. (1980). Asymmetry of the effective visual field in reading. *Perception and Psychophysics*, 27(6), 537–544.

Renandya, W. (2007). The power of extensive reading. *RELC Journal*, 38(2), 133–149.

Rensink, R. A., O'Regan, J. K. and Clark, J. J. (1997). To see or not to see: The need for attention to perceive changes in scenes. *Psychological Science*, 8(5), 368–373.

Révész, A., Michel, M. and Lee, M. (2016). *Investigating IELTS Academic Writing Task 2: Relationships between Cognitive Writing Processes, Text Quality, and Working Memory*. IELTS Research Report Series. Melbourne: British Council, Cambridge English Language Assessment and IDP: IELTS Australia.

Roberts, A. M., Stabler, J., Fischer, M. H. and Otty, L. (2013). Space and pattern in linear and postlinear poetry: Empirical and theoretical approaches. *European Journal of English Studies*, 17(1), 23–40.

Rossion, B. and Pourtois, G. (2004). Revisiting Snodgrass and Vanderwart's object pictorial set: The role of surface detail in basic-level object recognition. *Perception*, 33(2), 217–236.

Roy-Charland, A., Saint-Aubin, J. and Evans, M. A. (2007). Eye movements in shared book reading with children from kindergarten to grade 4. *Journal of Reading and Writing*, 20, 909–931.

Salverda, A. P., Dahan, D. and McQueen, J. M. (2003). The role of prosodic boundaries in the resolution of lexical embedding in speech comprehension. *Cognition*, 90(1), 51–89.

Salverda, A. P., Dahan, D., Tanenhaus, M. K., Crosswhite, K., Masharov, M. and McDonough, J. (2007). Effects of prosodically modulated sub-phonetic variation on lexical competition. *Cognition*, 105(2), 466–476.

Sanford, A. J. and Filik, R. (2007) 'They' as a gender-unspecified singular pronoun: Eye-tracking reveals a processing cost. *Quarterly Journal of Experimental Psychology*, 60(2), 171–178.

Sauro, S. and Smith, B. (2010). Investigating L2 performance in text chat. *Applied Linguistics*, 31(4), 554–577.

Schaffner, A., Knowles, K., Weger, U. and Roberts, A. (2012). Reading space in visual poetry: New cognitive perspectives. *Writing Technologies*, 4(1), 75–106.

Scheepers, C., Keller, F. and Lapata, M. (2008). Evidence for serial coercion: A time course analysis using the visual-world paradigm. *Cognitive Psychology*, 56(1), 1–29.

Schepens, J., Dijkstra, T. and Grootjen, F. (2012). Distribution of cognates in Europe as based on the Levenshtein distance. *Bilingualism: Language and Cognition*, 15(1), 157–166.

Scherr, K. C., Agauas, S. J. and Ashby, J. (2016). The text matters: Eye movements reflect the cognitive processing of interrogation rights. *Applied Cognitive Psychology*, 30(2), 234–241.

Schielzeth, H. (2010). Simple means to improve the interpretability of regression coefficients. *Methods in Ecology and Evolution*, 1(2), 103–113.

Schotter, E. R., Angele, B. and Rayner, K. (2012). Parafoveal processing in reading. *Attention, Perception and Psychophysics*, 74(1), 5–35.

Sedivy, J. C. (2010). Using eye-tracking in language acquisition research. In E. Blom and S. Unsworth (eds.), *Experimental Methods In Language Acquisition Research* (pp. 115–138). Amsterdam: John Benjamins.

Semel, E., Wiig, E. H. and Secord, W. A. (2003). *Clinical Evaluation of Language Fundamentals* (4th edition). Toronto: The Psychological Corporation/Harcourt.

Sereno, S. and Rayner, K. (2000). Spelling-sound regularity effects on eye fixations in reading. *Perception and Psychophysics*, 62(2), 402–409.

Sereno, S. C., O'Donnell, P. and Rayner, K. (2006). Eye movements and lexical ambiguity resolution: Investigating the subordinate bias effect. *Journal of Experimental Psychology: Human Perception and Performance*, 32(2), 335–350.

Shreve, G. M., La Cruz, I. and Angelone, E. (2010). Cognitive effort, syntactic disruption, and visual interference in a sight translation task. In G. M. Shreve and E. Angelone (eds.), *Translation and Cognition* (pp. 63–84). Amsterdam: John Benjamins.

Shukla, M., White, K. S. and Aslin, R. N. (2011). Prosody guides the rapid mapping of auditory word forms onto visual objects in 6-mo-old infants. *Proceedings of the National Academy of Sciences*, 108(15), 6038–6043.

Simpson, P. (2004). *Stylistics: A Resource Book for Students*. London: Routledge.

Simpson, S. and Torrance, M. (2007). *EyeWrite* (Version 5.1) [Computer software]. Osgoode, ON: SR Research, and Nottingham: Nottingham Trent University.

Siyanova-Chanturia, A., Conklin, K. and Schmitt, N. (2011). Adding more fuel to the fire: An eye-tracking study of idiom processing by native and nonnative speakers. *Second Language Research*, 27(2), 251–272.

Siyanova-Chanturia, A., Conklin, K. and van Heuven, W. J. B. (2011). Seeing a phrase 'time and again' matters: The role of phrasal frequency in the processing of multiword sequences. *Journal of Experimental Psychology: Learning, Memory, and Cognition*, 37(3), 776–784.

SensoMotoric Instruments (SMI) (2016a). *SMI BeGaze Manual Version 3.6*. Teltow: SMI.

SensoMotoric Instruments (SMI) (2016b). *SMI Experiment Center Manual Version 3.6*. Teltow: SMI.

Smith, B. (2012). Eye tracking as a measure of noticing: A study of explicit recasts in SCMC. *Language Learning and Technology*, 16(3), 53–81.

Smith, B. and Renaud, C. (2013). Using eye-tracking as a measure of foreign language learners' noticing of recasts during computer-mediated writing conferences. In K. McDonough and A. Mackey (eds.), *Language Learning and Language Teaching: Second Language Interaction in Diverse Educational Contexts* (pp. 147–165). Amsterdam: John Benjamins.

Snodgrass, J. G. and Vanderwart, M. (1980). A standardized set of 260 pictures: Norms for name agreement, image agreement, familiarity, and visual complexity. *Journal of Experimental Psychology: Human Learning and Memory*, 6(2), 174–215.

Spelman Miller, K., Lindgren, E. and Sullivan, K. P. H. (2008). The psycholinguistic dimension in second language writing: Opportunities for research and pedagogy. *TESOL Quarterly*, 42, 433–454.

Spivey, M. J., Tanenhaus, M. K., Eberhard, K. M. and Sedivy, J. C. (2002). Eye movements and spoken language comprehension: Effects of visual context on syntactic ambiguity resolution. *Cognitive Psychology*, 45(4), 447–481.

SR Research (2015a). *SR Research Data Viewer User Manual, Version 2.4.1*. Ontario: SR Research Ltd.

SR Research (2015b). *SR Research Experiment Builder User Manual, Version 1.10.1630*. Ontario: SR Research Ltd.

Staub, A. (2007). The parser doesn't ignore intransitivity, after all. *Journal of Experimental Psychology: Learning, Memory, and Cognition*, 33(3), 550–569.

Staub, A. and Rayner, K. (2007). Eye movements and on-line comprehension processes. In M. G. Gaskell (ed.), *The Oxford Handbook of Psycholinguistics* (pp. 327–342). Oxford: Oxford University Press.

Stevenson, M., Schoonen, R. and de Glopper, K. (2006). Revising in two languages: A multidimensional comparison of online writing revisions in L1 and FL. *Journal of Second Language Writing*, 15, 201–233.

Stickler, U. and Shi, L. (2015). Eye movements of online Chinese learners. *Calico*, 32(1), 52–81.

Stockwell, P. (2005). 'Stylistics: language and literature'. In B. Aarts and A. McMahon (eds.), *The Handbook of English Linguistics*. Oxford: Blackwell.

Stothard, S. E., Hulme, C., Clarke, P., Barmby, P. and Snowling, M. J. (2010). *YARC York Assessment of Reading for Comprehension (Secondary)*. Brentford: GL Assessment.

Strömqvist, S. and Karlsson, H. (2002). *ScriptLog for Windows: User's Manual (Tech. Rep.)*. Lund: Lund University, and University College of Stavanger, Centre for Reading Research, Department of Linguistics.

Sussman, R. S. and Sedivy, J. (2003). The time-course of processing syntactic dependencies: Evidence from eye movements. *Language and Cognitive Processes*, 18(2), 143–163.

Suvorov, R. (2015). The use of eye tracking in research on video-based second language (L2) listening assessment: A comparison of context videos and content videos. *Language Testing*, 32(4), 463–483.

Szarkowska, A., Krejtz, I., Krejtz, K. and Duchowski, A. (2013). Harnessing the potential of eye-tracking for media accessibility. In S. Grucza, M. Pluzyczka and J. Zajac (eds.), *Translation Studies and Eye-Tracking Analysis* (pp. 153–183). Frankfurt am Main: Peter Lang.

Tanenhaus, M. K. (2007a). Spoken language comprehension: Insights from eye movements. In M. G. Gaskell (ed.), *The Oxford Handbook of Psycholinguistics* (pp. 309–326). Oxford: Oxford University Press.

Tanenhaus, M. K. (2007b). Eye movements and spoken language processing. In R. van Gompel, M. H. Fischer, W. S. Murray and R. L. Hill (eds.), *Eye Movements: A Window on Mind and Brain* (pp. 443–469). Amsterdam: Elsevier.

Tanenhaus, M. K. and Trueswell, J. C. (2006). Eye movements and spoken language comprehension. In M. J. Traxler and M. A. Gernsbacher (ed.), *Handbook of Psycholinguistics* (2nd edition) (pp. 863–900). Amsterdam: Elsevier.

Tanenhaus, M. K., Spivey-Knowlton, M., Eberhard, K. and Sedivy, J. (1995). Integration of visual and linguistic information during spoken language comprehension. *Science*, 268, 1632–1634.

Thothathiri, M. and Snedeker, J. (2008). Give and take: Syntactic priming during spoken language comprehension. *Cognition*, 108(1), 51–68.

Timmis, I. (2015). *Corpus Linguistics for ELT: Research and Practice*. New York: Routledge.

Tincoff, R. and Jusczyk, P. W. (1999). Some beginnings of word comprehension in 6-month-olds. *Psychological Science*, 10(2), 172–175.

Tincoff, R. and Jusczyk, P. W. (2012). Six-month-olds comprehend words that refer to parts of the body. *Infancy*, 17(4), 432–444.

Tobii AB (2016). *Tobii Pro Studio User's Manual Version 3.4.5*. Danderyd: Tobii AB.

Torrance, M., Johansson, R., Johansson, V. and Wengelin, A. (2016). Reading during the composition of multi-sentence texts: An eye-movement study. *Psychological Research*, 80, 729–743.

Trueswell, J. C. (2008). Using eye movements as a developmental measure within psycholinguistics. In I. A. Sekerina, E. M. Fernández and H. Clahsen (eds.), *Developmental Psycholinguistics: On-Line Methods in Children's Language Processing*, volume 44 (pp. 73–96). Amsterdam: John Benjamins.

Trueswell, J., Tanenhaus, M. and Garnsey, S. (1994). Semantic influences on parsing: Use of thematic role information in syntactic ambiguity resolution. *Journal of Memory and Language*, 33(3), 285–318.

Van Assche, E., Drieghe, D., Duyck, W., Welvaert, M. and Hartsuiker, R. J. (2011). The influence of semantic constraints on bilingual word recognition during sentence reading. *Journal of Memory and Language*, 64(1), 88–107.

Van Hell, J. G. and Tanner, D. (2012). Second language proficiency and cross-language lexical activation. *Language Learning*, 62(s2), 148–171.

Van Heuven, W. J. B., Mandera, P., Keuleers, E. and Brysbaert, M. (2014). Subtlex-UK: A new and improved word frequency database for British English. *Quarterly Journal of Experimental Psychology*, 67, 1176–1190.

Van Lancker, D. and Canter, G. J. (1981). Idiomatic versus literal interpretations of ditropically ambiguous sentences. *Journal of Speech and Hearing Research*, 24, 64–69.

Van Lancker Sidtis, D. (2003). Auditory recognition of idioms by native and nonnative speakers of English: It takes one to know one. *Applied Psycholinguistics*, 24, 45–57.

Van Waes, L., Leijten, M. and Quinlan, T. (2010). Reading during sentence composing and error correction: A multilevel analysis of the influences of task complexity. *Reading and Writing*, 23, 803–834.

Varley, S. (2009). I'll just look that up in the concordancer: Integrating corpus consultation into the language learning environment. *Computer Assisted Language Learning*, 22, 133–152.

Vilaró, A., Duchowski, A., Orero, P., Grindinger, T., Tetreault, S. and di Giovanni, E. (2012). How sound is The Pear Tree story? Testing the effect of varying audio stimuli on visual attention distribution. *Perspectives: Studies in Translatology*, 20(1), 55–65.

Vitu, F. (2003). The basic assumptions of EZ Reader are not well-founded. *Behavioral and Brain Sciences*, 26(4), 506–507.

Wade, N. J. (2010). Pioneers of eye movement research. *i-Perception*, 1(2), 33–68.

Wade, N. J. and Tatler, B. W. (2011). Origins and applications of eye movement research. In S. Liversedge, I. Gilchrist and S. Everling (eds.), *Oxford Handbook of Eye Movements* (pp. 17–46). Oxford: Oxford University Press.

Wechsler, D. (1999). *Wechsler Abbreviated Scale of Intelligence*. New York, NY: The Psychological Corporation.

Weir, C. (2005). *Language Testing and Validation: An Evidence-Based Approach*. New York, NY: Palgrave Macmillan.

Wengelin, A., Torrance, M., Holmqvist, K., Simpson, S., Galbraith, D., Johansson, V. and Johansson, R. (2009). Combined eyetracking and keystroke-logging methods for studying cognitive processes in text production. *Behavior Research Methods*, 41(2), 337–351.

Whelan, R. (2008). Effective analysis of reaction time data. *The Psychological Record*, 58, 475–482.

Whitford, V. and Titone, D. (2012). Second language experience modulates first- and second-language word frequency effects: Evidence from eye movement measures of natural paragraph reading. *Psychonomic Bulletin and Review*, 19, 73–80.

Whitford, V., Pivneva, I. and Titone, D. (2016). Eye movement methods to investigate bilingual reading. In R. R. Heredia, J. Altarriba and A. B. Cieślicka (eds.), *Methods in Bilingual Reading Comprehension Research* (pp. 183–211). New York: Springer.

Wilkinson, D. (2012). A data-driven approach to increasing student motivation in the reading classroom. *Language Education in Asia*, 3(2), 252–262.

Wilkinson, G. S. and Robertson, G. (2006). *Wide Range Achievement Test 4 Professional Manual*. Lutz, FL: Psychological Assessment Resources.

Williams, R. S. and Morris, R. K. (2004). Eye movements, word familiarity, and vocabulary acquisition. *European Journal of Cognitive Psychology*, 16(1–2), 312–339.

Winke, P. and Lim, H. (2015). ESL essay raters' cognitive processes in applying the Jacobs et al. rubric: An eye-movement study. *Assessing Writing*, 25, 38–54.

Winter, B. (2013). *Linear Models and Linear Mixed Effects Models in R with Linguistic Applications*. Available online at arxiv.org/pdf/1308.5499.pdf

Winter, B. and Wieling, M. (2016). How to analyze linguistic change using mixed models, Growth Curve Analysis and Generalized Additive Modeling. *Journal of Language Evolution*, 1(1), 7–18.

Yee, E. and Sedivy, J. (2006). Eye movements to pictures reveal transient semantic activation during spoken word recognition. *Journal of Experimental Psychology: Learning, Memory, and Cognition*, 32(1), 1–14.

Zwierzchoń-Grabowska, E. (2013). Could eye-tracking help to reconstruct the translation processes? In S. Grucza, M. Pluzyczka and J. Zajac (eds.), *Translation Studies and Eye-Tracking Analysis* (pp. 67–83). Frankfurt am Main: Peter Lang.

Index